LEAVING RUSSIA

A JEWISH STORY

MAXIM D. SHRAYER

SYRACUSE UNIVERSITY PRESS

First Paperback Edition 2017

17 18 19 20 21 22   6 5 4 3 2 1

This work is a literary memoir. The experiences and conversations recounted here are the
result of the author's recollection and are rendered as a subjective accounting of events
that occurred in his life. His perceptions and opinions are entirely his own and do not
represent those of the publisher or the sponsors. Some names and identifying details have
been changed or omitted to protect the privacy of individuals.

∞ The paper used in this publication meets the minimum requirements of the American
National Standard for Information Sciences—Permanence of Paper for Printed Library
Materials, ANSI Z39.48-1992.

For a listing of books published and distributed by Syracuse University Press, visit
www.SyracuseUniversityPress.syr.edu.

ISBN: 978-0-8156-1088-5 (paperback) 978-0-8156-1024-3 (cloth) 978-0-8156-5243-4 (e-book)

Library of Congress has cataloged the hardcover as follows:

Shrayer, Maxim, 1967– author.

   Leaving Russia : a Jewish story / Maxim D. Shrayer. — First Edition.

     pages cm. — (Library of modern Jewish literature)

   Includes index.

   ISBN 978-0-8156-1024-3 (cloth : alk. paper) 1. Shrayer, Maxim, 1967—Childhood and
youth. 2. Refuseniks—Biography. 3. Political activists—Soviet Union—Biography.
4. Immigrants—United States—Biography. 5. Jews—Soviet Union—Biography.
6. Soviet Union—Biography. I. Title.

   PG3487.R34Z46 2013

   891.71'44—dc23

   [B]   2013034301

Manufactured in the United States of America

MAXIM D. SHRAYER was born in Moscow in 1967 to a Jewish-Russian family. With his parents, the writer and medical scientist David Shrayer-Petrov and the philologist and translator Emilia Shrayer (née Polyak), he spent almost nine years as a refusenik. He and his parents left the USSR and immigrated to the United States in 1987, after spending a summer in Austria and Italy.

Shrayer studied at Moscow University, Brown University, and Rutgers University, and received a Ph.D. at Yale University in 1995. He is professor of Russian, English, and Jewish Studies at Boston College, where he co-founded the Jewish Studies Program. Among Shrayer's books are the critical and biographical studies *The World of Nabokov's Stories*, *Russian Poet/Soviet Jew*, *Bunin and Nabokov: A History of Rivalry* (in Russian), and *I SAW IT: Ilya Selvinsky and the Legacy of Bearing Witness to the Shoah*. A bilingual author and translator, he has published three collections of Russian poetry and edited and co-translated three books of fiction by his father, David Shrayer-Petrov. Shrayer received a 2007 National Jewish Book Award for his two-volume *Anthology of Jewish-Russian Literature*, and a 2012 Guggenheim Fellowship for his research on Jewish-Russian poets and the Shoah.

Maxim D. Shrayer is the author of the literary memoir *Waiting for America: A Story of Emigration* and the story collection *Yom Kippur in Amsterdam*. His English-language prose, poetry, and translations have appeared in *Agni*, *Kenyon Review*, *Massachusetts Review*, *Partisan Review*, *Southwest Review*, *Tablet*, and other magazines. He has been the recipient of a number of fellowships, including those from the National Endowment for the Humanities, the Rockefeller Foundation, and the Bogliasco Foundation.

Shrayer lives in Brookline, Massachusetts, with his wife, Dr. Karen E. Lasser, a medical researcher and physician, and their daughters, Mira Isabella and Tatiana Rebecca.

A prequel to *Waiting for America*, *Leaving Russia* is Shrayer's second memoir.

To my daughters,
Mira Isabella and Tatiana Rebecca

CONTENTS

List of Illustrations   *xi*

Acknowledgments   *xiii*

Prologue   *xv*

PART ONE: **THE END OF CHILDHOOD**

1. Of Goat Milk and Marble Lions   *3*

2. Different   *12*

3. Becoming Refuseniks   *30*

   INTERLUDE: Dunes of Happiness   *53*

4. Cavalier of the Gold Medal   *76*

PART TWO: **THE EXPEDITION**

5. Moscow State   *101*

   INTERLUDE: Summertime   *118*

6. Poetry, Love, Persecution   *126*

   INTERLUDE: Facts and Arguments   *155*

7. Across the Steppe and into the Black Sea   *163*

PART THREE: **THE SHORT GOODBYE**

8. Last Autumn   *217*

   INTERLUDE: Readers' Reports   *238*

9. Purim-shpil   *248*

   INTERLUDE: Family Tree   *272*

10. Taking Leave   *284*

Epilogue: *In America?*   312

Index of Names and Places   315

ILLUSTRATIONS

Illustrations follow page 162.

1. Peysakh (Pyotr) Shrayer, David Shrayer's father, with parents and siblings
2. Borukh-Itsik and Fanya (Freyda) Shrayer, David's grandparents
3. Anna (Nyusya) Studnits, with her brother Grigory and relatives
4. David Shrayer with his parents, Bella Breydo and Pyotr Shrayer
5. David Shrayer and Bella Breydo
6. Captain Pyotr Shrayer
7. Emilia Shrayer with parents and sister Zhanna Volynskaya
8. David Shrayer, lieutenant of the medical corps
9. David Shrayer in Leningrad
10. Maxim Shrayer with his mother in Moscow
11. Maxim in Arkhangelskoye outside Moscow
12. Maxim at his father's typewriter
13. Maxim in Tbilisi, Georgia
14. 43 Marshala Biryuzova Street, where the Shrayers lived from 1971 to 1987
15. Rannahotell in Pärnu, Estonia
16. Jüri Arrak's *Corona*
17. Maxim with parents visiting Panga-Rehe, Jüri Arrak's summer home
18. Emilia and David Shrayer with Urve and Jüri Arrak
19. Maxim with Katya (Ekaterina) Tsarapkina
20. Emilia and David Shrayer at the Shrayers' apartment
21. Maxim with Emilia Shrayer, Urve Roodes Arrak, Jüri Arrak, and Vaïke Lubi

22. Maxim with classmates

23. Maxim's secondary school diploma

24. Maxim's field journal

25. David, Emilia, and Maxim Shrayer

26. Map of Russia with Maxim's expedition route

27. Maxim's expedition journal entry for 5 June 1986

28. Maxim's expedition journal entry for 8 July 1986

29. Maxim during an ascent to a glacier

30. Maxim drinking boiled water at the expedition camp

31. Maxim writing at the expedition camp

32. Maxim with Maxim Mussel

33. Maxim harvesting potatoes with university classmates

34. Emilia Shrayer at a demonstration in support of Yosef Begun

35. David Shrayer interviewed by Dan Rather of CBS News

36. Maxim, Emilia, and David Shrayer, and Anna Studnits

37. Maxim's travel document, issued in Italy

38. Maxim with Katya Tsarapkina and Max Mussel in Moscow

39. Maxim with Genrikh Sapgir in Paris

40. Maxim with David Shrayer

41. Emilia and David Shrayer

42. Yosef Begun, David Shrayer, and Emilia Shrayer

43. Maxim, Tatiana, Karen, and Mira in Newport, Rhode Island

44. Maxim, Tatiana, Karen, and Mira in South Chatham, Massachusetts

ACKNOWLEDGMENTS

EARLY PORTIONS OF THIS BOOK were written at the Rockefeller Foundation's Study and Conference Center in Bellagio, Italy, and at the Bogliasco Foundation's Liguria Study Center for the Arts and Humanities, and I thank both foundations for their support. The bulk of the book was composed during a leave made possible by the Boston College Faculty Fellowship, for which I give thanks. The final revisions of the book were completed during my tenure as a fellow of the Guggenheim Foundation, whose support I gratefully acknowledge.

Stephen Vedder has done a splendid job with preparing the photographs, and Michael S. Swanson and the generous staff of Boston College's Media Technology Services helped me design the map of my 1986 summer expedition. Maria B. Hosmer-Briggs has copyedited the manuscript with deftness and a keen understanding of what it's all about. I also thank all my friends and colleagues at Syracuse University Press.

Two of my Moscow school classmates have kindly consented to the reprinting of excerpts from their letters to me. Thank you!

Jüri Arrak, a close family friend and a great artist, has allowed me to reproduce his painting, a generous gift. Ivi Arrak, an artist in her own right, has been a gracious host during my family's post-Soviet visits to Estonia.

My dear friends Ekaterina Tsarapkina and Maxim Mussel read a draft of this book and offered generous comments.

• • •

My parents, Emilia Shrayer and David Shrayer-Petrov, have given me full access to their archive, including the family photos and videos. They have read drafts of the book and answered numerous queries. I am immeasurably grateful to them.

Karen E. Lasser, my kind and patient wife, has been an enthusiastic supporter of this project since its inception; I cannot thank her enough for reading and critiquing drafts of this book, and for inspiring me to tell this story.

My wife, daughters, and parents are my lifeline.

PROLOGUE

"WE JUST GOT A CALL from the Office of Visas . . . ," said my mother's voice. And then it stopped, choking on the unpronounceable words. "I can't. . . ."

The black receiver of the street payphone felt cold and heavy in my hands. On my left, Moscow's midday traffic flowed down Leninsky Prospect, one side of it forging ahead to the city center, the other moving in the direction of the city's southwestern outskirts. On my right, a tall wrought-iron fence marked the western boundary of the Moscow University campus. Such ominous iron fences typically surrounded Soviet institutions, giving their workers, students, and patients the feeling of enclosure.

"Mama, what's wrong?"

"They said they would be 'granting our request,'" my mother's voice laughed and sobbed into the heavy black receiver.

I sometimes telephoned my mother when I was about to leave the campus. I had been a student there for two and a half years, and unless it was bitterly cold outside, I liked calling from the street, the same pay phone outside the high wrought-iron fence, before turning right, toward the University Metro station. (Once as a freshmen, on a wager, I phoned my mother from a wood-paneled elevator going up to the top of the main university building, already past the thirtieth floor, and the clarity of sound was such that I wondered if instead of the bugged phone lines, some benevolent angeloids weren't carrying the signal in their cupped hands across the skies of the Soviet capital.) On a sunny day—and the day in the middle of April when our family's "emigration request" was granted was a sunny and breezy day—one attained a great view of the environs from where I was standing. Behind my back, inside the campus perimeter, the tower of the main university building dominated and dwarfed the surroundings: a magisterial product of Stalin's architects or simply a distant and imperfect echo of the Empire State Building. On the opposite side of Leninsky Prospect were the New Moscow Circus and the Children's Music Theater. As an impressionable Jewish preteen, how I relished the magic of Maeterlinck's *The Bluebird*, a staple of this theater's repertoire. On stage household objects, bread, fire, and water, turned into otherworldly beings who could vanquish the quotidian. Beyond the buildings of the Circus and the Musical Theater, the eye met grayish and brownish blocks of solid apartment buildings in what was one of Moscow's more desirable residential areas. In the ground floor of a Stalinist stone-laid apartment building was the Moscow University bookshop, which I frequented after classes. Books in general, and translations from Western languages in particular, were in tremendous demand, but every once in a while I would strike gold. Straight ahead was the marble puck of the University Metro station girded by various stalls and kiosks. My ride home took about an hour, with one or two transfers, depending on the route I chose. During the morning and especially the late afternoon rush hours, the train cars would be stuffed with people, like sausages are stuffed with meat, fat, and fennel seeds. Overcrowded subway cars usually carried at least one colonel, in the colder months clad in a thick greatcoat and a tall astrakhan with a cockade, or sometimes a general with a double red stripe running down his breeches. These were some of the coordinates of my Soviet youth: campus, bookstore, circus, and theater; Jewish luck; specter of the military service; brief escapes and forbidding wrought-iron fences.

I pictured my mother as her voice broke out of the black receiver, punctuating the transience of our Soviet living. Mother possesses the joyfully melancholic beauty of the Early Renaissance, a confluence of music and mystique, that sometimes expresses itself most completely in Ashkenazi women. It's as though centuries of her Jewish ancestors' wanderings across Europe, from Italy through Germany into the West Slavic lands, Lithuania, Ukraine, and finally into Russia, had endowed my mother with a quintessence of daintily timid and therefore ever more enchanting femininity.

"Come home as soon as you can," mother's voice said.

"I'll catch a cab, mamochka, I'll be there soon. . . . Is papa still at the clinic . . . ?"

We would be leaving, at long last, after nine years, I was thinking as I ran across Leninsky Prospect to the other side, in violation of traffic regulations. I felt that the walls and fences, which had stood in the way of my family's future, were falling. In the spring of 1987, when the authorities finally granted our request to emigrate, my mother was turning forty-seven; my father was fifty-one. The Soviet imagination had dubbed us *otkazniki* (from the Russian *otkaz*, "refusal"), meaning the ones who were denied, or *refused*, permission to leave the Soviet Union. In translation, the term "refusenik" had acquired an ambiguity, whose irony was hardly intentioned: the Soviet authorities, not the Jews, were refusing. Unless, of course, you consider the fact that we, the refuseniks, had refused the ticket to Soviet paradise.

After turning onto Garden Ring, downtown Moscow's inner beltway, we got stuck in traffic and crawled for the next fifteen minutes; the cabby lit another one of his vile *papirosy*. A cab ride from the campus to our apartment used to take half an hour to forty minutes. Sitting on the back seat and ignoring the cabby's attempts to chat me up about the prospects of the Central Army Club in the new soccer season, I underwent one of the most intense experiences of remembering. It was as though I was sitting in a projection room with two screens and two films rolling simultaneously before my eyes. The two films divided the almost twenty years of my life in two halves. One of them visualized the first eleven years of my life, starting with my early childhood and bringing the action to the late fall of 1978. The other film unraveled in time from the then-present (that April 1987 afternoon in Moscow and my mother's agitated voice in the receiver) back to the events of 1978 that had changed the course of my family's history. The winter of 1978–79, when we had first applied for exit visas, divided the footage into *before* and *after*.

A big part of me will always remain there in the projection room of my Soviet past, on the ripped vinyl back seat of a Moscow city cab taking me away from Russia. As I type these lines, Boston's capricious winter is coating the firs outside my window with the silkiest of snows. It's Monday morning, I have already driven my daughters to daycare, and my wife is at her clinic at Boston Medical Center, taking care of patients, many of them immigrants like myself. I take a sip of my tepid Ceylon tea with lemon, then peer into the milky-blue sky. A lot had changed since the spring of 1987. A lot has changed—in me and in my parents, and also in the country that held us captive. I was a different person back then, when I was leaving Russia for good. I was more brazen and desperate, much more judgmental and intolerant. An inveterate tomcat playing at chivalry, I was thinner and looked lankier, with a head of tall hair. I hadn't read *Lolita* or seen Paris or Rio de Janeiro. Accustomed to expecting antisemitic behavior everywhere, I was ready to fight for my honor. I believed, sincerely, that Ronald Reagan was good just because he fiercely opposed the "evil" Soviet empire.

To illustrate just how little I understood about my future country in the years immediately preceding emigration—or how flat my notion of the landscape of American life was at the time—I will briefly turn to an anecdote from the fall of 1984. I was seventeen, a freshman at Moscow University, and together with my parents I was already a veteran refusenik of six years. I was virulently anti-Soviet, staunchly pro-American. Through a friend from the refusenik community, my parents and I met an American historian of the Russian nineteenth century who was spending a semester in Moscow, researching his new book. This happened during the 1984 election, when Walter Mondale challenged Ronald Reagan for the presidency. I followed the election as closely as I could via the distorted coverage in Soviet newspapers and via the nighttime broadcasts of the Voice of America and other Russian-language programs reaching us from abroad. (The signal was usually obstructed by *glushilki* ["deafeners"], Soviet scrambling devices.) When, on a sleety November night at our apartment, the American historian told me that he had just cast his ballot at the embassy, and had voted for "Mondale, of course," my response was "How could you?!" At the time I linked President Reagan unequivocally with anti-Communism and anti-Sovietism, and appreciated him because of his support of the cause of Soviet Jews. Issues of Reagan's domestic politics had been of no interest to me as my family struggled for our right to leave Russia. When the American professor referred to Mondale as a "liberal democrat," my reasoning was: "liberal, left-wing, pink, pro-Soviet. . . ." I don't think this could have been otherwise at the time, given the country in which I was living and my family's ideological confrontation with its regime. My political recalibration would not occur for three more years, when, in the fall of 1987, I became a student at an American East Coast university.

Leaving Russia is a story of the life I left behind in 1987. The book takes its title from the knowledge that crystallized in me as I was writing it. From my birth in Moscow on 5 June 1967 until my emigration on 7 June 1987, my entire Russian (and Soviet) childhood and youth had been a protracted separation, a tearing away from my former homeland. Even before realizing it, around the age of eleven or twelve, I had already been waiting to leave and—unwittingly—conducting research for this book.

This book captures the first twenty years of my life in a way that suggests a loving ambition to alchemize the raw material of the collective, historical Soviet hours, months, and years into the timeline of an individual, private, Jewish story. My final severing from Russia took place roughly over the course of my first decade in the United States and predated my marriage and the birth of my children. Without the distance and perspective accorded by my immigrant years and by writing in a second language, I wouldn't have been able to undertake this memoir.

I'm forty-five as I prepare these lines for publication. I've lived in America for over half of my life—no small affair for a Jewish boy from Moscow. The world I once knew, the way one knows the air, sky, grass, and trash of one's home, is gone forever. My family's emigration in 1987 and the collapse of the Soviet Union in 1991 have rendered me a stranger there, where I was born and grew up. Gone from Russia and dispersed throughout the world are some of my oldest friends. Some of the kids I grew up with are no longer among the living: killed in Afghanistan and Chechnya; having drunk themselves to death; annihilated by the mob. While visiting Russia I now feel there like a comprehending alien. Still capable of appreciating many nuances of living there, I perceive today's Russia through a lens of foreignness, and this makes homecoming a surreal experience. I still feel a strong bond with the place and its people.

What I don't feel when I visit Russia is a sense of belonging. But did I ever? Was my having been born a Jew in Russia "God's mistake," as Isaac Babel put it in "How Things Were Done in Odessa," echoing Sholem Aleichem's Tevye the Dairyman? In real life, such retrospective judgments do not usually help one deal with the baggage of memory.

The finality of my separation from Russia struck me when I stood with my family at a small Jewish cemetery in Cranston, Rhode Island listening to the words the rabbi pronounced over a new grave, to which the remains of my maternal grandfather Arkady (Aron) Polyak were laid to final rest after being brought here from Moscow, where he had originally been buried. Leaving Egypt forever, Moses thus took the bones of Joseph from the crypt and carried them to the Promised Land. Having no roots in America, we have created deep attachments by bringing here the remains of our ancestors. My grandmother Anna (Nyusya) Studnits, who passed in November 2009, now rests with my grandfather after twenty-two Russian and twenty-two American years apart. Still, one cannot and perhaps should not seek to transplant all of one's roots. While visiting St. Petersburg (Leningrad), I used to go alone to the graves of my paternal grandparents and great-grandparents at the Preobrazhenskoe Jewish Cemetery and place pebbles on their granite headstones. Last year, my older daughter Mira, then a first-grader, stood there with me as I choked on tears and tried to hide my face. A year later, in June of 2013, I took my younger daughter Tatiana to Russia, and together we stood at our ancestors' graves on the outskirts of St. Petersburg. This time I did not hide the tears from my daughter.

My home and my life are now in America. Here I have become a New Englander and even developed traces of a Boston accent. Here I met and fell in love with my American-born wife Karen, herself a daughter of Jewish immigrants. Here I started writing in English. Here in America, my parents celebrated their fiftieth wedding anniversary. And here my daughters were born at Beth Israel Hospital in Boston, and were forever inscribed in the book of Red Sox fans.

Too much of a fatalist, I rarely feel nostalgia for the vestiges of my Russian—and Soviet—past. The world I left behind in 1987 was not at all like the pre-1917 paradise of sunlit country estates, otherworldly butterflies, and first love that my favorite of the Russian émigrés gorgeously

Anglicized in the 1940s, mollifying the pain of his own displacement. My Soviet years, almost half of which my parents and I spent as Jewish *refuseniks*, were hardly idyllic.

Save for the occasional fact-checking detour, in working on this book I have relied primarily on my own memory. Rather than attempting a historical account of the last decades of the Soviet Empire, I wanted to stick to my personal story. It is, of course, inevitable that in describing one's early childhood one cannot rely entirely on remembering, and resorts to reconstruction. However, my artistic and existential imperative throughout this book has been to describe mainly things in which I have directly participated. This overreliance on what I personally saw and witnessed should partially explain the reason why some of the most dramatic episodes in my parents' years as refuseniks are missing from these pages. I'm referring especially to the persecution and violence committed against by father and mother by the Soviet secret police in 1979–1987. A story of a young Jew leaving the Soviet Union might be starker and punchier if based on formal interviews with his parents. Yet to this day it remains painful, to the point of forbidding, for all of us to speak of the bitterest times from that Soviet life. My father had previously told about the refusenik years in fiction (his panoramic novel *Herbert and Nelly* and his short stories, some of them collected, in English, in *Jonah and Sarah*, *Autumn in Yalta*, and *Dinner with Stalin*), in memoirs (*Vodka and Pastries*; *Hunt for the Red Devil*), and also in poems and essays. But both my father and my mother have yet to tell the story of their refusenik years in discursive form. Lastly, there are important, even formative, individuals, episodes, encounters, and events that I had to omit from this book; the time has not yet come to speak about them.

I have benefited, in more ways than I can acknowledge, from conversations with my parents and from their recollections. To name Emilia Shrayer and David Shrayer-Petrov as my principal sources for this book would be a feeble truism; they are the co-authors of my being. The literary craft of my father and my mother's wise heart have served as my double compass.

I have consulted my parents' personal papers as I also drew on the photographic and archival materials we have been able to recover. These archival materials, among them my father's unpublished summary of our last months as refuseniks, were especially invaluable in the process of working on chapters eight, nine, and ten of this book. I did not keep diaries in the Soviet Union, the only exception being the journal of the 1986 expedition to the south of Russia. I brought this journal with me when I left Moscow for good on 7 June 1987, and sections from it appear in chapter seven. Although I have visited the former Soviet Union on a number of occasions since becoming an American citizen in 1993, I have not interviewed the protagonists (and antagonists) of this book. This book is not—or at least is not intended as—a medium of settling scores. Such scores could never be settled, either in a book or in the courtroom of history. To me this book has offered an opportunity to commit to memory a Jewish story of the receding Soviet past.

M. D. S.
December 2010–October 2012–July 2013
Chestnut Hill, Brookline, and South Chatham, Massachusetts

LEAVING RUSSIA

PART ONE

The End of Childhood

1

OF GOAT MILK AND MARBLE LIONS

SOMETIME IN THE MIDDLE 2000s I had a double dream, in which my father taught me poetry and fishing. Although the dream was about my Russian childhood, it was spoken in English. I was in our house in Chestnut Hill, where Karen and I lived from 2001 to 2011. It was in the spring, and definitely before Karen's first pregnancy and the birth of Mira.

In the dream I'm eight, a second grader, and my father and I are sitting in his den at a coffee table that looks like a World War I airplane. Pencils and a stack of paper are in front of us. My father shows me the basic classical meters, improvising various lines effortlessly, like a conjurer, creating seamless verse out of the mundane objects that surround us in the room and outside the windows: trolleybus, hospital, potholes, starlings on power lines. I like the four-foot iamb better, it feels like clay under my fingers, its verses want to be caressed. "Try a trochee," says my father, and it sounds like "try a truffle," try the chocolate of verses and you shall forever crave it, crave its taste upon your lips. Then I try a line of trochee, and it tastes like pure honey, pure nectar of delight. "Now add the rhymes, my dear," says my father loud and clear, "rhymes are signatures of style. But remember, son, you never should let your rhymes appear too clever, or decay, or go stale." Then he leaves me in his office and I scribble down an opus, "Going Fishing with My Dad." I can hear he is making Turkish coffee in the kitchen and conversing with my mother. "Ready?" asks my father sternly. "Ready," I reply and tremble, for I know he is fair. Then the colors grow dimmer, Moscow winter melts away.

We're now in Estonia, we're fishing on a river that on approach from the highway glistens like a wet grass snake and then vanishes without a trace, tucked away deep inside the valley. This is *our* river, and for years my father and I would drive here for the day from the coastal resort of Pärnu where my parents and I stayed for a month, sometimes two, in the summer. The steep high bank of the river, where we leave our car, is freshly mowed. Hayricks stand like sentries of our peace. We always catch fish in our river. And we're always the only ones around, just the two of us and the symmetrical hayricks reflected in the river's surface. We already have a pail full of standard European freshwater fare: bream, tench, roach, crucian. I rotate the pail, examining our catch, and I think of the evening, of how my mother would coat the fish in flour and pan-fry it in sunflower oil. Then a brief rainstorm interrupts our fishing, and we leave the rods and find shelter under a nearby hayrick. It's not simply a rick but a makeshift mowers' cabin. Inside, the fermenting air smells of our nearing return to Moscow, of the end of summer, of the brevity of miracle. The rainstorm passes and we crawl out of the rick, find our wet rods, hook on fresh worms, and cast our lines. Then my father lets out a victory sound and pulls out a golden fish bigger than any we've ever caught. The fish isn't a carp. It's a fish of some unknown or rare species, with perfectly chiseled scales which glitter in the afternoon sun like my mother's wedding ring, like onion domes, like hundreds of thousands of gold teeth that were ripped from the mouths of murdered Jews. The golden fish has gray, unblinking, plaintive eyes framed by round tortoise-shell glasses. The bridge of his refined nose has a bump. My father unhooks the fish and holds him on the palm of his open hand, and the fish's thin bloodless lips start chewing on some words in a throaty language. Father's left hand trembles, and he drops the fishing pole from his right hand and cups it to support the fish that rests in his left hand. "We must let him go, son," says my father. "He's the last one of them. The survivor."

I was born on 5 June 1967, and my father's first impulse was to name me "Israel" as he rejoiced over Israel's spectacular victory over Egypt, Jordan, and Syria during the Six-Day War. A first name like that would have doubtless rendered me an even more obvious target of antisemitism, and instead the name Maxim was chosen. It must have been in vogue in the Soviet Union in the middle to late '60s, judging by the number of other

Maxims my age I have met, including my best Moscow friend Maxim (Max) Mussel. My weight was also a factor: I was well over eight pounds and the labor was terribly painful for my mother.

I was born in my mother's bustling Moscow, not in my father's austere Leningrad. Otherwise, things might have been different. When my father met my mother in 1962, he was working on his Candidate of Science degree (Ph.D. equivalent) in microbiology at the Leningrad Institute of Tuberculosis while also writing and translating poetry and trying his hand at fiction. He pursued both of his lifelong careers, medicine and literature, which pulled him in different directions. Both suited him, each in its own way. Medicine and literature, literature and medicine. . . . Being a writer-doctor seems a particularly Russian marriage of trades. Not that the Anglo-American cultural world hasn't seen, in William Somerset Maugham or William Carlos Williams, its share of authors who took the Hippocratic oath. And yet, in the minds of many Russian readers the interrelationship of literature and medicine exists not as a dual professional appointment, but as a love, a marriage, a destiny. "Medicine is my wife," Chekhov used to say, "and literature, my mistress." My father embodies the view that literature and medicine are organically linked in purpose and method. He regards those around him as both objects of observation and subjects of imagination.

After marrying in the autumn of 1962, my parents lived in Leningrad for two years. My mother transferred to the Philology Faculty (School) of Leningrad University and worked part time as a linguistics research assistant. Leningrad's damp, icy winters and its atmosphere of a conservatory of time were not to my mother's liking, after Moscow's unstoppable, motley merry-go-round. Nor did my mother enjoy chance encounters with specters of my father's bachelorhood. She didn't feel at home in Leningrad and wanted to return to Moscow. My father, like many Leningrad writers and intellectuals of his generation who came on to the scene during the years of the so-called Khrushchev's Thaw, regarded Moscow as a space of larger opportunities and greater official liberalism. Moving to Moscow opened new horizons, and my father embraced the move, especially because by 1964 he had completed the experimental part of his dissertation. My mother transferred back to the Moscow Institute of Foreign

Languages (now Moscow State Linguistic University). My parents abandoned their Leningrad flat and moved to the Soviet capital, taking a single room in a communal apartment, in a grand old building off Gorky (Tverskaya) Street, their windows facing the arterial Garden Ring, earsplitting during the day, stridently humming at night. In Moscow they remained, until our emigration in 1987.

A Muscovite by birth and upbringing, I like excesses and absurdity in art, and, occasionally, also in life. Yet, as a Leningradian (St. Petersburgian) by heritage, I cannot live without some structure and order, and also crave a daily dose of classical beauty. Striving for a *measure of absurdity*, this is how I would describe myself, a child of Moscow with some Nevan blood in my veins. It wasn't until my student years that I discovered for myself and learned to like my father's native city, an architectural paradise where the mannered ways of its denizens, the Homeric slowness and glory of the past, and the ubiquitous memorial plaques all communicate to strangers a sense of their cultural imperfection.

My father appreciated Moscow for all she had to offer, for her largeness and openness and diversity, which his snobbish and inwardly insecure native city had lacked by nature and lacked even more after having been decapitalized (or is it decapitated?) in 1918, when, after the peace treaty of Brest-Litovsk, Lenin moved the capital of the new Soviet state to Moscow. Yet my father never ceased to love and miss Leningrad. Once, when I was about fifteen, which would have been in 1982 or 1983, my parents and I stopped in Leningrad on our way to Estonia. We had been driving all day (it's about four hundred miles northwest of Moscow, a long distance by the then-contemporary standards of Soviet driving), and we reached the limits of Leningrad in the evening. My father, who is quite nearsighted, and thus a very cautious driver, was operating the car in a way that was entirely unlike him. He let the car glide through the city, turning onto various streets and lanes without ever stopping at traffic lights. Was he breaking the traffic rules or had we hit a lucky streak of green? It was the end of June, the season of White Nights, and the setting sun lit the iron lace of bridges and set ablaze the water in rivers and canals. "We could go here," my father whispered as he turned the steering wheel. "But there's also another way," he muttered under his breath—to himself, to me and my mother, to our car—as we sailed across his city. Leningrad lived in my father's mind as a totality, the way Moscow never did even after two decades of living there. A blissful smile stayed on his face for the duration of that journey through Leningrad to the Lesnoye neighborhood in the city's Vyborg Side, where my father was born and grew up. The White Night led my father along the embankments of yore. The drive through Leningrad was enchanting, and even the youthful traffic police officer who pulled us over for some minor traffic violation couldn't spoil the fun of watching my father's homecoming.

People no longer say such things without a tinge of irony or sarcasm, but there you have it: I had a happy childhood. I was loved, encouraged, and supported at everything, except dishonesty, cruelty and assimilationism. The happiest shots of the early childhood capture me in the company of my parents. I see myself in my bedroom, on a sage-green sofa, having an English lesson with my mother. It's the spring before first grade, and I haven't yet started English at school. I'm six, and mother and I both laugh as I learn to pronounce the word "hedgehog." "Is this a cat?" she asks pointing to a picture of a needly creature with a sharp nose and jutting ears. "No mommy," I reply in English as my mother has taught me. "This is a hedgehog. A hedge-hog." My mother, a university lecturer in English, made this language an adventure of my life. It was my mother who first showed me how to play with English words, which she so adored. Strange, isn't it, that Russian is my mother tongue, my native tongue, and English my acquired, second language? Why can't English be considered my mother's tongue, and Russian the language of my father and his poetry lessons?

In the summer of 1969, when I turned two, my parents rented a cottage in the village of Mikhalkovo, about fifteen miles west of Moscow. The village and its peasants had once belonged to princely families, first the Golitsyns and later the Yusupovs. The Yusupovs built a luxurious estate, Arkhangelskoye (literally: "abode of Archangels"), its manor house having survived the flames of the Revolution and Civil War. Of the cottage, I recall a verandah with carved woodwork painted green and dark brown; a wooden stoop on which I sit with my mother, her light hair pulled back with a square head kerchief folded into a triangle; an oversized gray Flemish beret that I'm wearing. I also remember a tousled black dog I called "Dick-Dickoosha" tearing at a rusty chain; a nesting doll of a peasant woman from whom we used to buy goat milk still tepid from the morning milking; a flowering potato field we passed on the way to the whitewashed milestone where my father would get off the heaving bus, mesh sacks of groceries in both hands. And finally, a sun-pocked deer traversing a forest clearing where in the morning, amid mounds of dew-studded grass, mother and I would find young slippery jacks, those tenderest of wild mushrooms.

Mother and I are walking through the overgrown English park of the Arkhangelskoye estate. The main alley is perfectly straight and covered with red gravel, the kind that not only bloodies but also dyes your knees and palms when you trip and fall. Ahead of us lies the front lawn of the manor house, with columns thicker than elephant's legs, with emerald downpipes and tall glass doors. And there they are, the lions, my beloved creatures, guarding the entrance on either side of the front steps. "Mamochka, look," and I run for all I am worth, to hug and pet my marble friends. The lions look me straight in the eyes as I approach the manor house, but their grimaces are actually smiles, and their heavy front paws, stretched out in front of them, are not threatening. I run up the heavy steps, dash to the right to pet one of the lions on the neck and cheekbone, then run to the left and put my hand under the other lion's chin. Standing on my toes, I can reach their cool stone ears, but not the top of their heads with erect manes.

"Mama, come," I call her, and she hurries up the red gravel path in her pale green sun dress and keds.

"How are your friends this morning?" mother asks, and I know that I can now climb onto the lions' backs, something I'm not supposed to do by myself.

Mother leans against a white, peeling column, unties her kerchief and straightens her sunlit hair. The two of us are the only visitors at this hour, and mother kisses me and tells me something so affectionate that the lions purr like kittens and nod at her every word.

To my childhood self my mother was a standard of playful beauty. How I adored her as a young boy: her laughing eyes, her hairdos, her clothes, her gait, her perfume. Mother taught me about taste. Because of her training in English language and culture, she was the source of my then-intuitive appreciation of things broadly Western—not literature or art, but what one could call "Western lifestyle." She spoke to me of the streets and landmarks of London (where she had never been allowed to travel for work because she was Jewish), of St. Paul's or Trafalgar Square, as though she had lived there her whole life. As a young boy I heard myriad things about "the West" from mother. New York and San Francisco. Hollywood. Frank Sinatra and Ella Fitzgerald. These broadly Western leanings extended from style of clothes and appearance to music and dancing. I remember coming home from grade school and dancing with my mother, who taught in the morning and would usually be home by the afternoon, to one of the few precious American rock 'n' roll records that we owned. I remember twisting and shaking and imitating my mother, in the middle of my room, in broad daylight, to the sounds of "The Night Chicago Died."

The summer of 1969 was the last one we would spend as *dachniki* outside Moscow. We never owned a *dacha*. My parents weren't the types that desired to squat on a tiny parcel of land with gooseberry shrubs and a shack with a corrugated roof, surrounded by hundreds of other dusty dachas and thousands of Soviet men and women of property nurturing middle-class dreams. After the death of grandfather Pyotr (Peysakh) Shrayer in Leningrad, his spacious, pre-1917 summer house in Beloostrov, where I spent most of the summer of 1968, went to his third wife, and we never visited there again. My father inherited half of his father's mousy Moskvich automobile and his grandfather's gold Swiss watch. And also an ironic view of history and a love of painting.

In many episodes of my childhood I see myself going to art museums with my parents. Part of our routine was a walk through the impressionist and post-impressionist halls of the Pushkin Art Museum in Moscow. Some of the paintings from the museum's phenomenal collection have stayed with me since I first saw them at the age of six or seven. Pierre Bonnard's lush pastoral canvases of summer and fall, with haystacks, cows, and peasant girls; Renoir's portrait of the actress Jeanne Samary: bottle-green dress, mauve background, rusty hair. I remember standing in front of Cezanne's *Pierrot and Harlequin*, listening to my father's improvised tale about unrequited love, jealousy, and arrogant pride. A couple of rooms over, the ending of my father's tale was revealed in Picasso's heartsick *Harlequin and His Companion*, where two heavy glasses of alcohol, a smaller and a larger one, are lined up in front of the itinerant actors. And there it is, my favorite childhood painting. I can see it from the previous hall through the open door. Picasso's silver-blue girl balancing on a ball, and a sepia-blue African man with perfectly formed muscles and the grace of a titan.

Seeing those paintings for the first time, in my father's company, was a formative experience. Visualize the wet pastel crowd of Monet's *Le Boulevard des Capucines* or Matisse's hypnotizing, hungry goldfish swimming round in a room of blossoming walls. Or imagine the wondrous tropical forests, giant grasshoppers, and horse-eating jaguars of Henri Rousseau's fancy. These paintings gave me a protective dose of another perfection by placing me at some un-Soviet intersections of verity and beauty. I will never forget the time my father brought me over to see Rousseau's *The Poet and His Muse*. On the canvas I saw a middle-aged man holding a scroll in his left hand, and in his right, a goose feather. Standing to his right was a woman in a wreath of black flowers. She was wearing a lilac ankle-length flute gown, and her right hand pointed upward, to the sky, to Mt. Parnassus. With her left arm she gently embraced the man, whose gaze was focused on something that lay beyond the framed space of the canvas. "This is me and your mother," father explained.

In those magical paintings, in their imaginary worlds, my childhood would dwell eternally. Yet in real life, my childhood ended when we become refuseniks. A dreamy refusenik preteen, I wandered the halls of the Pushkin Museum alone, revisiting the paintings to which my father had introduced me. I now favored different canvases by the same artists. Some time in seventh grade, my eyes glided indifferently across the surface of Van Gogh's *The Red Vineyard at Arles*, which I had previously venerated, only to be glued to a different painting, *The Convict Prison*. We had already been refuseniks for at least two years. I couldn't help thinking about the ring of stooped prisoners walking endlessly and forlornly round the narrow courtyard of the jail. That was us, Jewish refuseniks. And even Picasso's *Girl on a Ball* no longer had power over me, its place taken by another painting, *Old Jew and a Boy*. I stared at Picasso's canvas for long stretches of time and imagined, reflected in it, myself and my father.

2

DIFFERENT

ONCE DURING A LITERATURE LESSON in seventh grade a note was passed to me from the back of the classroom. It was a sheet of paper ripped from a lined copybook and folded in half. "To the Jew from the Russians!" (*"evreiu ot russkikh!"*), was scribbled in Russian on the front of the folded sheet. And inside was a short note: "You Shrayer Juboy son of a beach etc." Nothing too creative, except the spelling errors. The note was signed by two of my classmates. One of them, Fedya M., now a yachtsman, used to live in our apartment building. As I later found out, Fedya M.'s maternal grandfather, a microbiologist and a victim of Stalinism, was Jewish. The other author of the note, Fedya K., was raised by a single mother. Fedya K. intimated to his classmates that his father, an air force pilot, had been shot down during the war, and we never questioned this information. I hadn't had any confrontations with the first Fedya and I rather liked the other one; from neither of the two Fedyas had I been expecting virulence.

As early on as at the age of four I felt my own *otherness*. Some realizations of difference were actually implosions of naïveté, as the time when I came home one day from kindergarten all excited, telling my parents about the elderly aide who had given me an extra helping of chicken at lunch. Placing a chicken leg on my plate, she said, in front of all the other kids: "Here's some chicken for you, with the skin. You little Jews like it with the skin, don't you." And already in kindergarten there were first direct contacts with the word *zhid* ("Kike," "Yid," and "Hebe" combined). The word would spring off the tongues of the Russian boys (mostly boys, because girls at that age baited less with words) with such ease, as though they had had a lifetime of Jew-hating. Why did they hate the Jew in me, some of my five- and six-year-old kindergarten mates? I had not even begun to look Jewish at the time. Like some of the Ashkenazi children with Baltic roots, until the age of nine or ten I had a small pug nose and light hair. I did not *look* Jewish. Was it my strange, foreign, Jewish last name? But how did they know, the little ethnologists, that it was a Jewish last name? And how did they know to single out the kid with a "Jewish" last name and to insult him with such ditties as: "One dirty old Jew sold worms and ate them too."

As a small child I had heard the word "Jew" in our home, from my parents, our relatives, and my parents' friends; I had also witnessed discussions of Jewish questions unfurling in our kitchen or living room. Yet it wasn't until my last year of Soviet kindergarten that my father had sat me down and talked to me about it. This must have been in the autumn of 1973; I was six years old; Israel had just defeated its enemies, yet again, during the Yom Kippur War. My father was cleaning and polishing shoes in the hallway when I asked him what *zhid* meant. My first lesson in Jewish self-awareness lasted about five minutes.

"There was once an ancient people, the Jews, or the Hebrews," my father told me after he put down his brushes. "We're their descendants. And there are people in the world who don't like us, and try to hurt us."

"I see, papa." My father's words seared my mind and filled me with pride.

"So the next time someone calls you *zhid*, you tell them you're a Jew and proud of it. Say it very calmly, and then, if it's a guy, hit him hard on the nose. Chances are they won't do it again."

At home I learned my first lessons of Jewish spirituality, tinged with resistance and zealotry. Yet, growing up in Moscow, I was far removed from the Jewish life that had enveloped my grandparents in their childhoods. Both my parents were born and raised in the Russian capitals. For as long as great-grandmother Fanya (Freyda) was alive (she died in 1962, outliving her husband by seventeen years), Yiddish was spoken in her household, which is why my father had a passive knowledge of it when he was growing up. As a young girl, my mother heard Yiddish when her parents spoke it with her maternal grandfather, and more often than not it was a language of arguments and discord. Even to my father and mother, their parents' past life in the former Pale of Settlement, in Ukraine and Lithuania, was part history, part legend. To me it was all legend, all wondrous tales of yore in which the number of mills my ancestors had owned in Podolia kept growing and multiplying, as they did in the recollections of elderly Auntie Polya Shaferman, first cousin of my paternal grandfather, whom my father and I would occasionally visit. This antiquated, tidily dressed old lady occupied two rooms of a Moscow communal apartment and spoke with a formidable Yiddish accent. When I last saw her around 1973 or 1974, she was living mainly in the world of yellowed photos from Kamenets-Podolsk. "Tell me, dearie, where are our mills? Our factories? What have they done to them?" Auntie Polya asked me, when we said goodbye.

Over the years of living in America, I have been asked on many occasions, by American-born Jews whose ancestors came from the Pale of Settlement, whether I speak Yiddish. To illustrate how limited was my connection with the living Yiddish language as I was growing up in Moscow, I recall a visit to Minsk, the capital of Belarus, some time in the late 1970s. My parents and I were returning to Moscow from a vacation in Estonia. Instead of going back by way of Pskov or Leningrad, we took a detour and drove back by way of Latvia, Lithuania, and Belarus. My father's Aunt Manya, his late mother's only remaining sibling, was living in Minsk with her daughter's family. At one point in between exhausting meals of rich Jewish foods like *cholent*, of which I had only read in Russian translations of Yiddish classics, the husband of my father's first cousin put on an old record. He was a corpulent, mustachioed man who had grown up speaking Yiddish and considered it his mother tongue. He put on the record and asked me to hear it without telling me what he was going to play. It was a screechy recording, baritone accompanied by the piano, and it sang with force in a language that I intuited to be Yiddish.

"Does this grab your heart, son?" the man asked in the middle of the song.

I blushed, turned away my gaze, and said "yes." What I said wasn't true, I just didn't want to offend my provincial relative. When I was nine or ten, Yiddish folk songs did not move me at all. Instead, listening to that recording of a Yiddish song only charged me with a vague sense of embarrassment. For me personally, there was no return to Yiddish as a living language, and to my ancestors' Ukraine and Lithuania. Soviet history and the Shoah had done their work of destruction. On top of that, my grandparents' individual life decisions and accommodations had made their culturally rich Jewish past largely inaccessible to me when as I was growing up in Moscow in the 1970s.

In September 1974 I started first grade in English School No. 34, situated in the northwest corner of Moscow, a short walk from the high bank of the Moskva River. It was a twenty-five-minute stroll or a short bus ride from my house. When the network of specialized schools was originally introduced, I believe in the 1930s, the intention was to offer Soviet children intensive training in foreign languages. The sign on the front entrance still referred to our school as a "specialized school with some subjects taught in English." However, by the time I was starting first grade, winds of the Cold War and forces of stagnation had reduced "the subjects . . . taught" to four or five weekly lessons of English and the occasional forays into the literature, culture, and geography of the English-speaking countries. Nevertheless, the "specialized" language schools continued to carry prestige in the days of my Soviet childhood, and to get in, one had to take an entrance examination. I recited the opening of Pushkin's "Song of Prince Oleg the Wise" and also a poem by my father.

About sixty students entered School No. 34 annually. I started in 1A, which, by the time of my graduation from high school in 1984, had become 10A. For ten years, Monday through Saturday, I went to school with a class of about thirty boys and girls. Except for two or three dropouts, the number remained virtually unchanged. About thirty in 1A, and about thirty more in the parallel class, 1B. Of about sixty of us . . . I hesitate to use the first-person plural pronoun. Was I ever one of "us"? Of about sixty students in my graduating year the bearer of the name "Maxim Davidovich Shrayer" was the only one officially registered and listed as *evrei* (Jew) in the school documents, class rosters, and various other files and dossiers. There was a girl in my class, Polya, who came from a Jewish family and carried a distinctly Jewish last name. I believe one of her grandparents had been a Yiddish professor before being fired and exiled in the late

1940s, during a ferocious antisemitic campaign. Polya's father was a stork of a Jewish doctor in black suits and oversize black-framed glasses slipping off the bridge of his nose. His first name was the Russian equivalent of Jesus's Hebrew name. Stooping and looking around as though he was being watched, he came to school once a month to discuss his daughter's wavering grades. He did favors for some of the teachers, procuring for them hard-to-come-by medications. Even as a grade-schooler, I always knew that there was something incongruent, something wrong in the fact that the nationality of this Jewish doctor's daughter was listed as "Russian," and not as "Jew."

One of the collective amusements in middle school was to steal the class roster and to rummage through it. The pupils would crowd somewhere in the corner, one kid would be positioned on the lookout for the teachers, and then the full names—first, patronymic, last—would be recited alongside the nationality and grades. This is how I learned the *official* ethnic make-up of my class. Of some thirty pupils, between twenty-two and twenty-four were listed as "Russian" (this included a girl with an Armenian last name, a boy with a Tatar last name, a boy with what seemed like a Greek or a Lithuanian last name, and the piteous Polya), between four and six were designated "Ukrainian" or "Belarusian," and one (myself) was a "Jew."

I'm not conducting a sociological inquiry. That has all been done to death. The official Soviet census data gives us the following numbers for the Jewish population: 2.151 million in 1970, 1.811 million in 1979, 1.449 million in 1989 (the attrition owes itself to the Jewish emigration). According to the Soviet 1970 census, the country's total population amounted to 240 million, which means that at the time when I started grade school, Jews constituted less than 1 percent of the entire population. Out of the sixty or so students in my school year, I was the only "official" Jew. The token Jew?

One in sixty (1.66 percent) exceeds the official nationwide data on the Jewish population in the Soviet Union around 1974. But in larger urban centers, such as Moscow, Leningrad, or Kiev, the Jewish populations vastly exceeded the nationwide averages, whereas in other, more rural or remote parts of the Soviet Union, the Jewish population could be minuscule. So was it my Jewish luck to have ended up in Moscow English school No. 34, in a class with a Jewish girl, whose Jewishness was hidden under the safety of her official "Russianness," and with no openly Jewish kids besides myself? Had my parents miscalculated by placing me in a competitive school without having first inquired about the presence of other Jewish students? But such inquiries, while perfectly normal in today's United States, would have been ill-advised in the Soviet Union.

I have met ex-Soviet Jews of my age who experienced little antisemitism from their classmates. My best Moscow friend Max (Maxim) Mussel had half a dozen Jewish classmates. Their whole ethnic climate was different. Several non-Jewish kids in Max's class had Jewish nicknames like Zalmanzon or Srulik, which were used with affection, not derision. As a result, Max remembers his school years with fondness, while I look back at mine with acrimony. In fact, even in "my" school, in grades above and below me, there were kids who identified as—and whom the others identified as—Jewish. Some time in high school a chubby kid with an ornate Germanic last name began to draw Stars of David in bathrooms and hallways and to scribble lists of Jewish students and teachers on the walls. He was quickly branded a "Zionist" and challenged to an open fight by another kid. The "Zionist" was two grades below me; I didn't know him well and to this day I'm not sure whether he was an agent provocateur, a foolish Jewish activist, or both.

This is a personal story, and I want to relate my own Jewish experience with exactitude. Despite being what they call a "popular kid," despite being involved in various activities at school, from drama to the International Friendship Club, I was always alone. I felt this aloneness at school every day, for ten years.

Now picture a Music Appreciation lesson in 6th grade. For the duration of the entire year we were studying Russian classical composers, starting with the "Mighty Bunch," with Glinka, Rimsky-Korsakov, Dargomyzhsky, and Cui. Mussorgsky's *Pictures at an Exhibition* was the topic of the week. Our teacher, Ms. Vinogradova, a haughty young woman wearing a tweed above-knee skirt and a tight white turtleneck through which one could see her bra and nipples, explained the titles of individual vignettes in Mussorgsky's cycle. Then, in turn, she played them on the phonograph. "This next piece," said Ms. V., "is called 'Two Jews.' It represents—" Before she had the chance to continue her explication about grave economic inequality in czarist Russia, one Jew being rich, the other poor, before she could go on about Mussorgsky's "class-conscious genius," half of my classmates exploded with the ugliest of laughs. Mostly boys, but also a few girls, laughed hysterically at the teacher's mere mention of the word "Jew." My classmates were laughing because to many of them the word "Jew," not even *zhid*, but "Jew," had the ring of something insulting, dirty, and laughable. Like a flavorful swear word. And now the teacher herself had used it. And there were not one but two Jews, as though one wasn't enough! Several kids kept turning and slashing me with their eyes. "Two Jews, two Jews," a boy at the desk right next to mine kept repeating as he laughed, rocking and slapping on the desk with both his rashy hands. Zoya, with whom I shared the desk, wasn't laughing, but turned crimson all the way to the roots of her hair. This humiliation, through which I sat frozen and pretending that it wasn't affecting me personally—that it wasn't the word *Jew* they were laughing at—continued as the teacher stood and observed us. She finally clapped her hands, restoring order and extinguishing the cascades of savage laugher. When I think about the episode, it occurs to me that my classmates' laughter was invited by the teacher's thoughtlessness. Would it have been too much for her to explain to the class that this piece about two Polish Jews, titled "Samuel Goldenberg and Shmuyle" in Mussorgsky's original manuscript, came to be known in Russian under the name "Dva evreia: bogatyi i bednyi" ("Two Jews: Rich and Poor")? Instead, Ms. V.'s presentation might have reminded my classmates of the beginning of an antisemitic ditty, to which most kids of my generation would have certainly been exposed. Translated literally, this ditty goes like this: "Two Jews, the third a Kike, run down a little rope." In English, the tone of the ditty could be rendered as this: "Two Jews and a Kike went to Israel for a hike." What stunned me at the time is that the music teacher didn't make any disapproving comments about my classmates' outburst. No one said anything to me after class. The beautiful daughters of a well-known Soviet immunologist, with whom my father had interacted professionally, filed past me toward the exit. Sergei and Vitya, the two boys I was quite friendly with in middle school (we visited each other's homes after school), also ignored me. In some respects the silences were more hurtful than the beastly, collective laughter.

It's almost impossible to talk about these things without self-pity or pathos. Baiting and taunting started in elementary school and continued all through middle school, culminating in eighth grade. Throughout those five or six years I asserted my Jewish pride with fists, sometimes on a weekly basis. There's a big difference between one's success at gym lessons and in fist fights. I can still remember that wild feeling of revenge that would possess me when I heard the word *zhid* directed at me or blabbed behind my back. In fist fights, my father's lessons never failed me. A former boxer who had to give up the sport in college due to deteriorating eyesight, he had taught me: "Hit on the nose. Hit them first, attack them, don't give them time to think. Surprise them. Overwhelm them."

I was never the strongest or the fittest among the boys in my class. I was never a jock by natural inclination, and despite figure skating and swimming lessons my parents encouraged me to take, until the age of ten or eleven I was athletically in the bottom part of the class along with Afanasy, a physics genius, and Venya, an aspiring military historian. It wasn't until sixth grade that I underwent a physical, athletic transformation. When I first read Isaac Babel's prophetic story "The Awakening," I realized that like Babel's violin-playing Jewish boy from Odessa, I, too, had my benevolent, physically strong, philosemitic Russian teacher who saw as his mission training Jewish kids to face the hostile world. His name was Vladimir Borisovich Markin, and he is the only teacher from my Soviet school whom I remember fondly and without reservations. Markin was our gym teacher, and for the first three years of school I was terrified of him. He addressed seven-year-olds with the formal pronoun *vy* (instead of the informal *ty* that was standard in the teachers' interactions with students).

Markin was about forty-five when I met him. With his perfectly groomed mustache, barrel chest, and flawless posture, he looked like an officer from the Imperial Guards. Referring to body parts during demonstrations of various exercises, he used Russian expressions that sounded most peculiar to me at the age of seven, such as *sakharnitsa* (sugar basin) in reference to one's behind. I believe he had been a champion gymnast before studying at the Moscow Institute of Physical Culture and Sports, which trained phys-ed instructors and coaches. He was also a chronic alcoholic, something everyone in school knew, and the administration condoned, because of his dedication. Cognac was Markin's expensive drink of choice, and by the end of the day he would have usually had several long swigs from a flat bottle he kept in the desk of his office, off the school's spacious gym. Alcohol didn't seem to affect Markin's physical form even into his fifties; when I was in high school, he could still turn on the bar like a Rumanian teenager. At the end of fifth grade, right before the summer break, my gym teacher summoned me to his office cluttered with soccer balls, trophies, and pieces of gymnastic equipment. "Shrayer, you of all people need to work on your muscles," he said and looked me right in the eye. "Have your parents buy you a chinning bar. Put it up over your door and do chin-ups every day, as many as you can. I want you to do six chin-ups in September."

The chinning bar was not a random recommendation. In gym classes all boys had to do chin-ups several times a year. The results would go on record as part of our fitness tests, and in fifth grade I could barely do two, while four or five of my classmates could do seven or eight. As though adhering to the stereotype of an intellectually developed but unathletic Jewish kid, I had been resigned to doing two chin-ups. Now I had to face up to the challenge. At home, my father and I put together a makeshift chinning-bar from a section of a broken hockey stick and two pieces of an old suitcase strap. We attached it to the upper frame of my bedroom door. I was able to do four chin-ups by the middle of summer, five by August, six by the end of the summer. At the opening round of gym tests in September, I astonished my classmates by doing seven chin-ups. From the athletic laggards I had suddenly moved to the top tier of my class, now competing only with two or three kids. "The all-time record of our school is twenty-four," said Markin and winked at me: "You might consider going for it." At the end of high school, on a good day I could do twenty-two chin-ups, more than anyone in my year. But I still never got much better in either soccer or hockey, the two team sports most commonly played after school and in the back yard.

My new place in the athletic hierarchy earned me more respect but also intensified the baiting. The gym was located on the ground floor of the school building next to the school cafeteria. In the locker room, where many fights took place, the nauseating fumes of sour cabbage soup and fatty cocoa were mixed in with the fresh smell of sweat. How many times I got beat up by Anton, a bodybuilder and student of karate, whose favorite pastime was to enrage me after gym classes! "Listen, guy," he would say. "I don't really care whether or not you're Jewish. It don't bother me. I just like to see you get all crazy when I call you 'Kike.'" I would hit him on the bridge of his nose, and there would be scarlet blood on his sweat-soaked T-shirt. Our classmates stood and watched as I fought in the middle of the locker room amphitheater. This was my moment of triumph. And it didn't much matter that I would come home with a black eye or caked blood on my lower lip. Anton loved to provoke me, but I don't think he was a visceral antisemite. He was jealous of my grades and of my improving athleticism, and he used the racial slurs to get back at me. In contrast, I think that my other chief tormentor, a slothful giant by the name of Kol'ka, hated me and ached to hurt *the Jew* in me. By ninth grade (the equivalent of junior year in American high schools) no one insulted me to my face. Even after the worst of the antisemitic episodes had subsided, I maintained the reputation of a dangerous fighter. Now that I haven't been in a fist fight for more than twenty-five years, exactly since the day I came to America, memories of those skirmishes sometimes strike me as mock-heroic. But they weren't at the time. I was fighting for my Jewish dignity.

Has the picture of my Soviet childhood and adolescence emerged as one of misery? This wasn't, of course, the case. One of the paradoxes of growing up Jewish in the Soviet Union, in the circumstances that surrounded me and my family, was that in many respects I was a regular kid. With my peers from the last Soviet generation, I shared an almost complete lack of illusions about the political system and the road to communism. In common we had our Brezhnev jokes (he reads out loud the five "o"s of the Olympic rings), our hunger for things Western. I shared with them our generation's heroic, compensatory narratives, among which the central one was the Great Patriotic War, where our grandparents had shed blood and defeated Nazism. With my classmates I had in common our unsentimental education at summer camps for the Young Pioneers. For ten years we wore almost identically abominable school uniforms: sackcloth gray in grade school, and later, navy with pewter buttons for the boys and burnt-umber orphanage dresses with pinafores for the girls. We knew the names of each other's parents and siblings, attended each other's birthday parties, and filled out each other's questionnaires fashioned from bound school notebooks and passed under the table during classes (. . . your favorite color . . . boy/girl name . . . favorite saying). Side by side with my classmates I participated in the mandatory mopping of classrooms and raking of leaves in the school yard. I sang the same songs in the school chorus ("Vienna Woods . . . tra-la-la-la / World of wonders . . . tra-la-la-la"). I acted in the same school plays (in an anti-colonial drama we staged in seventh grade, I played, in make-up, a black African among all whites). I admired the very same early Soviet rock groups—*Time Machine, Aquarium, Sunday*—that my classmates did.

Through ten years of almost daily contacts I never felt that I was one of them, I never felt accepted as one of their own. What I didn't have in common with my classmates was my Jewishness. Well do I remember going to the local police precinct soon after turning sixteen, in June of 1983, for a short interview that preceded the issuing of one's first Soviet passport. The youngish lieutenant studied me through his squinted, flaxen eyes, and finally asked:

"What nationality do you choose?"

"What do you mean?" I asked, unprepared for the bluntness of this invitation to assimilation.

"Jewish?" the young lieutenant asked again, almost sympathetically, as though he was referring to a malady. "Or Russian?"

"Jewish!" I blurted out, blood flowing to my head.

"Very well," the lieutenant concluded the interview. "Your passport will be ready in three weeks," he said. And he gave me a look that meant "you missed the opportunity to become like the rest of us."

Life itself added a postscript to this chapter. One of the most liberating moments in my life was my Soviet high school graduation ceremony in June 1984. After the official part with the parents present had ended, after the conifer-green diplomas had been handed to the graduates, after the prom lasting into the early hours of the morning, I finally walked out of the building where for ten years I had been spending six days of the week. I slammed the heavy door, swollen with yearly layers of maroon paint. Feeling rapturous, I ran down the cracked marble steps without looking back. I walked through the half-open wrought-iron gate toward the empty morning street lined with poplars shedding fluff. I was freed at last of the school and of my classmates. During the summer and early fall of 1984, as we were taking the entrance examinations for and starting out at universities, I would exchange an occasional phone call with two or three classmates. For the next three years I would sometimes bump into a classmate while riding the Metro or in the neighborhood. By the time I left Russia in June of 1987, I had had virtually no contacts with my classmates for the three years that followed our graduation. Nor had I any desire to stay in touch after leaving Russia. In 1993, after getting naturalized as a US citizen, I was able to go back for the first time. During the first visit, and also during the subsequent ones, I didn't seek out my former class-mates. Years went by. One time, in November 1999, during an academic conference in Boca Raton, whose attendance was depleted by Hurricane Georges, I bumped into Olga S., who had been in my year at school, but in the parallel class. After the fall of the Soviet Union Olga had left Moscow to attend graduate school in California and was now teaching political science at a midwestern university. We exchanged polite greetings, and that was the end of it.

In August 2000, on our honeymoon, Karen and I visited my child-hood haunts, including Moscow, St. Petersburg, and Estonia. I took Karen to see my old neighborhood, apartment building, and school, but I had no wish to look anybody up. I had moved on. What would be the point of rummaging through the past, I was thinking. For my wife to put older faces of my classmates against many stories and few surviving photos of my Soviet childhood? I didn't want Karen to meet them. They were like smoke over a dumping ground of memory.

In summer of 2001, Karen and I bought an old gambrel in Chestnut Hill and then spent over two years renovating it. We had painted it pale hyacinth. The house had empty bedrooms and was ready for a baby—both the house and us, its occupants. We were waiting and hoping. On 2 March 2004, *quite unexpectedly*, as my late grandmother Anna Mikhailovna might have put it, I received the first in a slew of e-mails from my former classmates that would reach me that spring. By then I had already written a draft of the first three or four chapters of this book. The first e-mail came from Nikita, with whom I shared a desk in high school. He was a solid fellow, gifted in physics and math, and I do not recall his ever engaging in antisemitic rampages. Nikita had found my Boston College e-mail address. His short, friendly e-mail reminded me that twenty years ago that spring we had graduated from high school. The following day, before I had even had a chance to respond to Nikita's e-mail (I hesitated), another e-mail arrived. It came from an assistant to my former classmate Nina R. (who must have become a business executive), and it contained a save-the-date; plans for a class reunion were already under way. Nikita's e-mail, coupled with the invitation, had stirred up what I thought had been buried in the past. In my short reply, dated 3 March 2002, I wrote to Nikita:

> Tell me about yourself. . . . We last spoke on the phone in the autumn of 1984. Those were hard years for my family. . . . I have not been in contact with any [classmates]. Is everybody alive? I embrace you, Max(im).

Nikita wrote back a week later. His letter offered a glimpse of many post-Soviet destinies of my generation. Nikita graduated from a prestigious university with a physics degree, following two years of military service. He didn't work a single day in his professional field. He had to forget about science and turn to commerce. At the time of the writing, Nikita was working as a drug rep. He was married, with a four-year-old daughter and a younger son.

Was it the trusting tone of Nikita's e-mail? The next day I responded with a longer e-mail, in which I further lifted the guard. Specifically, I decided to test the waters by turning to the subject of Jewishness and religious identity. I wrote about my professional interests (Jewish writers), about my wife's Jewish ancestry in Eastern Europe. And I concluded the e-mail this way:

> I have probably changed a lot—or, at least, you might think so. During our school years I shared very little with my classmates; I couldn't. This particularly applied to things Jewish—you probably understand what I

mean. But here [*here* refers to America] everything is different. I'm not the most observant [Jew], but [. . .] we have a real Jewish home. Soon, by the way, is Passover, and we're having family over for a Seder, that is, a Passover supper. And do you go to church? Nikita, and how are your brother and mother? —I remember them well. Do write about our classmates.

Yours, Maxim.

In the e-mail I also asked Nikita to give my regards to the other classmates and to share my e-mail address. I never heard back from him, although it's always possible that his e-mail was lost or junked. Two weeks later, already after my classmates had gotten together for their reunion, I received an e-mail from Karina. She and I had gone to school for ten years and always got along. Her mother was an ethnic Russian and her father an Armenian, and Karina had a Russianized Armenian last name. Karina's father was a chief engineer at a major factory. In September the entire class would get invited to Karina's apartment for the annual birthday bash, at which Karina's olive-skinned father, eyes radiant with love for his daughter, presented each of us with fancy party favors. My recollections of Karina were untarnished by the kinds of memories that had been making it hard for me to keep in touch with my other classmates. Her Armenian origins must have also played a part. When writing back to her, I was now speaking to Karina not only as one former classmate to another, but as a Jew to an Armenian, with the implicit awareness that we shared a common history of genocide. Karina had included a detailed report on all the classmates who had been at the reunion. In my response I referred to having been the only Jew in our class or about being Jewish in America. Karina didn't reply right away, and I immediately assumed the worse. In the meantime, on 9 April 2004, I heard from another former classmate, Sergei.

Sergei was one of my two best pals at school up until the sixth or seventh grade, and he often visited me at home after classes. His apartment was only three blocks from our school, and it was lined with bookcases. Some of their books had been published before the Revolution, and I also recall that they had religious books, including Psalters in Church Slavic. In middle school we pursued two sisters, and after school we would walk them home, carrying their satchels and canvas bags with spare shoes. I don't remember Sergei ever insulting the Jew in me, but I also don't think he ever stuck his neck out for me. Once, on the spur of a fight over a twenty-kopeck coin he had lost to me in a game of shaking coins, he said: "What, your own riches aren't enough for you?" We were about twelve and I thought that he wanted to say "your Jewish riches" but he held back. Even in high school, when Sergei and I had very different pursuits, good chemistry prevailed in our interactions. Sergei's e-mail included a long report on the reunion, replete with class photos of the classmates in attendance and with Sergei's gently humorous commentary. I hadn't seen those faces in twenty years. How much we had all changed, boys and girls pushing forty! I was moved by the photos more than by the words, and replied on the same day:

> Recently I heard from [Nikita and Karina]; I replied to both with detailed letters. After that both grew silent. I suspect that was because I had honestly written to both, that I associated school with rather traumatic memories, especially those of middle school. Perhaps you don't remember or you didn't pay attention, but some classmates taunted me as a Jew, and I resisted in different ways. You, by the way, NEVER engaged in this business, which I also haven't forgotten. Besides, you probably don't know that from 1978 [until emigrating in 1987] I lived a double life: my parents and I were refuseniks, my parents were persecuted (for real, KGB, arrests and so forth), and I couldn't share this with anyone. That's the way it is. Well, okay, enough said.

Sergei didn't reply. I had also assumed I would not hear back from Karina, but I had underestimated her. Whatever the reason for Sergei's silence, on 12 April, the former Soviet Day of Cosmonautics, Karina sent me an e-mail that opened this way:

> Hello Max! I congratulate you with the Pesach holiday—as you call it, and we call it Paskha! [The wordplay is lost in translation, as in Russian the same word, *Paskha*, as in "paschal lamb," refers both to Passover and Easter.] To be more precise, happy Christ's Holy Sunday. We celebrated yesterday, on Sunday. . . .

Two months went by, and at the beginning of July I unexpectedly heard from Fedya K. In school we were never exactly friendly, but I think each admired each other's abilities. Fedya K. has a foreign last name that I couldn't place. He was a spectacularly talented visual artist, who spent most of the class time drawing and doodling. I still have one of Fedya K.'s inkpen drawings, a caricature of our class, with most classmates pictured as alcoholics and reprobates. I always thought Fedya K. would go to art school. But he didn't. Instead, he matured earlier than all of us in high school, began to scrub his face crimson to promote beard growth, and already in ninth grade claimed to have had sex—something quite unheard of in our rather puritanical youth. Later Fedya K. got his act together and did well at the graduating examinations. The last I had heard of him was that straight after high school he served in the navy for three years. Other than his fabulous cartoons, my two strongest memories of Fedya K. were those of his grandfather, a handsome old gentleman with Alpine-white hair and refined features, and of the note "To the Jew from the Russians," which Fedya K. had coauthored and sent me in seventh grade.

In his e-mail Fedya K. wrote that he had read some of my Russian poems, that he was sorry I couldn't be at the reunion. He had become a successful lawyer, had a fourteen-year-old daughter. I asked about his mother and grandfather, both of whom I remembered well, and also about his foreign last name. Fedya replied that his grandfather had passed away at a very advanced age, and that their name was actually of French origin—an ancestor of his had come from France and joined the Russian Imperial service. Fedya's maternal great-grandfather, it turned out, had been a general in the czarist army. Now it was beginning to make sense— the name, the grandfather's aristocratic bearing, Fedya's Gallic nose and chin. Was the moment ripe for me to drop another e-mail shocker from across the Atlantic? On 7 July 2004, I wrote this to Fedya K.:

> Listen, you and I went to school together for ten years, and I want to tell you, without mincing words, more or less what I wrote to Sergei, Nikita, and Karina, after they had gotten in touch with me by e-mail. I told them this, and Sergei and Nikita immediately "signed off," only Karina continues to write. Namely: for twenty years I hadn't sought contacts with

former classmates, because the school years had been very traumatic for me. You, probably, no longer remember, but I (as the only Jew—Polya was registered as "Russian") was baited and taunted, especially in middle school. This was difficult . . . I write this to you because for a long time now I haven't been who I once was in school. In many ways Jewish identity defines my behavior and perception of the world. When I visit Russia (I still have my closest friends in Moscow and St. Petersburg), I run across people who pretend that none of this ever was: antisemitism, persecution, closing of synagogues, ostracism of "Zionists." Please understand, it's hard for me to get over all this stuff, so strong are the memories. I just wanted to write this to you. If it's easier for you not to reply, do as you wish. Of course I'm happy to be in touch with you. Yours, Max. Below see photo (Karen and me in Brazil . . .).

In a flight of weak-heartedness, I didn't say anything specifically about the wretched note "to the Jew from the Russians." Fedya K. replied immediately, on 8 July:

Dear Max!
What's with you? Can you really imagine that your nationality makes any difference to me?! From childhood I was raised, not least by my granddad, with deep respect for people. I was NEVER, even in childhood, when many things pass without us being conscious of them, permitted to place anybody beneath me, and especially on the basis of "skin color."[. . . .]

You know, I also cannot classify myself as a Russian, which I have never regretted. Among my present acquaintances there isn't a single person who would allow himself any sort of vile display of nationalism.

Enough about this. Please do not ever tell me about this! If you decide not to be in contact with me for some other reasons, tell me, I won't be offended. And one more thing, so that you would understand me correctly, I have no other goals but friendly relations with you. I need nothing else. Simply put, you're interesting to me, as a personality, as a person who has achieved much ON HIS OWN, unlike many others. I'm interested in reading your books, talking to you. As I wrote before, I'm myself thinking about leaving. And trust me, it's not the sated, comfortable life that I seek. My family and I have had to go through a lot here. In a letter one couldn't tell it all. Perhaps one day you will actually visit . . . and we can talk. I remain very happy to be in touch with you; write to me. And don't forget the photos.

Yours, . . .

I have every reason to believe Fedya K. was sincere. He has since emigrated from Russia and is now living in Europe. Our subsequent, friendly communications, more recently via Facebook, only confirmed that the adult Fedya K. was being himself when he wrote the letter. Had he, then, forgotten and moved on? Was it I, then, who was still living in the past? Fedya K. and some of our other former classmates must have the liberty not to remember. But I cannot unremember. Who will unburden me?

3

BECOMING REFUSENIKS

IN 1978, after several years of brooding, my parents decided to leave the Soviet Union for good. In early January of 1979, as the Soviet involvement in Afghanistan thickened, we formally requested permission to emigrate to Israel. My parents' decision to uproot themselves had been a long and tortuous one.

Despite the discrimination they encountered as Jews, my mother and father had both reached professional prominence. Neither one of them was a member of the Communist Party; both had attained their positions on merit. Two years prior to my parents' initial application for exit visas, my mother had been promoted to senior lecturer at the Higher Courses for Foreign Languages at the Ministry of Foreign Trade. Her duties focused on teaching advanced English to Soviet foreign trade specialists and also included interpreting and translation. My mother had co-authored a textbook of English for business. (Her name would be purged from the textbook when it would come out in the early 1980s.) Most language lecturers and instructors at my mother's institution would periodically be sent abroad, to the countries whose languages they taught, in order to perfect language skills. Not a single time was my mother allowed to go to England or to another English-speaking country. Off the record, the head of personnel openly told my mother: "You're Jewish, Mila, we just can't send you." And thus my mother continued to teach Soviet foreign trade executives about English business etiquette and about London's landmarks, including one Tavistock Hotel, a legendary establishment where Soviet commerce envoys would stay upon arriving in misty Albion. She was expected to command an in-depth knowledge of all sorts of things she had never experienced firsthand. In the fall of 1976, after fifteen years of teaching advanced English, my mother finally saw the "decaying world of capitalism" for the first time. Still not an English-speaking country it was, but Japan, where she interpreted, from English, for a delegation of Soviet engineers training at Mitsubishi. The trip to Japan lasted two months and catalyzed my mother. I was nine at the time and I remember her arrival from the airport at two in the morning; I stayed up, anxious to see my presents, colors markers and chewing gum, especially. There was something different about my mother, and not only in her new vogue-ish clothes and her haircut and perfume. It was as though in her mind she had crossed a boundary separating a Soviet past and a Western future. My mother couldn't stop talking about life *over there*. I remember shreds of adult conversations, in which words such as "privacy," "freedom of speech," "respect for human dignity" were being tossed about.

When my parents decided to leave Russia, my father was working as a senior research scientist at the Gamaleya Institute of Microbiology and Epidemiology of the Soviet Academy of Medical Sciences. He had published some seventy scientific papers, many of them on staphylococcal infections and phage therapy, and had done pioneering work in the treatment of mixed bacterial infections. His work had saved lives both of people and of livestock. In fact, in 1970 he had risked his life for Russia and her people when he worked, as part of a small team of epidemiologists, at the outbreak of cholera in Yalta. He had experienced his own share of prejudice, especially by the officials of the Academy of Medical Sciences. In 1975 he defended and submitted for attestation his dissertation for the degree of Doctor of Science, the highest advanced degree generally required in the Soviet Union for elevation to the rank of full professor. The process of conferring the degree by the VAK (acronym of the Higher Attestation Commission), was expected to be a mere formality, but became mired in antisemitism masking itself as bureaucracy. My father was asked to re-revise and re-submit for re-attestation what had already been a publicly defended, voted for, and approved dissertation. The process was taking two years and amounted to unabashed nitpicking by some members of the VAK. Even though, by 1978, the difficulties with my father's doctor's dissertation had been nearly overcome, the prejudicial treatment had injured his academic pride. It's one thing to be aware of systemic antisemitism at most Soviet institutions, but it's another to have become convinced that definite limits were being set by the system on one's own academic advancement. That it had taken my father longer than some of his peers to have shed academic illusions could be partly explained by the gains he had made by the middle 1970s in his other career.

A professional, published author and literary translator since the late 1950s, my father had only gained admission to the Union of Soviet Writers in 1976. Much more than a professional "union" in the Western sense of this word or a writer's organization like PEN or the Author's Guild, membership in the Union of Soviet Writers validated one's status as a literary practitioner. It was an elite organization, whose membership, limited to under eight thousand writers in a country of some 260 million, was highly coveted. Both an entitlement and a sinecure, the Writers' Union rewarded its members with benefits, such as well-paid readings and lectures, "creative trips," and subsidized vacations. The admitted writers received the Soviet system's imprimatur to contribute to the country's scripted cultural life.

Despite endorsements from and recommendations by such renowned writers as Viktor Shklovsky, admission to the Writers' Union had been an uphill battle for my father. Back in the late 1950s, upon the suggestion of the poet Boris Slutsky, he had adopted the literary penname "David Petrov," derived from Pyotr/Petr—a Russianized form of his father's first name, Peysakh. This assimilatory gesture, while camouflaging my father's Jewish last name, did not ease the publication of his poetry. His occasional, compromistic flights into official Soviet subjects (e.g., space exploration; construction of the Baikal–Amur Railroad) didn't help. Most of my father's poems were too richly experimental, lyrically denuding, and doctrinally untarnished for Soviet officialdom to allow their publication. By the time of his admission to the Writers' Union, he had only managed to publish one collection of his own verses and a short book of essays about the intersections of poetry and science. Most of his publications, and a significant source of his literary earnings, were in the area of literary translation, especially from Lithuanian, Serbo-Croatian, and Macedonian. He had been frustrated with being unable to publish the kind of poetry he was writing for the desk drawer. Some of his poetry had been circulating in the literary underground since the late 1950s, but this kind of publicity never was his cup of tea. My father had taken to heart and applied to his literary activity the aphorism of the Soviet general-turned-dissident Petro Grigorenko: "Only rats belong in the underground."

In 1975–76, as my father awaited the decision about his admission to the Writers' Union, he composed poems in which disharmonies of his Jewish and Russian selves adumbrated a conflict with the Soviet regime. He hadn't had a poetry book published since 1967. While relations between Jews and Gentiles had already became a principal concern of my father's writing, he couldn't dream of publishing these texts in the Soviet Union. In fact, not merely the fact of his own Jewishness but his open emphasis of the dual, paradoxical nature of the Jewish-Russian identity was the reason my father had been unable to place a new collection. The admission to the Union of Writers enabled him to sign three new book contracts, including one for a large volume of poetry. Titled *Winter Ship*, the new collection was to showcase many of my father's best poems and was probably as good a compromise between aesthetics and ideology as one could have expected in the Brezhnevite USSR. The collection had passed the editorial review and was in production, and I remember the trepidation with which my father awaited its arrival.

In a way, the scenario with my father's entrance to the Union of Soviet Writers mirrored the humiliating snags in the conferral of his Doctor of Science degree. When my father was finally made a member of the Union in 1976, he valued the newly-gained status but just could not feel ecstatic about it. To think of it. . . . He only got to drink the poisoned mead of the official writers' benefits for three full years. Unlike his academic life, which occurred in domains that were off-limits to me as a young boy, I did get a chance to witness my father's brief life as a full-membership Soviet author. My memories of the Writers' Union call for another brief digression. They may help to reconstruct how much—or how little—I understood, as an eleven-year-old, of my parents' decision to emigrate.

Between 1976 and 1980 I regularly went, both with my father and alone, to the Central House of Writers in Moscow (TsDL). I remember my childish admiration for the scarlet cushions and the gilt, carved armrests of the club's bottomless divans. There was an Olympic-size billiards room where certain writers practically lived, as well as two restaurants and two bars, replete with locomotive-like espresso machines. At these writers' feeding and watering places, my father treated me to canapés with salmon roe, smoked sturgeon, and veal tongue. On the way out of the building, on the right before the triple oak doors, there was a cloakroom where I would tip the attendants for getting my coat—the only occasions in my childhood that I would be allowed and expected to tip. I remember seeing in the flesh some of the writers whose personae millions of Soviet readers mythologized as they read their works. I saw these writers drink, gorge on food, and trade gossip just like ordinary mortals. I remember Andrey Voznesensky coming out of the Writers' House in winter, wrapped in a rich fur coat, one of his poetic flunkeys reverently holding the heavy door. A succession of shots and episodes: Bulat Okudzhava, dry, brittle, stooped, inhaling smoke and writhing as though his lungs were being filled with nerve gas. Yevgeny Yevtushenko walking across the lobby like a sprightly marionette; a woozy effigy of the beautiful and mellifluous Bella Akhmadulina; Fazil Iskander with the doubly ironic face of a tired dromedary; Vassily Aksyonov in wool turtlenecks framing the face of a gym instructor at the Noble Pension; the tall, emaciated Igor Shklyarevsky putting down his billiard cue to brag about a giant salmon he had caught in Karelia; David Samoylov confined to wearing thick lenses after a double cataract surgery, yet regarding the world with Napoleonic arrogance. Since the collapse of the Soviet Union, many names and faces from this literary panopticon have sunk into oblivion. They paid with reticence or silence for the comforts of the Writers' House, of subsidized resorts and other material benefits.

Several times I accompanied my father on readings and trips across the country. I witnessed how he transgressed the boundaries of official culture. Picture the closing night of Poezijös Pavasaris '78, a spring festival of poetry in Lithuania. Vilnius (Vilna), once the Jerusalem of Eastern Europe and now the capital of Soviet Lithuania; a lofty cathedral that doubled as an official concert hall. Grandmother Bella's Lithuania had vanished in the Shoah, and yet it continued to live in my father's heart through his Russian translations of Lithuanian poetry. For ten days a group of writers from different republics of the Soviet Union—Armenia,

Belarus (still Belorussia), Russia, Ukraine (still "the Ukraine")—had been touring Lithuania, stopping in villages and former market towns to read both their own works and translations of Lithuanian poetry. To my father, a Jew and a Russian poet, the Lithuanian poets he had translated into Russian complained behind closed doors about the Russian "Big Brother," whom they regarded as an oppressor and occupier. They also spoke of their guilt for their people's role during the Shoah, when most of Lithuania's Jews had been wiped out. (These Lithuanian writers never spoke directly of their fathers' and uncles' actions, only of complicity.) For the festival's closing night, the cathedral in Vilnius was overcrowded; TV cameras were placed in the aisles. I was almost ten, and I felt small and lost sitting by myself in a dark pew, surrounded by the sounds of Lithuanian, which I couldn't understand. My father was far away on stage, tall, tanned, his Levantine head like a crow astride hundreds of Baltic seagulls. He wore a blue denim suit that he had procured on one of his trips to Siberia, where in the construction area of the Baikal–Amur Railroad many "deficit items" were openly available for sale. After reciting his translations from the Lithuanian, my father turned to his Russian verses. The last poem he read bore the title "My Slavic Soul," and no Soviet magazine would print it. Without understanding everything, I knew every word of it by heart. My father's "Slavic soul" (*slavianskaia dusha*)—a feminine being in the gendered Russian language—abandons her owner's skin and hides in a hayloft, no longer capable of leading a double existence as both a Russian and a Jew. In English translation, the poem's opening would read as:

> My Slavic soul trapped in the skin of a familiar Jewish wrapping,
> Forswearing the daily strife that suffocates me all my life,
> One day will outsmart its lot, will turn a clever somersault
> And dashingly escape to burn like anthracite, the wondrous stone.
> I'll chase her: Wait! What shall I do alone amid this grove of birches
> In my perennial, banal, so typically Jewish wrapping?
> The ruts and roadside ditches that have viewed me as a solid fellow
> Will realize that I'm barren, like an abandoned charabanc.

A Jewish-Russian child, I cried unashamedly in the pew of this Lithuanian Catholic cathedral–turned–Soviet-temple-of-culture. When father finished reading, a roar of applause filled the cathedral, and an old woman in a mohair cardigan turned to me, contorting her mouth into a horrid smile; her bespectacled face had no flesh at all, no cheeks, chin or lips, just skin the color of a brown paper bag, as if sulfuric acid had been spilled on it many years ago. Was my father testing how far he could go in challenging the system without facing repression? I know from him that upon returning to Moscow he was summoned to the secretariat of the Union of Soviet Writers and given a major talking-to for having publicly recited "Zionist poetry." (In Soviet-speak the term "Zionist" had lost most of its distinct meaning, becoming synonymous with almost anything self-consciously Jewish or Judaic.) The scandal in Lithuania was one of the last straws.

As I think of everything my parents had worked so hard to accomplish in their Soviet lives and then lost in a wink, I anticipate naysayers' questions: A senior lecturer at a prestigious institution in Moscow? A senior scientist in the Soviet academy? A member of the Union of Soviet Writers? And that still wasn't enough for them? Weren't they just over-ambitious? In the final reckoning, it must not have been enough! The paradox of my parents' decision to emigrate was that they had come to it at high points of their careers, when both professionally and financially things were finally looking up, even if hurdles continued to stand in their way. To put this differently, my parents walked away from the Soviet battlefield when they might have already won the winnable Jewish battles of their careers.

There were two historical reasons behind my parents' decision to leave the Soviet Union: (1) the abiding state-sponsored and popular anti-semitism, (2) the ideological and cultural repression my parents experienced, *both* as Jews and as intellectuals living there. And there was a third, pressing, personal reason: to get me out of the country before I became an adult. As they hoped for better professional prospects abroad, in placing their Soviet careers on the execution block, my parents thought of me and my future. They wanted to save me from my Jewish aloneness at school, from the insults, from Soviet brain-twisting, from forced assimilation, and, finally, from the prospect of being drafted into the Soviet military after I turned eighteen in 1985.

In Chekhov's "Lady with a Lapdog," there's a line describing the feelings of Anna's husband about her trips to Moscow, to see Gurov. Anna tells her unloved husband she's going to Moscow to consult a gynecologist, and Anna's husband, the civil servant von Diderits, "believed and didn't believe" her (*"veril i ne veril"*). I love this line for its hopeless tendresse of diction and for the clarity with which Chekhov articulates the uselessness of rumination. While contemplating the prospects of emigration all through the middle 1970s, as the wave of Jewish emigration rose by tens of thousands, my parents continued to advance in their professional careers as though it would be possible *to stay* and *to leave* both together. After my mother's business trip to Japan, emigration became an *idée fixe*. In 1977 a family acquaintance, actually my mother's former suitor A.T., received permission to emigrate, and my parents asked him to arrange for an invitation (affidavit) from my father's uncle Munia Sharir (Shrayer), a former *halutz* who had been living in the land of Israel since 1924. (As a signatory of the Helsinki Accords, the Soviet Union outwardly endorsed the idea of "reunification" of families across the national boundaries, and one needed a formal affidavit from relatives in Israel to apply for an exit visa.)

As of 31 December 1978, my mother no longer had her beloved teaching job and my father his research position. Those sacrifices were a prerequisite for being able to submit the emigration paperwork. I remember so well the tempestuous 1979 New Year celebration at our Moscow apartment. The party was a symbolic break-up with the past, and three Americans were among our guests. There was a Jewish sociologist from New York with a divorced sister, who was dressed like Carmen (Bizet's, not Mérimée's). They knew our old Moscow friends who had gotten out in the early 1970s. The American brother and sister came to Moscow and looked us up. The third American guest was a businessman from Los Angeles who, I believe, had been working in Tehran, fled Iran as the revolutionary unrest grew by the day, and ended up passing through Moscow. The sociologist's sister and the businessman had met at the American Embassy a few days before New Year's and were now in the throes of a love affair. The adults drank black label Soviet champagne with smoked sturgeon and caviar, toasting the next year in . . . New York. My parents were euphoric as they embarked on a new life.

On 3 January 1979 my parents went to our district Department of Visas and Invitations (OVIR, in the lingo of Soviet acronyms) and submitted the official application to be "reunited" with family in Israel. As a historic note, I should mention that the Soviet Union hadn't had diplomatic relations with Israel since the days of the Six-Day War. Following the severing of the relations in 1967, the Soviet Union became an even greater backer of the Arab states and treated Israel as one of its arch-enemies. By declaring the intention to move to Israel, a Soviet subject formally sided with an enemy state.

Had we ever intended to go to Israel? America loomed large in my parents' imaginations, drawing them like a siren garlanded with neon lights of freedom and success. Photos of Hemingway and Robert Frost and a reproduction of Jackson Pollock's *Blue Poles* hung in my father's den alongside portraits of great Russian poets, among them Pushkin, Akhmatova, and Pasternak. My mother had abandoned the Queen's English in order to sound like a Yankee. And yet, Israel to us, and especially to my father, was much more than a legal fiction or a pretext to get out of the USSR. Israel, where my mother and father had living uncles, aunts, first cousins, and extended families, was both fact and phantom, reality and fiction, oasis and desert. We didn't know for certain where we would end up going, to America or to Israel.

Why did our family miss the ferry of emigration and get stuck in the Soviet Union for almost nine years? Was it meant to happen? Were we destined to become refuseniks, and could we have predicted it or prevented it from happening? We have spoken so many times about all the things that they might have done differently. They should not have ruminated for so long. They should have requested the Israeli affidavit earlier, not in 1977 but in 1976. They should have first quit their high-power jobs (especially my father, his job at the Academy of Medical Sciences) and lain low for a couple of years. They should have started the application process earlier, not in January 1979 but a year or two before that. They should have. . . . How clear everything seems in retrospect! Could we have anticipated the refusenik fiasco? Were my parents aware of the doctrine of "brain drain," in which not just visa applicants with prior access to "classified" information but thousands of Soviet Jews with advanced degrees or professional prominence were a Cold War strategic commodity? Had they seriously considered that the Afghan morass would exacerbate the climate of Soviet–Western relations? That the emigration trapdoors may close shut? In reconstructing those turning days and months in our lives, I keep returning to that convivial New Year's celebration with strange Americans dancing in our Moscow apartment, and my deliriously hopeful parents partying with them. The throbbing decision had finally been made. My parents were still young enough (father, forty-two; mother, thirty-eight) to adapt to new lives abroad, and they were getting me out before the army draft clock would start ticking. In their decision, clarity of vision was conjoined with dreamers' disregard of harrowing circumstances. For me, this is where Chekhov's articulation of both believing and disbelieving rings so true.

Just a few days before that New Year celebration, my mother had sat me down in the kitchen, where important family conversations took place around a blue Formica-top table.

"You know how things are difficult here for Jews," she said a bit matter-of-factly. "So papa and I would like to apply for permission to leave the country. To emigrate." After a pause she added: "This means that we will be moving, going to live abroad."

Of all my responses and questions, I remember two distinctly. "What about my school?" was one, and "What will happen to grandmother?" was the next one.

"Your grandmother, aunt, and little cousin will also come. Of course. We wouldn't want to leave them here, would we?" my mother said playfully but also with determination.

"We wouldn't. We'll take them with us."

"So that's settled, and over there" (*over there* was a euphemism for abroad), "you'll go to a great new school, and there'll be other Jewish kids and—"

"—I know, mama," I interrupted. "I understand."

"I know you do," my mother said. "And I also know you're a big boy, and this is something you will not discuss with your classmates or anybody else at school."

I had been fantasizing about America. Most kids of my Soviet generation fantasized about it despite being doused with anti-American propaganda. A miracle country, America held a particularly exalted place in the imaginations of Soviet Jews at the height of emigration. I was convinced we would be going to an absolutely perfect country, the best one in the world. In fifth grade I envisioned the United States and my would-be American peers as the complete opposite of the country where I was living and of my Soviet peers at school. I remember lying in bed and imagining a group of American kids and myself in their midst. I would be accepted and loved. How else, I thought, could it be in America?

The winter and spring of 1979, those galloping first six months. A shopping spree, often from under the table and at double mark-up: good clothes, leather suitcases, bed linens, fine china and silverware. Russian souvenirs. The excitement of selling off our possessions and buying things for the new life in the West. Then, as some of our fellow applicants were getting permission and leaving, and others were becoming refuseniks and staying, a mood of denial set in. "This won't happen to us, they just haven't yet gotten to our application at the OVIR, there are scores of applicants, there's a long queue, it simply takes time," my parents were saying to each other and to the new acquaintances they met through the Jewish emigration grapevine. Already the refusenik's grim reaper was swishing his scythe around us left and right, cutting down visa applicants with professional accomplishments. Pundits were talking in our kitchen and living room about the liability of having advanced degrees and about the "mechanisms" of the Cold War. Then, on 27 December 1979, the Soviet troops invaded Afghanistan. President Carter announced a grain embargo and issued an ultimatum that the United States would boycott the summer 1980 Moscow Olympics. Already expecting the worst, my parents spent the early months of 1980 like detainees awaiting their sentence.

Today we know that 1979, the year we first applied for an exit visa, was the peak year for Jewish emigration from the Soviet Union, with over 51,000 leaving. In 1980 almost 20,000 Jews were allowed to leave as the passage was already closing. Then the numbers quickly dwindled, and by the middle of the 1980s Jewish emigration was reduced to a paltry thousand per year. Even though the Jackson-Vanik Amendment, which had been signed into law in 1975, had made the release of Soviet Jews an exchange currency on the market of the "most favored nation" status, it hardly affected the outcome of emigration during the years 1981–86. The relations with the West would remain openly hostile until Mikhail Gorbachev's ascent to power in 1985, and a change in the refuseniks' lot—in our lot—wouldn't come until 1987.

One could say, in retrospect, that Soviet Jews were bargaining chips in Soviet dealings with the West. And also, that my parents and thousands of other future refuseniks who ended up missing the wave of 1977–79 should have counted the political omens and weighed their own professional accomplishments before applying for an exit visa. But life is not lived retrospectively, and the luck factor resists the simplistic causality of hindsight. Despite all the writing on the walls of Soviet history, and despite their resumes anchoring them to the Soviet Union, my parents could not have anticipated our refusenikhood. They had never planned to see me receive my own Soviet passport, graduate from high school in Moscow, and, worse even, turn eighteen with a prospect of being shipped to Afghanistan to fight the mujahideen.

We applied for permission to emigrate when I was eleven but finally left Russia when I was twenty. The condition of living in refusenik limbo defined my existence throughout those years.

Picture a crisp winter afternoon in the beginning of March 1980. Minus ten degrees Fahrenheit outside. An unripe orange sun rolls into the kitchen of our Moscow apartment as the table is set for a Sunday lunch. My mother has roasted a chicken, a plump young Hungarian chicken with fat thighs, the chicken every Soviet housewife dreamed of making for dinner, the lucky Eastern European cousin of the emaciated Russian hens that lay prostrated on the poultry counters. This is my favorite meal, roast chicken with potatoes. From the half-open oven, the chicken emits a divine smell of Jewish cooking, sweet like the promise of everlasting parental love. In the center of the table—an oval plate with mother-of-pearl pieces of schmaltz herring covered with white onion rings and sprinkled with vinegar. Herring, a salad of shaved white radish with fried onions, and also a dish of chopped liver with hard-boiled eggs are the *zakuski*. A hunk of caraway rye bread sits on a slicing board to the left of my father, who is at the head of the table. An iced bottle of vodka in the center of the table has come straight from the freezer. These Sunday lunches are usually reserved for private family time, for time alone with my parents (and my grandmother, if she's visiting). But the doorbell rings as we're about to sit down, and my father gets up to open it.

Who could it be? For some reason a guest has come over. It's a neighbor from our apartment building, Dr. Iosif Irlin. I've known him since I was four, since we moved to our co-op. A medical scientist like my father, he lost his lab and academic job after applying to emigrate. A strange aura surrounds Irlin and his wife Sveta, also an experimental scientist. They have been *refused*, the adults say about him. The authorities claimed that Irlin had access to classified medical information and had to be quarantined for an indefinite period of time. For two years now they have been refuseniks. *Refusenik* is a terrible word, it brings the taste of burned tires under my tongue. But I know it won't happen to us. We're just *waiting* for our permission to emigrate, my parents tell me. It's already been a year and two months since we applied. We should be hearing very shortly. I know my parents have thought of everything; they never make mistakes.

Our guest joins us at the kitchen table. My father pours vodka for the men and white wine for my mother. I drink golden grape juice. For a little while we eat quietly: fresh rye bread, herring that tastes like smoked salmon, radish into which the centuries of Jewish sorrow and joy have been mixed. The silence is becoming awkward, and Irlin decides to tell a joke about three animals planning to emigrate to Israel: a bear, a hare, and a fox. I already know this joke, but I listen politely. Someone has told the bear that in Israel all names end with *-uck*, and he suggests to the other applicants that they should change their names. "I'll be Buck," says the bear. "Great, I'll be Huck," says the hare. "And I ain't going," says the fox. My mother stares though the window at our street down below. There's a long queue in front of the liquor store. A trolleybus is making a stop with a tremor, like an old grasshopper. Despite the chill, windows of the VD ward of City Hospital No. 52 directly opposite our building are wide open for airing. My mother isn't laughing, but my father forces a laugh and pours himself and the guest some more vodka.

"There's something mama and I wanted to tell you," says my father.

I look up from my plate where a nacreous piece of herring swims across the blue porcelain sea. My father's eyes are running away from me.

"We got a postcard last week from the OVIR. Mama and I went there on Thursday. We have been refused. But we can reapply in six—"

"—I don't want . . . ," I scream as I propel myself from the kitchen settee.

"This is what I feared the most," my father says to his colleague Dr. Irlin. I bolt out of the kitchen. The serene flow of the present tense is broken. Broken is the peace of our Sunday lunch and the promise of happiness. . . . I dash out of the kitchen screaming and bawling, except that in my memory I did it in slow motion, so slow that I could see the cracks in the parquet floors, the caked mud on my mother's tall black boots parked in the foyer, the legs of the coat rack at which our dachshund Rusty had gnawed, the uneven golden ornaments of an alabaster Oriental war mask which I had made for my parents at sleepaway camp. I threw myself onto the bed. My parents followed me to my room and both sat beside me. "This is only temporary, we'll reapply in six months. And then we'll get permission," they kept trying to comfort me. I had a fit of hysterical sobbing. "I won't go to that school, I won't," I kept saying over and over again.

Perhaps I cried inconsolably because I knew there was no going back to childhood. In June of 1980, when I turned thirteen, I was to become a *bar mitzvah*, an adult according to Judaic law. That winter day when I learned I was a refusenik was also the day I fell, prematurely, into Jewish adulthood. It happened not through a religious ceremony but through losing faith in my Jewish parents' omnipotence. Clichés sometimes have curative powers, so here's another one: a perfect mirror had been shattered. Reflected in that mirror were my dreams of not being surrounded by peers who made me feel Jewish and alien. Were they dreams of a harmonious assimilation? Or were they simply idealistic fantasies of living in a better world?

Becoming a refusenik had deepened the rift between my classmates and myself. The secret I now carried inside had sealed my soul. There was no one at school I could open up to and trust with my secret. Only my best friends knew about my secret, but they weren't among my classmates. All through middle and high school, and later in university, I would lead a double life. Looking back, I wonder at times how it was that I never slipped, never betrayed myself. Twenty-odd years later it still amazes me that a young person's nature possesses such a plasticity and adapts to almost any kind of circumstances. At school I imitated a "normal" Soviet teenager, while at home I lived the illicit, dangerous life of a refusenik family. Of course, my parents sheltered, protected, and spared me. And like most preteens and teenagers, I was self-absorbed, and some of my parents' worst moments of danger and despair would pass me over.

A hangman's joke of the 1980 vintage told of a voice recording created at the Moscow OVIR: "*Zhdite otkaza*" ("Wait for your request to be denied"), instead of the conventional "*Zhdite otveta*" ("Wait for your call to be answered"). The joke signaled an atmosphere of hopelessness. The spring, summer, and fall months of 1980 belong to the blackest periods of our family history. Our visa application was denied for the first time in February 1980. In July of 1980 my father's last professional harbor, the Union of Soviet Writers, expelled and expunged him. A few months later, a hateful poem about him, titled "To the Poet Who Abandoned His Motherland," appeared in one of the biggest Soviet dailies, *Komsomolskaya Pravda* (*Komsomol Truth*), read daily by tens of millions. The author of the poem was then one of the secretaries of the Moscow branch of the Union of Soviet Writers, Stanislav Kunyaev. That Kunyaev had struck out at my father was particularly symbolic because in the 1960s and early 1970s he had been friendly with a number of Jewish-Russian poets, including Boris Slutsky, Aleksandr Mezhirov, and my father. As the wave of the Jewish emigration rose and then crested in 1977–79, Kunyaev had emerged as a leader of the Russian cultural chauvinists within the apparatus of Soviet literature. "To you this is a territory, and to me—Motherland, you son of a bitch," Kunyaev intoned, addressing my father from the pages of the Soviet newspaper. Kunyaev likened my father to a werewolf, the upshot being that he had been wearing the pelt of a Russian poet but now betrayed Russia by revealing his true, Jewish, alien self. My father wrote an open letter of protest, which Soviet newspapers refused to print. The expulsion and the pernicious poem were acts of direct ostracism against my father. Three of his books, a poetry collection, a novel for young adults, and a volume of poetry translations from the

Lithuanian, were immediately derailed. The novel had already entered the stage of corrected proofs, yet, barbarically, the galleys were "broken" and destroyed. I remember looking at the proofs and admiring the folio-size illustrations spread out across my father's desk. With this act of cultural violence the state was punishing my father for having attempted to emigrate, all the while preventing him from leaving. But even as he expected the system's revenge, my father was particularly devastated by the ban on the publication of his poetry collection *Winter Ship*. Even with the compromises and deletions my father had been forced to make (controversial poems such as "My Slavic Soul" being excluded), *Winter Ship* would have been a literary event had it appeared in 1980.

My father grieved the death of his books. Now that he was blacklisted, his literary earnings were cut off. He was unable to obtain commissions for new translations or give lectures. Having spent our family savings down to the last ruble, my parents faced financial hardships for the first time since the early 1960s, when my father was still in graduate school and my mother a university student. We sold off some of the most valuable possessions, including precious turn-of-the-century first editions, my great-grandfather's gold watch, some of my mother's jewelry, and what we had of antique furniture.

My parents needed a monthly check. Stigmatized, they couldn't return to their old jobs. Finding a half-decent professional job was a huge ordeal for a refusenik, which is why many worked as parking-lot attendants, boiler-room stokers, or warehouse clerks. After looking around, my father landed a job at the emergency room of one of Moscow's most crowded city hospitals. The pay was about one third of my father's old salary as an academic, and he was working a 24-hour shift every other day. To earn more cash, my father disregarded his severe myopia and astigmatism and worked at night as a "gypsy driver." A Doctor of Science and a published author, he would drive black marketers and prostitutes around Moscow, often picking up his clients in front of downtown restaurants. He sometimes came home in the early morning, a billfold in his pocket, twenty or thirty rumpled rubles smelling of liquor and sweaty palms. He was angry, humiliated, vengeful. My parents now hated the Soviet system with all their might—*hated* in contrast to being intellectually opposed to it. I remember the Moscow summer 1980 Olympics, the ones the United States and other countries had boycotted. My grandmother was over at our place, and we were all watching the opening ceremony. As a column of children in Young Pioneer's red kerchiefs marched around the Olympic stadium, my grandmother, an orphan of the Stalinist years, remarked: "Look, what lovely little children." My father's face turned sullen, and he said slowly and gravely, without looking at grandmother: "These are the children whose parents are oppressing us, and who will oppress your grandson when they grow up."

With the escalation of the war in Afghanistan, the relations between the Soviet Union and the West might have been at the lowest point since the Cuban Missile Crisis of 1962. Against this backdrop, my parents became actively involved in various refusenik activities, those ranging from cultural to political, while also seeking contacts with Western diplomats and journalists. Among the new activities were visits to the United States and British embassies to attend cultural events. My parents needed the extra breathing space and enjoyed the visits. Then, in December 1980 my father was arrested as he and my mother exited the British Embassy after a screening of a new British film. He was picked up right outside the embassy doors, separated from my mother in full view of the public, grabbed and thrown into an unmarked vehicle, and driven to a police precinct. There KGB officers gave him a severe interrogation. For several hours they threatened and intimidated him. My mother came home by herself, not knowing what to tell me, what to expect, and what to do. Late at night my father returned, shaken. I'm still scared to ask what exactly took place, but I know that among the chief threats which the KGB interrogators employed was to the safety of his wife and son. For about the next two years following the preventative arrest, my parents lay low. They waited for the political climate to change for the better, except it only got worse after Brezhnev's death in 1982 and the start of Andropov's term as the Soviet leader.

The KGB had temporarily intimidated my father, but they did not silence him. If anything, his energies and his protest were directed not outwardly, into anti-government political actions, but inwardly. In 1980, my father wrote the first part of a family saga about the mutilated destinies of Jewish refuseniks, which would eventually become his novel *Herbert and Nelly*. I read the first part in manuscript when I was thirteen. The initial prototype of my father's main character was Dr. Norbert Maga-zanik, a much-respected Moscow internist and a fellow refusenik. For my father's fictional protagonist Dr. Herbert Levitin, a Moscow professor of medicine, Jewishness evolves in the course of the novel from a prohibitive ethnic garb to a historical and spiritual mission. The Jewish professor is married to an ethnic Russian woman of peasant stock, and their decision to emigrate sets in motion a chain of destructive events ultimately result-ing in the killing of their son in Afghanistan and the wife's death from grief. "I will never recover," the dying wife says to her Jewish husband, "because I no longer believe in anything. . . . Neither in your awesome God, nor in my weak Christ." The Jews' marriage to Russia is doomed, the novel suggests. Emigrate or die! Those were the choices my father faced as a novelist while breathing life into his refusenik protagonist and charting the course of Dr. Levitin's destiny. The irony of it all, the irony of our destinies, was that unlike my father's chosen protagonist, who was slightly autobiographical, my father and his family weren't living out a novel. Book one of my father's refusenik saga ended, having exhausted its heroics. But the writer-doctor and his family lived on, hoping to survive the life that was both worse and better than fiction. Our family's prosaic imperative was to regroup, to preserve ourselves, and to wait. For how long? "If we could only know," Chekhov's Olga says at the end of *The Three Sisters*. If *we* could only know. . . .

How do you pick up and start a new life on the ruins of a previous one, the one you had tried, but failed, to abandon? In 1981 my parents concluded that instead of the emergency room meat grinder and driving an illegal cab at night, my father needed a solid job to support our family. In contrast to those working at research institutions and prestigious hospitals, rank-and-file clinicians were poorly paid and usually in demand in the Soviet Union. Yet my father hadn't practiced medicine in a clinical setting since 1961, when he completed his service in the army's medical corps. After looking around, he applied to do a clinical fellowship in endocrinology, an area he had always found fascinating. The fellowship program at the

Moscow Institute for the Advancement of Physicians was designed for training younger medical doctors. At the time, even without a background check, it would have been apparent that a former academic with advanced degrees and numerous publications could only have been a refusenik. It was a small miracle that the professors running the endocrine fellowship looked the other way and admitted my father.

Upon completion of the six-month fellowship, my father found a job at a clinic in the northwest of Moscow, near the Voykovskaya Metro station, or about half an hour by foot from where we lived. It was a typical Soviet neighborhood health clinic, with long lines outside the doctors' offices, with elderly feet-shuffling nurses who looked like so many of their patients, with rusty radiators overheating the corridors' putrid air. The clinic's medical director was a tough self-made woman of the sort that brings to mind permed yellow hair, plain skirt suits, telegraphic speech, and a Communist Party membership by default. She hired my father because she knew right away she was getting a bargain, a degree-bedecked medical scientist for a clinician's low salary. The chief remained my father's protectress even after my father's plain-clothes overseers from the KGB had begun to pay her regular visits. The clinic chief greased the system's gears while also pouring sand on those greased gears of oppression. Did she, daughter of a victim of Stalinist repressions, as we later learned, feel solidarity with our family as victims of the Soviet system?

My father worked as an endocrinologist at the same clinic from 1981 until the spring of 1987. Very quickly he gained a following among the patients, especially those suffering from obesity and infertility. He created individual treatment plans for diabetics and devised innovative diets. The patients were grateful to the good Jewish doctor and oblivious to rumors circulating at the clinic, where some of his medical colleagues were afraid of contacts with a refusenik. Coming home after a half-day at clinic, my father would open his briefcase and hand over the gifts of his patients: bottles and flasks of cognac; chocolate; caviar; occasionally a bill slipped into a pocket of his white coat. "Doctors don't eat flowers," my friend Max Mussel used to say when he saw my father unload the offerings in the manner of a country doctor whom peasants paid with chickens and honey.

As much as my father avoided administrative service and commit-tees at his clinic, he cared about his patients and had his own ideas about fairness. He had his nurse post a flyer on his office door announcing that, in addition to war veterans, who by law enjoyed privileges in the Soviet Union, educators and doctors could see him without having to wait, some-times for hours, outside his door. And fellow refuseniks always received VIP treatment from my father. I remember one case of a woman in her early thirties whose husband had become a very pious man over their years as refuseniks. A computer engineer fired from his job, he worked as a night watchman at a big trucking company and spent a great deal of time poring over the sacred texts. Skinny, with rusty-red hair and a skimpy beard, he cultivated the aura of a *tzaddik*. One day he brought his wife to my father's office at the clinic. He and his wife had been trying to conceive for five years, he told my father. My father examined the woman, who was thin and timid, with long graceful fingers and the velvet eyes of Shulamit. (I met the couple at a refusenik gathering.) He suspected a dis-order of the woman's thyroid, ordered a blood test, and a week later began to treat her for hypothyroidism. Four months later she became pregnant. She gave birth to a healthy boy, whom my father, chosen to be the *sandak*, held during the *bris*. The couple went on to have more kids. I've heard that in Israel, where they finally went in 1987, the pious man became a rabbi.

This was my father's routine for six years: seeing patients for half a day and writing at home, plus occasionally receiving private patients at home. Once a week he also consulted at City Hospital No. 4, which would play an important role at the peak of his troubles with the regime. Although my father's clinical work provided a modicum of financial stability for our family, it never was, and couldn't have been, a second career for him. Can one think of a career while teetering over an abyss?

As a refusenik my mother was having a more difficult time than my father finding a new professional niche. Being unemployed was both unsafe and demoralizing. As part of the intimidation campaign, my mother was summoned to the local police station and threatened that she would be charged with "parasitism," an article in the Soviet criminal code. No college or school would hire her with her credentials and an (eas-ily decipherable) employment gap. Trusting a "traitor" to teach, and not just any discipline, but the language of the country's principal ideological adversaries, was beyond the limits of what a Soviet dean or school principal could risk. Freelance interpreting work was also no longer available to her. Through the assistance of a benevolent friend who wasn't a refusenik, my mother tried but failed to gain employment as a night inspector of basements and boiler rooms. Finally, at the end of 1982, through the assistance of one of my father's patients at the clinic, she was hired to teach English, part-time, at a district House of Culture. Crooked mirrors of Soviet cultural life, "houses of culture" were part of an extensive network of public centers of leisure and education. They were a place where people saw performances and films and pursued hobbies and interests ranging from macramé knotting to poetry writing. For five years, my mother offered an English course for high school students whose parents wanted them to learn a foreign language beyond what was offered at a regular Soviet school. By and large, the students were unmotivated, and the atmosphere of the House of Culture stagnant. Coming home after an evening of teaching, my mother would tell us anecdotes about her colleagues or impersonate them down to regional accents and speech mannerisms. Her most piquant stories dealt with her boss, a barely literate, corrupt, but kindly Soviet bureaucrat. Coming from a family of the Moscow *lumpenproletariat*, the director of the House of Culture regarded my mother as a blue-blood intellectual who had somehow lost her way in the wild steppes of Soviet history. The director spent much of her time drinking tea in the company of two junior administrators, whose principal tasks were to brew tea and to pour it into cups. To this day I keep entreating my mother to write up an account of working at the House of Culture, an experience she wouldn't even have to satirize.

As my parents were becoming refuseniks, their social environment changed almost completely. Our family's isolation had occurred in stages. Immediately after my parents had first declared the intention to emigrate, almost all of my mother's coworkers and my father's scientific colleagues severed contacts with our family. At the beginning there had been plaintive phone calls and visits from my father's medical colleagues and former graduate students; those gibbering monologues of the "teacher, why are you leaving us?" variety first resounded across our apartment but then quickly petered out. Of my mother's closest friends at work, several of them going back to college, only one woman remained in contact. Another former friend would occasionally ring from a pay phone (this way, she probably believed, she wouldn't be traced to her home number), just to see if we were still alive, and breathe heavily into the receiver until my mother would recognize her breathing and say, "K., it's you?" Some of our relatives, including my father's cousins and my mother's aunt, had all of a sudden lost our address and phone number. But I'm not writing this to blame or expose, I must keep reminding myself. I can still feel, physically, that daunting sensation of life closing in on my parents. Like the elements eroding sand dunes, the isolation devoured our past.

Even bitterer for my father was the cowardice of his literary comrades following the expulsion from the Union of Soviet Writers. Not just writers in whose company I used to see my father at the Central House of Writers, but even the writers who used to come to our home, now feared, like the plague, contacts with my father. He needed them, at least their private support, after having been thrown out of the Union of Writers and having tasted KGB harassment. Shame for one's own spinelessness perpetuates silence and denial, and silences and denials feed on one another, breeding more shame and proscribing solidarity. This is one of the mechanisms of conformism I observed as a young refusenik, frequently a conformism sprung from fear. And yet this knowledge still doesn't help me make sense of the refusal of my father's close friend since medical school, the poet-turned-filmmaker Ilya Averbakh, to help my father when he had turned to Averbakh in a moment of desperation. And I can think of other such examples. To me this proves that the Soviet system worked, however crudely, on the individual human level, if the artistic and intellectual elite so facilely cooperated with the state in isolating the victims of persecution. And these were the late Soviet years, not the years of Stalinism!

By 1981 our social circle was almost entirely comprised of other refuseniks. Isolated by invisible fences of fear, distrust, and hostility that the mainstream Soviet society had built around us, refuseniks were largely confined to their own ranks. By some accounts, there were as many as 50,000 of them in the USSR in the middle 1980s, and as many as 15,000 in

Moscow alone. As an isolated community within the larger Soviet society, isolated even from many Soviet Jews who hadn't attempted to emigrate, the refuseniks had their own social codes and rituals, their clandestine institutions and seminars, their hierarchy and power grid, their elders dividing the pie of Western support, their politics and intrigues, and even their own matchmakers. There were families who had already been refuseniks for ten or fifteen years at the time we had joined their community. There were children who had been born to families of refuseniks. There were boys and girls who, like myself, came of age while living a double life, Soviet at school and refusenik at home. Plans were being made for family unions and marriages, and people joked that when young men and women from refusenik families would start having children of their own, we as a community would begin to grow and multiply *naturally*. After about a year of working at his medical clinic, my father had begun to speak of himself and of other refuseniks as foreigners illegally detained and awaiting release. "We are," he would say at refuseniks' gatherings, "foreign specialists temporarily employed in the USSR. We should have no relations with the authorities beyond the minimum that professionalism requires." In trying to rationalize his position as a refusenik and make the best of it, my father never stopped yearning for his severed scientific and literary connections. Double isolation was doubly painful.

As for myself, I recognized that the adult refuseniks were socially confined. Even though among ourselves, refusenik youths could speak openly about all the things that we would otherwise conceal from our peers, I was not keen on making children of refuseniks my social circle. This was one of the freedoms I enjoyed and my parents did not. At the time identifying as a Jew in broadly ethnic and historical terms, I wasn't particularly interested in the underground activities that some young refuseniks participated in: learning Hebrew; Torah study. The teenage refusenik in me wanted more than the glory of ghetto walls or a smoldering hope of Exodus; the faking Soviet kid stubbornly pushed on at school as though he had years and years of Soviet life ahead of him.

INTERLUDE

DUNES OF HAPPINESS

ESTONIA, a refuge from refusenik living. The source of my happiest youthful memories. When I add up all the summer vacations, I realize that between the ages of five and twenty I spent a total of three years in Estonia. Pärnu, the Estonian resort where we summered, sits on the West Coast of Estonia, about a two hour drive south from Tallinn, the Estonian capital. By the end of the nineteenth century, Pärnu became well known as a Baltic *Kurort*. It owed its reputation to the long strand, the curative mud baths, and its microclimate, steady and mild, most suitable for anxious city types with high blood pressure, raw nerves, and pallid faces.

The resort opens onto a double gulf, the Gulf of Pärnu being part of the larger Gulf of Riga. Still today the vacation capital of Estonia, Pärnu flourished during the pre-World War II interlude of Estonian independence. Then came the Soviet annexation in 1940, the Nazi occupation, and finally the Soviet "liberation," which lasted until 1991. Many streets were given Soviet names like Nõukogude "Soviet's" (now re-renamed Supeluse, "Swimming/Bathing"), but the town retained much of its prewar character. In the 1960s and early 1970s, Pärnu became the object of summer pilgrimages by the intelligentsia from Soviet cities.

When my parents and I first came to Pärnu in 1972—after having tried the rotten-apricot-smelling Crimea and the *shashlyk*-greasy Russian coast of the Black Sea—we were smitten by Estonia and its elegant culture of living. Years of Soviet rule couldn't take the Northern European breeding and memories of independence out of the local Estonian population. For them such things as work ethic, public interest, service, privacy, and efficiency were as natural as they were alien concepts to much of the population of the Soviet Union, raised in the spirit of brawny collectivism. Going to Estonia for the first time was like going abroad, and for years Estonia remained our foretaste of Europe and the West.

Less than a million ethnic Estonians were living within the republic's borders. The Estonians had never had a royalty or a nobility of their own, had always been governed by outsiders—Livonian knights, Danes, Swedes, Russians. The long heritage of being ruled by foreign powers might explain why, in the Soviet 1970s, the Estonians weren't particularly cordial to visitors. The general Estonian population abhorred Russians, while treating Jews slightly better. As Russians, we were part of the greater occupational forces; as Jews, we were fellow-victims of Russian—and Soviet—imperial domination.

One of the biggest opportunities I have missed in life was learning Estonian. In all fairness, there were no real venues to study the language formally while vacationing in Estonia, no summer courses for visitors. During my fifteen vacations in Pärnu, I didn't make more than half a dozen acquaintances among the local Estonians. There were exceptions—the librarian at the town children's library; the meek and saintly Evald Mikkus, whose studio apartment we rented for ten summers in a row; the drab-cheeked old Estonian woman who let me dig for trout worms in her kitchen garden. For years my parents and I would return to Pärnu and see the same faces of the local Estonians at the grocery stores, cafés, the telegraph office. We greeted them in Estonian—*tere* ("hello") or *tervist* ("health"); they curtly replied, never in Russian. An invisible wall separated the "Russians" from the Estonians. The "Russians" included the local occupant population and us, the summerfolk. While the Estonian landlords, postal workers, waiters, or sales clerks weren't especially friendly to the vacationers, they still treated us a thousand times better than those working in the everyman's Soviet office or establishment outside Estonia. Estonians showed constant solidarity with their own people, while treating the summer visitors with teeth-clenched aloofness. To the intelligentsia from Soviet cities, who were tired of being watched and supervised, the sensation of inscrutability was liberating.

I said "intelligentsia," but I should have probably said "Jewish intelligentsia." In those days, perhaps two-thirds of Pärnu's summer population was Jewish. How did it all start? Hundreds, perhaps thousands of Jewish parents from across the Soviet Union began to bring their progeny to Pärnu in the 1960s and early 1970s. It was a remarkable environment. Summer after summer, Russian-speaking Jewish kids who had known each other since early childhood would congregate on the beach, play charades and compete in ball games, or go to movies together. While vacationing in Pärnu, the parents would put aside perennial concerns about antisemitism. There were certainly non-Jewish parents and children among the vacationers—Russian, Ukrainian, Belarusian, Armenian, Tatar, Uzbek, Yakut. But the Jewish element prevailed. One of the summer jokes from the late 1970s went like this: In retaliation for the building of a new Jewish settlement in the West Bank, the PLO detonated a bomb . . . in Pärnu. Being surrounded by a majority of Jewish or part-Jewish peers was medicinal for wounded young hearts. During the year, when we were not in Estonia, most Jewish kids experienced one form or another of prejudicial treatment in their schools or back yards, on soccer fields, on buses or trams. In Pärnu, being Jewish was both "cool" and "hip," and this sometimes translated into absurd situations which would never have occurred back home. I remember a group of us hanging out in the seaside park, under the crown of a Tolstoyan oak tree. A blond and blue-eyed boy approached us. It was his first time in Pärnu, and we had briefly met him at the beach. He hailed from the northern Russian city of Vologda, and his last name bespoke his origins in the Russian Orthodox clergy. He stood in front of us and said in a straining voice: "I'd like to be friends. My grandmother is Jewish." The polar Jew was accepted to our gang and turned out to be a nice fellow.

The odor of the Old Hansa still hangs under the vault of Pärnu's old town gate where we occasionally played. We were spending most of our time at the beach or in the seaside parks with secluded benches, inside the wooden orchestra shell when it rained, on the tennis and badminton courts when it didn't, and regardless of the weather, in the children's amusement park with its somnolent carrousels and sagged, low-hanging swings. Inspired by the East German–Yugoslavian Westerns starring the debonair Gojko Mitić, we were all mad about Mohegan warriors. But I also recall a period when my Pärnu friends and I became fascinated with

Hanseatic seafaring merchants, with Lübeck and The Hague, with Brabant cuffs and wooden clogs, and also with what we heard from the local children's librarian about Pushkin's great-grandfather, the Blackmoor of Peter the Great, who had spent some time in Pärnu in the 1730s.

In addition to its surviving gable-roofed buildings, Pärnu also prides itself on its late 1920s and 1930s architecture, including the Mud Baths Clinic, the *Kursaal*, and Rannahotell. Taken apart from their surroundings, these sites would never appear matchless. To a visiting European, the whole town would give the habitually pleasurable sense of recognition, a little like Ostende, Binz, Harlingen, Cuxhaven, Sopot, Palanga, Jūrmala and other coastal resorts of the North or Baltic Sea. But to me and to my closest childhood friends there is nothing like Pärnu anywhere in the world. In our memories of those summers, we dwell in the kind of happiness that is beyond the reach of language—especially an adopted language.

Throughout the pre-college years, I used to go to Estonia for two, sometimes almost three months. My parents would ship me off soon after my birthday in early June. They usually joined me in July, and the three of us would be together in Pärnu for part of July and August. Only three times, between the ages of nine and twelve, my parents sent me, for the month of June, to summer camps for Young Pioneers in the environs of Moscow. In those camps I tried all sorts of things normally out of reach for a city kid from a "good family." I smoked cigarette butts that my fellow campers and I would pick up from ditches and asphalt. I was swearing like a son of thieves. I drank cheap cologne borrowed from a guitar-playing long-haired camp counselor. And I missed Pärnu, the summer comfort zone of my childhood.

For the first two summers we rented an old cottage on the other side of the Riga Road, a long walk from the beach across the bowels of Pärnu, where the streets smelled of burning coal and raspberries. The cottage belonged to Luule, a beautiful Estonian woman who was living in Tallinn and later married a Finn and moved across the sea. Luule charged a token rent, but the house had no gas or running water, and swarmed with mice and silverfish, while the yard was a jungle of gooseberry bushes and stinging nettles. I remember eating lots of whipped cream with berries.

Every morning Grandmother Anna Mikhailovna and I would walk to the beach past the gray stucco building of the public baths, past the town market with rows of cucumbers, jars of pickles, mounds of ornate lettuce, black, red, and yellow currants, sugar snap peas, and early summer apples (including the slightly oblong aromatic fruit the locals called "Fox's Nose"). Along the way we recited Russian poetry, mainly from the repertoire of nineteenth-century love lyrics by Pushkin, Lermontov, Tyutchev, Nikitin, Nekrasov, and Fet, but also by the great twentieth-century poet Esenin, whose folksome, bluesy lamentations infected me for life with a nostalgia for the destroyed pastoral. At the beach, grandmother encouraged me to recite our treasure trove of poems to willing audiences of vacationers. My earliest Pärnu memories are sweet like the Estonian jelly rolls that we used to eat at the beach as a five o'clock snack.

Coming to Pärnu year after year from 1972 to 1986, one got to know a whole community of peers as well as their siblings, parents, and extended families. The core of our Pärnu *kompaniia* was formed around 1975, when we were seven or eight. On days deemed unfit for beaching, the adults would hide from the newspaper-flopping northern winds behind the protective wall of the concrete parapet separating the beach from the seaside park. The grownups placed their chaise-lounges in concentric circles and spent the mornings reading, smoking, discussing politics and the arts. In loud whispers they talked about Brodsky, Nabokov, Neizvestny, Sakharov, Solzhenitsyn and other forbidden subjects. The kids would brave the chilly wind and play in the tidal plane. When I was eight, our gang of Pärnu friends expanded to about ten permanent members and remained virtually intact until our university days. During the rest of the year some of us didn't live in the same cities, but in Pärnu we were inseparable. Many parents were also friendly, forming their own *kompaniia*, congregating in the same spot at the beach and gathering at night for little soirées, where they told racy jokes ("anecdotes" in the Russian parlance) and consumed large quantities of Cinzano Bianco, available in Soviet liquor stores in the middle 1970s. On many days we would spend not only the mornings and afternoons in each other's company, but also the evening, as our parents took turns in hosting suppers or after-suppers, at which not only the Italian vermouth but Estonian-made rowanberry wine and Benedictine

liqueur were abundantly consumed by adults. The kids were served rhubarb juice, and the fare included smoked herring, smoked cheese with
caraway seeds, and red currant tarts. We only dreaded the end of August.

Between the ages of ten and fourteen, the time when children become sex-
ual subjects, Gosha (Igor) was my best friend. My senior by five months,
Gosha was the only son of two music professors, an older Jewish man and
a younger non-Jewish woman. As a young boy, he looked perfectly Slavic,
light-haired and pug-nosed. Around puberty, Jewish genes rebelled, and
Gosha suddenly looked like a Jewish-Russian mutt, a face combining his
father's crooked nose and sharp chin and his mother's smile of a mar-
tyr, pale Slavic eyes, and high round cheekbones. His father, Yuzef Kon,
an escapee from wartime Poland, had a mouth full of hisses and spikes,
the gray bristling head of a Roman senator, and sardonic dentures that
led their own exilic lives, independent of their owner's. Gosha's mother,
Lyala (Olga) Bochkareva, whose artisan Russian last name he carried as
a protective gear against antisemitism at school, had grown up in Central Asia, in Tashkent. She had been her husband's doctoral student at the
Tashkent Conservatory of Music, and they both later moved to Petrozavodsk, a smaller city about 200 miles north of Leningrad. Petrozavodsk,
which I once visited during winter break, sits in the heart of Karelia, a
land of lakes and forests originally populated by the Finns' half-brothers,
the Karels. Both of Gosha's parents were professors at the Petrozavodsk
Conservatory of Music, a branch of the famed Leningrad Conservatory.

At its most intense period, ours was the purest and most innocent
friendship I have ever experienced. Since Gosha's parents were friendly
with mine and remained our trusted family friends even after we had
become refuseniks, the topic of emigration was something he and I openly
and frequently discussed. (Gosha's father had never shed his foreignness,
read German-language detective novels at the beach, and had living relatives in Poland). We told each other everything. We complimented each
other, Gosha a lover of physics and math and a student of saxophone,
I a consumer of poetry then contemplating a career in natural sciences
or medicine. And both of us were enthusiastic readers of historical fiction, from Sir Walter Scott and Prosper Mérimée to Vassily Yan, Heinrich

Mann, and Lion Feuchtwanger, whose novel *The Spanish Ballad* we both
read not as fiction but as a true story of Jewish pride and valor.

During the school year, when we didn't see each other, Gosha and I
exchanged long illuminated letters. Our *epistolaria* became an outlet for
our shared admiration for gangsters. Why gangsters? It was probably
an antidote to the drivelish Young Pioneer decorum that we were fed at
school. As twelve-year-olds, Gosha and I read *The Odessa Stories* by the
genius Isaac Babel. We admired Babel's princely gangster Benya Krik
(Benya "the Scream"). Benya Krik and his Odessan criminal underworld
fueled our imaginations. After reading Babel, Gosha and I discovered a
culture of old thieves' songs and their contemporary versions and imita-
tions. Sung in a Russian colored by thieves' lingo, Odessan jargonisms,
and Yiddishisms, these songs circulated widely in the form of amateur
tape recordings, without being released on official Soviet record labels.
Some of them were being recorded by Russian émigré *chansonnier*s in New
York and Paris and smuggled into the country. In the 1980s the Leningrad doctor-turned-songwriter Aleksandr Rozenbaum gained fame with
his cycle of colorful Odessan songs. Gosha and I knew by heart dozens
of songs about bank heists and gangsters' harlots. Singing in chorus, we
walked Pärnu's streets and park alleys. We discussed the taste and impact
of various liquors and narcotics. We observed professional card sharks
at play in shady corners of the beach or in seaside parks, under canopies
of old limes. We even tried our own game of poker in the orchestra shell,
until my father caught us at the crime scene. And we fantasized about our
mutual friend, the young ballerina Katya Tsarapkina.

I remember walking with Gosha in the direction of a sagging cottage
with yellow peeling paint, which Katya and her parents rented for many
summers. Without a shade of irony or jealous rivalry, Gosha and I delib-
erated who would be the chosen by our Beautiful Lady. We were both
exploding with energy, and we wrestled a lot on the beach, like two lion
cubs. And yet I don't remember any discord between us, any arguments,
any fights or disagreements, except a few times during fishing expeditions on which we would go with my father. Gosha's father, the old music
professor, was an urbanist to boot. He detested sylvan pleasures and was
more than happy to place Gosha in the care of my father, who treated him

like his own son. Once a week the three of us would go fishing off the mile-long jetty built in the 1860s to protect the Pärnu beach from erosion. And once or twice every summer we would drive to a lake in Central Estonia and stay there overnight, fishing, swimming, and frying fish over a camp fire.

One summer, I believe this was after we had both finished seventh grade, Gosha and I discovered an activity that we kept a strict secret. Even our parents didn't know at the time. Only our friend Katya had an inkling about our secret walks. The resort of Pärnu prides itself on having a women's nude beach, an area marked by warning signs but directly accessible from the general part of the strand. "If you need tomatoes, take a walk to the women's beach," was the joke all the Pärnu kids had been hearing from the grown-ups. One day Gosha and I brazenly crossed the boundary, descending from the dunes overgrown with tall rushes and dwarf weeping willows, and took a long walk along the fringes of the women's beach. We were wearing nothing but swimming trunks, and our young masculinity raged at the sight of so many naked female bodies. It was absolutely incredible, unlike anything we had seen, and a thousand times better than the steamed-over body parts peeked through a chink in the bathhouse on girls' day in summer camp, or the occasional page ripped from a West German pornographic magazine that boys passed around in washrooms. The naked women and girls on the nude beach in Pärnu— hundreds of them, old, young, slender and not, lazing in the sun, reading in the shade, snacking on tomatoes, cucumbers and cheese, splashing in the shallow waters, running into the sea like nymphs—seemed totally and happily oblivious to our presence. A couple of older women muttered something like "Don't you boys have another place to walk!" But the majority of the nude sunbathers paid no attention to our voyeuristic postures and pastures. I remember the two of us staring, enchanted, at a group of Estonian girls coming out of the water and drying each other with double towels. They had budding breasts like melting vanilla ice cream and glittering golden fleeces running down their laps. They saw us and looked in our direction, without even covering themselves, laughing and saying something loud and playful in Estonian. Did we look too innocent, uninitiated, unthreatening? Was it so apparent that we hadn't

experienced more than a few lip kisses and a few minutes of pressing ourselves to girls at dances? Those walks to the women's beach continued for
several weeks, populating our reveries with more material than we were
probably capable of storing. Our walks ended abruptly when our friend
Katya, grown jealous of our pastime without her, threatened to expose us
to the parents.

In senior high school Gosha took up a new hobby: boxing. When we
were reunited the summer following our tomato-gathering expeditions,
things were somehow no longer the same between us. Gosha became more
reclusive, eminently introverted like his own father. I was going through
a stage of romantic extrovertism. I courted girls, was passionately interested in theater, Silver Age poetry, and The Beatles. I also suspect that our
cooling off had something to do with my growing realization that I was
a Jewish captive in the Soviet Union. Gosha's father never spoke of Jewish topics and of losing his family in the Shoah, and his self-preserving
instinct increasingly clashed with my own father's Judaic self-awareness,
until one day they got into a serious fight. Gosha and I were still spending
a lot of time together that summer, out of the inertia of habit and a sense of
loyalty to our past friendship. Then, on a breezy Baltic evening in August
of 1983, when the air brings a briny taste of sadness to one's lips, destiny
knocked over and shattered the magic lantern of our friendship.

One of the main reasons I treasure Estonian memories has to do with not
feeling alone among my peers. My two closest friends, Max Mussel and
Katya Tsarapkina, come from the gang of the kids I met in Pärnu in the
early 1970s. My father and Katya's mother, Inga Kogan, are the same age
and grew up in adjacent buildings in Lesnoye, a neighborhood of Leningrad's Vyborg working-class district. When I first met Katya's mother,
she had the bluest of cornflower blue eyes. A movie buff, Inga had had
what they used to call a "tempestuous" youth. She never finished college,
and married a man four years her junior, a chemical engineer and former
member of his university's water polo team. When I first saw him over
thirty years ago, Katya's father, Volodya, was tall and dapper. Katya is
forty-three as I type these lines, married and a mother of a teenage boy,
and to this day she insists that her father represents the gold standard of

male beauty as Dr. Freud smiles upon them from his heavenly clinic. Both of Katya's grandfathers were Jewish, both of her grandmothers not-Jewish, and Katya looks most of all like her West-Slavic ancestors. From her father she inherited his slenderness and long-leggedness, from her mother the enchanted half-smile of an absinthe-drinker. The melancholy of her shtetl ancestors dwells in Katya's eyes and on her brow. Having studied classical ballet from an early age, Katya gave it up altogether at the age of fourteen. Over a quarter of a century later, she still possesses the lilting gait of a ballerina. I met Katya in 1975, on the quartzy Pärnu beach, where my father and her mother had run into each other after a hiatus of ten years. And as if this connection wasn't enough, it turned out that in Leningrad, Katya and her parents were living in an apartment house erected next to the site of a razed eighteenth-century building where my father had grown up. When we stayed there during our visits to Leningrad, my father was carried back to his boyhood in the siege-ravaged Leningrad, but also to the youth and Thaw that he and Katya's mother had in common.

Katya and I have always felt that our second-generation friendship was fated. We fought a lot in the early teens, Katya being a year older and also, at twelve and thirteen, the object of my affection. In high school our friendship became harmonious, like that of two loving siblings. I find it difficult to write about Katya in connection with our past, as it forces me to put closure on her story. Instead I close my eyes to give them rest, and I see our white Zhiguli sedan parked on the roadside. We have just returned to Pärnu from a blessed pine forest. We have been picking bilberries, wild raspberries, and mushrooms. We have been picking berries while simultaneously eating off the plants, gorging on the tart, dark-purple bilberries and the sweet, scarlet raspberries. Fatigued after several hours of work, Katya is sitting in the back seat by the window, her long contortionist arms locked in a perfect geometrical figure. She squints at the camera as though all of the world's allure and surprise have been concentrated in her face. Images like that one are forbidding of closure, as is my Estonian childhood.

In 1983, as Gosha faded out of the picture, Max Mussel became my best male friend. It might seem that Max had ousted Gosha, assuming his vortex in the triangle of childhood friendship that had bound Katya,

Gosha, and me together. Actually, Katya and I had both known Max for a long time as one of the founding members of the Pärnu Jewish Mohegans. Max Mussel is still remembered by the Pärnu kids as Max *Krolik,* Max the Rabbit. He earned his nickname because as an eight- and nine-year-old he had retainers on his teeth and sported gold-frame round glasses. This combination evoked an association with Rabbit in Milne's *Winnie the Pooh,* the book we adored. Max *Krolik,* or simply "Krol," looked the most intellectual among us and was usually seen with a book in hand. I envied his spectacles, associating them with mental prowess and refinement. As a youth he was unathletic, skinny, oversensitive. Slavic blood flowed in his veins, calming his explosive self the way a peaceful Russian river cools a hot summer landscape. Max's origins call for a brief pause because of the way they illustrate the workings of mixed marriages in my former homeland. Before World War II, Max's maternal grandfather, Israel Abolits, married a Russian woman. Her first name and patronymic, Olympiada Nikitichna, made one think of a merchant's wife in a nineteenth-century Russian vaudeville show. He loved his Olympiada (Lipa) breathlessly his whole life, and she, too, adored her Izya. Max looked a lot like his grandfather Israel, an engineering professor. Every summer Max came to Pärnu with his grandparents and cousin Zoya, a pianist who practiced for hours on end at a local school. Max's parents divorced when he was in his teens and led their own lives, and I mainly remember young Max summering with his grandparents. His grandfather had an old-fashioned professorial briefcase the size of a small pig, and he used to carry it with him to the beach, to the park, and to the public baths, which he frequented. Folded newspapers jutted out of its half-zipped compartments like giraffe necks. Even on hot days, Max's Russian grandmother went around the resort in dark floral dresses and a shawl wrapped round her shoulders.

As a teenager Max was a tireless reader of any foreign fiction he could find in translation. In senior high school he was the only person I knew who actually "finished" Proust and Musil. He was the first to have "discovered" Julio Cortázar and Pär Lagerkvist, and he also put me onto Hermann Hesse. I remember the two of us walking along the beach and trying to figure out how to play the glass-bead game. Max dreamed of becoming a film director. The passion for manipulating visual images likely stemmed from his myopia. His vision became quite bad when he was in high school, and strong glasses gave him migraines. Max resorted to weaker prescriptions, which limited the clarity and sharpness of his vision, especially from a distance. This was a source of gentle teasing by his friends, as Max often assumed a girl was attractive when he saw a nice figure from afar, only to be disappointed after going over to meet her and seeing her face up close.

In senior high school and college, my friends Katya and Max flirted with each other, sometimes behind my back, sometimes right under my eyes, but abstained from amorous entanglements. Both are married and have children, and their Pärnu flirtations remain a perennial subject of private jokes. Our lives have been joined together, forming a triangle of friendship. Each of us is as different from the other two as three people can be. Katya is phlegmatic, obsessive, sometimes unstoppable. She's also boundlessly generous. Although Max is given to moments of apathy and disbelief, he is a gentle soul, which is a rare quality among men. In our three-way dynamic, I tend to be the decider and organizer, and in my ego-centrism I can sometimes be an overbearing friend. It's been twenty-five years since I left Russia, and I still miss the presence of Max and Katya in my daily life. We make every effort to see each other—in St. Petersburg or Moscow, in Milan, in Marbella, in Boston. Three times we have met in Pärnu for summertime reunions. When we get together, putting aside our families, marriages, countries, formed habits, and tempered predilections, time drops its shackles. Forever fifteen or sixteen, we find each other on the amber alley that takes us to the seaside amusement park and the art nouveau mansion of the former casino. Katya runs ahead of us, always slightly *en pointe*. I'm next, clutching badminton rackets. Max, his asthma acting up in the pine-infused air, lags behind. Under his arm he clutches a Russian translation of Remarque's *Three Comrades*. "Look, boys," Katya turns her head and waves her arms, "Look, they've fixed the Ferris wheel. Please let's go up!"

The story of my Estonia wouldn't be complete without an homage to Jüri Arrak and his artistic freedom. Prior to returning to Moscow by night train, we used to stop in Tallinn for a day or two. This was one of our annual rituals of parting with summer and Estonia. While my parents shopped for Estonian-made clothes and household goods that had the semblance and the quality of things Western, I roamed around Vyshgorod (Upper Town), Tallinn's medieval center. I loved to stand on the castle's observation landings, whence one could take in the entire seaport and the steely semicircle of the Baltic Sea. Ecstatic, I would mouth the quaint names of the castle towers: Fat Margarita, Long Hermann. Our family friends, Russian Jews who lived in Tallinn, treated me to my favorite sandwiches with anchovies and hard-boiled egg and also to delectable cheese pastries and milky, chicory-flavored coffee.

At the end of August 1975, our family friend Boris Bernshtein, an art critic and a post-World War II transplant from Odessa to Tallinn, took us to the annual fall *vernissage* of Estonian artists. At the annual shows of Estonian art, non-representational and abstract paintings were freely exhibited alongside commonplaces of socialist realism that one could see all across the Soviet Union (an Estonian fisherman in a valorous pose would replace a Kazakh rancher or a Ukrainian farmer). At the art show, Bernshtein brought us over to a painting titled "Corona." "It's by Jüri Arrak, who is, perhaps, the best living Estonian artist," Bernshtein explained.

"*Corona*" is an Estonian folk version of billiards. A square table is made of smooth pinewood. There is a hole in each corner. Instead of the regular balls, one uses wooden pucks with holes in the middle, and the nine-ball is a larger-size puck. Arrak's painting employed bright unmixed colors and depicted four humanoids playing *Corona* (see ill. 16). I said humanoids because they had human faces and human bodies. Yet all of the creatures in the painting had the same, bunched-up hair, arranged in braids, which stood up and extended around the back of the head, forming wondrous crenellations. These orange, blue, and aquamarine humanoids were simultaneously primordial, medieval, and alien, but their gaping mouths and frozen eyes had contemporary, Soviet expressions. The *Corona* players possessed a secret knowledge, which trembled on their faces like water on melting icicles. But they didn't know how to use this secret knowledge, sequestered as they were within the confines of the small pool hall. Seeing Arrak's *Corona* for the first time at the age of nine was something of a culture shock.

That evening, on the train taking us back to Moscow, I drew from memory a copy of *Corona*. My father got the artist's address from Boris Bernshtein and mailed him my drawing and a personal letter of introduction. Jüri Arrak sent my father photos and slides of some of his paintings, and my father mailed him poems and translations. (He had translated several Estonian poets, including Ellen Niit, Mats Traat, and Jaan Kross.) Later my father composed and dedicated to Jüri a poem about Soviet escapists playing *Corona*. In the course of their early correspondence they discovered many affinities, which paved ground for a lifelong friendship. Both Jüri and my father were born in 1936, the Year of the Rat according to the Chinese calendar, and they felt that their affinities were not coincidental. To this day Jüri and my father fondly refer to each other in Russian as *staraia krysa* ("old rat"). Born in very different places and in different countries (Estonia was still independent in 1936), both hated change and adored routine, were superstitious, and were given to hypochondria. Both Jüri and my father allowed for a dose of the mystical in their daily lives, and, of course, both were creative artists.

The following summer, in late July of 1976, Jüri Arrak drove down from Tallinn to Pärnu to fetch us. In his rattling Zaporozhets mini car we drove north and west along the coast to his summer house, the homestead Panga-Rehe in the Tõstemaa region. Even today, after the post-independence boom of the Estonian economy, the paved road remains a narrow ribbon looping through forests of mast pines. Back in 1977, for much of the way from Pärnu to Tõstemaa we drove on a tractor-beaten gravel road. Like its big brother Pärnu, in its heyday Tõstemaa had been a flourishing local seaport. Round stones of the old merchant homes and boat drops sunken to their knees are what remains of its Hanseatic glory. When we first visited the area in the 1970s, the local population was poor and, with a few Soviet-era adjustments, continued to live like their forefathers, working the lean rocky soil, fishing, foraging mushrooms and berries. This was as far off the beaten tracks as one could get in Estonia, and Jüri needed such a place for his summer studio. From a local fisherman, a widower who was too old to winter there alone, Jüri bought the homestead with an adjoining field, a large nineteenth-century house, a barn, remains of a sauna, and an apple orchard. Panga-Rehe is about one-third of a mile inland from the Baltic coast. Farmers and fishermen had lived on this homestead, raising sheep, growing barley, oats, and potatoes in the field, apples and gooseberries in the garden, making honey, smoking perch, salting herring, sun-drying flounder. When Jüri bought the place in the early 1970s, he repaired the straw-covered roof and did some electrical and structural improvements, but kept the interiors unchanged. Most of the old, rough-hewn furniture, including the hard beds with straw mattresses, had come with the house. There was no running water, and several times a day we walked to the well, where a slippery green echo made its home. One half of the house was taken up by main living area, combining kitchen, parlor, and dining room, with a hearth and a wood-burning stove; a long oaken table, its surface blackened and smoothed out by a century of daily repasts; long benches on both sides; narrow beds around the walls. Old peasant tools and utensils were everywhere on the walls. Bunches of drying herbs and flowers hung from the massive central rafter over the dining room table. On some of the walls and doors Jüri had painted his creatures, illustrating stories from the Estonian national epic, *Kalevipoeg*. He was at the time very interested in mythology, not just Finno-Ugric and Graeco-Roman, but also Indian and Far Eastern, and I remember him working on a large painting to be entitled *Gigantomachia*, the battle of giants. The cold floors of the Panga-Rehe house were laid in rocks that were slightly smaller and rounder than the cobblestones paving the courtyard. The foundation and bearing walls of the house were built from round granite stones to last for centuries. Attached to the right side of the house was a barn with a hayloft. Off the main room was a guest room, where we slept, and a big pantry. Jüri's summer studio, the master bedroom, and the children's bedroom formed the left wing of the house. The recessed windows were small, and it was always shimmering-dark and cool inside the house.

An old black mutt by the name of Rex used to greet the arrivals with cascading, cheery barks. Rex was succeeded by a cocker spaniel Lonni, a busybody who dashed about the outlying fields and looked from afar like a partridge. Jüri and his then wife Urve Roodes Arrak, an artist working with leather media, had two boys. The younger, Jaan, was my age; Arno, his brother, was two years our senior. Both had long pale yellow hair and looked like young Vikings. The summer we first came to visit Panga-Rehe, Jüri had built and decorated a house on stilts in the middle of the apple orchard, and the boys slept there at night. Although the Arrak parents both spoke Russian fluently and were more cosmopolitan than many of their fellow Estonians, the boys weren't encouraged to learn Russian, despite the official requirement at school. Not pushing children to master Russian was simultaneously a form of the occupied Estonians' civil disobedience and a means of cultural and linguistic self-preservation. The young Arraks and I had to resort to English, which they knew much better than Russian and which I had been learning at home and at school. I felt even more *abroad* in Panga-Rehe than in Pärnu. Both brothers, especially the younger, more gregarious Jaan, struck me as free, relaxed, and comfortable in their skin. Thinking of our impending return to Moscow and of being a Jewish black sheep among my Russian peers, I envied the Estonian boys.

Memories of Panga-Rehe and the Arraks are golden, untouched by the patina of time. In the morning Jüri would paint, and Urve and my mother did some cooking, while my father sat outside taking notes or composing poetry. The Arrak kids and I would bicycle to the coast and dive into the cold open sea from a huge boulder the size of a fat bull; sometimes we would also fish for yellow perch and anchovies off the sleeping bull's forehead. The seaside landscape was rough and angular, all pale green and gray, with juniper trees and lichen-coated rocks. Years later, when I first tasted gin, it brought back memories of putting a purple Baltic juniper berry under my tongue and slowly sucking its scrumptiously unsweet juices.

If it rained the night before, we would walk to a nearby "mushroom" forest, lugging back baskets of red- and brown-capped aromatic boletuses for soup and orange chanterelles for pan-frying with butter, onions, and dill. Sometimes Jüri would bring out a wooden table, chairs, paper, and paints and give his sons and me a lesson in the middle of the courtyard, under the tall mid-August sky. I should have saved those feeble watercolors and drawings of mine with Jüri's corrections! Both Jaan and Arno inherited artistic genes, and Arno Arrak later became a professional artist. While Jüri didn't purposely invite his guests to see unfinished paintings, he also didn't close the door to his studio. During our second or third summer visit to Panga-Rehe I observed stages of Jüri's work on a canvas he called *Conversation of Self-Portraits*. Four of Arrak's bearded selves, two of them still outlines, two already given some flesh and blood, were sitting around the room, engrossed in a four-way discussion.

One summer Jüri and my father spent several days behind closed doors in Jüri's studio, working on a book of stories for children. They were variations of old Estonian folktales about a prankster swamp-goblin who assists poor waifs and punishes greedy farmers' wives. Jüri called him "Majv" and attributed metaphysical prowess to this creature. After they had hammered together a rough draft of the stories, my father was going to write it all up in Russian, and Jüri illustrate it—for a book they hoped to publish in Moscow. Nothing came of the project, probably because we soon became refuseniks and Soviet publishing houses closed their doors to my father.

Because of the level of trust between the Arraks and my parents, from the very beginning the Arraks were privy to our plans. Like many Estonians who remained in their country after World War II and throughout the Soviet occupation, the Arraks had close family abroad, including Jüri's uncle and first cousins in the United States. At night, when the kids were already in bed after a supper of fresh peasant bread, cottage cheese, milk from under the cow, honey, fried mushrooms, vegetables, and tea brewed from fresh herbs and berries, the Arraks and my parents would stay up and talk. I slept in the guest bedroom, udders of creamy fog hanging outside on branches and wood shutters. It was so quiet all around, the nearest homestead not for half a mile away, that I could hear every word. The subjects of emigration, artistic freedom, and position of minorities dominated their nighttime conversations. Sometimes the Arraks and my parents listened to evening programs on the Voice of America, Kol Israel, Radio France, and other short-wave broadcasts from abroad. The forbidden programs reached those sparsely-populated parts without being scrambled.

Throughout our years as refuseniks, the Arraks remained our close friends and openly supported our family. Unlike many of my parents' old friends, Jüri and Urve weren't afraid of associating with refuseniks and dissidents, even though it may have caused repercussions for their own

Soviet careers. They got along seamlessly, my parents and the Arraks. Only once did I overhear a dissonant late-night exchange between my father and Jüri. They were talking about World War II, evacuation from the siege-encircled Leningrad to the Urals, about my father's wartime childhood amid Russian peasant children who hadn't seen a Jew prior to his arrival, and also about the meaning of privation and not seeing sugar and meat for months.

"Where were you during the war?" my father asked Jüri.

"I was in Tallinn, with my mother," Jüri replied, unperturbed.

"It was hard, wasn't it?" my father said automatically, probably thinking of a boy exactly his age living through the war in a Nazi-occupied Russian city.

"Well, actually, we had a normal life," Jüri answered, growing a bit tense.

A burdensome silence of disharmony set in the old farmhouse, and sensing my father's bewilderment and Jüri's discomfort, Urve offered to boil up some water for a fresh pot of herbal tea. At the time I didn't make much of the exchange, chalking up the tension to the amount of Calvados the two men had consumed. I hadn't yet learned that Estonia was the first country in Europe to become *Judenrein*, during the time that Jüri called "normal life." I also didn't know about the 20th "Estonian" Division of the Waffen-SS or the Klooga concentration camp located southwest of Tallinn. Should I embitter the perfect memories of Estonia by staining them with the blood ink of my afterknowledge?

Visits to Panga-Rehe crowned our Estonian vacations. We would take in the healing silence of the homestead and rest our eyes on the severe beauty of the Nordic landscape. Because we visited every year between 1976 and 1986, we witnessed changes in the Arraks' interests and tastes. Those changes prefigured the ruptures in Jüri and Urve's marriage, which, when we first met them, seemed so perfect and idyllic. From a cultivated appreciation of Estonian folk customs and traditional daily living, the Arraks turned to Buddhism and, Urve especially, to astrology. One summer in the middle 1980s we drove into Panga-Rehe to discover a tall limestone stupa with a bright-colored downsloping eye painted on its front. Jüri had built it with the help of his new associate Vello S., also an Estonian painter. On strolls to the secluded coast, Vello talked to my parents about the dissident movement in Estonia and about attempting to cross the Finnish border illegally someplace in Northern Karelia. From there he planned to reach Helsinki, take a ferry to Stockholm, and ask for political asylum in Sweden. Vello quoted *Animal Farm* from memory and nicknamed his hippyish girlfriend "Molly," after the horse in Orwell's novel. That summer, for the first time, a sense of foreboding had invaded the tranquil air of the Arraks' homestead. Vello's own canvasses, painted in turbid colors, had subversively dreamy titles such as *Memories of a Zoo Superintendent*. Jüri, who was chairman of the graphic arts—and later, the painting section—of the Estonian branch of the Union of Soviet Artists, tried to help Vello exhibit his work. I suspect that Vello played a part in the chain of events that eventually led to the dissolution of Jüri's marriage to Urve and a period of Jüri's heavy drinking and darkness. . . .

During our honeymoon in August 2000, I visited Panga-Rehe with Karen, my American-born wife. Since our first visit together we have been back to Estonia three times, during nostalgic summer vacations in Pärnu, which we have shared with my dear Max and Katya. In the old Panga Rehe kitchen, under the smoked beams, amid rusty peasant scythes, husky cowbells, and leaky copper pots displayed on the blackened walls, not Urve but Jüri's lovely second wife, Ivi, now makes herbal tea. The walls haven't been whitewashed for many, many years, and the memories of the Panga-Rehe I once knew still hover over the heavy dining room table. In the late 1980s, Urve Arrak and the Arraks' elder son Arno with his family left Estonia to spend almost two decades in Canada and the United States. But they couldn't live forever without their Estonia. Arno Arrak paints landscapes with more than a dash of his father's manner in their colors and lines. Jüri's younger son Jaan, my peer, who never left Estonia and became an entrepreneur, died in a tragic accident in 2006. Urve eventually returned home to Tallinn, where she died in 2012. It's a different Panga-Rehe today, a different wife and family routine, and also a different Jüri who still paints mesmerizing canvasses that transport me to another world. He has grown older and quieter, and also more sentimental, just like my own father and other artists born in 1936, the Year of the Rat.

During our first visit to Panga-Rehe, Karen and I walked far on paths along the Baltic coast, and she tasted juniper berries while I shared memories of Estonia. I also told her the most fantastical of all the Panga-Rehe stories, which she didn't believe, of course. In August 1983, my parents and I drove up from Pärnu to visit the Arraks. The first thing Jüri said after we got out of the car and hugged and kissed was: "Tomorrow we'll go visit Väike Lubi." "Väike" means "little" in Estonian; during our first summer in Pärnu we had rented a cottage in a street called Väike-Sepa, or "little grasshopper."

"Uncle Jüri, so who is this Little Lubi?" I asked.

"She builds towers," Jüri answered. "A local wonder. You'll see."

The next morning, after fortifying ourselves with a gargantuan omelet with mushrooms, dill, and scallions, we drove inland for about half an hour on dirt roads. We first came to a large clearing, its boundaries marked on two sides by tall pine trees, on the third by a rivulet studded with yellow water lilies, and on the fourth by the road by which we arrived. Along the road, which girded the clearing and then disappeared in the pine forest, edenic raspberry bushes stood heavy with fruit the size of a prune. Sheep wandered in the tall grass, grazing. In the far end of the clearing we saw a vegetable garden and four or five beehives constructed of odd boards and parti-colored planks. One beehive was built from carved pieces of an old armchair. In the center of the clearing stood Väike Lubi's towers.

Visualize a structure, which is about three stories high, built of thin vertical logs and various horizontal boards and cuts of plywood. The horizontal sections were somehow woven into the vertical ones, forming a grid, each wall like a piece of roughly knit cloth with large loops and holes. The roofs were covered with sundry materials, including shingles of different shapes and colors, corrugated metal, plywood, straw, and tarpaulin. There were no hung doors or framed windows. Wooden ladders built from young mast pine trees were attached to the towers at different heights, in places where gaping openings in the walls offered access to the structure's interior. All the outlandishness of the construction aside, each of the towers was intended as a living space and carried a semblance of an architectural style. One looked like a contemporary barn; the other, a functionalist summer house; the third, a chalet.

As my parents and I marched in place near the car, ogling the towers, Jüri ran to the vegetable garden and came back in the company of a woman who looked between forty and forty-five. She was under five feet tall, with muscular arms and hips, and tufts of gray in her sandy hair. She was dressed in black rubber boots and a worn-out button-front gown made of green fabric with a printed pattern of yellow daisies. The woman and Jüri were walking toward us, laughing, conversing jovially in Estonian. A smile never left her typically Finno-Ugric face with its sharp nose and triangular cheek bones. This was Väike Lubi, builder of the three towers and mistress of the forest clearing.

Väike Lubi surprised us by speaking very fluent, and only lightly accented, Russian. After learning that my mother was a specialist in the English language, she addressed her in an accurate English.

"I studied architecture in Canada," Väike Lubi told my mother. "For five years." My mother did her best to conceal her bemusement, as this couldn't possibly have been true.

During the entire visit with Väike Lubi, Jüri and Urve never treated her like a lunatic. It wasn't until later, in the car while driving back to Panga Rehe, that Jüri told us that Väike Lubi had spent her twenties and thirties in various mental institutions. Then one day she showed up at this clearing, which belonged to a nearby collective farm, and started building. The locals initially helped her with food and building materials. She grew into a folk deity and an object of adoration. She healed with herbs and incantations. Infertile couples used to come to her for counsel and cure. Väike Lubi's clearing became a regular stop for wedding parties in the area, and she blessed bride and groom and gave them wreaths of flowers to wear during the ceremony.

Estonia was Christianized only in the late twelfth century by foreign invaders, and to this day native folk traditions nourish Estonian culture. Should it be surprising that in the 1980s, after forty years of Soviet occupation, the adherence of the Estonians to their ancient pagan rites would find expression in the creation of a wondrous figure like Väike Lubi? But I saw her with my own eyes, not just a creation of local Estonian lore but a real person in flesh and blood. She was a living miracle that one could stand near, speak to, or photograph. I witnessed Väike Lubi's healing powers. Jüri had complained to my father of a bump on his neck. The bulging, fatty growth was about the size of a large cherry, and my father suggested that Jüri have it checked and surgically removed. Väike Lubi examined Jüri and tugged him by the sleeve to the bank of the rivulet. Sheep ran after their mistress, bleating triumphantly. The rest of our party followed Väike Lubi, Jüri, and the sheep. Väike Lubi stepped into the water, and I saw hundreds of minnows dash to her feet. She didn't feed them but said something to them in Estonian. She pulled a pen knife out of her gown's side pocket, cut a bunch of plants with dark green leaves growing near the bank of the rivulet, and chopped them up on her callused thumb. She then rubbed the chopped plant against the growth on Jüri's neck, and it started to disappear right before our eyes. It was astonishing. Väike Lubi shook our hands, hugged Jüri and Urve and gave them cuttings of the healing plant to take home. Then she turned around and minced up the path toward the center of her clearing, where another group of pilgrims was waiting. . . .

After I finished telling my wife about Väike Lubi, she looked at me with a scientist's skepticism, as if thinking: "You're a hopeless fictionalizer!"

"It's true, I swear to you," I said.

"Then let's visit her."

"Fine, we'll stop there on the way back to Pärnu," I agreed.

Later that afternoon, when we were saying goodbye to Jüri and Ivi Arrak, I asked what happened to Väike Lubi.

"She's gone," Jüri said pensively. "Disappeared about 1990, right before independence."

"And the towers?"

"The towers, too, are gone. Someone, they say a rich Estonian from Canada, bought the whole property and built a grand summer house there. And the locals have forgotten about Väike Lubi. Where is she? Who knows?" Jüri's voice dropped, he coughed with vexation and turned to Ivi, drawing her to his side.

Karen and I got into our rental Opel and drove through the sunlit pine forest back to Pärnu, where other ghosts of my Estonian childhood guarded the quietest dunes of happiness.

In some ways, I miss Estonia and Pärnu more than I miss Russia and my old home in Moscow. I realize now that our summer visits, between 1972 and 1986, were a release. Especially during our refusenik years, the Estonian summer months gave us a temporary escape from an oppressive Soviet reality. A vacation in Estonia, away from Moscow's officialdom, charged us with enough spirit and energy to last a whole year.

After Estonia's white beaches, soft colors, and understated elegance, the arrival in Moscow left me with a gnawing sensation of entrapment. Rainy season would have already set in in central Russia. Waddling Moscow buses would greet us with splashes of cold mud. And one more acute sensation of returning to Moscow from Estonia: watermelons. The city streets reeked of rotting watermelons. The watermelons would arrive from the south around the end of August or early September. Street corners and areas in front of food stores would be filled up with cage-like metal containers full of watermelons. People congregated in front of the large metal containers, picking and choosing ripe watermelons, sniffing them, tugging at their twisted piggish stems, tapping and pressing at them like doctors giving an abdominal exam. Parents would lift up children and put them inside the containers, and children crawled over the mounds of white and green stripy balls. Emotions ran wild and people would get into fights over watermelons. Women would lean over dirty edges of the metal containers in order to reach for watermelons, and boys would peer at the "panorama," as we called in our jargon, of underwear and garter belts. Streams of pink watermelon juice flowed down pavements and mixed with the Stygian waters of the city streets. "Moscow again," I used to think, refusing to forget Estonia. "Now it's ten more months before we go back to Pärnu."

4

CAVALIER OF THE GOLD MEDAL

MY LIFE AS A YOUNG REFUSENIK was a fight, a Jewish boy's desperate ascent. Between the ages of ten and eighteen I didn't attempt a single line of poetry. My main interests were in the natural sciences, especially in biology and medicine. First it was anything about fish that I could lay my hands on. I bought books on ichthyology in Czech and German that I couldn't read—just for the illustrations. I bred tropical fish in my bedroom. Later it was genetics. And in the middle of high school, doctoring became my obsession. My father discussed medical cases with me on our evening walks around the neighborhood. I knew about types of diabetes and thyroid disorders, and in eighth and ninth grades I could only envision my life as a physician. Literature was and had always been my love, but never in high school did I think of writing as a future profession. (In retrospect, it occurs to me that it must have had something to do with the fact that after expulsion from the Union of Soviet Writers, my father made a living solely as a medical doctor while writing for his desk drawer or for unsanctioned publication.) Determined as I was to get into medical school, at the age of fourteen I had to devise a plan for the ninth and tenth grades, then the last two years of Soviet high school. Such a plan was supposed to carry me, against all odds, over the barriers of anti-Jewish institutional quotas. It also meant that I had to prepare myself for complications stemming from our status as refuseniks.

In practical terms, the yearning to get into medical school translated into several resolutions I made around the spring of 1982, two months shy of my fifteenth birthday. One was to acquire practical experience and recommendations that would help me get into medical school. Opposite from our apartment building was the campus of Moscow City Hospital No. 52. In the spring and summer, stupendously bored patients amused themselves by taking down large bathroom mirrors, holding them outside the windows of their wards, and directing reflected sun rays at our apartment building. Many times I would be blinded in my own bedroom by a ray of light dispatched from the hospital ward—a warning not to venture into medicine, or a trite metaphor of fate. I didn't take heed. Instead, I landed a summer job as a medical orderly on the nephrology ward. My monthly salary was eighty rubles, and it was strange to think that some people actually subsisted on the meager sum of money I was paid. (For comparison, my father's modest salary at his medical clinic was about two hundred rubles per month.) It was uncommon for Soviet kids my age, especially in big cities, to work in the summer. Unlike our peers in the capitalist world, we were supposed to "enjoy" our Soviet childhood—by going to sleepaway summer camps, dachas, or resorts, or by simply loafing around the city. At the hospital, where I worked for parts of two summers, I didn't meet a single employee my age. I was initially supposed to clean rooms, wash bathrooms, and change bed linens. However, my lot changed after the head nurse, a medical school dropout by the name of Marat, took me under his wing. Marat, who was in his middle thirties when I met him, came from a family of diplomats and had had a privileged Soviet childhood. He was the spitting image of the Russian Romantic poet Lermontov, with small hazel eyes, at once fearless, melancholy, and mocking, a tall forehead, pudgy cheeks, and a hussar's curled mustache. Because of his suave air of confidence in dealing with patients, I had originally thought Marat was a doctor. Indeed, because of Marat's intelligence and medical experience, the doctors, especially the medical residents, often deferred to him. Marat was also sharp-tongued and quite the thespian, and his mind stored an incessant supply of jokes. No one told Brezhnev jokes more burlesquely than did Marat, and still today I entertain my students with what I remember from Marat's treasure-trove. Brezhnev is riding to the airport on his way to India, to visit Indira Gandhi, and his aid notices that one of the General Secretary's shoes doesn't match the other one. "Comrade Brezhnev," he whispers, "there's a small problem. One of your shoes is black, and the other, brown." "Young man,"

Brezhnev replies calmly. "Back home I have the exact the same pair." On many occasions Marat told a joke instead of answering a question. Such was his defense mechanism. He never spoke about his past or his marriage and family. And the only time he got angry with me was when I asked him why he had dropped out of medical school. "Do not ever ask me that again," Marat snapped during a cigarette break.

The nephrology ward could easily have provided a playwright with material for a tragic comedy à la Maxim Gorky's *The Lower Depths*. Set against the backdrop of very sick and dying kidney patients, such a play would feature a cast of charismatic characters, many of whom, like Marat himself, were escapees from Soviet life. This group included the chief physician Raisa Iosifovna Gordon, a wise old Jewish lady with yellowish, poorly dyed hair and depressed halibut eyes; the alcoholic nurse aid Muza who had done time for selling alcohol on the side at the liquor store where she used to work as a sales clerk; the gentle nurse Antonina who routinely did "favors" for the male patients. All the nursing staff ate lunch together in the staff room, compliments of the cook who stole lean beef and good vegetables from the patients' table.

Such an unglamorous apprenticeship might have deterred another person, but I took pleasure in being accepted by these people. There were several Jewish doctors, but no Jews among the nursing staff. I didn't experience antisemitism from any of the nurses or the "lower medical personnel," and I enjoyed Marat's patronage and the camaraderie. Above all, I loved the work and taking care of the patients. After having trained me, Marat soon changed my job description, and I started carrying blood and urine samples to the hospital lab, preparing needles and syringes for sterilization, and even drawing blood under supervision. I got to have the most fun on Mondays when Marat, fighting off the hangover after boozing on the weekend, was given to purple-gray asthenia. He would sit on a metal stool in the phlebotomy room, smoking Marlboro (he smoked only American cigarettes he got through his parents and his older brother, who was also a Soviet Foreign Service officer) and giving me directions ("this long needle here"; "that tube yonder") in a low, husky voice. On those days of being in low spirits (sometimes his drinking weekends spilled over onto the work week), Marat would try to talk me out of going to medical school. "It's all a scam, our glorious Soviet medicine," he would drawl out. "A low-paying scam for idealistic Jewish boys like you. I was once such a boy—well, almost, except line 5, so you'd better believe me." "But I love it, I love patients," I would counter. "I loves it, you loves it, they loves it," Marat would mock me. ("Line 5" refers to the nationality listed in one's Soviet passport.)

Working at the hospital and earning some money made me feel older than my classmates and peers. I walked around the hospital campus in a white coat, and people mistook me for a medical student. During the summer of 1983 I could think of nothing but pressing ahead through another year of high school and applying to medical school. In my last day on the job, I picked up a recommendation signed by several attending physicians and went to say goodbye to the nursing staff. I was in high spirits, and in the evening my mother and I were taking a night train to Estonia. I went around the ward looking for Marat, but he was nowhere to be found. It was the end of the afternoon and I assumed he had left early for the day, especially since it was on a Friday. As I walked down the hospital corridor past the phlebotomy room, I heard cascades of a smoker's cough. I peeked in: Marat was lying on the oil-cloth–covered cot, smoking and staring at the matte white ceiling.

"Close the door," Marat said softly.

"I've been looking for you, I wanted to say goodbye."

"Sit down," he pointed to a metal stool.

I sat there, crossing my legs and folding my arms.

"Listen to me, kiddo. It's only because I'm fond of you. I know you like this, you love it, whatever," Marat was gasping. "Listen to me, don't do it."

"Do what?" I asked, while in my head I was already smelling the tarry air of the train station and feeling the white cool Baltic sand with my toes.

"Don't even try it. These bastards, they don't accept you folks into med schools, that's the sorry part. The best doctors I know are all Jews, but these fucking morons don't want to train more Jewish doctors. You guys leave, because you don't feel wanted here."

A thought flashed through my head: Does he know about me? Like an experienced conspirator, I pretended not to follow the drift of what Marat was saying.

"I'm not sure what you mean," I said and even rolled my eyes.

"You're not sure what I mean?" Marat raised his voice. "They think you Jews are ungrateful. That's a bloody lie. Imagine working in this shitty hospital your whole life, for two hundred and thirty rubles, like our own Dr. Gordon? She loves the patients like her own kin. And the pigs call this ungrateful!"

I was still trying to decide how to respond.

"Come on, pal, don't pretend you don't know what I'm saying."

"Marat?" I said, but it was too late.

"A stupid, twisted country," Marat exhaled and turned away to face the scratched tiled wall.

I walked home trying to shake off Marat's warning, and I never told my parents about our conversation. Over the summer of 1983, both in Moscow and during our Pärnu vacation, my parents and I had many grueling conversations about medical school. I knew that for a Jew, especially in Moscow and with a refusenik background, the chances of getting into medical school were extremely low. Yet I wouldn't hear of an alternative career path. I still believed, stubbornly, naïvely, that with top grades at school and my hospital experience and recommendations, I should be able to gain admission.

A historical note helps me reconstruct what the world felt like as I prepared for the trials of my last high school year. On 31 August 1983, two days after my parents and I returned to Moscow from Estonia, Korean Air Lines Flight 007 was shot down by a Soviet fighter aircraft over Sakhalin Island. The plane was on its way from New York to Seoul via Anchorage. US Congressman Lawrence MacDonald was among the 269 passengers onboard. The official Soviet version was that the Soviet Air Force acted to protect its airspace, which the South Korean Boeing 747 had allegedly violated. At refusenik gatherings there was talk of yet another escalation of the Cold War, of dreadful prospects for emigration. Although Andropov was rumored to be very sick, we didn't think this would stop the Soviet leader from pushing the levers of repression.

In anticipation of trying to get into medical school, my main goal in senior high school was to receive straight As in all terms and on all finals. This would have made me eligible to receive the so-called *gold medal* (*zolotaia medal*), a high-school diploma with the highest distinction. In the Soviet Union the gold medal accorded special privileges to those applying to universities. The way the application process was set up at the time, one could only apply to one university at a time. One usually took four entrance examinations. Standardized tests weren't practiced. An unwritten system of "passing scores" was in place. A *passing score* (*prokhodnoi ball*) was a minimum cumulative score one had to attain. For instance, a passing score of 16 meant that one needed to get four Bs, or two As and two Cs, and so forth. Having a high school gold medal entitled an applicant to take only one of the four required entrance examinations. If an applicant got an A on the first examination, he or she would normally be admitted without having to take the other three examinations. Competition was high even at moderately prestigious universities. The stakes were inexorably higher for boys, who, upon reaching the age of eighteen, were drafted into the military for two or three years, unless they were already full-time university students eligible for a deferral and training as officer reservists. In addition to the regular horrors of the Soviet military service with its hazing and abuse of recent draftees known as *dedovshchina*, in the early 1980s serving in the Soviet military meant the prospect of being sent to Afghanistan (which the Soviet secret police could arrange, as a punitive measure, for a son of dissenters). During my first year out of high school, a kid from a nearby apartment building, someone with whom I used to play soccer and ping-pong, was returned home in a "zinc casket" from a tour of duty in Afghanistan. He was his parents' only child.

My dream of becoming a physician aside, I couldn't afford *not* to get into a university. I needed top grades and solid recommendations, and I was making a run for it. In the autumn of 1982, age fifteen and a half, I joined the Komsomol (Young Communist League). Although it was nominally a volunteer organization, in my time the vast majority of Soviet young men and women between the ages of fourteen and twenty-eight were Komsomol members. In my high school year, every single person joined. Still, despite pressure from the school administration and cajolement of peers, strictly speaking I didn't *have* to join. This was a deliberate decision on my part, calculated in cold blood and executed with precision.

I became a *komsomolets* in the late fall of my junior year, rather on the late side as compared to many of my classmates. Joining was a key part of my university admission plan. A non-member, I reasoned, would instantly stand out of the torrent of applications, and a Jewish non-member was the kind of a black sheep that would be immediately slaughtered on the altar of admission quotas.

How absurd, one might say, that a child of refuseniks applies to become a member of the Komsomol. At the entrance interview I was grilled by members of the school Komsomol committee. A few of those young activists were what we used to call *ideinye*, or "ideologically-minded ones." They believed—or pretended to believe—in the official Soviet ideology and spewed chunks of semi-digested *Komsomol Truth* editorials. Other Komsomol activists at my school were cynical operators already contemplating a career in the Party and government. One of them, a young man who was planning to apply to the Moscow Institute of International Relations, where career diplomats and foreign journalists were trained, asked about my "view of the state of Israel." I remember standing there, acting the part, giving them the Soviet-speak answers about Israel's "military aggression" and the "freedom-loving, oppressed" Palestinian people.

I recall senior high school as a constant effort of will, as though I was constantly flexing all my muscles without ever unflexing them. At the beginning of the senior year I was still hopeful about becoming a doctor, working extra hard on the sciences (getting As in physics was a struggle), being tutored in advanced math by a college professor, and aiming, still naïvely, for the gold medal and for medical school. "What happens if you don't get into medical school?" my parents began to ask, echoing my own fears, which I was shoving under the rug. "Then what? Afghanistan?"

The majority of Soviet institutions of higher learning had their entrance examinations in August. If rejected, one would have to wait a whole year and then reapply. At prestigious universities, the numbers of applicants exceeded the numbers of spots many times over. Even without "complicating" circumstances such as the Jewish nationality on one's passport, one mentally adjusted the number of anticipated admissions for various advantaged applicants, such as children of the Party elite, preselected candidates from the Soviet ethnic republics or enclaves, and army veterans, as well as beneficiaries of connections and bribes.

After weeks of deliberations, after making all sorts of inquiries and visits, my parents and I scrapped the medical school plan. This was a very hard decision, but the likelihood of my getting into medical school in Moscow did not justify taking a chance. By the autumn of 1983 we had arrived at what we felt would be a watertight scenario. Moscow State University held its entrance examinations during the month of July, a month earlier than other institutions. This offered a salutary opportunity. Moscow University was comprised of about a dozen schools, which were called "faculties": physics, chemistry, philosophy, history, and others. Medicine not being in the cards, at least for the time being, I chose the next best option. Among the "faculties" of Moscow University, the smallest one was the School of Soil Science. Historically part of the much larger School of Biology, in 1973 it had gained an independent status. The only such institution the entire Soviet Union, the School of Soil Science was supposed to train experts on soil, agriculture, and ecology. I have yet to meet a seventeen-year-old vying to study soil science. Applying there was a compromise between an interest in the natural sciences and a desire to study at the best university in the country. Two factors influenced my choice. One was that during the first two years, students at the School of Soil Science were educated very broadly in the natural sciences, which vaguely left open the prospect of a pre-med training. But the deciding factor was that out of a class of roughly one hundred students, the School of Soil Science was said to admit one, sometimes two Jews annually. Professor Gleb Dobrovolsky, founder of the School and its dean at the time of my application, was known as a liberal, and the School employed several Jews among its faculty and research staff. In fact, one of its most senior scholars was Professor Viktor Kovda, a Jew. At the School of Soil Sciences the unspoken *numerus clausus* seemed lower than in the other divisions of Moscow State University, and my parents and I reasoned that I would have a chance. The back-up plan, in case I didn't get into the Moscow University in July, was to apply in August to the Moscow Automobile and Road Construction Institute, to which I was likely to be accepted. In the last Soviet decades, the ubiquitous colleges of engineering, with the exception of a few strategic ones, were the refuge of young Jewish men and women. The prospect of joining the ranks of Soviet engineers nauseated me, but I needed a safety school in view of the upcoming military draft. Thus, by the middle of my senior year, dreams of medicine had been pushed to the sidelines, and I prepared myself for applying to Moscow University to study soil science, with engineering as the next best option.

On 5 June 1984 I turned seventeen. The Soviet secondary school graduation exams took place during the month of June. The exams at my school, some of them written and some oral, were in eight disciplines: written composition, biology, chemistry, foreign language (English), literature, history, mathematics, and physics. At stake was the gold medal, something I had been aiming for all through senior high. Physics was the last exam of the graduation series, and physics didn't come naturally to me. Over the years I had to work extra hard to maintain all As in physics, and in my senior year I got help from a disenfranchised refusenik physicist who made a living by tutoring college applicants at his apartment. In the morning, as I rode a city bus to school, I knew high school physics better than my own name. I had received As on all the previous graduation exams, and I relished the sensation of a gold medal on my open palm.

Scene: a physics classroom on the fifth floor of the school; half-open door revealing an adjacent physics lab; electrical equipment, weights, measures. Outside the windows the wind gently rustles in silver poplar branches. Two blackboards; at each of them a student writing or waiting to be examined. Between the blackboards and the classroom desks, four examiners sit around the teacher's long casket of a desk. Three of the examiners I know well: the literature teacher from middle school, the biology teacher, and the physics teacher. The physics teacher, Zinaida Rudzish, is a Latvian or perhaps a Baltic German, judging by her last name and her lisping accent in Russian. But the fourth person, who is she? What's she doing there, this strange woman with short gray hair, a snout nose, and small pale eyes floating under thick lenses? I come in and walk to the back of the classroom and sit to the left of one of my classmates, Alina, who had the biggest collection of Beatles tapes in our school. Alina's face is chalky, and her neck is covered with crimson spots that look like love bites. But they are fear bites. Alina can't figure out the problem.

"Who's the lady, the one with thick lenses?" I whisper.

"An inspector from the district board of education. They tell you this when you're called to the blackboard. I overheard."

"What's she doing here?"

"I can't figure this out," Alina whispers and flashes her *bilet* under the desk. A *bilet* ("ticket") is a strip of notebook paper with two theory questions and a problem written out in the neat longhand of our physics teacher. Everyone pulls the tickets out of a small stack on the teacher's desk.

Alina has a moderately difficult problem from mechanics, of the sort that my physics tutor has trained me to solve almost automatically. I whisper the solution and then lean back on my chair. I watch a classmate of mine attacking the battered blackboard with chalk, nailing numbers and formulas into its dark emerald surface. Then my name is called out. I come up to the examiners' desk and draw my lot.

"You can go straight to the board, Shrayer," says the physics teacher. "With your preparation, I'm sure you'll breeze through this."

I don't care for the way she pronounces the word "preparation." I'm embarrassed to ask for time to prepare, even though I'm entitled to ten or fifteen minutes, and I walk up to the blackboard.

The theoretical questions, one on thermodynamics, the other on structure of the atom, unfold in my head as chunks of text complete with paragraphs and italicized formulas. My brain readily responds to the problem, something or other about calculating the velocity of a hot air balloon. While Alina, her face now turning the color of parchment, is being raked over the coals at the other blackboard, I write out the solution to the problem and underline the answer. The benevolent literature teacher, who has the answers to my *bilet* in front of her on the examiners' desk, quickly turns to me and winks with both her eyes, as if saying "yes, correct." She's rooting for me, as is the biology teacher, who is still hoping I will apply to medical school. Good, I'm thinking. The problem's all set. The two questions are straightforward enough, and I'm better with theory anyway. And then it's all over. To my left, Alina enters the final stage of her execution. Poor Alina. How I detest optics!

In a few minutes the lifeless Alina comes off the elevated platform in front of the blackboard and exits the classroom. My name is called again, as a formality, since everyone knows I'm next. The physics teacher, chunky, pressed inside of a green suit that almost matches the blackboard, approaches me.

"So, let's have a look," she says. "The problem looks good, yes, very good." She turns to the other examiners and says: "The problem is solved correctly. Shall we move to the theory part?" And then the physics teacher looks toward the lady from the board of education and asks her: "Perhaps you would like to examine our almost gold medalist?"

The lady with short hair grins, revealing her teeth, perfect albeit stained a dirty yellow. She gets up from her chair and makes several steps in my direction, looking straight in my eyes. I lower my gaze and see her nicely shaped legs clad in body-color nylons and her red shoes on high heels. She emits a strong smell of cigarettes and Red Moscow perfume.

"Your physics teacher has told me a bit about you, Shrayer," she says. "I've been watching your progress for the past two years. You seem very confident, just like your father. I once heard him read at the Poetry Book-shop downtown, in 1975 or 1976, I believe. I'm a great lover of poetry, you know. Is he writing much these days?"

"I don't know . . . The usual amount," I answer, because I can't ignore the examiner's questions, however implausible they might be, with my gold medal and university admissions at stake. But why is she asking about my father?

"Well, those creative minds, we all know how they are, don't we?" she gives out a lecherous laugh and turns to the literature teacher, who is not looking up and minces a handkerchief. "I'm sure you know the thermodynamics question perfectly," says my chief examiner, taking another step in my direction. "Let's hear about the more exciting matter, the structure of the atom."

I speak for about two or three minutes, a bit nervously, and at one point misspeak—electrons instead of neutrons, but correct myself instantly. The lady from the board of education stops me with a nod and an affirming hand gesture.

"Attaboy," she says, turning to my physics teacher. "A tiny mistake in the middle, but he corrected himself, didn't he? Will there be additional questions for the candidate?"

Silence. I wait for twenty seconds and walk towards the examiners' desk. I put my *bilet* face down and say a faint "thank you" to my teachers. Hard to believe, I'm done. I turn around and walk to the door. My hot left hand reaches the sticky knob when I hear: "Wait, Shrayer." The voice belongs to the chief examiner.

"I don't believe I have released you. Actually I do have one more question."

I return to the blackboard.

"Might you tell the committee how a fluorescent lamp works? What physical principles engender its functioning?"

We had never studied this in high school; one only asked a question like that to shoot a student down. The rest of the morning is a grayish blur. I recall saying something about particles moving in a gaseous environment, something of which I had but a vague intuition. Afterward there was a whole hour of waiting outside the physics classroom in the company of my classmates. Then we were all invited back and seated, and the physics teacher read out loud three sets of grades for each one of us: the year, the graduation exam, and the grade going to the high school diploma. When she read my grades: *A, B, A,* a collective sigh of disbelief circled the room, and Alina said from the back row: "He just lost his gold medal."

Years of living a refusenik double life were supposed to have prepared me for the gold medal fiasco. Skeptics had been predicting that *they* would never give the gold medal to a child of refuseniks. From a rational point of view it didn't make sense for the Soviet system to reward its defectors and internal enemies, and my parents had tried to warn me of the possibility of something running amok. But such arguments usually make sense after the shock has subsided, after there is no going back to the time preceding the offense. Earlier that morning, when I was on my way to take my last graduation exam, I really thought I had done it. And I couldn't imagine that my plan would be crushed literally on the brink of its realization. How melodramatic this must sound today. But melodrama is largely about telling, not about experiencing. The experience itself was devastating, and the shock did not come from the two years of scholastic efforts having instantly gone to waste. The shock I experienced on the day of the physics exam was the shock of being powerless. What made it all the worse was the cruel balderdash of the scenario which the Soviet system had orchestrated to punish my family. And it was only a high school physics exam! Why did the system care so much about a seventeen-year-old Jewish kid's graduation prize? A gold medal that wasn't even made of gold?

Walking home after the physics exam, I kept replaying in my head the entire *scene*: the classroom, the examiners, the questions, the lady who had been dispatched to my school with the purpose of undercutting my plan for happiness. I remember stopping at an ice cream kiosk just a block from my apartment building and buying a fruit sorbet for seven kopecks: a flimsy paper cup filled with frozen pink sugary stuff that Soviet kids so loved because this cheapest of ices smelled of wild strawberries. I ate the fruit sorbet in the middle of the square named after the Soviet physicist Igor Kurchatov, head of Stalin's nuclear project, which produced the first Soviet A-bomb. At the center of the square, in front of the Institute of Atomic Energy, stood a monument to Kurchatov, a bearded block of stone on a black pedestal. About the size of an elephant's head, the head of the Soviet nuclear physicist towered over the square with its trashed public park, the old movie theater "Orient," the newspaper and ice-cream kiosks, the vehicles, and the people rushing about their daily business. Licking my fruit ice, gazing at the physicist's totemic head, I knew once and for all that what had happened to me was perfectly "normal" in a police state like the Soviet Union, just as normal as grabbing my father, a doctor and a writer, from the arms of my mother, throwing him into a Black Maria, and taking him to the precinct station for a KGB interrogation. The physics exam had rid me of my last illusions about the country of my birth. Was it my final loss of civic innocence? As I realized that the system was now aiming its gun at me, I also knew that I had to defend myself from the system, not just some of its individual citizens.

I came home, intent on telling my parents soberly what happened at the exam and putting it behind me. As soon as I crossed our threshold, uncontrollable tears flooded my face. I hadn't cried like that since the day in the winter of 1980 when I learned we had become refuseniks. My parents, who in moments like that only blamed themselves for everything that happened to me, listened to my account and helped me change into pajamas. My father gave me a drink of Armenian cognac with a cup of tea, and I went to sleep in the middle of the day, in my parents' bedroom. When I woke up three hours later, there was a note on a tray to look in the fridge. I looked and found my favorite delicacies, including crabmeat. My parents had to go out, and they left me a novel by two Russian émigré authors. Titled *A Journalist for Brezhnev*, this thriller about the defection of a Soviet journalist had been published abroad and given to us by an American diplomat. I lay in bed for the rest of the day, swallowing the forbidden thriller, noshing on the delicacies, and trying hard to put the gold medal out of my mind.

To the high school graduation event I didn't wear a suit and tie like most of my male classmates. Instead, I put on my best American clothes: a pair of Wrangler blue jeans, a pale-blue denim shirt, and a beige "members only" jacket. It was a statement: I was a young foreigner temporarily held in Russia. I wanted to look and act differently. Not I but Olga S., a student from 10B, received the gold medal. An ethnic Russian, she had the face and dress of a Komsomol bride and was applying to Moscow University to study political economy.

On stage, as the principal cleared his throat and he handed me my high school diploma, he mumbled something about my "excellent achievement" and "perfect grades." When the official part was over, parents of several classmates came up to me and my parents to express disgust with how "unfairly" I had been "treated." What's more, many of my classmates, including the very kids who used to taunt me in grade and middle school, walked up to me to say something encouraging, along the lines of "never mind those slime-balls."

The teachers were split into two camps: those who looked away and those who tried to pull me aside and express their sympathy or embarrassment. The gym teacher, Vladimir Borisovich Markin, he who had pushed me to build muscles and stamina, was the only one who openly expressed loathing for the system. My father brought a flask of cognac to give him as a token of gratitude. Father looked for the gym teacher during the reception following the official part, but Markin was nowhere to be found. Then father went down to the first floor and knocked at the door of the gym teacher's office. He later told me he found Markin sitting in his chair, amid basketballs and athletic diplomas and trophies, stooped like an artillery officer, staring at a half-empty bottle of cheap port. My father opened the cognac and poured some for both of them. They drank in silence, and then Vladimir Borisovich grabbed my father's hand with both of his and cried out: "I'm ashamed to be working here. Those bastards, how they've hurt your boy."

A week after graduation from high school, in the early days of July 1984, I was walking from the University Metro station to the admissions office of the School of Soil Science. I felt like a Jewish tank. The Lenin Hills, upon which sprawled the campus of the "new" Moscow University, were the enemy heights I had to storm in order to survive. Land was burning under my feet. I was furious, thirsty for revenge. I was determined to win and exercise my right to be treated as an equal to non-Jewish applicants. My parents, who were worried sick that the Moscow University experiment might turn into another gold medal fiasco, later told me that during the admission season I would wake up and go to sleep with the face of a zealot.

At the School of Soil Science I filled out an application form and delivered my papers into the hands of the admissions officer, a lanky fellow with chestnut eyes, sorrowful like the land of Armenia herself. He told me he was a lecturer in soil chemistry and a member of the admission board. After looking over my application materials he paused, closed my green-clad high school diploma, and gave me a bewildered look.

"Shouldn't the cover be red?" he asked.

"Why?" I replied, defiant.

"Don't you have a gold medal?"

"No, I don't. Straight As, but no medal."

"Oh, I see," the admissions officer replied and put the diploma back in my file. "Well, with such grades, I would think . . . ," and something like a momentary blush of sympathy flashed across his face.

Of about 100 students admitted annually to the School of Soil Science, some 25 spots usually went to the preselects and army veterans. If, hypothetically, 700 regular candidates applied to 75 spots, this amounted to the competition of about 9 persons per admission slot. The "passing score" fluctuated a bit, based on competition and other factors, but usually stood around 16 (A equals 5, B, 4, etc.) A D received on any exam automatically disqualified one from continuing. About a third of the applicants dropped out of the race after mathematics—the first, written exam. I was well prepared, and by getting a B I not only made the first cut but also put myself in the serious running. Next came physics, the exam I feared the most. Sparks of universal justice touch us a few times in a lifetime, and for me the entrance physics exam was such a spark. I got an A, a solid A, on the oral physics examination. My lot was in the hands of two professors from the School of Physics. Not only did they give me an A, but they also complimented me on my "advanced understanding" of electromagnetic theory. Having expected a B if not a C in physics, I began to feel jitters of hope, especially because the third exam was chemistry. Chemistry was definitely the subject I knew best among the natural sciences. I already had nine cumulative points (a B and an A), and with another A and another B, I felt I might even exceed the expected "passing score."

The third exam was the tipping point of the examination series. Imagine a sunny morning in July, applicants and families crowding the front steps of the grey tomb of a building shared by the schools of Biology and Soil Science. "Young genius, young genius," my parents and I hear loud whispers coming from several directions. I turn around and see a boy of about 14, rotund, with blues eyes and black curly hair. To me he looks distinctly Jewish, Ashkenazi, and an eagle nose clashes with his chaste eyes and cherubic cheeks. Dressed in a suit and striped tie, the boy carries a school satchel. A whole *mishpacha* surrounds him as he makes his way through the crowd up the granite steps and toward the heavy oak doors. "Comes from Minsk. Skipped several grades. Little Jewish wunderkind," I hear behind my back, and I feel goose bumps sprouting up on my limbs.

By ten in the morning I'm already sitting in one of the top rows of a large auditorium, a "ticket" with a problem and two theory questions laid out on the desk in front of me. I have it all figured out in my head. The chemical problem is familiar, and I've jotted the solution down on a sheet of paper stamped in the upper right corner; all paper must be surrendered at the end of the exam. I'm waiting to be called to one of the double desks where examiners exchange glaring glances and open rubber mouths like actors in silent era films. Patience is not my natural virtue; waiting is torture. When my name is finally called, loudly, as it echoes across the auditorium, I'm struck by its foreign sound. I look down to the bottom of the auditorium and my eyes catch sight of the young Jewish genius from Minsk. He's one of the applicants with whom I'm supposed to compete for the one or two "Jewish" spots in the class of about a hundred students. The genius is stooped over his desk like a bear cub over a beehive. The theme of "Two Jews" from Mussorgsky's *Pictures at an Exhibition* flutters in my head as I approach my examiners.

My examiners are two men, one in his early forties, the other in his early fifties. One is a furtive red clown, the other a lazy white clown. Very soon it becomes obvious they have been doing this routine together for a while. I can tell right off, from the way they look at me, that both clowns are bigots.

"So," says the rotund cynic, who reeks of pipe tobacco and rancid sweat. "Got lucky today, right? Easy problem, little kid's stuff." My examiners probably consider deodorants a Russophobic Jewish invention.

I look at my funny reflection in the examiner's front gold teeth.

"The solution to the problem appears to be right," says the sluggish examiner, lifting his pallid eyes from the page. "But does the applicant know chemical theory, that's the question? Well, speak, youth."

I talk for a few minutes about something I know and understand as well as I do some of my favorite Russian poems, until the red clown stops me with a quick impatient gesture of his short stubby fingers.

"Okay—okay, rote memorization, but all correct," he says and turns to his partner, who is slouched in his chair.

"Yes, sure, I suppose we're done with the applicant. Unless my colleague has any further questions," the red clown says and furrows his brow.

"Only if you insist," the white clown replies, grinning. "Young man," he says looking at his perfectly groomed nails. "Can you tell us about the structure of polymers?"

I start answering and then draw the basic structure of a polymer, although this is only mentioned in the senior year chemistry textbook. I feel that I'm turning red down to the roots of my hair.

"Oh, that will do, young man," the red clown interrupts me. He and his partner look at each other, both nod, and the white clown removes a fountain pen from his front pocket and slowly writes "good" in my examination sheet next to the word "chemistry." It's a B. I've been counting on an A. And there's still composition. What if the score . . . ?

"Excuse me," I press sandy words out of my dry mouth. "I thought I answered everything correctly. Why a B?"

"The answer about polymers might have been a bit more vivacious," the younger examiner maliciously replies. "After all, you're applying to the best university in the country, young man."

"Don't be greedy," the white clown picks up, and I hear prejudice in his use of the word "greedy." "But then again, you always have the right to appeal our grade. If I were you, I wouldn't, but that's entirely your decision."

Walking out of the building onto the granite steps, I tasted vengeance on my caked lips. "I got a B," I told my parents. "I'm going to appeal the grade."

"Can you eat something first?" my mother implored.

"No, not now," and I was already leafing through the textbook looking for the chapter where polymers were briefly discussed.

"Look here, I knew it, I knew it. There's less than a page on polymers in the entire textbook. It's college-level stuff they were asking of me. That's discrimination."

Walking up the steps, I caught a glimpse of the young Jewish genius that was standing in the circle of his relatives. Disheveled and damaged, he was wiping tears with the sleeve of his striped suit.

In the Admissions Office, the sympathetic lecturer explained to me how the process worked.

"You need to submit a written appeal explaining why you think your grade needs to be raised. Listen," and he lowered his voice, "I just want to warn you that sometimes they actually lower the grade. B is good, so why risk it?"

"Who's on the appeal committee?" I asked.

"Two chemistry full professors, an official from the rector's office, and our very own dean of admissions. Tough crowd."

"I'm going," I replied.

After submitting the handwritten appeal and waiting for about forty minutes, I was invited to come into an office with an oval table, on one side of which sat three men and a woman. Aleksandr Manucharov, the dean of students at the School of Soil Science, presided over the appeals committee. With a gesture of his pianist's hands, he motioned me to sit down at the other side of the table, facing my judges.

"We have looked over your exam sheets and your appeal," said the woman on the far right of the table, a chemistry professor. "You're a strong candidate. We concede that the examiners may have been a little harsh—"

"—but," a man in a polka dot tie interrupted her, "we want you to know that they are both distinguished members of the School of Chemistry and first-rate scientists, and we can't overturn every decision our trusted colleagues make. Especially when we're talking about a B, already a fine grade."

"But this is grossly unfair, and you all understand it," I yelled in their faces. "I deserve an A, not anything lower than that."

Silence descended upon the room, like an angel of death. Then the dean of admissions, a middle-aged tall man in a black rumpled suit, cleared his throat.

"Look here, Shrayer," said the dean. "You've got an A and two Bs, you're way ahead. Go home and rest, and don't mess up the composition. Your score is good so far, and you seem to be passing. Though I can't make any promises."

Two or three days later, I took the last examination: written composition. After two more days of waiting, on a rainy late July afternoon, my parents and I were having tea at home. All three of us were used up after the almost two months of my examinations. The composition grades and the list of admitted students were supposed to be posted on the doors of the School of Soil Science by noon of the following day.

"Call," my father told me.

"I don't want to. It's too early."

"Okay, I'll call," my mother offered.

She dialed the number of the admissions office and asked to check if the composition grades were in. "She's checking," my mother whispered to us, covering the receiver with her palm. "B? Are you sure. Admitted? Oh my God! Are you absolutely sure? Oh thank you, thank you," and my mother dropped the receiver.

"You got a B on composition and you've been admitted to Moscow University. The lists will be posted tomorrow."

The three of us embraced and performed an "Indian" victory dance in the middle of the room. "We beat them, we won," father, mother, and I kept screaming. "Victory!"

We opened a bottle of champagne, toasted, then started telephoning: my grandmother and aunt, refusenik friends, my friends who were still in town.

The following day I went to the university to look for my name in the typed list of the freshmen. The list was pasted with tape to the oaken front doors. Twice I scanned the pages with my eyes, twice without finding myself. Then, putting my index finger to the top of the list, I slowly brought it down almost all the way to the bottom, where my name, Шраер, Максим Давидович, shot in black amid other black letters. "Hey, I'm in," I said to myself.

Later that day my father drove me to the Leningradsky railway station and bought me a ticket for Tallinn for that same evening. My parents were coming two days later. I had never traveled to Estonia alone and had only taken long-distance trains unchaperoned twice before that. Going to Pärnu alone was my prize for having gotten in. I shared the four-berth compartment with a Jewish couple and their little boy. They were also going to Pärnu. I felt like an adult. A Moscow University student. It sounded so unreal, so fantastical. And yet, the image of my name in the column of newly admitted students was constantly before my eyes, printed on the double glass of the compartment window, superimposed onto landscapes of fir trees, greening fields, and rickety peasant huts.

I left my luggage under the care of my sojourners, who had offered to share their fried chicken and hard-boiled eggs. I walked to the restaurant car. The Estonia, one of the best trains in the Soviet railroad fleet, was supposed to have a decent menu. I was seated at an empty table for four, with a fresh, heavily starched tablecloth, a little dish of unmistakably Estonian mustard, and a plate of *sepik*, the ashen-gray Estonian bread that smelled of charcoal, barley, and the Baltic Sea. I ordered a bottle of Estonian sawdust-colored beer, three fried eggs, a cucumber and tomato salad, rhubarb cake, tea with lemon, and a shot of Vana Tallinn liqueur—why do I remember all this? The waitress had a white lacy piece pinned on top of her head. Her de-voiced, accented Russian immediately transported me to a space where I felt more at home. Sipping my beer and slowly eating my supper, I achieved a sense of retrospective vision that liberated me from the strain of the previous two months. Later, as I chewed on the rhubarb cake and brought to my lips a snifter of Estonia's famed liqueur, which tasted of wormwood calm and chocolate oblivion, the maître d' brought over a couple of retirees and seated them at my table.

Her hair pomaded and dyed snow-blue, the pouty lady looked exactly like I would have imagined the wife of a retired air force general to look. The general himself was a bulldog with a shiny bald head, fleshy ears, and jovial, hairy hands. Next to his matronly wife, the general looked like a footman. And yet, the left side of his beige summer suit was adorned with five or six rows of ribbons of military decorations, and on his right lapel dangled a gold-faceted star. The retired general was in his early seventies, the same age as both my grandfathers would have been, had they lived to see their Jewish boy triumph against the Soviet odds. The general was a Hero of the Soviet Union, bearer of the highest distinction given for military valor. Despite my jaded sense of Soviet values, the general's gold star brought back a wave of memories of my grandfathers, stirring up a mixture of useless awe and sadness.

Later that night, as I lay on my upper berth, listening to the tetrameter of clanking and clashing wheels, I thought about the retired air force general I had met at the restaurant car, about his gold star and about his patrician wife, who had immediately bristled up after having one look at me. I also thought about my own gold medal, the one I never received, and about the defeat of Nazism. My grandfather Pyotr Shrayer, a thirty-four-year-old lieutenant-commander, smiled gladly at his descendant standing next to him on the bridge of his torpedo boat. Charging full steam ahead, my grandfather's vessel carried me toward Tallinn and the end of the war. Studenthood. . . .

PART TWO

The Expedition

5

MOSCOW STATE

THE MAIN CAMPUS of Moscow State University sits atop an elevated area on the right bank of the Moskva River. Once lying outside Moscow's city limits, this picturesque area used to be known as Vorobyovy ("Sparrow") Hills until 1935, when it was renamed Lenin Hills. The Lenin Hills campus with its main tower, once the tallest building in Europe, owes its erection to the post-World War II explosion of Stalinist Empire style. In 1999 the Lenin Hills were re-renamed, or rather their historic name was restored. Yet in my memories I keep ascending not the Sparrow Hills but the Lenin Hills on my way to Moscow University, and descending to my other life that lay beneath the Lenin Hills.

Having become a university student at seventeen, for the first time in my life I didn't feel alone among my school peers. Also for the first time I experienced real diversity in the classroom. The one-hundred-odd members of my class at the School of Soil Science made up a composite image of the ethnic make-up of the Soviet Union. The Russian element still predominated, followed by Ukrainian students (I can't say that Belarusian classmates expressed a strong sense of identity). But the Eastern Slavs weren't a dominant majority. There were members of at least a dozen other ethnicities in my class. Students from the Caucasus: an Armenian, a Georgian from Abkhazia, two Azeris (one of whom called himself "Turk"), a Chechen, and a Lakh (from Daghestan in Northeast Caucasus). Despite different religions and centuries-old conflicts, while away from their home the students from the Caucasus region formed (I couldn't resist the pugnacious pun) a *caucus* of their own and stuck together. My classmates from the Volga basin included a Tatar and a Bashkir, while a Kirghiz and an Uzbek represented Central Asia. Two Estonians and a Lithuanian flew their lowered Baltic flags. Add to that a Moldovan, a Pole, and also two foreign students from Bulgaria, and you will find yourself in the cauldron of ethnicities and languages which I experienced in September 1984. While Russian served as the obvious *lingua franca*, many other languages were spoken. Ukrainians from Western Ukraine conversed with each other in Ukrainian, and members of the Turkic language family communicated with one another in their native tongues: a Bashkir with a Tatar, a Tatar with an Azeri, an Azeri with an Uzbek, and so forth.

There was one other Jewish student in my year, Ilia Salita, also a Muscovite (and now also an American). Two classmates with Jewish mothers but Russian fathers and Slavic last names would later reveal themselves to us, the open Jews. Our year was divided into eight subgroups or discussion sections, and the ethnically savvy administration placed both of the Jews, Ilia and me, in the same discussion section. Ilia and I didn't become close friends, but we did look out for each other. I know that behind our backs, some of the classmates referred to us as the "Jewish lobby." Antisemitism hadn't entirely disappeared, nor could the two of us ferret it out even if we tried. But the prejudice had assumed subtler or quieter forms.

Besides the multiethnic and multilingual richness, which surrounded me at Moscow University, there was also geographic and class diversity. About half of our class were non-Muscovites. They lived not at home with parents but in the university dormitories. In terms of their lifestyle and collective identity as "provincials," they formed a community of their own vis-à-vis the Moscow students. As was to be expected, parents of several of my classmates from the provinces were members of the regional Party elite. While some of the non-Muscovites had grown up in families of provincial intelligentsia (a high school teacher of literature in a small town; a scientist at a regional research institute), other classmates came from working class and peasant families and were the first in their families to go to university. Finally, there were students from military families, who had spent their childhood on military bases and garrisons.

My classmates hailed from all over the vast Soviet Union, from as far east as the Kamchatka Peninsula in the Far East, as far west as Kaliningrad (the former Königsberg in the former East Prussia), as far north as Murmansk (beyond the Arctic Circle on the Barents Sea), and as far south as Astrakhan in the Volga delta, Baku in Azerbaijan, and Tashkent in Uzbekistan. For the first time I was exposed, on a daily basis, to the dialectal lushness of the Russian language. I'm not referring to non-Russians from ethnic Soviet republics and autonomous enclaves, who spoke Russian with accents: the guttural and glottal Caucasus accents; the yogurt-gulping Central Asian pronunciation; the humid, wheezing *h* sound of the Ukrainians speaking in Russian (instead of the hard and crunchy *g* of the standard Russian); the de-voiced consonants and sing-song intonation of Russian-speaking Estonians. Perhaps even more absorbing to me, given my perpetual fascination with ethnography and dialectology, was the lexical and accentual diversity of the way my provincial Russian peers spoke Russian. For instance, I quickly befriended Vanya Govorukhin, son of a reporter at a regional newspaper in the Gorky (now Nizhny-Novgorod) Province. Vanya spoke with the characteristic *okan'e*, a pronunciation common in the north of Russia and in parts of the Volga region. Not only his stressed *o*'s, but also the unstressed *o*'s, came out as deep, round vowels, sort of like the trumpet of Jericho pointing at the listener's ear.

One more formation of students, a caucus of its own kind, deserves a quick digression. About a dozen male students in my year were army veterans who had entered Moscow University through a special back-to-school program. Returning home after two mandatory years of military service (three in the navy), many of these men required a year-long remedial course in high school disciplines. The program extended these men's path to a university diploma from five to six years, but as a trade-off the veterans were accepted to the university with a lower "passing score." The army veterans were on average four, some even five or six, years older than the recent high school graduates. As compared to the seventeen- and eighteen-year-old boys, they were definitely "men," mustached and some even bearded, filled out, weathered, tough. The veterans treated us, the unseasoned kids who hadn't served, with a mixture of condescension and older brothers' brio. In the eyes of these seasoned classmates, Muscovites from the families of the intelligentsia represented an entitled, privileged, glamorous metropolitan life. We, the young city slickers, viewed the army veterans as roughnecks or country bumpkins—or both.

Two of the veterans had been in the Afghan War theater. Now and then they would drop a shocking detail about being parachuted into a remote mountain village and left there to fight the mujahideen amid hostile local populations. The *afgantsy*—the Afghan War veterans—told about breeding dogs they would slaughter and eat during the winter months. The unwinnable Afghan War would be obdurately fought until 1989, and the presence of our *afgantsy* made perfectly real the prospect of being dispatched to Afghanistan.

Despite initial friction and a gap of years and experience, by the end of my first university year I had befriended two veterans. One of them was Sergei Khudoleyev, a pockmarked giant from a Cossack *stanitsa* (village) in the fertile southern Kuban region, where he longed to return after graduation. He was so big and mighty that his body required regular naps to replenish its energy. Sergei used to doze off and snore during the lectures and in the cafeteria after lunch. Benevolent and calm, he never took offense at being teased for his sleepiness and snoring. He sang folk songs, was obsessively neat, and was terribly shy with women. My other pal among the ex-servicemen, Lyonya (Leonid) Chumachenko, was Khudoleyev's total opposite. A *bon vivant* from the coastal city of Kherson on the Black Sea, Lyonya moved to Odessa after finishing high school. Before he was drafted into the navy, he painted houses with a partner who was Jewish (a "little Jewish fellow," *evreichik*, as he called him, and he meant this not pejoratively but fondly). Lyonya was a drinker, a charmer and ladies' man, and a gifted comedic actor in amateur productions. Soon after we became friendly, he offered to give me medicine for "clap" just in case I ever needed some ("A buddy of mine back home is a doctor, he gets the pills for me," Lyonya explained.) Practically in the same breath he also revealed to me that he planned to stay in Moscow, that the south was too "narrow" for him, the Black Sea too "shallow," even though he missed a "to-die-for girl" still waiting for him in Odessa.

On 23 February, Soviet Army Day, the veterans would don their enlisted personnel's uniforms with decorations, pins, and chevrons. Although they tended to represent a unified group to the rest of their classmates and the faculty, there were all sorts of divisions in their midst. In addition to obvious differences of ethnicity and place of origin, the veterans wanted different things from their experience and education in the Soviet capital. Going to Moscow University offered a ticket to a good job, a Moscow residency permit, a place better than their home in the provinces. In this connection, a melancholy anecdote about one of my former classmates comes to mind. His name was Maksud, and he was from Tatarstan, a large and populous autonomous republic in the Volga basin. Maksud's plan was to get into graduate school and stay in Moscow. He was smart and unmerciful. At the beginning of our freshmen year, Maksud started courting Ninochka, a petite girl with butterfly eyes, wavy blond hair, and typically Muscovite speech mannerisms. Ninochka's father was, if I remember correctly, a head curator at one of Moscow's art museums, an icon specialist, and a descendant of a noble family. For several months Maksud pursued her, bringing her flowers and walking her home, until she succumbed. But she set a condition: he couldn't tell her parents he was an ethnic Tatar. Her parents would never let her go out with a non-Russian, she told Maksud. And especially a Muslim or a Jew. Ninochka chose a substitute Slavic name for him, Serezha (Sergei, the name of Russia's patron saint, St. Sergius of Radonezh). She began to supply him with the Russian classics and take him to the theater and to music recitals. When Maksud phoned Ninochka at home and her parents answered, he identified himself by his code name. Teeming with hatred for the Russian intelligentsia, Maksud jealously and venomously disliked me, a Moscow Jew. It amazed me then that he failed to recognize in me a fellow victim of the grand imperial Russian prejudice against all aliens.

While at Moscow University I would see my classmates five or six days a week during the school year. Some of them became my "pals" . . . in the American campus sense of the word. In Russian I thought of them as my *priiateli* (*priiatel'* means "pal"), rather than *druz'ia* (from *drug*, "friend"). My university pals never became close friends and trusted confidantes. Even during the physically taxing expedition I would undertake after my second year at the School of Soil Science, where we had to trust one another with our safety during ascents to the mountains, a distance remained. This distance that was keeping me apart even from my closest classmates was the secret of being a refusenik. Even if some of my other university pals did know in the end, they didn't hear it from me. Why was I being so cagey, why couldn't I just tell them? Was I suffering from a Jewish-Soviet paranoia? I don't think so. In fact, still today my life in 1984–1987 strikes me as a fairly normal double life of someone who is both a Soviet university student and a young Jewish refusenik. My university life was teeming with classes, lectures, research, expeditions, poetry, and romance. I experienced the usual intricacies of human sympathies and antipathies; cliques; intellectual and amorous competition. There were weekly games of volleyball, there were parties, skit nights, and even amateur plays I acted in (a spiteful king in a play about François Villon). There were, finally, the two summers during which I slept in bunks and tents, ate atrocious food, and longed for home and family, side by side with my classmates. What I'm trying to commit to words and having some difficulty with is the sense that despite the unloved and underwhelming studies, my life as a Moscow University student was full and stimulating. And yet the refusenik part of my world—the one I concealed from my university peers—never let me feel a oneness with them. Like lovemaking on the eve of breaking up, my refusenik secret both hurt and excited, both tormented and pleasured. I can think of a number of times when I was tempted to tell a classmate about my *other* life. We would be sitting at a Saturday morning lecture on Marxist philosophy. (What "basis"? What "superstructure"?) As we traded jokes and gossiped, I would look outside the auditorium's embrasure windows at February's rat-gray snow and think of a presentation by a Canadian Jewish activist. It was to be held at a refusenik's apartment later that day. I was going with my mother, but how could I possibly share any of this with my classmates? I remember feeling impulses to open up. And then, immediately, I would strangle these impulses: while walking with Pyotr Tsanava, a tall Georgian with a sensualist's guilty smile, along the empty Leningrad Highway late at night; while sharing a beer with Yulya Galkina, a Moscow jackdaw intolerant of bigotry and falseness; there were other occasions and other classmates to whom I wanted to open up. I can well imagine that despite the sunny disposition I possessed when I was eighteen, my classmates remember me as somewhat aloof. And I can even imagine the trappings of a negative stereotype of a "calculating, secretive" Jew in the way some of my university classmates judged me behind my back. But there was no question in my mind that the two lives, my university life and my refusenik life, must be kept separate, without mixing and meshing. In living this double life at the university, I took to heart my father's advice: If you don't tell them, and if your classmates are ever questioned by the authorities in connection with your political troubles, they would be able to answer, with honesty: He never talked about it; I really didn't know.

Very few students came to study at the School of Soil Science because they loved soil, ecology, or agriculture. There were exceptions, to be sure. One of my classmates, Pyotr Tsanava, came from a dynasty of tea-growers and indeed wanted to train in Moscow and return to Abkhazia to work on the land. Among us there were only a few born lovers of soil like Tsanava. Given that field work and expeditions to remote and exotic areas of the country were a regular part of our training, the School attracted various dreamers, Soviet hippies, "granolas" and environmentalists, and even aspiring bards and songwriters. Many of those men and women had come to the School because they sought to escape the tedium of Soviet living. I felt grateful that I didn't end up attending a college of engineering like my best friend Max, who was studying telephone communications while dreaming of filmmaking.

It's not easy to learn unloved subjects even in the best of surroundings. And yet a young mind possesses a supreme resilience, and this resilience, constantly reinforced by the excitement of going to school at a great university and having found a new social niche among my classmates, helped me get through even the most unattractive of courses. For the first two years, the whole one hundred of us had lectures together, Monday through Saturday, in one of the two grand auditoriums of the Biology and Soil Science building. For the labs and discussion and problem-solving sessions we broke into subgroups. The building where we had most of our classes and labs was about a ten-minute walk to the west of the famous main tower of Moscow University. These smaller Moscow University buildings now make me think of the grand sepulchers of knowledge on the campuses of Land-Grant universities, such as Vanderslice Hall of the University of Wisconsin–Madison. The Soil Science auditorium had expensive woodwork, blackboards built for goliaths of science, and hardwood amphitheater seats forbidding of comfort. Large oil portraits of the founding fathers of Russian soil science (naturally, Mother Russia had birthed both soil science and its leading lights) hang in a semicircle around the front of the auditorium. Dokuchaev, Pryanishnikov, Rodé . . . The time-shined dark portraits of bearded long-haired fierce men. Gilded heavy frames. Devotion to the cause of Russian science. This was supposed to inspire us, but instead bored most of us like stories of Lenin's childhood.

For the first year our studies consisted mainly of general courses in the natural sciences. (Three years later this would come in handy when I entered Brown University as a transfer student. Brown didn't have a core curriculum, and I received credit for two years of my Moscow University courses and was able to complete a wholly new major in comparative literature and literary translation.) Unlike an American university where undergraduates choose courses from multiple offerings without much coordination, our schedules were mandated and posted at the beginning of each semester, with no flexibility whatsoever. In the 1980s, everything was still being done in a starkly old-fashioned, manual fashion: typed or handwritten schedule announcements, no course catalog of any sort. And absolutely nothing was computerized. Of the subjects I took in the first year at Moscow University, I enjoyed Geology and Mineralogy, and also liked Botany and even tolerated Introduction to Soil Science with its vestiges of ecology, geography, evolutionary biology, and microbiology. I remember most fondly working with rocks and gems in the vast geological collections in one of the top floors of the main Moscow University tower. I could bear Organic Chemistry, although the long hours I had to spend at the lab, titrating and purifying, were tedious, notwithstanding all the rainbows and firebirds I bred in the captivity of my vials. I despised Advanced Calculus, taught by a former military pilot whose hands had been so severely burned during World War II that he had to wear leather gloves to hold a piece of chalk. And I couldn't abide General Physics. I confess that of all the material I was taught in advanced science courses at Moscow University, I remember almost nothing concrete, despite the fact that I studied hard for my exams and got only As and occasional Bs. I used to be able to play with differential equations as though they were words of prose and sounds of poetry, but I have forgotten it utterly and completely.

In the second year, the courses became more specialized, and included such monsters as Physical and Colloid Chemistry, Statistics, and Analysis of Soil. At the same time, I rather liked Land Surveying, which for decades had been taught in the school by "Babushka" K., an iron lady in her seventies who glided up and down the long parquetted corridors on high heels; permed, perfumed, and perennially young. It was said about her that as a young graduate student in the early 1930s she had been a champion skater and a research assistant to several then-ageing luminaries of soil science.

Some of our male professors cultivated Olympian looks. Among them was the dean of the School, G. V. Dobrovolsky, a slender man with perfectly ironed collars and cuffs. His twin brother was also a professor of natural sciences, teaching at the Moscow Pedagogical University. The professor who made the biggest impression on me as a freshman was the Soviet grandee Boris Rozanov, an imposing man in his fifties dressed in foreign-made suits and ties, with a Mephistophelian profile and the large, jutting mauve ears of a pedigreed Chihuahua. Rozanov had worked in Nairobi, Kenya, heading the anti-desertification section of the United Nations Environmental Programme. Laureate of the Soviet State Prize and author of monographs and textbooks on soil science and ecology, Rozanov spoke good English and capably acted the part of an official Soviet liberal. To the astonishment of students, he told sexy stories of visiting the pleasantly decaying West during international conferences, and described travels across Patagonia and adventures in the African savanna. One of his favorite anecdotes was about attending an international conference in Chile—this was during the Pinochet years—and chanting revolutionary songs in the company of "progressive" Western colleagues. With their slow measured speech, barometric irony, cologned faces, and manicured nails, Rozanov and the older male professors among the School's elite were like supporting characters in a Soviet academic play.

Continuing with the study of English was a refuge. Together with my Jewish classmate Ilia Salita, also a graduate of an English school, I placed out of required foreign language classes and enrolled in a two-year laboratory of advanced English for science majors. Our instructor was an attractive woman in her late thirties who wore silk scarves and pearls, spoke what I thought to be the Queen's English, and appeared on TV in an experimental program for language learners. She provided an all-immersion environment and insisted on speaking only English with her students, even when we would bump into her on campus. Initially, she tried to correct the pronunciation I had learned by imitating the Americans I had met. But soon she left my American phonetics alone, interpreting my refusal to speak like an Englishman not as a political choice, but an act of delayed teenage rebellion.

After quickly going over some translation exercises introducing advanced scientific vocabulary, our group would spend most of the weekly *para* (double class hour) discussing an English novel of our instructor's choosing. Not many English and American novels were available in print in the Soviet Union. They were mainly published, as learners' annotated editions with Russian-language vocabulary notes, and in violation of copyright, by the Moscow publishing house Progress. Of the novels we read, I remember best our discussions of Somerset Maugham's *Theatre*. Our instructor, who certainly didn't come across as a prude, avoided even the mention of the novel's lesbian theme. Several of us asked innocently phrased questions, pretending not to understand why one woman would want to kiss another or desire to see her naked. She couldn't stop or even admonish us, because in doing so she would have had to transgress a taboo. One of my strongest memories of that English course is the deliciously schematic ending of Maugham's novel. The famous actress Julia Lambert has finally freed herself from loving a much younger, self-serving man who was unworthy of her. She goes into her favorite London restaurant, sits by herself, and, foreswearing her diet, orders a fattening meal: "It gave her a pleasant sense of independence to sit there unknown and unnoticed. . . . Her steak arrived. It was cooked exactly as she liked it and the onions were crisp and brown. She ate the fried potatoes delicately, with her fingers, savoring each one as though it were the passing moment that she would bid delay. 'What is love beside steak and onions?' she asked." I read Maugham's novel in the early spring of 1985, craving after both the meal and the sense of anonymity that was so lacking in my Soviet existence. How long would it be, I wondered, before I, too, would sit in a London restaurant and order steak and onions? In fact it would be eight more years before I, as a newly-minted US citizen, would visit London and look back at my Moscow University years as scenes from another, distant life.

How accustomed we've become to thinking of the years 1984–86 as occurring *on the brink*. . . . This is retrospective thinking, a memoirist's fallacy, and I would like to avoid it at least in some chapters of this story. When I recall my first university year, I'm struck by the fact that the collapse of the Soviet system did not pose even a remote eventuality. As I think of how my friends and I perceived our Jewishness, I'm amazed at the readiness with which we assumed that since the Soviet system would always be there, so would official antisemitism and restrictions on Jewish self-expression. An acute sense of both visible and invisible ghetto walls defined our Jewish studenthood and many of our public activities. This brings me to the Moscow Choral Synagogue, without which a portrait of Jewish life in Moscow of my youth would be incomplete.

The popular parlance referred to this synagogue in the center of Moscow as *gora*. *Gora* means "hill" or "mountain" in Russian, and the name owed its origins to the location of the synagogue. This turn-of-the-century building with a classical fronton and Ionic columns stood in Arkhipov Street, one of the steepest streets in old Moscow. Going uphill to the synagogue from the nearby Nogin Square Metro station, we envisioned ancient Jewish temples and were filled with pride. The Metro station has since been renamed Kitay-Gorod, having deposited on the trash heap of history the name of the Bolshevik revolutionary Viktor Nogin. Arkhipov Street, too, has been re-renamed, and is once again called Spasoglinishchevsky Lane, a name covered with a patina of Russian Orthodox memory. A member of the circle of the Russian Itinerants, Abram Arkhipov made a name for himself with colorful, perhaps too-exuberant scenes of Russian peasant women in their floral shawls and headscarves. Painting Russian peasant life was for the Jew Arkhipov a way of entering the mainstream of Russian cultural life, of becoming a Russian artist and therefore culturally a Russian. While approaching the Moscow Choral Synagogue today, one no longer feels that special, Jewish-Russian irony we felt while treading Arkhipov Street. Jewish boys and girls who were Russian by culture, we came to Arkhipov Street in order to hear the sound of our Jewish voices.

I had started going to the *gora* with my father, on Jewish holidays and sometimes on Friday night, when I was around ten or eleven and we were becoming refuseniks. Father and I would go in and sit for awhile in the main sanctuary, where prayers for the Soviet governments were posted behind the *bimah* in large letters in Hebrew and Russian. During the festive holiday of Simchas Torah, we made sure to stop by a smaller chapel off the right side of the synagogue, where men in black hats and kaftans danced and sang their wordless songs of ecstasy. Later, when I became a university student, my friend Max was my regular companion. Parents cautioned us against going to the *gora*. The risk of being expelled from the university was too high, they believed, to justify our expeditions to Arkhipov Street. I knew all this, and yet I refused to know any of this.

It's hard to imagine that one main synagogue served some 200,000 Jews of the Soviet capital as well as visitors. Referring simultaneously to the building and the hilly street on which it stood, *gora* (or its diminutive, *gorka*) was a private code we employed to avoid using the word "synagogue." *"Ty idesh' na gorku?"* (literally, "Are you going to the little hill?"), a Jew might ask another one in the university hallway, some time around the end of December. To the uninitiated, this very specific question about going to a Chanukah celebration probably suggested going skiing. The degree of punishment a Jewish student faced if informed on or apprehended in a crowd outside the synagogue depended on the climate at his or her educational institution, varying from severe official reprimand to expulsion. Not only plainclothes security agents, but also Komsomol and Communist Party "activists" from within the ranks of the students, were dispatched to the environs of the Moscow Synagogue on Friday evenings, and especially during Jewish holidays. The "activists" would meander up and down Arkhipov Street, trying to identify fellow students. For Jewish students the experience of being stopped by a school "activist" and warned, or even reported, was not unfamiliar. Yet thousands of young Jewish students still took their chances.

We were being watched and exposed, and this made the experience more enthralling. The main action was not inside the synagogue but in the street, where we would form circles, hands over each other's shoulders, and sing Jewish songs in Hebrew and Yiddish, "Hava Nagila," "Shalom Aleichem," "Tum-Balalaika," sometimes humming the melodies and only chanting or roaring the refrains. Towards the end of the evening on a Jewish holiday, the crowd grew so thick that it was no longer possible to dance, and we would just march in place, embracing and rocking to the melodies erupting from thousands of young gullets. Now and then photo flashes dashed across the crowd, illuminating the enraptured Jewish faces chanting "Shalom, Shalom, Shalom Aleichem," and one never knew for sure if these stolen images would be smuggled outside the country by foreigners or entered in KGB files.

It was not an observant Jew's formed habit of communal religious practice that drove me and many other young Jews to the *gora*. What drew me there, at the age of seventeen and eighteen, was the thrill of being part of a crowd of young Jews. Going to the *gora* was an affirmation of identity, a Jewish pride parade, and a form of protest. But it was also a massive Jewish singles night, to which Jewish mothers would sometimes bring their timid debutantes. Despite the natural fear of informers and "activists," young Jewish people would meet without hindrance and exchange phone numbers, forming new friendships and relationships. I knew couples that met outside the *gora*, married, and later emigrated together. Outside the synagogue on a Friday night in July 1984, the summer I was applying to Moscow University, I met a Jewish girl I would date during the summer between high school and university.

On many occasions over the years I have been living in America, I have encountered American- and Canadian-born Jews who regard me and other ex-Soviet Jews with a mixture of solidarity, skepticism, and condescension—as somehow a lesser Jew. I understand that behind this response lies a stereotype of a Russian-Soviet-Jew as someone devoid of Judaism. Besides the perceived superiority of a "native" Jew toward a recent immigrant Jew from the old country, what indirectly feeds into this perception is ideas of historians and sociologists who speak of the disappearance of religious self-awareness among Soviet Jews. On the surface of it, someone might say, I, too, fit the profile when I was a young Jewish man in the Soviet Union: I hadn't had a formal Judaic religious education, I didn't know Hebrew, I was never bar-mitzvaed in shul. And yet, this parametric perspective does no justice to my experience of being a young Jew in the Moscow of the 1980s. In terms of the fifty-eight centuries of Jewish spirituality, the seventy Soviet years were but a flicker of time. I refuse to believe that millennia of Jewish religious memory could have been erased from our identities. What might be more to the point is to say that we expressed our Jewishness not in the religiously observant, but in broadly Jewish spiritual ways.

About ten years ago, a congregational rabbi in an affluent Boston sub-urb, a peer of mine in age if not experience, told me, upon hearing that I was originally from the Soviet Union: "We're going to grow you as a Jew." My wife and I sat in the rabbi's study, in deep comfortable chairs, and I was overcome with quiet rage. To "grow" me, a Russian Jew—like some flavorless hothouse tomato? I recalled the sensation of standing in a crowd of hundreds, sometimes thousands of Jewish men and women filling a hunchbacked Moscow street on *shabes* or on Jewish holidays. I thought of how we were ready to overflow the police cordons. I told this American-born rabbi that we Russian Jews don't need to be "grown," we who had made a conscious choice to be Jewish and act Jewish even though in danger. Left to my memories and my rage, I never returned to the rabbi's congregation, still a Russian Jew among my American co-religionists. . . .

Like a moth over a streetlamp, I am hovering over the thought that my life as a young Jewish university student and a refusenik was in some ways exceptional, while in others not atypical of the lives of my peers in large Soviet cities. Centripetal forces drove me into the student main-stream while centrifugal ones pushed me out, to orbits of refusenik sin-gularity and Jewishness. Besides my parents, and our family's love and shared sense of refuseniks' plight and mission, what kept me more or less grounded in that double life was the loyalty of my closest friends Max Mussel and Katya Tsarapkina. One makes such friends only once in a lifetime, and then struggles not to lose them in the currents of emigration.

Max, Katya, and I had already become each others' best friends by the time we started college. Katya lived in Leningrad, and during the school year Max and I saw her only three or four times, mainly when Max and I came to Leningrad for the weekend. The two-month summer vacations in Pärnu had been reduced to three weeks in August, during which the three of us did our best to make up for the time apart.

In Moscow, Max and I lived about an hour from each other. We saw each other sometimes as often as every day of the week, except when I was away on an expedition or when Max was at officer reservists' training camp. Lefortovo, where Max was living, was an old district in the eastern part of Moscow, where ancient park alleys still remembered Peter the Great. Our most common downtown meeting place, Pushkin Square, was a halfway point between Moscow University, located in the southwest of the city, and my neighborhood of Oktyabrskoye Pole in the northwest of Moscow. Weekdays, unless we were cutting classes, we would meet in the late afternoon, and on weekends we often got together in the late morning and spent a whole day wandering about our city.

There are certain youthful memories that transcend the past in a way that makes it appear too perfect. This perfection of the past, especially if it occurs in a foreign language, both corrects for immigrant anxieties and compensates for exilic losses. I remember a particularly fine Sunday morning in April of 1985, one of those liberating mornings in Moscow when everybody knows that winter is over. Max and I met outside the Taganskaya Metro station, across the street from the Theater at Taganka, famous for its Brecht-inspired performances, and followed the streams of molten snow down Taganskaya Street to the Yauza River Embankment, past the Foreign Languages Library and in the direction of the Boulevard Ring, a succession of boulevards encircling the center of old Moscow. On their long necks, the waters carried down into the Yauza pieces of small urban debris, candy wrappers, sticks from Eskimo Pie bars, and beer caps, as we talked of Hesse's *Steppenwolf* and *The Glass Bead Game* and also of Cortázar's story "Blow-Up," which inspired Michelangelo Antonioni's film. I was mainly reading Russian authors of past and present, instinctively distrusting translations. Max concentrated on non-Russian literature, especially Anglo-American, German, Latin-American, and

Japanese—anything decent he could get his hands on in the Soviet book market. We complemented each other: I a convinced Russophile in my reading habits, Max a sworn Westernizer; I a reader of poetry, Max of prose and screenplay translations; I a theater-goer, Max a fanatical film lover. He wouldn't go to the theater, regarding it as a conventional and obsolete art form, while I went to see plays once a week. Max was the main source of my knowledge of early Soviet and of Western cinema. He also knew most Beatles songs by heart. Max associated the Russian classics with mandatory high school reading lists, and the Russian-language Soviet authors were to him either sell-outs or imitators. Max only made an exception for the poet Vladimir Mayakovsky, whose stepladder verses and lyrical montage, he believed, resembled the early pictures of Eisenstein and Dziga Vertov.

Max and I lingered for a little while on the bridge over the Yauza, studying the brackish, sun-splashed water. Then we decided to hit the boulevards. We strolled for awhile on a fragment of the Boulevard Ring, until we came upon a *stekliashka*, a cafeteria-bar with glass-paneled walls. It was about eleven in the morning and the *stekliashka* had just opened. Through dirty glass walls we could see early clients holding faceted glasses and resembling old lizards in a dusty terrarium. We entered the *stekliashka* and inquired at the bar (it was a self-service establishment) what they had to eat and drink.

"We've got *jerez*. And dumplings," answered a tall, tartly woman of about thirty-five, dressed in a low-cut lacy blouse and a pleated skirt. A bespattered apron was tied across her waist, while a semblance of a doily adorned the top of her head, like an Orthodox cross sitting on top of an onion dome. She uttered the short sentence and burst out laughing, coquettishly covering her mouth with both her hands like a true daughter of the Russian urban lower classes. The word *jerez* seemed so out of place in this establishment. Or did the barmaid laugh because not the wondrous word *jerez* but the awakening of spring intoxicated her, like a sniff of ether that a bored nurse snatches away in an empty operating room?

"*Jerez*, 80 kopecks," said the woman, whom the drunks congregating in the *stekliashka* called Valyushka (a diminutive of Valentina). In pronouncing the word *jerez*, Valyushka stressed the *jer*-syllable so sprightly that both Max and I thought she was testing the innuendo on us, two students who looked like they came from the Jewish intelligentsia.

"Excellent Crimean *jerez*," she repeated again, now obviously stressing the *jer* (*kher*) part—*kher*, a Russian subliterary term which, in tone, would be equivalent to the American *dick*.

Max and I each got a faceted glass of *jerez* and a plate of dumplings. We moved to a high table near the front of the cafeteria, from where we could see the boulevard. There were no chairs, and we stood there for awhile, like two horses, drinking our fill of this Soviet *jerez* and eating our vinegar-drizzled, clayish dumplings. We were happy on that April morning. Max had just turned nineteen, I was turning eighteen in June. Both of us longed to be someplace else, inside an abstractly composite long shot of a bar or a waterfront café, scents of good cigarettes, perfume, and whiskey tickling our nostrils. We talked, as we often did in those days, of what it would be like to find ourselves abroad. In the spring of 1985 the chances of this happening seemed nil, just as the prospects of change in the Soviet Union seemed non-existent. Yet we still wondered what it would be like to sit in a bar overlooking Narragansett Bay. Max was finishing Thornton Wilder's *Theophilus North*, a novel set in and around Newport, Rhode Island. (He would see Newport for the first time in the summer of 1989, when he first visited me in America.) We had both just seen *Death in Venice* with Dirk Bogarde at a Visconti retrospective, and we let our imagination run wild and pictured ourselves relaxing in a café in the Laguna. (In August of 1987 I would see Venice with my parents and a group of Soviet refugees traveling in Italy.) Once Max and I managed to transform the Soviet grunge and gruffness of our surroundings and inscribe ourselves into an imaginary shot of that fantasized Western bar or café, we went on talking about our lives' most pressing issues: each other's romantic adventures, books and cinema, Jews and refuseniks.

In some memories of my Moscow youth I feel so at peace that I start wondering why I left in the first place. Had I experienced the best of friendships in the wrong place at the right time so I would then go on remembering the time even as I forget the place?

INTERLUDE

SUMMERTIME

MY FIRST YEAR AT MOSCOW UNIVERSITY ended not after the spring semester finals but two months later, at the beginning of August. After the first year, all students at the School of Soil Science were required to do a summer semester at a research and study facility in Chashnikovo, about thirty miles north of Moscow. Although considered a "small town" (*selo*) because it had a school (and had earlier had a church), it was really a village with geese ambling along the unpaved streets. Chashnikovo was right off the Leningrad Highway and getting there by car was easy. It was more complicated to get into or out of Chashnikovo by public transportation. City buses only circulated between Moscow and Zelenograd, the local district center; once in Zelenograd, you were left to your own devices. Rural buses, those prehistoric animals, ran irregularly. The most viable option was to stand on the curb of the Leningrad Highway, trying to hitch a ride with a trucker. Telephone cards (or any other plastic cards) were unheard of in what was then the Soviet Union, and students had telephone access on the Chashnikovo campus only in case of a dire emergency. Staying there for two months, we felt severed from civilization—that, despite Chashnikovo's close proximity to Moscow.

The living conditions on the summer campus were basic, although not as primitive as the ones I would encounter in a year's time during a summer expedition to the south of Russia and the Caucasus. We were staying in rough-hewn unheated bunks with walls and floors made of unfinished wood painted green and maroon. Each bunk had about a dozen beds in it. Mosquito nets, a form of capitalist decadence, were missing on windows. There were two sheds with unlit and unventilated pit latrines, and a row of faucets outside the sheds, where men and women performed their ablutions. There were no showers. The day started at 6:30 a.m. with cheerful songs thrusting out of a mounted loudspeaker. After breakfast we would line up for a military-style briefing. The campus refectory served food of average repulsiveness: clumpy cream of wheat and rainy tea for breakfast, and for lunch and dinner, some creative combination of depressed-looking cabbage soup, grayish village macaroni, pieces of fat in gravy over mashed potatoes, and compote, always compote, made from fresh apples or dried fruit. Vegetarians or those with other dietary restrictions would have had a rough time. Back then I was still eating pork, and the challenge was simply getting enough nutrition. (I can't recall whether my Muslim classmates—and there were at least eight of them—also ate pork and I suspect they did.) We were young and eternally hungry, and we continued to practice the same old tricks many of us had learned in summer camp: stealing an extra dish for a "sick friend" or confusing the server, a local girl, with flirtatious urban chatter, so that she would lose count and hand the charmer an extra dish of Stroganoff to be split several ways.

Upon arriving in Chashnikovo, we were divided into units of eight to ten students, and each unit was assigned a field instructor of botany. I will call our instructor Elena Olegovna Blinova. She was a self-effacing tortoise with tender eyes. Out of breath, she would arrive late in our classroom verandah, clutching notes and books to her expansive chest as though they were a baby. How old Blinova was—thirty-five, forty-five, fifty?—we didn't know. It was rumored that her late husband was her former dissertation adviser at Moscow University, but such rumors often circulate around female academics with broken lives. Blinova's unkempt hair was straw-gray, her skin sallow. She was a heavy smoker and sometimes bummed cigarettes from students. All of us became very fond of Blinova. She was incapable of malice. Despite her sloppiness, messy clothes, and chronic unpunctuality, she was a first-rate botanist with discoveries to her name, and also an exciting speaker. Of all my studies at the School of Soil Science, botany was easily among my three favorite subjects, in no small measure thanks to Blinova's guided daily excursions to fields and forests.

Plants were as godly to her as human beings. They were as alive as people, had souls. Plants were also characters in some endless play of

Blinova's composition, and she spoke of cornflowers, chicories, bluebells, or masterworts as jealous lovers, martyred princes, betrayed wives, or smothered babes. By the end of the botany course we must have learned a hundred Latin taxonomic names, and some of them still float up to memory's surface: *Rosa rugosa* (source of rosehips), *Quercus robus* (great European oak), *Viburnum opulus* (whose red delicate berries can prevent attacks of asthma). Every day except Sunday during the botany part of the summer semester, unless it was pouring rain outside, we would go out into the field to study Eurasian flora and collect samples. Blinova taught us how to prepare a herbarium, and as a final project, we were supposed to put together an album of about a dozen perfectly dried and mounted plant species with extensive labels. Herbarium is *gerbarii* in Russian, but in our student folklore it was known as *gul'barii*, a combination of *gerbarii* and *gul'ba*, an evocative Russian word that means spree, wild festivities, carousing, galavanting. A herbarium was also a *fornicarium* in our student folklore. The botany instructor was tolerant of the couples that would occasionally stay behind in a forest clearing under the pretext of looking for specimens for their final projects. Early in June the festival of Ivan Kupala is celebrated in the countryside. Ivan Kupala is the folk name of John the Baptist, yet the festival goes back to Slavic paganism and celebrates oneness with nature, love, nudity, and abandon. The celebration has botanical significance, as it's believed that on the night of Ivan Kupala, ferns blossom in the forests. On the eve of Ivan Kupala, Blinova found a pretext to pull the male students in our group to the side and said, with a long sigh: "Be gentle with the girls."

In contrast to the tender if dozy Blinova, our geology instructor was a sprightly old man with the last name Vipert. A geology professor, he arrived from Moscow in his own car, a gray and winged 1960s Moskvich. The compulsively tidy Vipert was pushing seventy, dry and pale-green-eyed, energetic and witty. For some reason Vipert resembled my paternal grandfather's younger brother Abrasha, although he was not of Jewish-Ukrainian but apparently of Baltic-German stock. Vipert was misogynistic in an old-fashioned, gentlemanly sort of way, and the women in our unit couldn't take him too seriously. Standing in the middle of a ravine, holding a sample of a mineral in his cupped right hand,

Vipert liked to reminisce about his ancestors, gold-epauletted military officers and loyal servants to the czar. Vipert was one of the first people I encountered in Russia who openly spoke of the émigré writer Vladimir Nabokov, who in America would become a subject of my research. In fact he claimed that he was somehow related to a woman by the name of Svetlana Zivert, Nabokov's first fiancée, who broke off the engagement in Berlin, in 1922. Several times during our five- of six-hour-long excursions on foot, Vipert returned to the subject of Nabokov and his first fiancée. "He kept writing about my relative in novel after novel, poem after poem," Vipert would digress. And then he would go on lecturing about the local basalts and granites. None of us dared ask the old geologist how he got hold of Nabokov's books, still banned in the Soviet Union. Vipert also told us he was finishing his *magnum opus*, a study that would turn on its head the prevalent theory of the geological origins of central Russia. He had been working on his project for over thirty years, and that was the main reason he liked to teach summer school at Chashnikovo, where he conducted his own field research. Vipert's favorite saying was: "Don't piss into the wind."

During the summer of 1985, the Chashnikovo summer, I was only learning the Russian grammar of love and longing. When I think of my summertime romance with Polina, the Russian word *nadlom* leaps to mind, a noun that desperately resists translation. Literally, *nadlom* means "a fracture or split which is a beginning of breakage or rupture," but to me it represents a romantic predicament when dark sensualism seeps out of the foreknowledge of doomed love, of wanting the wrong person and being unable to resist.

Polina was a divorced second-year graduate student in agrochemistry. She arrived in Chashnikovo in the middle of July, for a month of experiments at the research facility. She was twenty-three and already had a three-year-old daughter. Polina's daughter was spending the summer with her grandparents in a small town in the north-eastern corner of Moldova, near the border with Ukraine, not far from Kamenets-Podolsk where both of my grandfathers grew up. The name of Polina's hometown literally means "magpies."

She was staying in a two-story decrepit cottage, which must have been at one point occupied by hired managers of the Chashnikovo estate. The manor house itself had been completely destroyed and razed, and the campus refectory later built in its stead at the end of the main alley lined with old, overgrown elms. Polina's window faced the old stables that had survived the fires of the 1917 Revolution. Her room, where other female graduate students also stayed while working in Chashnikovo, was long and abnormally narrow, probably a result of communal partitioning. There were three spring metal-frame beds against the walls, two on one side, one on the other. A light bulb descended from the ceiling on a black cord. Spiders wove their webs in three of the four corners of the ceiling. In addition to the three metal-frame beds, there was also a three-legged table propped up against the wall, a corroded sink and a faucet, and a cracked old mirror over the sink. Polina had been assigned a plot of land at the far end of the campus, where she was supposed to be growing experimental crops and taking daily measurements. I never found out what exactly Polina grew or studied. She never spoke about it, and I didn't ask. Nor did I show curiosity about Polina's background.

When unbraided and let loose, Polina's long straight hair shined like anthracite. She had olive skin and dark-brown, almost black eyes. One of the first things I asked her was whether she had Roma blood. She answered that she was half Moldovan, half Roma. She wore dark low-cut floral dresses without bras, or long dark skirts with round-necked white blouses. Her legs were long and her ankles slim, and her hips bore the curving promise of heaviness. We had met at the refectory, in line to get lunch. To the others, those were just banal circumstances—how she returned my long stare, how we struck up a conversation about a new production of *The Three Sisters* at the Taganka Theater, how I stole out of my bunk after midnight and tapped at her door. But I gleaned mystery in the way she appeared, like a charcoal drawing, in the opened second-floor window, the way she lowered her gaze, as if summoning me upstairs into her unlit room.

After Polina and I had already spent a few nights together and a few days apart, she took me on a long stroll. We left behind the campus and walked for a while on a dry clay road. Then we cut across a meadow to the edge of the forest. I saw a campfire and people's dusky silhouettes.

"Do you know them?" I asked Polina.

"They are my father's people. They've been coming here every summer. They set up an encampment and stay for a couple of months. There's a small Roma community here in Chashnikovo, if you can believe it."

When we approached, Polina greeted the twenty or so men and women sitting around the campfire. A strikingly handsome young man with long hair was playing guitar and singing. He looked up, bared his teeth, and waved at Polina between two chords. After he finished the song, Polina said to him:

"Ilya, this is my friend, a Moscow boy. I want you to sing for him."

Ilya threw back his hair and began to play. It was a tango tune, "Bésame Mucho," except Ilya only sang the words "Bésame, bésame mucho" in Spanish, but the rest of the lyrics in Russian. Scraps of those home-grown lines are still with me today: "Bésame, bésame mucho, / Today you and I are spending our farewell night. / Bésame, bésame mucho. . . ." And then the refrain, fashioned in a passionately tacky Russian: "That evening . . . champagne, fruit, and cognac crowd the table. . . . / In you there was something of the Gypsy, / you smiled only for me. . . ." We sat for a while in front of the fire, listening, and then Polina brought her index finger across my palm and towards my elbow: another one of her invisible, sensuous signs.

We returned to Polina's dark room, where time stood still, waitfully. When she pressed my head to her body with both hands, mouth against her hot shoulder, she whispered: "Don't roar this time." "Why not?" I asked, obliviously. "The bitch can hear everything," Polina replied, scrappily. It turned out that the "bitch" was Polina's dissertation advisor, a divorcée in her forties, who had come to in Chashnikovo for a few days to check on the progress of their experiments and was staying next door. With the advisor arrived her smiley daughter, who walked like a pelican. Later on I kept bumping into the advisor and her daughter in the corridor, and I would entertain the teenage child with improvised tales about the local wood sprites.

Our nightly trysts continued for another week. Less than a week before the end of the summer program, Max came for a visit. He was originally planning to return to Moscow the same day, but one of my bunkmates got sick with the croup and was moved to the infirmary. There was a vacant bed in our bunkhouse, and Max ended up staying for the whole weekend. On Saturday, Polina invited Max and me to her room for supper to celebrate the conclusion of my semester in Chashnikovo. She also invited Emmochka, an Estonian classmate of mine, with whom she had been independently friendly. Max brought a bottle of vodka from Moscow, and we also procured a couple of bottles of fruity wine in a local liquor kiosk. Polina opened a jar of home-made pickled vegetables: red peppers, pattypan squash (known in Russia by its French name, *pâtisson*), cucumbers, tomatoes, pickled with garlic and Moldovan spices. On a small electric stove she fried up some meat with onions and boiled new potatoes, which she served sprinkled with dill and rolling in butter. In the middle of our feast another bottle of vodka emerged from a secret drawer. All four of us got drunk and played strip poker. When I woke up at dawn, Max was sleeping on one of the beds across the narrow aisle from Polina and me. Slatternly in the morning light, Max was wrapped in the sheet like a Roman senator in a toga. The Estonian girl was sleeping in the other bed, without her shirt, but still wearing her faded blue jeans. My initial reaction was to get out of bed, find my scattered clothes, and flee before Max and the Estonian could wake up and see me. As I pulled the edge of the blanket, Polina whispered: "Wait, don't go yet." As we lay in the narrow single bed pressed to each other, Polina whispered again: "I know about you."

"You know what?" I said, feeling goose bumps on my arms and legs.

"You don't have to pretend. I never told you this, but my mother's mother was Jewish, her last name was Kaplan. Which makes me a Jewess, according to your religion. Both me and my little girl."

"Do you have? . . ." I started asking, in disbelief.

" . . . Jewish relatives?" Polina guessed my question.

"Yes."

"It's possible that I have distant cousins in Israel. But most of my Jewish relatives were killed in the camps. In Transnistria," Polina said, no longer whispering. "From the whole big family in Bessarabia, my grand-mother was the only one who survived."

"Polina," I said sternly. "Tell me what you meant when you said 'I know about you.'"

"That you and your family have been trying to emigrate," she answered.

"How did you know?"

"Through the rumor mill at school," Polina whispered.

"Don't believe everything you hear . . . ," I muttered.

"Did I upset you, my boy?" Polina asked. "Well, life isn't always easy." And she added, after a pause: "But you and I had fun, didn't we?"

Once again, politics had invaded a part of my life that I hoped would remain clear of refusenik circumstances. It was inevitable and to be expected, and yet I felt as though sacks of lead pellets had been tied to my feet. And I also felt betrayed. Betrayed by whom? The nearness of Polina and the fresh memories of our summertime romance made me think of the fragility of privacy.

Polina kissed me on the cheek, this time just the cheek. "Dearheart, could you pass me those," she said, pointing with her eyes to her lingerie lying, like a crushed black bird, on the scratched green floor next to the bed.

I got up and dressed, found Max's scattered clothes, and then woke him up. Polina lay, curled up in the green woolen blanket, facing the wall. Max quickly pulled on his pants and T-shirt, and we walked out on tiptoes, without waking up the Estonian girl.

Polina and I avoided each other for the rest of my stay in Chashnikovo. Four or five days later the field semester ended and I returned to Moscow.

6

POETRY, LOVE, PERSECUTION

WHILE I WAS IN CHASHNIKOVO for part of the summer, my parents undertook to renovate our apartment, which hadn't been upgraded since we moved there in 1971. Decent wallpaper and tile had been procured for double the official prices, and an enterprising contractor who ran a virtually private business on the side was hired to do the work. Upon returning home at the end of July 1985, I found our place completely redone from floor to ceiling, replete with new living room furniture and bookshelves.

It may seem odd that my parents, then refuseniks of almost seven years, would decide to do it. Did the renovations symbolize a surrender, an acknowledgment that we were giving up our hope of emigrating?

As of the summer of 1985, the political situation in the Soviet Union didn't promise a change of fortune for the refuseniks. The "rule of corpses"—Brezhnev's latter years followed by Andropov's brief stint on the Soviet throne—had ended in March 1985 with the passing of Konstantin Chernenko. At the March 1985 Extraordinary Plenary Meeting of the Central Committee, the fifty-four-year old, power-hungry Mikhail Gorbachev had succeeded Chernenko as General Secretary of the Communist Party. Gorbachev was elected over his Brezhnevite rival Viktor Grishin by a narrow margin, and his grip on power still seemed very tenuous. It was known that the new Soviet leader Gorbachev had been a protégé of both Mikhail Suslov, the Party's Grand Inquisitor, and Yuri Andropov, the former chief of the KGB. To put this in a refusenik's perspective, my parents first stood on the path of emigration and tasted of political persecution at the end of the Brezhnev period. Throughout the Andropov and Chernenko years (1982-1985), we continued to reapply for exit visas, and

126

the authorities promptly denied our requests. As my parents renovated our apartment, the dawn of Gorbachev's rule brought forth not a promise of reforms that would later transform and undo the country, but only the recent, chilling memories of Andropov.

The renovations of the apartment hinted at a modicum of comfort in our lives. My father was working as an endocrinologist at a neighborhood clinic, and also consulting at another hospital and seeing private patients, and my mother was teaching English part-time at a district House of Culture and giving private lessons. A fragile equilibrium had set in. The refuseniks had become an isolated community with some economic stability but not much hope for emigration and still a hanging threat of persecution.

When we drove to Estonia for our August vacation, I sat next to my father while my mother napped or read in the back seat. I remember thinking, as we crossed the rolling Valdai Hills, that we would always live in Russia, that every summer I would be going to Pärnu, that my future children would grow up in a country that would be fundamentally unchanged and would always hold its Jews as captive aliens.

In the middle of our August vacation, my father had to leave Pärnu for a week and drive back to Moscow. He then left the car in Moscow and took the overnight train back to Estonia. Two weeks later my parents and I traveled back to Russia by train. We took an early morning bus to Tallinn and spent the whole day with Jüri and Urve Arrak, who were still married and living in a state of teetering harmony. The Arraks were fully aware of my parents' circumstances. Yet on that sparkling Baltic day we never spoke of being refuseniks and of the dangers of dissent. Instead, we feasted on the gifts of Tallinn's best patisserie, including my favorite strips of moist coffee cake layered with whipped cream and topped with glazed cranberries. The Arraks drove us to see the spot on the coast outside Tallinn, where episodes of Grigory Kosintsev's *Hamlet* had been filmed in the early 1960s. We stood on an observation platform, looked down over the toothy cliffs on the beach below, and spoke, like characters in a Chekhov story, of time that churns our lives into granules of fine white sand.

A farewell dinner at the Arraks' Tallinn apartment crowned the day, a farewell dinner and an adventure. We had been taking the same

"Estonia" express train No. 34 for years, and it had always left Tallinn at the same time past seven in the evening. The dinner at the Arraks had been so relaxing that even my father, who liked to get to the train station well in advance, didn't urge Jüri to go until about half an hour before the departure. The Arraks lived less than fifteen minutes from the Tallinn train station, and when we arrived on the platform, the train had just started to push off. We ran up to the train, then my mother saw a policeman and dashed to him, screaming "Stop the train!" "It's too late, citizen," he replied with an Estonian accent. We stood on the platform, suitcases, fishing rods, and a box of pastries in hand, watching our train pull off and unable to get on board. Pärnu acquaintances of many years stared at us in complete disbelief from the departing train. We, the Shrayers, were not known to miss trains. It turned out that the timetable, which had indeed remained intact for at least fifteen years if not longer, had been changed that year, and we had missed our train by only a few minutes. It all worked out in the end and we managed to rebook ourselves on the train leaving later the same evening. I cannot think of a more tired or clichéd allegory of fate than missing a homebound train. Lying awake in the luminescent darkness of our sleeper compartment, too wired to fall asleep, I thought of what lay ahead in Moscow. The coming school year would be the most turbulent time in my entire Soviet life.

In September of 1985, soon after returning from Estonia, I surprised myself by returning to poetry. Between the ages of eight and nine, under my father's tutelage, I had composed a dozen or so poems and a verse epic titled *The Royal Hunt*. Then I gave up writing poetry—just as gladly as I had given up playing piano. I didn't write a single line even in my mid-teens, when impressionable Jewish-Russian boys tended to bolster their ego by fashioning themselves after lyrical heroes of Russian Romantic poetry. Imagine my father's great pleasure at his son's embracing, as a sophomore in college, his lifelong métier, and especially at a time when my father was living in isolation, unable to publish in Russia, abnegated by most of his literary brethren, cut off from readers or poetic interlocutors.

Pages describing the magic of artistic self-discovery or the act of composing one's first poem almost always result from an attack of narcissism.

In my experience, readers gloss these pages over or skip them altogether, and especially so when such scenes are spiked with nostalgia for artistic innocence. My first poem in the autumn of 1985 burst out of a mundane argument with my mother. The argument was about freedom and independence; my father was observing the interchange from the sidelines, silently. Like most Soviet students my age going to university in their native cities, I was living at home. My mother had a hard time not worrying when I would stay out very late or go away for the weekend. In retrospect I can see that her anxiety was fueled by the real danger that surrounded refusenik activists. She was afraid of my getting into trouble, and being expelled from the university and drafted into the army. In the midst of our kitchen fight I said unfair things about a "blind motherly instinct," about "vicariousness" and "envy that your son has fun." After slamming the door to my room I grabbed a sheet of paper and wrote out, practically without pausing to think, a poem of five stanzas, which I then typed out on my father's Olympia and delivered to my mother as terms of reconciliation. In the second stanza, the cementing conceit was that of my mother as Phemis, the Goddess of Justice, and the word Phemis ("Femida") end-rhymed with *obida* ("hurt," "offense"). I had resorted to lofty Romantic diction as I predictably composed the poem in iambic tetrameter with feminine and masculine endings alternated. My rhymes were, for the most part, exact and grammatical, and the texture of the poem wasn't particularly exciting. I had almost instantaneously purged out of my system a longing for the aesthetics of nineteenth-century versification. It wasn't, of course, as simple as that. Yet I remember feeling how in the course of the argument with my mother and the ensuing reconciliation via poetry, I had leapfrogged from composing the prescribed classical verse I had been taught as an eight-year-old to aiming at something more deliberate.

Trying to capture, especially in translation, the laboratory of my early poems would be a doomed proposition. About a dozen of those poems would later appear in émigré magazines and also become a part of my first collection, *Tabun nad lugom* (*Herd above the Meadow*), published in New York in 1990. Re-reading the poems from the autumn and winter of 1985-86, I recognize in them a resistance to the poetic culture of the Silver Age, with which many of my peers were intoxicated. This adoration of the

Silver Age struck me as a bit tacky. When a young author I would meet in 1985 or 1986 spoke of the resplendent tetrad—Akhmatova, Mandelstam, Pasternak, Tsvetaeva—as his or her deities, I turned the other way. I found jarring the emulation of the inimitable genius Marina Tsvetaeva by aspiring women poets. And I had a particularly hard time tolerating Jewish-Russian boys fashioning themselves after Osip Mandelstam, as if by imitating Mandelstam one also took upon himself the aura of poetic martyrdom.

As I sought my poetic orientation elsewhere, I tried to marry the explosively experimental urbanistic verses of the Soviet 1920s with poetry imbued with Russian folklore and peasant traditions. I suspect that in me, an acculturated Russian Jew from a big Soviet city, two centuries of Jewish disenfranchisement in the Russian lands were seeking expression. The Jewish Moscow boy in me wanted to write like a native Russian lad, while this phantom of a Russian lad burned up with dreams of city living. I understand now that I pursued a synthesis of two poetic traditions. On the one hand, I set my roots in the poetry of Russian constructivists, Eduard Bagritsky, Ilya Selvinsky, and Vladimir Lugovskoy, with their pulsating metaphors and articulation of the creator's authorial powers. On the other, I regard as a major influence the folkloric verses of Sergei Esenin and Nikolai Klyuev, and also the pantheistic poetry of Nikolai Zabolotsky. When I started writing in 1985, my efforts naturally fell on the fertile ground of the verse aesthetics of late 1950s through early 1960s Leningrad poetry, where my father had started out as a poet. Both teacher and older poetic peer and friend, my father was my living link with poetry. He was also a judge whose verdict I feared and trusted, perhaps too much. We had daily conversations about the craft of poetry, and even during the late autumn of 1985, when a real threat of arrest and imprisonment hung over my father, he maintained his calm when reading and discussing my newly-minted poems.

I did not actively seek literary mentors or poetry workshops. This was probably a mistake, but I couldn't help it at the time. My father's horrendous experience with the Union of Soviet Writers made me apprehensive of collective literary organizations and activities. A youthful snobbery

("I come from it, I know what it's like") was also a factor in my avoidance of workshops. Once or twice in the autumn of 1985 I visited the literary seminar (*lito*) at Moscow University, led by Igor Volgin, a timid poet and a Dostoevsky biographer, who cultivated a pliant atmosphere of non-confrontation. He encouraged his protégées to write about safe, not ideologically marked subjects, such as family traditions or bird-watching or circus-going, and much of the poetry they produced sounded like a provincial spinster's rhymed journal. I participated in two sessions of Volgin's seminar and never went back.

Until the age of twelve, through my father, I had had access to writers. My father brought me along to the Writers' House, and fellow authors used to visit him at home. By the time I had started to write in 1985, my father's literary contacts had drastically diminished. While he felt strongly that a young poet needed both a literary environment and the advice of older writers, he no longer had many literary friends to whom I could turn with my poems. In November of 1985 I showed some of my poems to Evgeny Reyn, my father's friend from their literary youth in Leningrad. Reyn, a veteran poet and screenwriter, hadn't been able to publish his first collection of verse until 1984. In the autumn of 1985 Reyn still hesitated about voicing strong opinions and said some complimentary but nondescript things about my poems. He topped his comments with an anecdote about an old Silver Age poet who had told the young Reyn that poems should be like "troops during a parade." The anecdote, delivered in Reyn's bellowing voice, was supposed to serve as a tongue-in-cheek warning that I not forget to polish the brass and shine the leather of my verses. I was naturally disappointed that Reyn didn't have anything specific to say about the texts I showed him. Around the same time I gave a batch of my poems to Rostislav Rybkin, a literary translator who had begun to frequent the refusenik salon that my parents had been hosting at our apartment. Rybkin, a diminutive man with a nervous smile, was known in the Soviet Union as a leading translator of science fiction from English, and, specifically, as Ray Bradbury's translator. Rybkin corrected a couple of typos, and questioned the use of a case ending in one poem, but had nothing else critical or complimentary to say. These experiences had confirmed my instinct that a father's literary acquaintances wouldn't feel comfortable telling it like it is to a son. I kept waiting to meet an older poet who would inspire me though word and action.

For a few weeks during October and November of 1985 I attended a basic computer class in the main tower of Moscow University. One day, as I was crossing the enormous red-carpeted university foyer, hurrying to catch an elevator, my eye caught a flyer. It announced that a "noted children's author Genrikh Sapgir" would be reading from and discussing his works in the "parlor" of Moscow University's "house of academics." I remembered Sapgir from my childhood and had preserved autographed copies of his books for young readers. Like millions of other Soviet children, I had been exposed to Sapgir's brilliant, richly orchestrated, verbally inventive poems full of puns and wordplay, and also to animations based on his screenplays, among them *Horseloon* and *My Green Crocodile*. My father and Sapgir, who was his senior by almost eight years, had been friendly since the late 1950s, yet I hadn't seen Sapgir at our house or heard about him from my father for a long time, and definitely since we had become refuseniks. Sapgir's was in some respects a typically pathological story of a Soviet artistic career: a phenomenally successful children's author in poetry, cinematography, and theater; a major Russian poet who couldn't publish in Russia. By 1985 Sapgir had become a patriarch of the Moscow literary underground, his unsanctioned texts circulating widely at home and available in print in the West. Yet he had been unable to place his poetry for grown-ups in Soviet publications. Running ahead of myself, I should explain that during the late 1980s Sapgir the adult poet would be legitimized in the Soviet Union; when he died in 1999 in Moscow, he was a legendary and widely published author. When I saw that small flyer announcing Sapgir's reading at Moscow University, I became instantly drawn to his un-Russian, foreign name, the first name like that of Heinrich Heine, the last name Eastern-sounding, Hebrew-infused, marked with exceptionality.

Imagine this scene as I saw it in the middle of November, a sophomore studying soil science and writing poetry, an eighteen-year-old refusenik and son of a banished writer. It was a fairly large room with a stage, a heavy curtain of red velour and matching upholstery on cushioned chairs, a table with two chairs placed in the proscenium. A tall man looking and speaking like Stiva Oblonsky, just the way I imagined him from Tolstoy's novel—unhurried, even-toned, witty, aristocratic—came out to introduce "our guest." In his remarks he alluded to a "greater openness" and also to stepping over the footlights separating the stage and the audience. A mustached, heavyset man then in his late fifties, Sapgir resembled Honoré de Balzac. He nodded all through the introduction, plump fingers locked and resting on the tabletop, then hung a brown suede jacket on the back of his chair and began to read from typed pages. He read from a performative cycle titled *Monologues*. It was shocking to hear, especially in an official setting, a poetic dialogue between two members of the Soviet intelligentsia who wear masks in public and remove them from their faces when they come home at night, only to discover one day that the masks won't peel off. I remember literally jumping up in my chair at the punch lines, both in disbelief that this was actually happening and from the sheer pleasure of hearing it. Then Sapgir read, almost in its entirety, a book of his poems, *Terverses of Genrikh Bufarev*. Genrikh Bufarev was Sapgir's poetic alter ego, an invented persona, an alcoholic poet-prophet. *Terverses* (*tertsikhi* in the Russian) is Sapgir's coinage, from *terzina* and *verse*, and the poems' classical roots (in Dante's *terza rima*) clash with their postmodern meanings. One of the poems, for instance, was about a visit by a group of writers (it was clear enough that these were Soviet writers) to a collective farm. The writers were using invented, hybrid words, both to satirize Soviet-speak and to underscore how words had lost their meanings because they no longer described familiar objects. Sapgir prefaced another poem, called "House of Dumpdogs," with an explanation that "dumpdogs=dumplings+hotdogs," since "our" cafés serving dumplings are usually out of dumplings, whereas hot dog cafeterias are commonly out of dogs. Finally, as if to show that he was not just a Russian poet but a poet of the world, Sapgir read his translations of Blake's sonnets. There were only eight or nine people in the audience, and in the middle of the reading an ageing lady with a thin battered briefcase walked out, demonstratively slamming the door behind her. Sapgir read with such passion and power; the lines rolling off his tongue were made of some other poetic matter, different from the drivel dominating Soviet literary publications.

At the end of the reading, I came up to Sapgir and gave him my father's regards. We exchanged phone numbers and a promise to keep in touch. I remember coming home that night in a state of ecstatic restlessness, telling my father that I heard a real "genius" of poetry. How could this be possible, I though during the long Metro ride home, tossing in my head some of the lines I had memorized? I was inspired, finally, by an older living poet other than my father, in a way that would catalyze my own writing and poetic thinking.

In the autumn of 1985 I experienced a sensation which I had previously known from reading novels and autobiographies, a sensation of fullness of life. In addition to being a university student and having a circle of friends outside the university, I was writing poetry, constantly, consummately. And I found myself in the midst of a refusenik romance set against my parents' growing troubles with the regime.

In 1984 my parents returned to open refusenik activism by organizing and hosting at our apartment a series of monthly cultural events. Various refusenik seminars had been a feature of underground intellectual life in the Soviet Union since the 1970s and had come under attack by the authorities. Refusenik seminars tended to focus on scholarly and scientific activities or on carrying out Jewish educational missions (learning Judaism and Hebrew). My parents' seminar focused on literature and the arts. People would gather at our apartment, often on a Saturday night, to socialize and to enjoy a reading or performance. It was a refusenik seminar coupled with a salon. While my parents' idea was to give refusenik artists, musicians, and authors a venue in place of the official opportunities they had been deprived of, the seminar was by no means limited to refusenik presenters or guests. From a couple of dozen refuseniks my parents had befriended over the years, attendance grew to a larger audience of guests, not necessarily friends of friends or exclusively refuseniks. There was, inevitably, an overlap between the activities of our refusenik seminar and the orbits of Moscow's underground dissident and artistic scene. (Sapgir read at one of our gatherings.) In the autumn of 1985, when my parents' seminar was regularly meeting once a month, we started noticing that uniformed policemen would stand outside our apartment building during the events. Policemen would stop our guests downstairs and ask them to show their passports. In the meantime both of my parents were becoming aware that now and then plainclothes individuals indiscreetly followed them.

In the middle of October I met a young woman from a refusenik family at one of my parents' events. I will call her Lyuba. Her pale face had the grace not of Jewish but of Georgian women, the kind of somber beauty that peaks between twenty and twenty-three. Lyuba had dark hazel eyes and a bob haircut and was sporting a hooded navy sweatshirt with the name of an American East Coast college in white block letters. I later found out that the sweatshirt and some of Lyuba's other casual American clothes were gifts from an American student of Russian she had dated and rejected. Lyuba was over three years my senior and, as it turned out, a junior at Moscow University. Her story was quite extraordinary.

Lyuba had been in senior high school when her parents lost their good jobs and joined the refusenik caste. Like everyone else in her class, she had already joined the Young Communist League (Komsomol) and was making plans to study mathematics and computer science after high school. She was actually a person of many gifts, including one for poetry, but had a special talent for numbers and ciphers. Lyuba's plans were undercut when the news of her parents' fall from the Soviet ladder reached the school. In my own case, the high school administration either didn't know for a while or else sought to avoid a scandal that would somehow mar the school's reputation. Though a son of refuseniks, and even though I lost my gold medal, I graduated from high school still a Komsomol member. In Lyuba's case, her school held a public meeting, akin to a Stalinist show trial, at which she was expelled from the Komsomol as a daughter of ungrateful individuals (read: Zionist Jews) who had chosen to go to Israel. Except the "ungrateful individuals" weren't allowed to go to Israel, and after the expulsion from the Komsomol, Lyuba's chances of getting into university were annihilated. Unlike her university-bound classmates, Lyuba ended up going to a two-year technical college. With her top grades from the junior college, she applied to Moscow University and did brilliantly on her entrance exams. A small miracle took place: a non-Komsomol-member, Lyuba got in entirely on merit.

The next day after meeting Lyuba, I sought her out at the glass-and-concrete building about one-third of the way from the University Metro station to the building of my School. I looked up the junior year lecture schedule and stood outside the auditorium, waiting. Lyuba came out in the company of two very pretty girlfriends and a solicitous, blonde man holding an unbuckled leather briefcase. It was refusenik romance incarnate, where nothing needed to be said or explained about our double lives. Lyuba and I ditched what remained of that Monday's classes and headed for the center of Moscow, where we spent the rest of the day and most of the evening walking the streets in a state of happy aimlessness, grabbing pancakes with chocolate sauce at a little café by the Nikitsky Gate, going into the ticket office of the Moscow Conservatory of Music, and then standing for an hour in the dimly lit courtyard outside her second-floor apartment. The windows of her bedroom faced the inner courtyard, and in the months to come I would get to know this view of antediluvian benches, swings and a seesaw, and also a fountain choked on rotting leaves. Lyuba and her family were living in an old Moscow working-class area. On my way to and from the city center and to the University and back, I passed through or connected at Lyuba's Metro station. It was named so in memory of the poorly armed Moscow workers who rose in December 1905, first for a general strike, then to erect barricades and oppose czarist troops in street fighting, only to be pushed back by gun fire and mauled by artillery shelling. Lyuba and I started talking about the first Russian revolution. I remember Lyuba taking my hand and saying, about the two of us, how odd it was that we were refuseniks, our families had been oppressed by the Soviet regime, and yet we still remained brainchildren of the Revolution and subscribed to its myths. Outside her dun windows on a November evening, she told me we would have to keep our trysts a secret, or at least a secret from her parents.

"*No kak?* (How, then?)" I asked, in my youthful naïveté. "Our parents are friendly. And what's to hide?"

"I'm twenty-one already. My mother thinks I should be married and having children. She would never approve of us."

And that's how it would be, my parents knowing everything, with Lyuba's family either not knowing or pretending not to know. In her mother's eyes I was not "marriable," still too young and looking for roman-tic adventure, and it was hard to fault her for such sinewy practicality.

Lyuba herself liked to make fun of our age difference. "You're still a raw youth," she would say with a chortle, revealing her habit of playing on the titles of Russian literary works. Lyuba was right, and being with her initiated my transition from the boyish (and, I believed at the time, chivalrous) idea of playing at love to get sex toward a more complex pic-ture of love in all its beauty and vulnerability.

We had been dating for less than three weeks, and yet Lyuba now rivaled Max's presence in my daily life. I knew the faces and names of many of her classmates and professors and became friendly with her girl-friends. Almost every day, and certainly if we didn't already have after-school plans, I would speed across the campus to see her. I remember an evening at Lyuba's apartment in late October or early November, mud and chilly rain in the street, Lyuba's parents and younger sister out visiting friends. We were having a carpet picnic in the living room, and along with tea and bread Lyuba served scrambled eggs with cheese she had learned to cook from the American student who had pursued her while spending a year in Moscow. Apparently he still kept calling her, wanting to bring her to America. I didn't like the eggs, and I told Lyuba they tasted nothing like the Russian eggs fried sizzling with butter, sunny side up.

"Why didn't you go for him?" I then asked.

"You don't understand," Lyuba answered, thinning her lips the way she did in moments of flaring anger. "I couldn't. . . ."

Winter had arrived early that year; there was snowy sleet on the ground. Lyuba walked with me to her Metro station, its façade adorned with bas-reliefs of rioting Moscow proletarians. Neon clouds of breath fluttered over the heads of other couples saying goodbye. The declaration sprang out of me with such sudden force that I wavered and nearly fell onto Lyuba. A few days later, on a Saturday, I hosted a party. My kind par-ents went to sleep over at my grandmother's, and Lyuba stayed over. The night before, she had phoned and mysteriously asked me to buy lemons. "Do you like to have tea with lemon or to eat them sliced with honey?" I asked, cluelessly. Even in my generation ancient methods of contraception still had a stronghold on young Soviet women. French letters didn't reach our shores easily, and Soviet-made prophylactics were only spoken of in jokes about shy young men coming into a drugstore. . . .

My studies at the School of Soil Science had entered a critical phase as the texture of my life kept expanding to encompass Lyuba, new poems, and my parents' growing troubles. Of the tracks available to Soil Science students (Soil Chemistry, Soil Physics, Soil Biology, Agriculture, etc.), I was leaning toward majoring in General Soil Science. Professor Boris Rozanov, whose lectures had been a highlight of our freshman year, chaired the Department of General Soil Science. It enjoyed the reputation of offering a tolerant, relaxed academic atmosphere, and employed several Jews as instructors and researchers. In his sumptuous office, under a heavy piece of glass protecting his desk top, Rozanov kept not only family pictures but also a photograph of Marilyn Monroe, pleated skirt raised by a lecherous gust of wind. I was still trying to figure out how to use my education as a stepping stone toward some sort of a non-scientific path or career. One possibility was getting into science writing, covering other people's research, going on and reporting on travels alongside ecologists, geologists, or other field researchers. I negotiated with the monthly magazine *Rural Youth* to do interviews with several distinguished professors at my School, but nothing was panning out. Aside from the impediments of having a Jewish name, the barrels of Soviet science writing were brimming with pickled natural scientists and fermenting engineers.

During the fall semester of my sophomore year, physical and colloid chemistry already coming out of my ears, I already found my classes actively revolting. Going to school every day, chugging along through classes, measuring soil chemicals during long lab hours, and still remaining remotely engaged was costing me a great deal of emotional energy. I obtained permission to sit in on a Renaissance course at the Art History branch of the School of History. It was taught by the art historian Viktor N. Grashchenkov, a tall, muscular man with the face of Marcus Aurelius. History was quartered next door to Lyuba's building, and I could see Lyuba before or after the Renaissance. After being force-fed the pork feet and millet of science in the morning, I relished every morsel of the Renaissance course, every word coming out of Grashchenkov's mouth, every slide he showed. As I lost myself in the world of the Italian Renaissance, I was visited by all sorts of strange ideas. In retrospect, these were desperate attempts to arrange for some sort of a marriage of science and art. "Wouldn't it be interesting?" I remember thinking as Professor Grashchenkov discussed a painting by Filippino Lippi, where the Virgin Mary appears to St. Bernard as he writes outdoors against the background of staggering slabs of weathered rock. "Wouldn't it be fascinating to study the changes in natural landscape on the basis of their representations in painting, starting from the Middle Ages and the Renaissance?" After two months of lectures, I finally confided to Grashchenkov that my heart wasn't in science, especially soil science, and that I only loved art and literature. "Why don't you transfer to our program?" he suggested. "You'll only lose a year, you're young, you've got plenty of time." Elated by the prospect, I filled out a transfer application form. I must have been so excited about the flight from natural sciences into the arts that I didn't pause to consider my chances or confer with my parents. Grashchenkov looked over the application, his eyebrows furrowing as he came upon my last name (he had only known me as "Maxim"). He paused, cleared his throat, then calligraphized in the upper right corner of my application: ". . . the department . . . doesn't object to the transfer of student Shrayer, Maxim Davidovich. . . ." The language of his resolution now strikes me as tortured—"doesn't object" instead of "supports." At the time I didn't make much of Grashchenkov's language. Only a formality remained: the signature and official stamp of some pencil-pusher, an associate dean in the School of History. The dean sized me up, rolled his eyes over my application form, and refused to approve it. That afternoon Grashchenkov didn't take my call when I telephoned his secretary. Nor did he talk to me when I called him at home and spoke to his wife. At the next lecture he avoided eye contact with me. When the class—on Tintoretto—ended, Grashchenkov coughed dramatically and swept out of the classroom. When I caught up with him down the long corridor, he mumbled something about "unforeseen complications" and disappeared into his office, hugging a slide carousel and a cognac leather briefcase. I never came back, thus ending my brief apprenticeship to Soviet art history. Grashchenkov probably forgot about me the way one forgets about sour milk in one's morning coffee. But the administration and some of my professors at the School of Soil Science didn't take lightly to my attempt at defection. I had made a mistake, and I had to face the consequences.

Already in the middle of November I was feeling excessively scrutinized. Aleksandr Manucharov, the dean of students who remembered me from my appeal after the admissions chemistry exam, stopped me in the corridor in between lectures. "Watch out, Shrayer," he said, severely and cryptically. But as is often the case in schemes of repression, my main nemesis was not a professor or dean but a nobody with administrative responsibilities. The name of this woman in her late forties escapes me, but even now I would recognize her in a crowd of other buxom women with buns of cheaply dyed hair, over-rouged cheeks, and ghastly earrings with violet gemstones. Her official title was "senior inspector" at the Office of Student Services, and her role was to monitor attendance and grades, and to enforce discipline. A classic Soviet Nazi lady. The way she pronounced my last name, lips pouting with contempt as though tea from her beloved samovar suddenly tasted rancid, gave me an idea of her racial preferences. It was one thing after another in the course of two weeks in November. First Ms. Hairbun summoned me to her office to inform me they were about to cut my monthly stipend for having missed more than two lectures. Then she decided that I hadn't passed a foreign language exam (I had placed out of regular English my freshman year and was taking an advanced class). But the worst of all for my future at the School of Soil Science was Ms. Hairbun's speculation that I may be physically unfit to do field work and spend the summer after sophomore year on an expedition required for all the students. She mandated for me to undergo an extensive physical examination at the Moscow University clinic, where the doctors were suddenly looking to find something in my health. This, in turn, created a medical and administrative fire that took my parents and me the rest of the year to put out. As the mess at school grew serious, looking more and more like an orchestrated plot, of which Ms. Hairbun was a willing executor, I still couldn't think clearly about the ramifications of what was happening. Was I a twig carried by the Soviet alien waters toward my own undoing? The whole art history transfer fiasco, then the troubles at the School of Soil Science, were paving the way for expulsion and to becoming a draft-age Soviet young male without a deferral. I knew this, and yet I wasn't thinking clearly and rationally about my university standing and the threat of military service. Somehow, everything was converging upon me, I remember feeling. But all I really wanted to do was to write poetry and be with Lyuba.

Through syntax and silences, a surviving poem registers my inner strain. The poem came out of a midday walk in Kolomenskoye. Standing on a high bank of the Moskva River, since the fifteenth century Kolomenskoye had been a royal summer residence. It was renowned for its architecture, especially the Church of the Ascension, built by Czar Vassily III to commemorate the birth of his heir, the future Ivan IV (the Terrible). As Lyuba and I strolled through its park amid white stone churches and towers, two young Jewish lovers trapped in a Soviet museum of history, we both felt centuries removed from the modern city rambling across the river. When I reread the poem today, I think of how epic proportions of our lives often come as an afterthought—as they do here in English, in a literal translation: "We talked of something as we rustled on a lumpish alley, / A timorous leaf licked clay off shoe soles, / And some spectral beings headed for the peeling palace, / Vanishing for a long time within the black-and-white quarters. / The treasonous sun danced on cupola gold, / Or was it then it crawled over dusty clouds? / Our hands wove into each other and gray birds screamed / Their wobbly calls tearing away into a rickety sky / Off the shoulders and arms of the routinely undressed models— /The yellow aspen trees with long ashen ankles. || How did it happen, our gaits dashing to meet each other, / And disobedient fingers wandering amid fingers, / And us making some distant conversation, and the high slope of the river? / And on a wooden bench an old lady in an enormous lilac hat? || You were straightening your hairdo, while silence hid in the park. / We talked of something, and the city coughed with vexation."

What did the two young people in the poem talk about? What was being left unsaid? The poem knows, without saying it directly, what I couldn't share even with Lyuba.

On some level, my parents had probably seen it coming. I recall a visit by two Canadians who traveled to the USSR in order to show their support

142 | THE EXPEDITION

for refuseniks. One of them, Michael Posner, was at the time a reporter for *Maclean's* and now writes for the *Toronto Globe & Mail*. My mother, customarily the spokesperson for the family, was telling Posner about the refusenik gatherings we hosted at our apartment, and about the risks involved. By that time our refusenik seminar-salon had been going strong for a year. Also, the first part of my father's novel *Herbert and Nelly* had found its way to the West. I remember coming home late from a party some time in the autumn of 1984, to find my father and a photographer working in the bathroom on developing and hanging rolls of film to dry on the shower rod. In due course, the films were smuggled out of the country in a diplomatic pouch, reaching the United States and then traveling to Israel, where my father's uncle Munia Sharir facilitated the novel's publication. By the autumn of 1985 the upcoming publication, under the title *Being a Refusenik*, was announced by Aliya Library, a prominent publisher of Russian-language books based in Israel.

My parents knew they were being followed around, yet they spared me some of this knowledge. I wasn't told but surmised that my mother was struck in a crowded street by two men who, under their breath, threatened graver punishment if my parents wouldn't stop "sticking out." Then, in the last days of November, a subpoena (summons) was deposited in our mail box. Dated 27 November 1985 and printed on the stationery of the Moscow City Prosecutor, the subpoena requested "Shrayer, David Petrovich" to "appear" on 2 December 1985 at 11 AM, at the office of "prosecutor N. B. Tsirkunenko." This slip of paper has survived among my father's personal papers, and I'm looking at a photocopy of it as I type these lines.

In the early evening of the day the subpoena arrived, still trying to process the whole thing, my parents and I held a family conference. Various scenarios were considered and different options weighed, from a public protest or hunger strike to ignoring the subpoena and buying time (my father called the latter the "tactic of crushed glass"). The situation was urgent and obviously dangerous. My parents and I decided to seek the immediate advice of seasoned friends and acquaintances from the refusenik and dissident circles. That evening I went to see the Slepaks, while my parents visited Valery Soyfer. Soyfer, formerly a successful Soviet geneticist, had substantial experience with dissident actions and many connections with Western scientists; my parents thought his counsel would be helpful.

A former Prisoner of Zion, Vladimir (Volodya) Slepak was a legend within the refusenik and dissident movements and abroad. He and his wife Maria (Masha) had been among the leading refusenik activists since the early 1970s. Refuzeniks spoke of his fearlessness and valor, of charging KGB thugs at demonstrations before they had a chance to strike him. I had heard from eye-witnesses of the day in June of 1978 when the Slepaks along with another celebrated refusenik activist, Ida Nudel, flew banners with protest slogans from the balconies of their apartment buildings in Moscow. They were arrested; Vladimir Slepak and Ida Nudel were sentenced to five years of forced exile, while Masha Slepak received a suspended sentence. My parents met and befriended the Slepaks by the time of Volodya's return to Moscow from Siberia.

Volodya Slepak was in his late fifties when I got to know him, and the weighty silver curls of his hair and beard made him look like a cross between a biblical patriarch and a Judean zealot. Now retired from the kind of open activism for which he had paid with a prison sentence, Volodya was still one of the refusenik elders. Like a mighty bull having miraculously survived years of fighting, he would doze off during after-supper conversations in our kitchen, looking imposing and strong also in slumber. The bespectacled round face of Masha Slepak carried a special dolorous beauty sometimes given to ageing Ashkenazi women. Even in her lightest moments, sadness never left Masha's face. Both of the Slepaks' sons were living in the United States. Held hostage by the Soviet state and separated from their boys, the Slepaks, Masha especially, treated me with parental kindness. In Masha's big eyes I read an unspoken reproach addressed to all refusenik parents.

The Slepaks were living right on Gorky Street in a communal apartment they shared with another family. My parents and I had last visited them just a week before the subpoena came, on a Friday night. As Masha lit the candles, she whispered, eyes closed, "Please let me see my boys this year." (She wouldn't see them for two more years, until the autumn of 1987.) After dinner, which was always accompanied by jovial drinking and the opening of the Slepaks' bottomless trove of activist stories and prison camp anecdotes, my father, Volodya, and I stepped out onto the balcony for some air. Down below, Gorky Street pulsated, Red Square on our right, the Pushkin monument on our left. The equestrian statue of the medieval Grand Prince Yuri Dolgoruky, often called the founder of Moscow, stood in a square below, across the lanes of streaming traffic. My father and Slepak were talking about prospects of arrest and imprisonment. "The earlier you go to jail, the earlier you'll get out," Slepak said, smiling relentlessly. My father didn't care for the comment but said nothing. . . .

Now that the subpoena had landed on our doorstep and my father was in danger, we needed the Slepaks' help. As I rode the Metro from our Oktyabrskoye Pole station into the center, I was going over in my head what the Slepaks might say or do after hearing about the subpoena. Call their connections in the diplomatic corps? Get in touch with foreign correspondents? Alert their contacts in Israel and in the United States? I was sure they would do something to help us right away. I ran up the escalator and all the way to the Slepaks' apartment building. I didn't want to call them, on the theory that their phone line was always bugged, and simply showed up at their door and rang the bell. It was around 8 p.m.; Masha was wearing house clothes; a neighbor's face materialized in the far end of the communal corridor and vanished. Masha and I kissed and embraced, and she led me to their quarters to the right off the communal corridor. Volodya was sitting on the sofa, reading. Without saying anything, I gestured for a pad and pencil. I knew the Slepaks always had one ready so as to avoid sharing information with the good "listeners."

"Father received a subpoena," I wrote. "Should he go?"

"Right," Masha said, hands fluttered up; Volodya calmly nodded. They put coats on, and we walked downstairs and went outside through the back entrance. The Slepaks' car was parked in the back yard, and we sat in it, engine running to generate some heat, and strategized. I actually don't know why the car was any less secure than their rooms. The gist of the Slepaks' advice was that my father had better show up as summoned. That a subpoena was serious and could be made more serious. That playing games with *the KGB* wasn't a good idea, as it could only make things worse in the long run, even if it may delay things in the short run. "My dear boy," Masha said as we parted. "Be careful." Being careful was the last thing on my mind as I walked to the Metro station and rode the train home. I felt both proud that I was finally a part of real political action and disappointed by the Slepaks' reaction and advice.

In the preface to his selected memoirs of Soviet writers, published in St. Petersburg in 2007 as *Vodka and Pastries: A Novel with Writers*, my father sketched out the days after the first subpoena was delivered to our apartment, when he was expecting arrest and hoping to escape it: "I decided not to volunteer myself into the hands of the KGB. If they are summoning me with a subpoena, if they don't bring themselves to arrest me at home or in the street, then something is preventing them from doing it, something must be limiting their lawlessness. That is, the KGB wants for me to say or write something during a meeting with a prosecutor, something that would accord them greater freedom to arrest me. I understood this and decided to go into hiding. . . . I wasn't sleeping at home. The prosecutor's office continued sending me their subpoenas. . . . I walked the icy streets of Moscow. On my heels were the black shadows of the KGB vehicles. . . ."

The pressures of being hunted by the Soviet secret police were mounting as November crawled into December, light days reaching their annual lowest limit. Cornered and gravely exhausted, my father ended up in the hospital with a heart attack. He was hospitalized at the Fourth City, where for several years he had been serving as a consulting endocrinologist. The Fourth City Hospital had been founded by Emperor Paul I as a public hospital for the poor. In the early 1800s the distinguished Russian architect Matvey Kazakov had revamped the main ward in neoclassical style, and thus the edifice stood unchanged for over two centuries, surrounded by a campus of newer buildings. The Fourth City (formerly "Paul's Infirmary") was one of the city's better medical centers, and a teaching and research hospital. Several attending physicians on the floor of the intensive cardiology unit knew my father from having previously done rounds with him, and he was receiving decent care. The first few days of my father's hospitalization were especially trying. I will rely on my father's words, also from the preface to *Vodka and Pastries*: "Of course the KGB people knew my whereabouts. My attending told me they had insisted on conducting an interrogation directly in the intensive care unit. She replied: 'If you want his death, go and interrogate!' They wanted my death, but by the hands of others."

The plainclothes thugs left the ward, but they weren't prepared to leave my father alone. For the first several days, mother and I worried the most about nighttime, when visitors, even family members, weren't admitted. The floor of the ward became deserted save for a nurse on duty, and my father, lying on a hospital bed with an oxygen mask, was especially vulnerable.

We took turns visiting during the day, mother in the morning, I in the afternoon, on the way back from the university. The hospital campus was located in an old section of Moscow's Zamoskvorechye district, where nineteenth-century and even older buildings, some of them one- or two-story stucco mansions, had survived Soviet-era architectural revamping. I usually took the snail tram from the bustling Paveletskaya Metro and Railroad Station, down Dubininskaya Street and almost to its intersection with Danilovsky Val, part of an old thoroughfare traversing, from west to east, the area south of Moscow's historic center. From the hospital campus on Pavlovskaya (Paul's) Street it was a short walk to the ancient Danilovsky Monastery, seat of the Patriarch of Moscow. Not far from there was the Moskva River embankment. The Torpedo soccer stadium rose from across the river. My father, who was to turn fifty in just over a month, looked forlorn, cheeks sunken, graying mustache covering a bloodless upper lip. After he was moved from intensive care to a regular cardiology floor and allowed to go outside for fresh air, he started walking me back to the tram stop. I will never forget our daily good-byes, and the feeling that father was already in a prison camp across the tracks and I was visiting him in the "zone." And after an hour in the zone with my father I would cross, as if speciously, into a life that had the trappings of normalcy. I would rendezvous with Lyuba and go see a movie or a play, or visit one of her girlfriends or my friend Max, whose mother was often out in the evenings. Lyuba sensed something about our troubles at home, but she didn't know exactly what was happening, nor was I free to share it. I felt it would be simpler this way.

During my father's first two weeks at the hospital, two or three other subpoenas were delivered to our mailbox. Mother spent several days trying to clarify my father's predicament. She spoke with more veterans of the refusenik and dissident movement, including an old-time refusenik who had been a practicing attorney before losing his job. We weren't living in a land of respect for the law, and yet we wanted to know exactly what legal options, even if on paper, my father had, in view of the subpoena. Between cooking for and visiting my father, crisscrossing Moscow to meet with various contacts on my father's behalf, and teaching part-time at the House of Culture, my mother hardly had a moment to herself. Through connections at the American embassy, she had gotten in touch with several journalists accredited in Moscow, including a reporter for CBS News and a *New York Times* correspondent. She was also on the phone with activists of the Soviet Jewry movement from the US, Canada, Great Britain, and France, who had previously visited us in Moscow, and also with old Moscow friends who had gotten out in the late 1970s and were living abroad. All of them pledged support through Jewish and human rights organizations and their local and national politicians. This sounded inspiring but also a bit nebulous—could a senator or MP indeed pressure the Soviet authorities into leaving my father alone?

We were getting different advice from different people, including acquaintances with histories of arrest and imprisonment. At least for now, our tactic was to win some time, to give my father a chance to gain strength as he recuperated. He was feeling a little better, and finally, perhaps against better judgment, he took a taxi home from the hospital. It was around noon, a sunny winter day in the middle of December, and father wanted to have a bath and shave and spend a couple of hours at home before returning to the hospital ward. My mother was actually out, and I don't remember the reason I happened to be home; university study days must have already begun. I recall down to the minutes how my father had come in, how we kissed and hugged, how he took his coat off and began to undress outside the bathroom when the doorbell rang. Father must have still been in such a state of nervous restlessness that he didn't even look in the peephole first before turning the deadbolt and opening the door. It was too late. Wearing only pants, socks and an undershirt my father opened the door, and we saw a police junior lieutenant standing there in a winter greatcoat and snow-powdered jackboots, clutching a green slip of paper in his left hand. The lieutenant had pale yellow eyebrows and eyelashes and blue eyes. He looked unthreatening, except that he was in a uniform and obviously executing an order.

"Citizen Shrayer?" he asked my father.

"Yes," father replied, quietly.

"Sign for a subpoena," said the lieutenant, mustering notes of authority in his thin voice.

"You see, lieutenant," father said, gesturing to the lieutenant to come into the hallway. "I've been ill, stuck at the hospital for two weeks, just came home to have a wash."

The lieutenant, who was only a few years older than I and looked younger than his years, seemed unprepared for normal human words to come out of my father's mouth. He hesitated, as if considering whether or not to let my father be, and finally said "Just sign here." Perhaps I imagined it, but I thought that he was a bit ashamed of his mission.

The appearance date written on the new subpoena was just around the corner.

My father went back to the hospital ward that afternoon. The doctors still planned to keep him under observation for at least a week, but we weren't sure for how much longer the hospital could serve as a sanctuary. The tactic of ignoring the subpoena had exhausted itself. We needed to undertake decisive actions to protect my father.

In the hospital my father wrote a personal letter to Gorbachev, protesting his persecution and harassment. My mother took the letter to the post office and sent it, half-heartedly, as a telegram to the Kremlin. We weren't putting much stock in this action, and my father next composed an open letter of appeal to writers and artists abroad, detailing his condition and asking for support and protection. My mother translated it into English. On a chilly December night mother and I went by Metro to the center of

Moscow. She had wanted to go without me, but I was adamant. It wasn't a long ride, first to Barrikadnaya, Lyuba's Metro station, where we changed trains and rode one stop to Belorusskaya, where we changed trains once more and rode one more stop to Mayakovskaya. The stop was named after the genius of the revolutionary avant-garde, whom Stalin, not without prompting, posthumously deemed the "greatest of Soviet poets." I had admired the interior of this Metro stop with its succession of vaults and brightly lit rotundas, its floor and walls clad in rose stone. Mayakovsky's statue, placed in the middle of a square right outside the Metro stop, was a popular meeting spot. Anti-Soviet protests, readings, and demonstrations had taken place in front of the Mayakovsky monument. It was past nine in the evening when we got out of the underground station, mother carrying a purse with the protest letter. After my parents had newly moved to Moscow from Leningrad in 1964, they lived in a communal apartment a few steps from where we now stood, near the intersection of Garden Ring and Gorky Steet. The double presence of Gorky and Mayakovsky cast a note of darker irony on our enterprise: there we were, heading to a meeting with a US journalist to deliver a plea for help. An appeal from my father to literary brethren abroad. Silently we headed east, walking on the south side of the wide Garden Ring.

My parents had seen the American journalist only once before, I believe at the apartment of an American diplomat with whom they were friendly. On the phone the journalist and my mother had agreed that we would be walking from the direction of Gorky Street, and he would meet us on the block of the Garden Ring where the *New York Times* had its offices. We approached the designated block, well-lit as most of the Garden Ring yet deserted at the weekday evening hour. Only a few cars were parked here and there. There was no journalist in sight, and we filed past the meeting point, then turned around and walked back. We had to repeat the maneuver two or three times, knowing that we were making ourselves obvious targets. "There he is," mother said, finally, her breath shortening, and we hurried toward a tall figure in a dark wool coat, who had emerged on the other end of the block. Still on approach, the bespectacled, bearded American journalist greeted my mother with a nod, and with something of a smile as we got closer.

"You left this," mother said, in English, and handed him the envelope with my father's open letter.

"Thank you," the journalist replied, slipping it in his long coat. He walked past us and ducked into a lane.

"Let's get out of here," I said, pulling my mother onto the edge of the pavement to flag a taxi. A cab stopped almost immediately. "It's the opposite direction, now I've got to turn around," the driver grumbled. "We'll take care of you, let's just go, chief," I said. As I recall the incident today and share it with American friends or the occasional reporter still curious about those Soviet days, it gains a James-Bondian, celluloid quality and somehow loses its gravity. As I got into the cab next to my mother and slammed the door, I saw an unmarked car parked not too far behind on our side of the street come alive with headlights. How can I explain, twenty-five years later, that I felt a mixture of fear for my mother and of a breathtaking spirit of adventure as I stole glances of the unmarked vehicle through the rear window. It was a Zhiguli, a Soviet-made Fiat, not even a top model, and there were two men in it. I didn't want to alarm my mother or especially the cab driver, but I couldn't help turning around. I worried, given the ease with which we had stopped our cab, that we were in a trap on wheels. I worried but couldn't say anything out loud. Our cab made a U-turn at the intersection with Tsvetnoy Boulevard, just a couple of blocks from the Old Moscow Circus. As we sped along the Garden Ring, heading back to Mayakovsky Square and moving in the right direction, I no longer had any doubt that the unmarked vehicle was following us. "Hurry, my good man," I told the cabbie as we turned right onto Gorky Street. "We'll make it worth your while."

I was counting the landmarks. Gorky Street became Leningradsky Prospect, a speedway that ultimately flows into the Leningrad Highway. We passed the Dynamo soccer stadium, near where my grandmother, aunt, and cousin lived, then sped past the ornate, red and white Petrovsky Castle, where Catherine II and her successors stopped when visiting Moscow, and where the Air Force Academy was now quartered. We had left behind the Automobile and Road Construction Institute, where I would have probably gone to study if I hadn't gotten into Moscow University. Just outside Aeroport Metro station were apartment buildings where

Soviet writers and filmmakers enjoyed privileged housing and other services. A few minutes later, just past the Sokol (Falcon) Metro station, the chasing vehicle still on our tail, we got off the speedway and turned onto Alabyan Street. From there, over an echoing bridge above multiple railway tracks, it was a straight shot to our street, Marshala Biryuzova. Streets and squares in my neighborhood bore the names of Soviet wartime generals or military commanders. We were just a few minutes away from our apartment house. The cab driver was going full-throttle, and the pursuing car had run a couple of red lights so as not to fall behind. Mother and I didn't speak throughout the chase. I gave the cabbie directions where to turn off the street. Each section of our long twelve-story apartment house had its own front entrance. The cabbie pulled up all the way to the door. The unmarked vehicle stopped just behind us. We dashed for the entrance, rode the elevator to our seventh floor, unlocked the apartment, then locked the bolts and chains. I glanced down from my bedroom window and saw that the vehicle was still there, both men sitting inside. A few minutes later they were gone. They could have asked for backup, perhaps for a police car with a siren, mother and I reasoned with each other. They could have stopped the cab, had us arrested and interrogated. But they didn't, only chasing us to our doorstep. We had concluded that the men in the unmarked vehicle must have been watching the offices of the *New York Times* or the journalist himself, and followed any suspects so as to identify them—which they did by getting our street address. We had accomplished our mission, getting father's letter to an American journalist, and the Soviet secret police knew about it, too. In the morning my mother went to see my father at the hospital and described the events of the previous night. I spent the first part of the day at school and the late afternoon and entire evening with Lyuba. It was ever more tempting to tell her about the letter and the night chase, but I didn't, deflecting Lyuba's question with another half-truth about having been "occupied" on account of my parents' troubles. She didn't press me on the issue.

A week later my father was moved from the hospital to a rehab center just north of Moscow, in the village of Bratsevo. At first he refused to ride in the van the hospital provided, but the chief cardiologist, the courageous woman who had taken my father under her wing, personally assured him it was "safe." After convalescing there for over a week, father returned home on New Year's Eve. My parents had a quiet celebration at home. Father wanted a respite from all the stress of the past month and a half. He told mother and me that, as he lay in the intensive care unit following the heart attack, KGB thugs waiting outside to interrogate him, a new book had gained shape in his head. It was to be a story of my father's literary youth in the Leningrad of Khrushchev's Thaw, the late 1950s and early 1960s. During the weeks of recovery and rehab, father had had a lot of time to think about the future book, and he now just wanted to wake up at home on New Year's Day, get to his typewriter, and work, work on without interruption. The book, which my father rapidly composed in the winter and spring of 1986, would be called *Friends and Shadows* and form the first part of his memoir *Vodka and Pastries*. I witnessed its composition and, along with my mother, was privileged to be its first reader.

Lyuba and I spent New Year's Eve at the apartment of an old Pärnu friend, Galya. Galya's father, an architect, spent many days at the racetrack. Her tolerant parents threw incredibly abundant parties for their daughter and readily made their three-room apartment, located a short walk from the Ostankino TV tower, available for her use. Some of the guests at the New Year's bash had known each other for years, mainly from Pärnu. We drank and partied with an ease I hadn't felt since when I was a student in the Soviet Union. Was there, perhaps, a vibe of new hope in the air as we chimed in the year 1986? I remember discussing with Max and a couple of other guests that the winds of political change might be finally blowing in our direction. It was widely rumored that in late December 1985 Gorbachev had gained full control of the Communist leadership and of the country, supposedly gearing up for a vaguely defined course of "liberalization." We had also heard that at the end of December, Boris Yeltsin, the future dissolver of the Soviet Union, had been elected First Secretary of the Moscow City Party Committee. In fact, I believe it was then that I first heard of Yeltsin, from one of the guests at the party, a student at the Institute of Oil and Gas. "I heard on the Voice of America that this is a very promising sign," he whispered to me, in a conspiratorial fashion. "Yelstin is not a retrograde, and they say he is definitely not an antisemite. And he plays tennis." We were doing such a good job getting drunk that the hostess became worried and asked her boyfriend to pour out the two remaining bottles of vodka into the toilet bowl. The next morning, when I walked Lyuba home from the subway station, we had one of those tremulous conversations one can only have in one's youth or dreams—about perfect plans for life, about living in California on a sunlit beach—and I felt a special closeness to her. In my experience, such conversations, in the very impossibility of realizing the perfect plans the lovers tend to conjure up, signal the imminence of breaking up.

Indeed, Lyuba and I were drifting apart. There were no fights or acrimony, but just a growing sense that we wanted different things. I was too young and immature for marriage or even a shared domesticity. I was also still hungry for romantic adventure, for fuller amorous experience. Another factor was the two-month expedition I was to participate in during the summer, and the prospect of forced separation, during which Lyuba would have to wait for me like a soldier's bride. Our relationship was petering out, as though it was only meant to thrive on the hardest of times, with subpoenas dropping at my family's doorsteps.

Some time in February, Max and I went to Leningrad for a weekend. "Oh, just to change the pace and visit some old friends," I told Lyuba. We saw Katya and also spent time with other Pärnu friends who were living in Leningrad. "We all thought we had lost you," said our friend Vika as a group of us shared two bottles of gum-gripping Algerian red wine on the ice of the Gulf of Finland. Max, my loyal friend who had never said anything throughout the time Lyuba and I were together, only nodded in agreement and took a gulp from a green bottle. My friends hadn't lost me, but Lyuba and I had spilled our love over February ice and snow. Upon returning from Leningrad I learned that Lyuba had spent the weekend with a classmate from Moscow State, the tall Teutonic man who always looked at her with timid longing.

The subpoenas stopped coming either to our mailbox or our door. My father was left alone, at least for the time being. Even though he was still weak after all the stress he had endured, he went back to work at the clinic and was spending long hours in front of his Olympia, typing away at the new book. My parents had resumed the refusenik salons, still unsure how long the interlude of peace would last. In the meantime, on 12 January 1986 the prominent Prisoner of Zion Anatoly (Natan) Sharansky was exchanged for two Soviet spies and released to the West. Sharansky had been arrested in 1977 and held in a labor camp since 1978. He and his wife Avital had been apart for almost a decade, she in Israel, he in Soviet captivity. The refusenik community was abuzz with details of Sharansky's release. We heard about the way Sharansky walked across the Glienicke Bridge from East Berlin into West Berlin, not in a straight line but in a zigzag, to show his defiance. Was Sharansky's release a hopeful sign or simply another East-West spy deal? We wondered about that, as we also wondered about the significance of Gorbachev's consolidation of power. One thing that notably increased in our lives following those horrendous December events was the number of foreign visitors. In the winter and spring of 1986 we received a slew of such courageous guests. Our visitors included a California state senator, a Protestant minister, and an Italian-American medical student. They brought us gifts, usually clothes and books, and took back our pictures. An undated photo from this period would eventually reach us from abroad. It has survived among my parents' papers, although we don't know who took it. Father, mother, and I are photographed in the living room, which doubled as my father's den. To the left, behind our backs, is a china cabinet with white-and-blue Russian porcelain mugs, out of which tea with lemon always tasted so good. To the right from where we're sitting is my father's desk with photos of the poet Aleksandr Blok, and of my grandfather Pyotr in wartime uniform, and a stone paperweight in the shape of an owl. On the edge of the coffee table, in front of us, is a plate of what looks like matzo meal cakes, a dish my mother often served to the foreign guests who kept kosher. I look serious, perhaps a little anxious, while my father and mother both have a stamp of exhaustion on their faces from fear of new troubles. For how much longer could they endure being refuseniks?

INTERLUDE

FACTS AND ARGUMENTS

MY POSITION AT THE SCHOOL OF SOIL SCIENCE remained shaky, especially following my failed defection to art history. Throughout the autumn of 1985, as poetry-writing, Lyuba, and my parents' persecution had all taken center stage, I had been neglecting my studies. Something had to change in the new semester, or else I would face more problems. When classes resumed in January, I plunged myself into exploratory research, spending long hours at the library. By the end of the spring I needed to build up a research agenda. It was a challenge to search for research ideas that would excite me enough to keep me going. About once a week in January, February, and March I went to see Professor Rozanov, the brightest academic star at my school. We brainstormed about topics for a research term paper and a senior thesis I was going to write under his mentorship. What if we measured the impact of the decreasing salination of the Black Sea on the fertility of soil in the coastal areas? (I wanted a pretext for doing field work in the environs of Odessa, the home of my beloved writers from the "South-Western School," Isaac Babel, Eduard Bagritsky, and Yury Olesha.) Has anyone studied the relationship between the changing pattern of massive bird migrations and the soil content in the areas of natural habitat where large numbers of migratory birds congregate, molt, and leave their droppings? (I could already picture myself traveling to the Volga delta, the largest in Europe.) Rozanov listened approvingly and specifically asked for bibliographies of articles published in Western journals. I ended up perusing almost the entire run of *Soil Science* at the university library. Unwittingly, I must have been searching for some compelling travel narrative, a story, even a fantasy, to shape my research in a more or less literary or artistic direction.

As I was trying to distill my ideas down to a list of two or three topics with bibliographies, to present them to Rozanov, a historical event was taking place in Moscow. The Twenty-Seventh Congress of the Communist Party convened at the end of February and the beginning of March 1986. There was talk at the Congress about "acceleration" of the Soviet economy. The terms *perestroika* ("restructuring") and *glasnost* ("openness") were not spoken of directly, but a new, reformist economic course was guardedly publicized, and "democratization" was hinted at. In this atmosphere that augured a new political Thaw, another fiasco occurred at school. In the middle of April, after months of listening to my research ideas and encouraging me, Professor Rozanov unexpectedly turned down the formal request to serve as my advisor.

This happened at a public meeting of the students with the entire faculty and research staff of the Department of General Soil Science. At such annual meetings students presented research ideas and advisors were formally assigned and announced. As the chair of the department, Rozanov presided over the meeting. Going down a typed list of about a dozen of my classmates, he would pause to say something about each student and identify their would-be advisor. I was always nearly at the bottom of the alphabetical list, not an easy thing for someone born to be on fire with impatience. Finally Rozanov had reached my named and cleared his throat. Imagine my shock when he muttered something to the effect that "Shrayer had come by once or twice with some raw ideas," and that "Shrayer would benefit from working with one of our junior research colleagues." I was so shocked I couldn't contain myself. I jumped up and addressed Rozanov in front of the whole gathering: "But Boris Georgievich, I don't understand. Just a few days ago you and I had firmed up a research plan for next year, and you acted as though I was already your advisee." Some of my classmates turned toward me with strange looks. Neither hostile nor unsympathetic, their looks rather made me feel like a condemned man.

With his tobacco-stained fingers, Rozanov tied a loop in the air and only said this: "Shrayer, I shall please see you in my office, privately." And he moved to the last person on the list.

Why did Rozanov wash his hands of me? Had he known all along, or been finally "warned," about my refusenik background? My parents' recent troubles? All or any of this was in the range of possibilities. Or had Rozanov figured out that my heart was not fully in soil science? But why had he been stringing me along? Why had he acted as though we were future research collaborators? Why would a powerful Russian professor feign enthusiasm for the research ideas of a Jewish sophomore? This didn't make much sense to me.

A likelier explanation had emerged by the end of the day, after I came home and described the meeting at which Rozanov had turned me down. My parents listened to my account and both lowered their gazes. "We should have told you right away," said my father. "But we didn't want to upset your mood," mother added. "You seemed so taken with your research project . . . finally so enthusiastic. . . ." It turned out that on 8 April 1986, just about a week before the meeting, the Moscow weekly review *Fakty i argumenty* (*Facts and Arguments*) had published a nasty article that implicated my father and several other refuseniks in anti-Soviet and subversive activities.

A copy of this article is before me on my desk, taking me back almost exactly twenty-three years, from this wet April 2009 morning in Boston to those April days of 1986 in Moscow. Titled "Repentance of the Deceived One" and signed "R. Lesnykh," the article appeared in the Moscow weekly under the rubric "Unmasking." A note prefacing the article explained that it had been originally printed "at the end of the previous year" in *Pravda Ukrainy* (*Truth of Ukraine*), the central organ of the Communist Party of Ukraine. The note in the Moscow weekly also quoted from—and reproduced a facsimile of—the opening sentence of a handwritten denunciation that had been submitted to the Ukrainian paper by one Evgeny Koyfman, a Jewish man from the city of Dnepropetrovsk. Koyfman, reportedly a former refusenik who had seen the light of day and changed his mind about leaving his "Motherland," described how it had taken him some time to realize that the activities of those "striving to introduce him to learning Hebrew and Judaism" would "in fact amount to surreptitious, careful attempts to implant Zionist ideology in his consciousness." The opening section of the article described how Koyfman had found himself involved in activities that begin with "preaching the 'exclusivity' of Jews," then proceed to "discredit the Soviet nationalities policy," and finally lead to "open slander and anti-Sovietism." These were serious charges and accusations, and in his denunciation, Koyfman reported a number of encounters with Jewish activists. According to the article, in May 1982 "Koyfman went to Moscow and found himself in the apartment of a certain Shrayer": "'To learn the language? We'll help, of course we'll help,' the host condescendingly promised. 'And not only with this. Be firm in your desire to leave the USSR.'" This was pure unadulterated fiction. My father didn't know Hebrew and was never involved in the underground network of teaching Hebrew or Judaism. Furthermore, the years 1981-82, following my father's arrest outside the British Embassy, were the lowest point of my parents' involvement in any sort of refusenik activism.

In cooking up a fabricated charge, the article accused my father of "anti-Sovietism" and "Zionism." In fact, Koyfman alleged that in May 1982 in Moscow he encountered "somebody who called himself Yuli Edelstein" the day after meeting "a certain Shrayer." A prominent refusenik activist and a Prisoner of Zion, Edelstein was arrested in 1984 for a fabricated charge of "drug possession." In the spring of 1986, Edelstein was still serving a three-year sentence of hard labor; he wouldn't be released and allowed to go to Israel until 1987. Even as a vernal wind was blowing in from the Kremlin, the KGB was still in the position to use its well-tested methods, and the threat of my father's continuing persecution and imprisonment remained real.

If we attempt to reconstruct the events of November-December 1985, with the subpoenas and my father's intense persecution, it seems quite likely that a trial had been in the works. Publication of my father's novel about refuseniks had been announced in Israel by the time the first subpoena had arrived. The prospect of a publicized trial of a "Zionist writer" gave my father reason to fear for his arrest. To our family, the April 1986 article in *Facts and Arguments* was a delayed aftershock of the November–December events. As I try to make sense of the way Professor Rozanov dropped me like a sack of potatoes, I can see how to him and others at the School of Soil Science who might have read the article, the name Shrayer was likely to point not to an abstract Jewish target of denunciation, a "certain Shrayer," but to my father and to his family.

The next morning, armed with the knowledge of the denunciatory article in *Facts and Arguments*, I went to see Rozanov again, this time in the privacy of his office. He listened till the end of my tirade about unfairness and commitment, vigorously shaking off cigarette ashes into an urn of professorial dimensions.

"I'm assigning you a great advisor," Rozanov said. His shapely fingers tapped on a pack of smokes lying in front of him on the table. "Professor Samoylova is a fine specialist, a fabulous teacher, trust me. You'll thank me one day."

What else could I say to him? What else could I do?

Even if I wanted now to find out the truth and decided to contact Rozanov—and even if he might have been willing to tell me the truth about his maneuver—I couldn't do it today: he passed away in 1993, aged sixty-four.

Elena Maximovna Samoylova, whom Rozanov assigned as my advisor, was a full professor and a renowned expert on the evolution of soils. She and Rozanov were known to have a tenuous relationship, laced with competition: he the chair, she the "second" professor, and a woman at that. Going to Samoylova's office for the first time, I felt that she and I were being thrust into each other's hands as a punishment for both. Professor Samoylova was a smileless woman in her early fifties, with a puffy face, and short hair dyed the color of weak black tea. She usually dressed in plain wool cardigans over floral blouses with long collars and in monochromatic skirts. Her office looked like a cross between a map depository and a book reshelving station. Samoylova, who had been expecting me, hardly concealed her contempt for Rozanov and his academic politics. She was a person of few words. I gleaned compassion in her remarks, and also in the ironic twinge of her bottle-green eyes. With slicing motions of her hands, Samoylova unfolded a map of Eastern Kazakhstan and Western Siberia over a table in the center of her office, spreading it over layers of maps, books, and journals. She pressed her left index finger to a spot on the map and then circled it with her right index finger; her nails were short and ungroomed.

"There," she said, referring to the point underneath her left index finger. "This is Kulunda. Geographically speaking, you're in the center of the Kulunda Steppe."

Sensing my bewilderment, she added some background. "This is southeast of the Barabinsk Steppe, surely you have heard of it. About 200 kilometers west of Barnaul, 200 kilometers southwest of Novosibirsk, some 400 kilometers southeast of Omsk, almost exactly 200 kilometers north of Semipalatinsk," Samoylova explained with unflinching precision, indicating and measuring out these directions on the map. "Any questions so far?"

"No," I replied.

"Splendid. There are salt lakes all around here, and all sorts of fascinating things in the soil," Samoylova continued. "Plus the foothills of the Altai are fifty kilometers to the southeast. The Kulunda Steppe is what my research group is focusing on for the foreseeable future. We have an expedition going there every summer. We go by plane to Barnaul, then take a chopper to Kulunda. This coming summer you're going on a trip to the Black Sea. But the summer after your third year, we'll send you to do field research in Kulunda. This means you have less than a year to become very familiar with the literature and form a research question. Now any questions?"

"No questions," I said and jotted down a couple of things in my notebook.

"Well, you should try to make the best of your years here," Samoylova said. "And try to learn as much as you can about transformations of soil types across geographic zones," she added. "Very soon, during your summer expedition, you'll be traveling from Moscow all the way to the Black Sea. That's a great opportunity to learn more about field research."

I thanked Samoylova and left. The long, earthy corridor of the School of Soil Science loomed before my eyes like the endless expanses of West Siberia, round metal light fixtures shining on the wood-paneled walls like saucers of salt lakes on the surface of the steppe. For the time being, my scientific lot had been drawn, and I now looked forward to two months of summer travel and to getting away from my Moscow life.

When you are young, you possess a remarkable mechanism of inner self-defense, which uncannily helps you get over almost anything, even if you acquire emotional scars. In the course of six turbulent months, I had experienced the enchantment of poetry writing, the dread over persecution of my parents, the ebb and flow of romance, a curtailed apprenticeship as an art historian, and even the beckoning of scientific exploits. As I think of everything the events of the autumn and winter of 1985–86 had meant to me, I wonder how much a young person's heart and mind can encompass before this young person ceases to be himself. I'm still wondering, after over twenty-five years in America.

1. Peysakh (Pyotr) Shrayer (front row left), Maxim D. Shrayer's paternal grandfather, with his parents and four siblings. Kamenets-Podolsk, Ukraine, 1924. Photographer unknown. Courtesy of Emilia and David Shrayer.

2. Borukh-Itsik Shrayer and Fanya (Freyda) Shrayer (née Kizer), the paternal grandparents of Maxim's father, David Shrayer. Leningrad, 1930s. Photographer unknown. Courtesy of Emilia and David Shrayer.

3. Anna (Nyusya) Studnits, Maxim's maternal grandmother (back row third from the right), with her brother Grisha (Grigory; on her left) and relatives on their father's side. Gorodok, Ukraine, 1931. Photographer unknown. Courtesy of Emilia and David Shrayer.

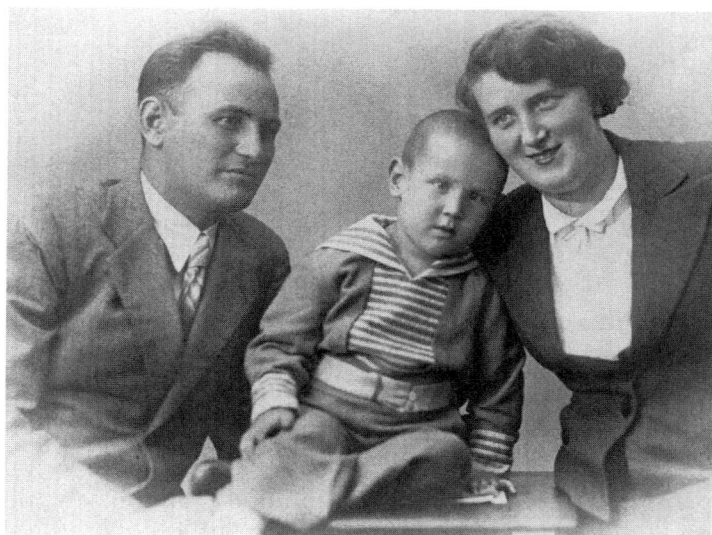

4. David Shrayer with his parents, Bella Breydo and Pyotr Shrayer. Leningrad, ca. 1939–40. Photographer unknown. Courtesy of Emilia and David Shrayer.

5. David Shrayer and Bella Breydo. Village of Siva, Molotov (now Perm') Province, 1942. Photographer unknown. Courtesy of Emilia and David Shrayer.

6. Pyotr Shrayer, captain, ca. 1943. Photographer unknown. Courtesy of Emilia and David Shrayer.

7. Emilia Shrayer (née Polyak), Maxim's mother (second from the right) with her parents, Aron (Arkady) Polyak and Anna Studnits, and her sister Zhanna Volynskaya (née Polyak). Moscow, 1951. Photographer unknown. Courtesy of Emilia and David Shrayer.

8. David Shrayer, lieutenant of the medical corps. Borisov, Belarus, 1959. Photographer unknown. Courtesy of Emilia and David Shrayer.

9. David Shrayer. Leningrad, early 1960s. Photographer unknown. Courtesy of Emilia and David Shrayer.

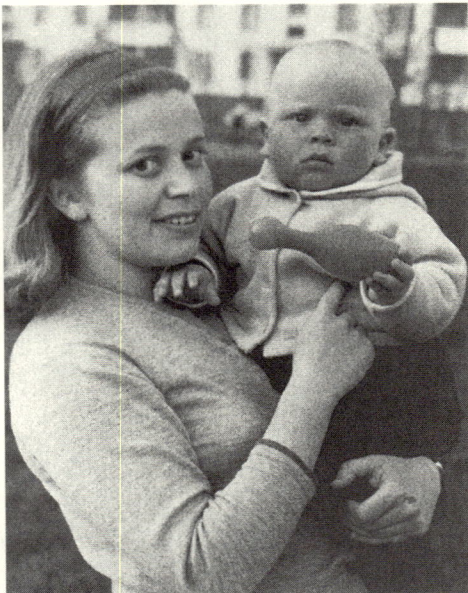

10. Maxim with his mother. Moscow, 1968. Photograph by David Shrayer. Reproduced by permission of the photographer.

11. Maxim. Arkhangelskoye outside Moscow, 1969. Photograph by David Shrayer. Reproduced by permission of the photographer.

12. Maxim at his father's typewriter. Moscow, 1971. Photograph by David Shrayer. Reproduced by permission of the photographer.

13. Maxim. Tbilisi, Georgia, 1977. Photograph by David Shrayer. Reproduced by permission of the photographer.

14. 43 Marshala Biryuzova Street, the apartment building where the Shrayers lived from 1971 to 1987 (photographed in 1998). Photograph by Maxim D. Shrayer.

15. Rannahotell. Pärnu, Estonia (postcard), ca. 1938. Photographer unknown. Courtesy of Maxim D. Shrayer.

16. Jüri Arrak. *Corona* (oil on canvas, 97x120 cm.). 1975. Photograph courtesy of the artist. Reproduced by permission of the artist.

17. Maxim with parents visiting Panga-Rehe, Jüri Arrak's summer home. Estonia, summer 1977. Photographer unknown. Courtesy of Emilia and David Shrayer.

18. Emilia and David Shrayer with Urve Roodes Arrak (on the left) and Jüri Arrak (second from the right) with their spaniel Lonni. Panga-Rehe, summer 1979. Photograph by Maxim D. Shrayer.

19. Maxim with Katya (Ekaterina) Tsarapkina in the Shrayers' Zhiguli. Pärnu, summer 1980. Photograph by David Shrayer. Reproduced by permission of the photographer.

20. Emilia and David Shrayer. The Shrayers' apartment. Moscow, ca. autumn 1980. Photograph by Maxim D. Shrayer.

21. Maxim with Emilia Shrayer, Urve Roodes Arrak and Jüri Arrak, and Vaïke Lubi (on the right). Estonia, summer 1983. Photograph by David Shrayer. Reproduced by permission of the photographer.

22. Maxim (top row on the left) with classmates. Grounds of School No. 34. Moscow, May 1984. Photographer unknown. Courtesy of Maxim D. Shrayer.

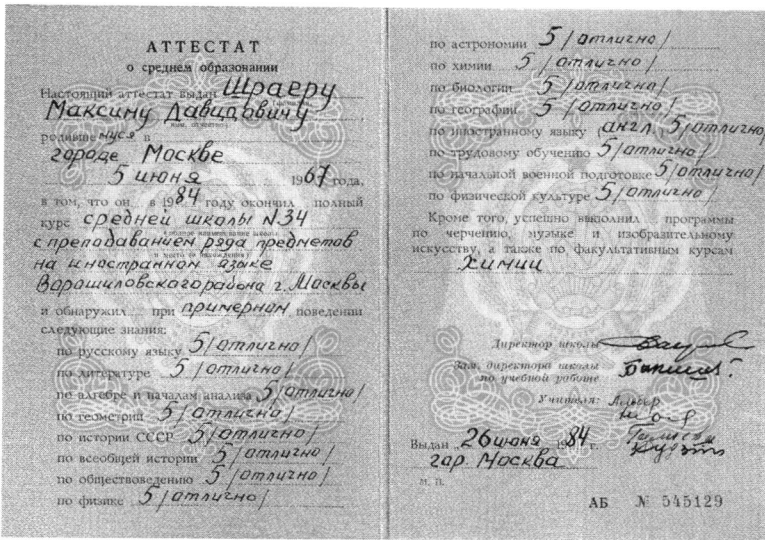

23. Maxim's secondary school diploma. School No. 34. Moscow, June 1984. Courtesy of Maxim D. Shrayer.

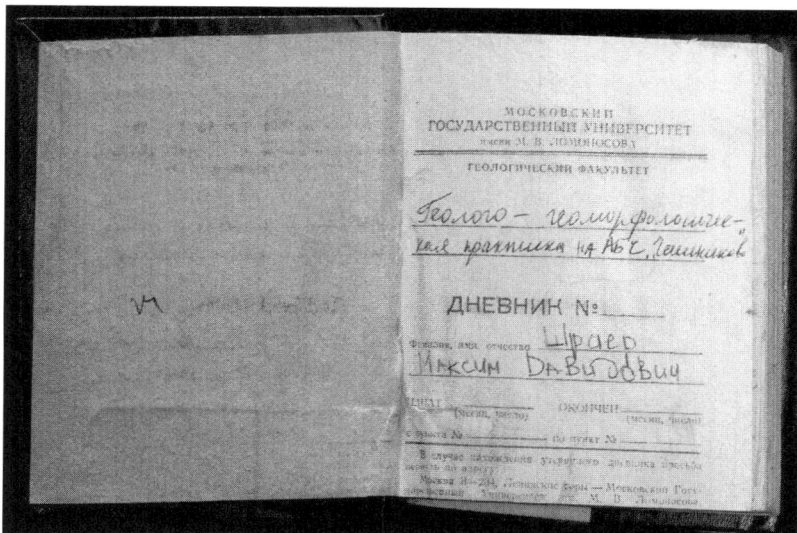

24. Maxim's field journal with summer notes on geology and botany. Chashnikovo, Moscow Province, summer 1985. Courtesy of Maxim D. Shrayer.

25. David, Emilia, and Maxim Shrayer. The Shrayers' apartment. Moscow, winter 1986. Photographer unknown. Courtesy of Emilia and David Shrayer.

Expedition Route, Summer 1986

1. Moscow University, Moscow
2. Lopasnya, Chekhov District, Moscow Province
3. Tulskie zaseki forest, (outside) Krapivna, Shchekino District, Tula Province
4. Spasskoe-Lutovinovo, Mtsensk District, Orel Province
5. Kursk Nature Reserve, (outside) Kursk, Kursk Province
6. (Outside) Melovoe, Melovoe District, Voroshilovgrad (Lugansk) Province
7. (Outside) Proletarsk, Proletarsk District, Rostov Province
8. Teberda, Karachai-Cherkessk Autonomous Province, Stavropol Region
9. Pshada, Gelendzhik District, Krasnodar Region
10. Khrenovoe, Bobrov District, Voronezh Province
11. Chashnikovo, Solnechnogorsk District, Moscow Province

26. Map of Russia with Maxim's expedition route. Summer 1986. (The expedition route features only the principal stops and points.) Created and copyrighted by Maxim D. Shrayer.

27. Maxim's expedition journal with the entry for 5 June 1986, his nine-teenth birthday. (The first expedition stop, Lopasnya, outside Moscow.) Courtesy of Maxim D. Shrayer.

28. Maxim's expedition journal entry for 8 July 1986. (Leaving Teberda, Karachai-Cherkessk Autonomous Province.) Courtesy of Maxim D. Shrayer.

29. Maxim during an ascent to a glacier. Teberda, July 1986. Photographer unknown. Courtesy of Maxim D. Shrayer.

30. Maxim drinking boiled water at the expedition camp. July 1986. Photographer unknown. Courtesy of Maxim D. Shrayer.

31. Maxim writing at the expedition camp. July 1986. Photographer unknown. Courtesy of Maxim D. Shrayer.

32. Maxim with Maxim Mussel. Pärnu, August 1986. Photographer unknown. Courtesy of Maxim D. Shrayer.

33. Maxim (first on the right) harvesting potatoes with School of Soil Science class-mates. Chashnikovo, September 1986. Photograph by Aleksandr Golovkin. Courtesy of Maxim D. Shrayer.

34. Emilia Shrayer (second from the left) at a demonstration in support of Yosef Begun. On her left, with the poster "Freedom to my father Yosef Begun," is Boris Begun. February 1987. Moscow, Arbat Street. Courtesy of Emilia and David Shrayer. This photograph by Andrew Rosenthal appeared in *Newsweek* magazine on 23 February 1987. Reproduced by permission of the Associated Press.

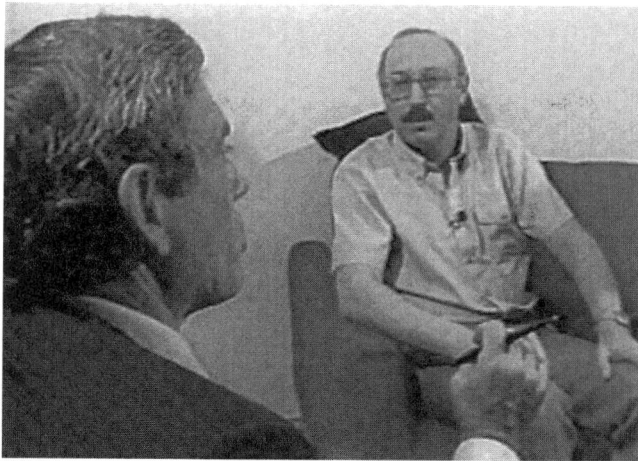

35. David Shrayer being interviewed by Dan Rather of CBS News. The Shrayers' apartment. Moscow, May 1987. From *Seven Days in May: The Soviet Union* (CBS, 1987). Courtesy of Emilia and David Shrayer. Reproduced by permission of CBS News Archives, a division of CBS Broadcasting Inc.

36. Maxim, Emilia, and David Shrayer, and Anna Studnits at Moscow's Sheremetyevo-2 Airport, 7 June 1987. From *Seven Days in May: The Soviet Union* (CBS, 1987). Courtesy of Emilia and David Shrayer. Reproduced by permission of CBS News Archives, a division of CBS Broadcasting Inc.

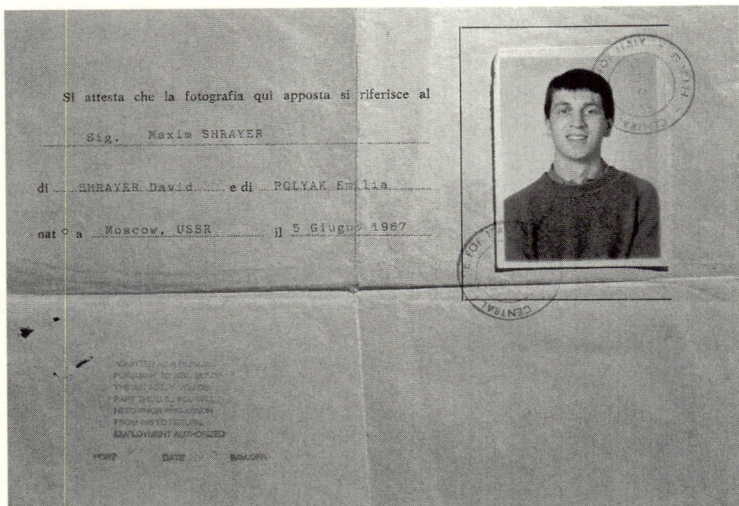

37. The travel document issued in Italy, with which Maxim entered the United States as a refugee on 26 August 1987. Courtesy of Maxim D. Shrayer.

38. Maxim with Katya Tsarapkina and Maxim Mussel. Moscow, November 1995. Photograph by Maxim D. Shrayer.

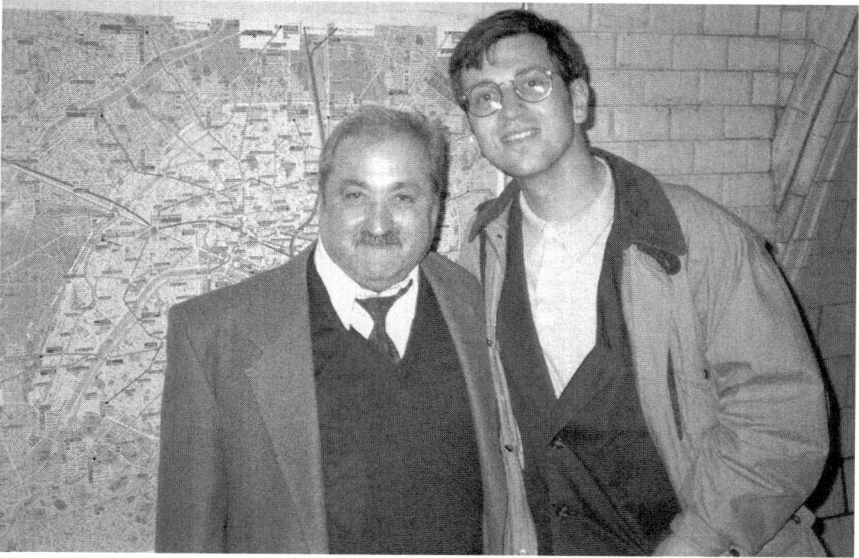

39. Maxim with Genrikh Sapgir. Paris, May 1995. Photograph by David Shrayer. Reproduced by permission of the photographer.

40. Maxim with David Shrayer. Providence, Rhode Island, May 2003. Photograph by Gary Gilbert. Reproduced by permission of the photographer.

41. Emilia and David Shrayer. Chestnut Hill, Massachusetts, July 2006. Photograph by Maxim D. Shrayer.

42. Yosef Begun, David Shrayer, and Emilia Shrayer. Boston, April 2010. Photograph by Maxim D. Shrayer.

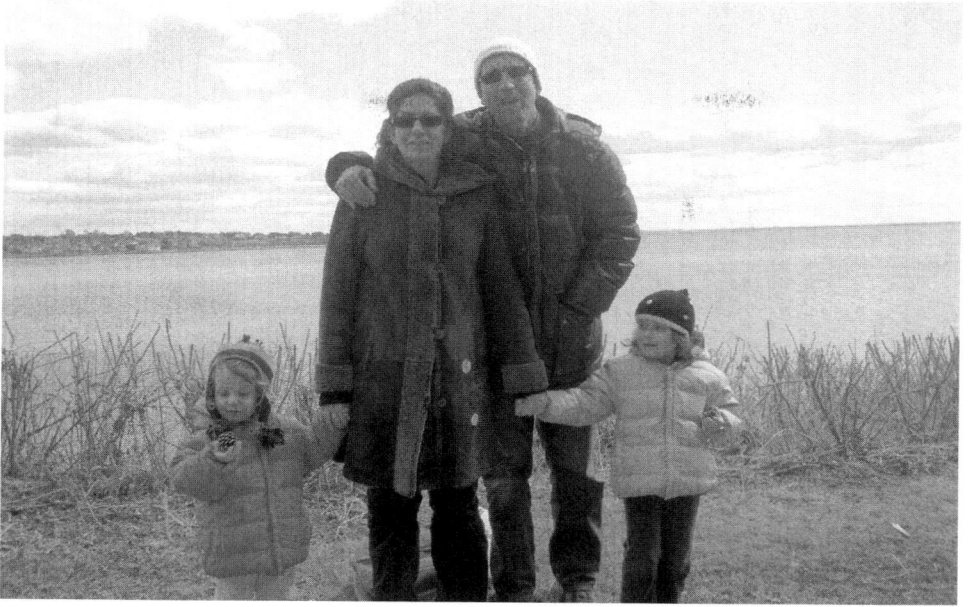

43. Tatiana, Karen, Maxim, and Mira. Newport, Rhode Island, March 2011. Photograph by Maxim D. Shrayer.

44. Maxim, Tatiana, Karen, and Mira. South Chatham, Massachusetts, August 2012. Photograph by Maxim D. Shrayer.

7

ACROSS THE STEPPE
AND INTO THE BLACK SEA

ONE OF THE VERY FIRST THINGS I LEARNED, back in high school, when I made inquiries about the School of Soil Science, was that it prided itself on its *zonalka*. Students from other schools within Moscow University, including the snobs from Law and Journalism, usually knew about the *zonalka* and envied the would-be soil scientists. *Zonalka* is a casual abbreviation of *zonal'naia praktika* (literally: zonal practicum), a two-month summer expedition, which soil science students participated in after the sophomore year. There were two established routes, Moscow–Crimea and Moscow–Caucasus, and each year a class was divided into two groups according to one's future specialization. We traveled in two separate columns from Moscow due south in the general direction of the Black Sea. Each half came back from the journey convinced that their route was more exciting, and factions of "Crimeans" and "Caucasians" continued to argue the point. As a future "general" soil scientist, I traveled to the Caucasus (for details of the route, see the expedition map in ill. 26).

The logic behind the *zonalka* was to introduce us to zonal transformations in nature. We observed both horizontal and vertical changes of climate and vegetation zones. We experienced variations in landscape, soil, flora, and even fauna, from north to south, then into the high mountains of the Caucasus, and finally from the mountains down to the coast of the Black Sea. In terms of the specific vegetation zones, we began our journey in the area of mixed forest, traveling through the area of broad-leaf forest and forest steppe to the area of meadow steppe and southern and even arid steppe to the western foothills of the Greater Caucasus mountain range. Once near the mountains, we were able to see how altitude and elevation above sea level created vertical variation, from steppes and grasslands to forests to Alpine meadows, and to permafrost and glaciers. Finally, after a week of mountaineering we descended to the coast, for some rest amid lush maritime forests and wild, scraggy beaches. Different instructors had different expectations of us and taught with varying degrees of rigor; I recall one professor telling us right away that he wanted us to master one hundred plant species, both Russian and Latin names, by the end of the journey. Geobotany, ecology, geology, geography, soil classification, and other subjects were taught in context, and nature itself was our classroom.

But there was also cultural and historical logic to the *zonalka*, which made the experience particularly meaningful for someone like myself, a humanist who thought not of iron oxide but of Adam the primal man when digging up and measuring a red soil section. The journey from Moscow took me through the black soil belt of central-southern Russia. This area, known in Russian as *chernozem'e* (from *chernozëm*, black soil, a humus-rich fertile topsoil) forms a near tetrangle or rhomboid on the map, its vortices marked by the great Russian cities of Orel, Tambov, Kursk, and Voronezh. The black soil belt is simultaneously Russia's breadbasket and its cultural heartland. Especially in the nineteenth century, a great number of Russian writers came from former country estates we passed on the route or visited. South and southeast of the black soil belt, along what had once been the frontier of the Russian state, I encountered the heritage of the Don, Kuban, and Terek Cossacks. And once we reached the mountains of Northwest Caucasus in the area of Karachai-Cherkessia, the rich ethnic and linguistic diversity and the Muslim patrimony of the region came alive before my eyes. The experience of North Caucasus revealed the oozing legacy of Russia's colonial conquest; only a few years later, Chechnya would explode in a violent revolt. Finally, a respite on the Russian coast of the Black Sea at Pshada, some thirty miles down the coast from Gelendzhik, was a minor window onto an ancient Hellenic past opulent with mythology.

For me personally, the expedition took place against the backdrop of what had been a turbulent year. But for all of the participants of the expedition, including the former marines and paratroopers who acted like they had seen it all, leaving Moscow in June of 1986 meant trying to put behind ourselves the ever-present signs of the Chernobyl nuclear catastrophe. It had taken place on 26 April 1986, just a little over a month before our departure from Moscow. Refugees from the disaster area in Ukraine and Belarus had been arriving by the trainful and crowding Moscow's railroad stations. For weeks there had been talk of Hiroshima and Nagasaki, of thousands of victims, of children and pregnant women with radiation sickness. Everybody seemed to know somebody with a connection to an exposed person. A sense of panic had given way to a dulled sensation of the whole huge country cracking at its seams.

On this journey, which took me almost 1000 miles to the south of Moscow, I was getting to know the kind of Russia that I had never seen before. Once as a three-year-old I had been to Crimea, and later, as a six-year-old, to Sochi on the Black Sea coast, traveling to both places by plane and train. When I was eight, my father took me with him to Georgia for over three weeks. Otherwise, the Baltics, mainly Estonia, had been the annual destination of our family vacations since the time I was five. From driving to Estonia and back I had an idea of the landscape and local color in the areas lying northwest of Moscow and en route to the Baltic lands. But never once, both as a child and a young man, had my travels given me a chance to observe, freely and unhurriedly, the ways of provincial Russia south of the Moscow Province. This was a kind of antidote to a Jewish city boy's vision of the world—and probably to my whole existence as a refusenik. To this day, memories of the expedition inform my perception of Russia. To this remarkable experience of slowly traversing the Russian heartland in the direction of south and sea, often taking smaller roads and making frequent stops, I owe much of what I know first-hand about the daily life in rural Russia and inside Russia's southern boundaries.

Throughout the summer 1986 expedition I kept a journal. When I was leaving Russia in June 1987, I carried the journal across the border in a sky-blue backpack. A customs officer examined the contents of my backpack and asked about the "notebook." "Notes from school—on soil science and botany," I replied, and the officer looked the other way. I was very lucky.

Impressions of that summer 1986 expedition have been living within me for many years, waiting to be described. But they have also been stored in the journal, a surviving written record of my Soviet past. As I set out to write these pages, gasoline prices have been teetering above the four-dollar-per-gallon line while a humid and unusually rainy Boston summer has turned my cucumber plants into tropical vines. The journal, about a hundred pages in a mouse-grey thread-bound vinyl notebook, now lies on my desk, next to my daughters' and wife's photographs. It's the only journal or diary I ever kept throughout my Soviet years. Diary-writing wasn't a habit our family cultivated, and to this day I haven't become a systematic journal-keeper.

This is the only chapter of this entire book for which I'm relying heavily on surviving written records of my own keeping. In my expedition journal, factual details are interspersed with notes for future poems and even complete drafts. I must have intended the journal both as an act of witnessing and as a literary exercise. As I read through it, I come across not only factual bits and details that I would not have been able to recollect from memory alone. I also see that in so many ways I'm no longer the person who authored these entries. How strange to be making use of the journal's characterizations and ideas, and especially so as I try to render its voice in a more or less literal English translation while also furnishing the journal excerpts with commentary. The process has its charms and its perils.

We departed from the main campus of Moscow University on 2 June 1986, traveling on the Simferopol Highway. Our group of "Caucasians" consisted of about fifty students, eight or nine faculty members, two bus drivers with some family members, and three truck drivers. A military field kitchen, drawn by one of the trucks, completed our procession. The students were divided into five groups with faculty leaders, each group referred to in Soviet-speak as a "brigade" and assigned a folding table, an oilcloth, aluminum bowls, mugs, and dinnerware, and a tea kettle that looked prehistoric. Each group had its own field classes, digs, and research projects, and carried out various chores.

The three truck drivers, anarchic fellows in their early thirties, lived for beer and sex with university girls. One of the two bus drivers was a misanthropic middle-aged man who regarded his ochre-colored bus as a submarine under his command. The other bus driver was a ruddy alcoholic in his late fifties who brought his wife and grandson on the trip. Every night he would get drunk and vomit before passing out on the floor of the bus, his poor wife doing her best to keep the bus hygienic. He was rehired every year because of his phenomenal knowledge of Russian roads and his ability, when he was sober, to procure provisions for us at any old food store along the way; we were having to replenish our supplies in provincial towns and villages with bare shelves.

Our faculty included three unmarried women, old maids according to the Soviet norms of the time but still young by today's American standards, and not averse to summertime romance with come-who-might. Of the male faculty, one fashioned himself a macho rebel and socialized only with the army vets, another was a quiet, mild-mannered researcher who traveled with a preteen son and kept to himself during the respites from classes and field work. Our expedition director was a colorful individual by the name of Lev Bogatyrev, a respected researcher and also an accomplished vocalist. His ambition had been to become an opera singer, but life made different arrangements. In his spare time in Moscow, Bogatyrev was a soloist with the chorus of the Academy of Armored Forces. He knew a vast repertoire of songs, ranging from Italian opera to Soviet pop. Every day he gave mini-performances at meals or pit stops or evening campfires. Bogatyrev was hardly a tyrant; next to performing, he especially enjoyed open-air massages that a couple of my female classmates offered him at the end of a long day. Even though there was supposed to be military-style discipline with line-ups three times a day and permissions requested to leave the camp, Bogatyrev didn't enforce it strictly. For the most part, the atmosphere on the journey combined that of an academic expedition, reservist military exercises, and an itinerant circus.

We set up our first encampment on the edge of a field abutting a forest and a swamp, between the villages of Myshkino and Semyonovskaya. This was outside the town of Chekhov, a district center which used to be called Lopasnya, in the southwestern tip of the Moscow Province. It was pouring rain and, as we soon discovered, some of the tents, large enough to accommodate ten people, had holes in the roof. By the end of the first stop we had repaired or consolidated the useable tents and figured out the routine. The day started at six, which meant that the "brigade" on service would get up around 4:30, fire up the field kitchen, make the morning gruel and tea, and also cook up the soup for our midday meal. Our food supplies consisted, predictably, of dry goods such as oatmeal or cream of wheat, Soviet black tea of the cheapest kind (the "sweepings"), and dried fruit for the compote. Whatever we could we bought locally—butter, eggs, fruit and vegetables, even fresh chickens once or twice. We fished in waters we passed and we also picked whatever edible products we could find growing in the wild or in abandoned orchards, including berries, wild garlic, and wild plums. Gruel and pea soup (dubbed "musical") were the foundations of our diet. We had sunflower oil, condensed milk, and a limited supply of *tushenka*, canned pork stew. At breakfast and supper each brigade of about twelve people received a heated-up can of the coveted, lardy meat, which came to about a tablespoon per person. This was not exactly enough to get fat on, and we were constantly craving meat. The faculty ate with us; the drivers received cooked porridge and soup from us but had their own (I suspect, richer) table.

About once a week each student would carry out campfire duties and stay up all night, guarding the encampment. In the first few days of the expedition, permanent duties were also determined: some of us pitched tents and assembled tables and benches, others unloaded and loaded the trucks, yet others set up the field kitchen and communal washing area with buckets and push-up water dispensers. My communal duty was to oversee the loading and unloading of suitcases, backpacks, and crates with equipment and soil samples. I suspect that the safekeeping of valuables had been deemed a Jewish mercantile talent; I was the only Jew on the trip, and the job went to me.

These excerpts from my journal convey some initial impressions of the expedition:

2 June 1986. The first rooster crows in the village of Myshkino.[1] Amazing, the roosters are definitely communicating. The unknowable

---

1. I was the last one on the alphabetical list, and of course we started from the bottom. On the first night a classmate and I kept a vigil at the campfire, and I penned the first journal entry.

village ways. A gluttonous fire. Baked potatoes burning the lips. And the birds have started screaming. Now where's the sun?

4 June 1986. Road to the farm. Empty village—girls in short identical dresses. A little church. Domes—one a normal dark brown poppy-head, the other strangely shaped, a dried pear turned upside down. Church from about the 1840s. Red brick. The fence is well preserved. Cast iron. . . . Shielded by fat meaty limestone, all covered in warts with green hairs, in folds of skin-bark, large wrinkles, elephant-like. . . . Inside, two main iconostases, faces of saints, and teenage drawing on top of the faces. . . . I really cannot abide published diaries. Either you write them for yourself, or a priori for publication. . . .

5 June 1986. My birthday. We went to a swamp. I do like nature to be wild and quiet. Bog orchid[2]—lilac-pink, sharp, sort of like a sterlet's little muzzle; in general a swamp in its colors is somehow close to a tropical sea. Strange??? Perhaps I'm just different, but I feel some sort of alienation from these boors, and not just the former servicemen. Maybe it's really the barrier of coming from the intelligentsia—what barrier? It couldn't be because of the refusenik thing! . . . This is difficult, although not burdensome. A smoke screen.

Leaving behind our first encampment and the confines of the Moscow Province on the morning of June 7, I felt as though I had already been gone a long time. We were just over one hundred miles south of Moscow, crossing from the area of southern taiga into the broad-leafed forests, but we might as well have been hundreds of miles away from my native urban civilization. Except for the obvious desolation of churches, the rural landscape seemed untouched by Soviet time. Through mud-speckled windows, the life of the small towns we observed on the way also seemed unperturbed by history. We passed the city of Tula, heading for our next stop, the famous Tulskie Zaseki forest tracts in the Shchekino District, the southwestern section of the Tula Province. In my journal, the following entry dates to the first morning in Tulskie Zaseki:

2. Russian: *iatryshnik* (*Orchis palustris*).

7 June 1986. After Tula, the river Upa, about 8 meters wide—grown shallow. Factory pipes of the somber Tula shining at the horizon (military factories). A childhood memory: Yasnaya Polyana.[3] . . . In front of our eyes nature is warming up and there are no more fir trees. Birch— *Betula pendula*. . . . Morning in an apple orchard . . .

The tracts of Tulskie Zaseki go back to the fifteenth and sixteenth centuries, when their founders envisioned them as defense lines on the southern boundaries of Muscovy. Tall trees, especially European oaks, were felled in such a way that the fallen trees wouldn't be separated from the trunks, forming extensive areas impenetrable to mounted troops. In Peter the Great's time the lumber from these trees was considered highly valuable. By the nineteenth century, Tulskie Zaseki had emerged to become a protected reserve, with alternating sections of oak, lime, and ash trees. It was a naturalist's dream, and we spent three days there, taking foot excursions through forest groves more beautiful than I had ever seen, digging up soil sections, observing the changes in vegetation. After the vicious mosquitoes and swampy mud of our first stop, the abandoned apple orchard where we stayed in Tulskie Zaseki offered relief. It was dry and sunny, and a warm, southerly breeze brought with it the relaxing aroma of aged oak barrels.

9 June 1986. A section of gray forest soil. Wild strawberries. Wild garlic.[4] . . . In general, there's nothing to observe and study, or I don't feel like it. Grass snakes, field mice, gray heron at the swamp, bugs and grasshoppers.

I preferred unstructured contemplation, and for me the joys of the Russian countryside were matched, if not exceeded, by the ethnographic and literary pleasures of soaking in the small-town life as I had never seen it before. We were staying outside the old town of Krapivna, its

---

3. Yasnaya Polyana—estate of Lev Tolstoy outside the city of Tula. In Yasnaya Polyana Tolstoy was born, later lived as an adult, and was buried; now a memorial museum.

4. Wild garlic, also known as bear's garlic or ramsons (Russian *cheremsha*; Latin *Allium ursinum*).

name derived from *krapiva*, Russian for stinging nettles. The legend had it that after the Tatar-Mongol troops swept across the area, causing desolation, dense nettles grew across the ravaged Russian villages. Krapivna had once been an important military outpost with a fortress and large garrison, then a county seat with a textile industry and wealthy grain merchants, but already in the nineteenth century it was a true backwater, only remembered for its Junior College of Forestry. When I set foot in Krapivna, I felt like I was back in the early nineteenth century, except for the emptiness of food stores—a salient marker of Soviet times:

> 10 June 1986. Town of Krapivna. Too bad Gogol isn't around—it's just like in D.S.[5], about 150 years ago. Dusty square, warehouses, muzhiks, black-and-red [faces]. Drunks. Women are trying to talk their men—all of them in identical untucked shirts—into something: to buy, do, say something. Not a whit to eat in the stores, but lots of textiles. Architecture in its primordial fashion. And three churches, one of them big, navy-white-blue, stone-white, eighteenth century, St. Nicholas, an empty courtyard, cold, the sexton is sleeping, only in such Russian towns do you see such churches. An old woman is kissing all the icons and crossing herself—strange, like an alien I'm watching from the corner. Logs of smoked cheese.[6]

On June 11 we left Tulskie Zaseki and drove southwest in the direction of the city of Orel. Our next destination was Spasskoe-Lutovinovo in the Mtsensk District of the Orel Province, and our double goal was to study the ecology of the forest-steppe area and to visit the estate-museum of Ivan Turgenev. But before we bid farewell to the Tula Province and entered the famed Black Soil belt, our expedition took a detour and stopped at Yasnaya Polyana. Tolstoy asked to be buried here, near the manor house where he had been born and spent much of his life. His grave is unmarked; in my mind I have the image of a greening mound in the middle of a lawn on the

---

5. *D.S.*: Gogol's *Dead Souls*.

6. I am not entirely sure what this refers to; I guess there was smoked cheese for sale in a food shop, and the locals were not buying it.

edge of a ravine, with trees forming a live fence on one side. Or perhaps the later image had been superimposed on an earlier memory. My father had taken me to Yasnaya Polyana for the first time when I was about seven, on a one-day trip from Moscow. This time, standing near Tolstoy's grave and looking downward, I envisaged a map of Russian literature extending across south-central Russia down the area we planned to traverse over the coming two weeks. It was a map of former country estates, of gentryfolk culture from which came Turgenev, Leskov, Bunin, and many other great Russian writers. Destroyed by the fires and tractors of the Revolution, this culture now lived on in the books and in the memorial estate-museums like Spasskoe-Lutovinovo, which had been spared the fate of many country estates because of its old master's literary fame.

In Spasskoe-Lutovinovo we camped on the border of Turgenev's estate, and I recall a meadow with a nearby low-lying area of grassland dotted in blue and yellow. The small valley was now dry after the spring torrents, and couples descended there during the midday respite. I don't recall much of what we dug for and studied, or, perhaps, all the other impressions had paled in comparison to a half-day-long visit to the estate-museum:

> 12 June 1986. Excursion to Spasskoye-Lutovinovo. A pale-purple manor house. A bathhouse. A cellar . . . An almshouse at the entrance to the manor house. Horses—half-draft ones—grazing in the park. A drunk old man leads a gelding. 'What do they call you?' — 'Gramps; I'm old.' — 'Well, and what's your name and patronymic?' — 'Timofey Andreeich. And yours?' — 'Maxim Davidovich.' — 'Vladimirovich?' — 'No, Davidovich.' — 'Vladimirovich?' — 'Yes' (to hell with you)[7]. Back through the village. Dead, although this used to be a large prosperous village—[now] a big cemetery. Roosters and hens walk anywhere they like; in the pond, geese and ducks . . . The little village drowning in poplars / Has dropped its windows into the pond. . . . Portraits of Tyutchev,

---

7. I gave up on trying to impress upon the old man that my patronymic is Davidovich, "son of David"; he couldn't fathom that such a name was even possible.

Shchepkin, Belinsky[8] in the manor house. Turgenev was 192 centimeters [about 6 feet 3 inches] tall—a giant. Our tour guide—whitish, long, slightly greasy hair; beardless face either practically without growth or shaven clean like a sheet of paper; glasses in a black frame bent inward. Corduroy black slacks, ugly, drooping, and a blue shirt with a front panel; big hands with long-grown nails and fat fingers. Speaks with confidence and is generally rather sure of himself. Something unmanly . . . perhaps, but perhaps not. Led us around the house, told me to take off the 'head garment'—whispering tenderly. For the most part commented about furniture, but kept silent about Pauline Viardot[9]. . . . Night over a crucian carp pond. A one-armed tousled angler (formerly a gardener, himself stocked the pond with carp), looks like a wood sprite, black-swarthy-bristly. . . . In the village a photo shop—a shack with a straw roof. Chickens and geese. On the main street Roma children, beautiful and colorful. . . . Campfire. Local folk. A fat, mustached man with a gold tooth, meaty nose, palms of hands with little pillows. With him, lads aged twenty-two to twelve, even the youngest one smokes. The man got worked up without anybody prodding him, trashing the decline of morality, deforestation, bureaucratic civil servants, in a word, everything. . . . Recalled the old days, the forests and natural riches of the local Orel Province, even as compared to the Lipetsk Province to the west and the Kursk Province to the east. He had gone back to school at a late age and did a low-residence math and physics degree at Orel. His discourse touched on everything, from abundance versus non-abundance of mushrooms to ecology, viruses, and educational systems and programs. Strange, but he probably has no one to talk to, hence his unleashed tongue.

8. Fyodor Tyutchev—major nineteenth-century poet; Mikhail Shchepkin—dominant Russian actor of the first two thirds of the nineteenth century; Vissarion Belinsky—preeminent literary critic of the Russian 1830s and 1840s.

9. Pauline García-Viardot—celebrated nineteenth-century singer and composer, object of Ivan Turgenev's passionate admiration, his close friend and—according to some sources—his lover.

Not surprisingly, as I learned during the expedition, museums at former country estates and also nature reserves were magnets for various escapees from the jaws of Soviet reality serving as guides or forest wardens. Chance campfire conversations with local oddballs and hidden dissidents would spark our own political discussions, which would go on for days. In connection with the Spasskoe-Lutovinovo stop, I recall a group of us debating the role of Stalin. The cult of personality and the purges were not forbidden subjects, yet in the late Soviet years, young people weren't exactly encouraged to re-examine Stalin's legacy. Ours was not an argument of "fathers and sons," but of members of the same generation raised in opposite ways with regard to Stalin. There were two principal "Stalinists," a woman from Volgograd (still remembered by many in the West as "Stalingrad") by the name of Ira Muravyova and an army veteran from a Kuban Cossack town, Sergei Khudoleyev. I was on good terms with both of them and was shocked by an ideological divide that had quickly formed between the Stalinist twosome and the rest of our "brigade." Ira and Sergei romanticized a mighty Soviet state. They couldn't very well deny the Great Terror, but they comfortably justified it as a means of a building a strong industry. For both of them, even in the late 1980s the Soviet victory over Nazism remained not only Stalin's crowning achievement but a principal coordinate of ideological orientation.

While Ira and Sergei were *gosudarstvenniki* (from the Russian noun *gosudarstvo*, "state"), patriotic proponents of a powerful (and, they argued, strong and unyielding on the international arena) Russian/Soviet state, they were not Russian nationalists or xenophobes. In fact, on one occasion I witnessed Ira Muravyova's voiced contempt for antisemitism. One of their most vociferous critics was a former marine, originally from the Kamchatka region. The girls in my year had affectionately nicknamed him "Stepasha," after his last name and also after a puppet dog in a nightly TV show, "Good Night, Kids." Stepasha aspired to be a stage director. At the time, I knew the repertoire of Moscow theaters like my own back yard, and we cultivated a connection despite major differences. Stepasha struggled, oscillating between Russian ultranationalism and love of world culture, especially theater of the absurd. I suspected, although I didn't know it for sure, that his family had been exiled to the Far East.

Stepasha bitterly clashed with the Stalinists and detested anything Soviet, placing his cultural roots in an era predating the 1917 revolutions. He was torn, as were many educated Russian nationalists, between a vision of Russianness based in ethnicity and Russian Orthodoxy, and a realization that one cannot be a Russian *intelligent* without an openness to other cultures and traditions. Visiting the Turgenev estate and hearing about the two decades the Russian liberal Turgenev had spent in Western Europe, in the 1860s through the 1880s, had unbottled Stepasha. On our last night at Spasskoe-Lutovinovo he launched a campfire monologue about the "Russian intelligentsia." Russian intelligentsia was a phantom, Stepasha argued. It was gone. By that he meant, although he preferred to remain cryptic, that the "Russian intelligentsia" had either emigrated or been destroyed in the purges, or else had been Sovietized beyond recognition. He didn't quite put it this way, but in his words I heard (or the Jew in me heard?) Stepasha's doubts that a cultural entity known as Russian intelligentsia could still be considered "Russian," given the prominence of other backgrounds—Armenian, Georgian, Jewish, Kazakh, Tatar, Ukrainian. Ours was an ethnically diverse group of students, and I suspect I wasn't the only one hearing something disturbing in Stepasha's words.

The following day we left the Orel Province and drove in the direction of Kursk, heading for the Kursk Nature Reserve:

> 13 June 1986. Mtsensk—founded in 1147. River Zushcha. Three ivory churches on hills above the river. Small gold (honey) domes. And nearby chimneys and factories . . . After Kursk already the river Seim. The nature reserve is about 1 kilometer from the village of Selikhovy Dvory.

Mtsensk, an ancient Russian town, figured prominently in Russian culture, past and present. Nikolay Leskov memorialized his native *orlovshchina* in the short novel *Lady Macbeth of Mtsensk County* (1865). Shakespearean notes resonate in the titles and themes of other Russian tales set in the Black Soil belt, including Turgenev's own *King Lear of the Steppe*. It was a chain of cultural associations, in which Russian writers, composers, and visual artists took something from the West and gave back so much more. Stopping in Mtsensk made me think not only of Leskov and Turgenev, in some ways each others' stylistic opposites, but also of Dmitry Shostakovich's opera based on Leskov's *Lady Macbeth of Mtsensk County*, subsequently reworked and renamed *Katerina Izmailova*. Stalin attended a performance in 1936 and targeted Shostakovich for a denouncing *Pravda* editorial. This opera of forbidden passion and murder in nineteenth-century Russia was deemed redolent of "petit-bourgeois formalism" and a slap on the face of Russian classical traditions; it was banned. Passing through Mtsensk, with its picture-perfect churches and ugly Soviet factories, I was sitting just a couple of seats away from my Stalinist classmates Ira and Sergei and the Russian nationalist Stepasha. We were but temporary fellow travelers, and I wanted to shun useless politics. I only wanted to keep my eyes on the Russian steppe, which beckoned from across the horizon.

We were leaving behind the forest-steppe with its leafy groves and water meadows, and entering the Kursk Province, where the northern (meadow) steppe truly began. This region had once been Muscovy's southern and southwestern frontier. The steppe was a buffer and also a boundary. The Russian word steppe (*step'*) means "flat and arid land." In these grasslands, trees naturally grow around and along rivers and lakes. In European Russia, belts of steppe grasslands extend from the area where we spent the next three days to the south and southeast and east, all the way to the Black and Caspian seas and to Kazakhstan. The types of steppe change according to latitude and also to climate, and on our expedition route we would observe a variety of them, from the lush, meadow steppes outside Kursk to the arid, semi-desert steppes near Proletarsk, close to the border with Kalmykia. The word "steppe" brought forth associations with freedom, openness, wild expanses, and natural beauty.

On the evening of 13 June we set up camp outside Kursk, only a short stroll from one of the entrances to the Central-Black Soil Nature Reserve, which we called the Kursk Reserve and the locals simply "the reserve." The reserve was celebrated as one of the few places where one could still experience virgin steppe, its soil never ploughed or upturned. The topsoil layer here was supposed to be three feet deep—a wealth of humus as compared to the paltry few inches in the boreal forests of Russia's northern latitudes where we had started our journey. Relic plants grew on the reserve; wolves and red foxes still roamed around as they had done in the days when wild cattle dominated the habitat; the *zubry* (European bisons) had been hunted down by the seventeenth century. From a distance, the virgin steppe was a patchwork of colors, mainly yellow and blue. In the landscape one could discern flat circles known as "saucers," with a bumpy surface in between them. On our first night in the Kursk Reserve I only managed to sneak out for a little bit after we had finished pitching tents and unloading. I ran to the fenced boundary and stood there, astonished by the sight of the blossoming steppe. The next morning I wrote this down:

> 14 June 1986. Steppe. Waves of feather grass or shocks of gray; saw-worts perfect as if they came from a pastry shop; wondrous bloody-crimson thistles; prickly plums with slits of eyelets; dwarf almonds. Volga fescue—the legacy of the Pechenegs and the Polovtsians.[10] Velvety salvia, pliable flax, soft lashes of the pink-purple *knautia*. A steppe viper whistles something in synch with the swaying of the feather grass. The steppe is all breathing; it overwhelms you, merging with the sky, the distant horizon, the air, all of it. You steep yourself in the steppe, give yourself to it, becoming forever its slave and master. I want to go to the steppe. Flax is blue.

During the first half of the expedition, up until reaching Teberda in Northwest Caucasus at the end of June, we were moving southward at a rather fast clip. I would have gladly stayed on around Kursk, not only because of the splendor of virgin steppe, but because the climate was lovely, with dry even heat during the day and cooler, breezy nights. We spent one entire day inside the reserve, observing and taking notes. On the morning of our second day at Kursk our director announced that we would be going into the city. This was, as Bogatyrev drew out during a morning lineup, to address our "bodily needs." Indeed, we hadn't showered since leaving Moscow. A couple of times we took dips in ponds and

10. Pechenegs and Polovtsians (as the Kumans were known in Russian)—semi-nomadic peoples inhabiting the steppes along the southern and eastern frontiers of medieval Rus and raiding Russian lands in the ninth through the twelfth centuries. Here I used the term allegorically to represent a people of the steppe.

rivers along the way. Men routinely washed the upper part of their bodies right in the public washing area; women had it much harder. Groups of two or three women would walk to a nearby forest with buckets of water and aluminum mugs. The only reason bodily odors weren't constantly on our minds is that all of us without exception were sweaty and dirty. And now we would be going into the city of Kursk to visit a public bathhouse. What good fortune!

Of Kursk, a provincial capital, I had been aware in connection with one of the decisive operations of World War II; every Soviet kid learned in school about the defeat of Nazi troops in the summer of 1943, in a tank battle south of that city. I knew, vaguely, that this city of under half a million prided itself on a magnetic anomaly, the area's world-class deposits of iron ore. What was revealed to me as we approached was the charming view of a city on an elevated plateau, its domes, bell towers, and spires laced with bright green verdure. Many years later, I had a similar reaction when, on a visit to Tuscany from Genoa, my wife and I walked toward the old walls of Lucca from the city's railroad station.

A blessed visit to a public baths came first; we scrubbed our bodies up and down and walloped each other with besoms in the steamroom, this despite a hot summer day outside. I can well imagine that I liked Kursk so much because after two hours at the bathhouse and a couple of beers in the locker room, even a peeling barracks with a weeping willow and deep puddles all around would seem picturesque. I recall a pleasant stroll from the bathhouse through the old city center, where a few of us had lunch. Bright yellow lemon ice was sold in the streets. We saw a splendid city cathedral built in Baroque style. An educated-looking man with a black briefcase stopped for a moment and said to our group: "A real beauty, hmm, our cathedral. Rastrelli[11] himself worked on it." One just had to ignore the local monstrosities of Stalinist Empire style and also to avoid making eye contact with typical apartment buildings of the Soviet 1960s and '70s that dotted the city's outskirts.

---

11. Francesco Bartolomeo Rastrelli, famous eighteenth-century Russian architect of Italian origin, designer of the Winter Palace in St. Petersburg.

When I as a young person in the USSR, coming from a place like Kursk would automatically deem one a provincial. Not geographically, but culturally speaking. I toured the Kursk city center with three classmates. One was Dmitry Ladonin, son of a Moscow professor. The other was Vanya Govorukhin, my best pal on the expedition. The third was Lyonya Chumachenko, an ex-serviceman who had lived in Odessa and considered himself a connoisseur of fine food and ladies. Children of the Moscow intelligentsia, Ladonin and I shared a curiosity about the neglected urban culture of the Russian provinces. For Govorukhin, who came from a smaller town farther away from Moscow, Kursk was impressive for what it had to offer: several universities, a symphony orchestra, museums. Chumachenko was only interested in finding a restaurant to "rub elbows with Europe," as he put it. He quickly polled passers-by and led us to an old hotel with an empty dining room. Vanya Govorukhin peeked inside and refused to go in, opting to tour yet another former monastery. The hotel dining room had retained some of its pre-Revolutionary gubernatorial glamour, although the menu was typically bare, save for consommé and fried pike-fish with potatoes. The three of us celebrated a temporary return to civilization, washing down the food with some vile port. I was sad to leave Kursk and vowed to return there some day and spend more time wandering its rutted, verdant streets, and enjoying the brightest-colored lemon ice in all of Russia. . . .

From Kursk we traveled to the Voroshilovgrad (now Lugansk) Province of Ukraine. We were taking what seemed like a bit of a detour on the map: instead of driving directly south from Kursk, we first headed east as far as the outskirts of Voronezh. Voronezh was another prominent city of the Black Soil belt. Osip Mandelstam had been exiled there in 1934–37 and immortalized the city in his "Voronezh Notebooks." Voronezh was also the birthplace of Andrey Platonov, one of my favorite fiction writers of the twentieth century. But there was no time for a stop in the city, the alcoholic bus driver announced, and we only made a pit stop before reaching Voronezh, in a village with a melodic name, Devitsa, which means "maiden" in Russian. At Voronezh the Don still looked quite narrow, a maiden stream rather than the matronly river I had been imagining from the Don Cossack lore. We turned south and spent the night in the sandy valley of a withered stream, its banks grown with crooked pines. This was in the Bobrov District, not far from where, one month later and already on the way back to Moscow, our expedition would have its last principal stop. We had pitched our tents late at night in a glen, under pouring rain, and the next morning someone, perhaps a local person we encountered, mentioned that we had just slept on the ground with a residue of radioactive rain caused by Chernobyl's plume. The mood became somber at the breakfast table, but we were young and unwilling to give in to ominous warnings. I stood up and announced that in Moscow I had grown up next door to the Institute of Atomic Energy, and look—I still had two legs and one head. It was a stupid and careless joke, but it brightened the spirits as we prepared to continue on our journey.

Just shy of scraping the easternmost tip of Ukraine, we crossed the Russian Federation border at Chertkovo and pitched our tents. Melovoye, the nearby district center on the Ukrainian side, got its name for the area's principal natural attraction, mounds of chalk (chalk is *mel* in Russian). My journal entries from this stop give a detailed account of the natural environs:

> 19 June 1986. Our camp 10 kilometers from Melovoye, in a low-lying area in the Streletskaya Steppe.[12] All around us are mounds, the chalk baring its deadly pallor; the steppe looks scorched—chess squares of fescue, little wild-apple trees gone wild, their carmine leaves all covered in with webs. . . . From behind a mound the steppe's low sky juts out. And early on in the evening, a lemon-yellow moon smolders over a crushed sky. A mound of beastly, desperately sweet wild strawberries, crimson and whitish; in the steppe, yellow and lemony [plants] with a fine, fruity scent: feather grasses, thistles, saw-worts, tenderly pink with a pastry-shop smell, waxen flowers of Jerusalem sage, artemisia, a whole wild world of scents. To lie down in the grass and remain there— a grasshopper. To propel yourself above tall grass like a dragonfly with

---

12. Streletskaya Steppe is a section of the Lugansk (Luhansk) Nature Reserve with the characteristic habitat of middle steppe grasslands.

smoky wings, like a tiger butterfly or a bee; to buzz like a yellow mos-
quito-giraffe—to vanish in Henry Rousseau's grass jungle like a pan-
ther ant, an antelope wasp. . . . *Baibaks*—steppe marmots—a civilization.
Idea for a book about a search for their hidden civilization. . . . Steppe
marmots are red-straw-brown, very emotional, furtive; with curiosity
they peer at the people in the bus and run off when the people get closer
to their holes. They resemble people: eyes burning, hiccupping, chuck-
ling and whistling. Yellow and lemon cornflowers smell of orchard and
refuse to fade under Anastasia's pillow. Chalk mound, belemnites and
ammonites. Growing right over the precipice are small half-withered
purple thyme plants; they give out a spellbinding, enticingly sweet
smell—no wonder they grow over the precipice—precipice of life, of
fate. . . . St. John's wort—king of the grasses, gold of the grasses, mead
of the grasses; stems like strings. . . . Tea with the music of grassland.

We were in Ukraine, but I didn't get much of a sense for the local
color. Melovoye was too close to the Russian border, and the only thing
that distinguished the Russian language spoken here was the use of *he*,
a Ukrainian glottal fricative instead of the standard Russian *g*, a velar
plosive. Of all the stations of our expedition route, this one focused the
most on nature and the least on culture. An organic experience, one might
call it. We didn't even go into Melovoye, whose claim to fame was a sunflower oil factory. In addition to excursions to a local nature reserve and
to climbing chalk mounds and collecting belemnites, or "devil's fingers," I
remember two things most vividly. One was the anxious courtship of the
marmots on the nearby mounds. The other was an overgrown orchard of
sour cherries, which we pillaged and then sat in front of our tents, relaxing and gorging on bucketfuls of the small scarlet berries bursting with
sour liquid. Our bodies craved vitamins after weeks of subsisting mainly
on grains. Our bodies also craved other things, and a couple could walk
for half a mile, get over a chalk mound, enter the steppe, and disappear
amid its tall scented grasses. After consuming hundreds of sour cherries
our mouths were dry with desire and tasted of summer languor. At sunset our camp looked emptier than usual, and this dissonant entry from
my journal hints at a rendezvous having gone sour:

20 June 1986. Chameleon sunset instantly responds to moonlight. A huge moon—full and alive, like an eye. The sunset is now reluctant to talk, now rattling off, now rustling its lips, now screaming. Steppe marmots listen to the sunset. The crows here are vultures. Flying low. . . . The evening heals one's thoughts, sharpens one's thoughts. Glowworms are unpleasant-looking. Larvae—beauty and ugliness both together. Where's the boundary between those things? In general, where's the boundary . . . ?

I never got to see the great city of Rostov-on-Don: we turned east about a hundred miles north of it and made an overnight stop near the town of Morozovsk. A perfunctory entry records some impressions of the long drive from Melovoye to Proletarsk, the site of our encampment in the area of southern arid steppe:

22 June 1986. Departing for Proletarsk. The river Seversky Donetsk— town of Kamensk-Shakhtinsky—the highway to Volgograd—town of Belaya Kalitva. Fields of corn and wheat. *Cerapadus* growing—hybrid of sour cherry (*Cerasus*) and birdcherry (*Padus*), selected by Michurin.[13] Its pits contain bombs of the poisonous prussic acid. The landscape is boring and monotonous—field after field, occasional strips of forest and fruit orchards . . . rich lands, one can tell right away. A memorial rally in the town of Morozovsk: June 22.[14] Slogan: "For the beloved Motherland / Committing acts of glory / The village for the city, / The city for the village." . . . Stopping for the night in a cornfield outside Morozovsk . . . next to currant shrubs.

Still on the way to Melovoye we had already crossed into the historic territory of the Don Cossacks. But now, as we traversed the Rostov Province from northwest to southeast, diagonally across, moving in the direction of Kalmykia, Astrakhan, the Volga delta, and the Caspian Sea, we found ourselves in the heart of what had once been the Don Cossack Host. (Later, on the way back from the Caucasus, we would pass through

---

13. Ivan V. Michurin, a famous Russian selectionist and pomologist.

14. Commemorating the day of the Nazi invasion of the Soviet Union on 22 June 1941.

the historic territory of the Kuban Cossack Host along the Kuban River valley.)

The Cossacks held a special place in the Russian cultural imagination: riders and frontiersmen, loyal servants of the czar and dispersers of student and workers' protests in Russian cities. The Cossack lands were both Russian and un-Russian. The Russian word *kazak* (Cossack) is actually of Turkic origin and means "free man." Formerly professional warriors, the Cossacks had settled on the southern frontiers of the Russian state, establishing themselves in the very steppe region we were now studying. The Don gave its name to Don Cossacks, one of the two original groups. Their origins were still disputed: descendants of Kurgan people or even Khazars; runaway peasant serfs; a hodgepodge of ethnicities and backgrounds finally mortared together by their spoken language (Russian), faith (Orthodoxy), and mission (border guards). As Russia expanded its territory, the Cossacks moved south toward North Caucasus and the frontier of the Ottoman Empire and Persia, and later as far east as Siberia and the Far East. They split into further groups around the new areas of settlement, often taking their names from the areas' rivers. In Imperial Russia, the Cossacks enjoyed privileges in exchange for service in special regiments.

One of my classmates, Sergei Khudoleyev, came from the Kuban Cossack town of Nevinnomyssk, close to Stavropol and the foothills of the Caucasus. Even though his hometown was still some four hundred miles away, Khudoleyev, a soft-spoken fellow, became animated as the word "Cossack" reverberated through our bus. He stood at the helm of the bus, next to the red-faced driver already dying for his first glass of rotgut even though it was barely past noon, and gave all of us a crash course in Cossack history. Smiling bitterly, Khudoleyev unpacked some of the Soviet-era pseudonyms of the towns we would pass, revealing their former Cossack names. Like the other army veterans among my university classmates, Khudoleyev tended to overuse the collective mode and the "we" pronoun. I never felt integrated into the various types of "we" or "us" that claimed me as their own: the students, the expedition members, the Russians, the Soviets. We had already left behind the Tsimlyansk Reservoir (Sea of Tsimlyansk), stretching north and east to link up with the Volga–Don Canal and take in the Volga waters at Volgograd. Outside Tsimlyansk we passed the vineyards where the champagne of the Don is produced. As we crossed the Don at the town of Volgodonsk and drove along the Sal, one of the Don's eastern tributaries, I noticed that the "we" in Khudoleyev's speech had gained a different significance, not "we the veterans" or "we the expedition members" or even "we" the Russians. It was now "we" the Cossacks. I had been aware, mainly from reading Tolstoy's *The Cossacks: A Caucasus Tale*, of the extent to which the Cossacks had historically cultivated a sense of their non-Russianness and disparateness. The change I now observed in the way Khudoleyev perceived and expressed himself stirred up my own sense of distinctness. Around me were former Cossack towns and villages with Soviet names, and yet Jewishness mysteriously flowed back into my thoughts, seeking an outlet for expression.

By the middle of the afternoon, we had reached the town of Proletarsk, a district center in the southeastern part of the Rostov Province. Here, on the shores of the Proletarsk Reservoir, we planned to stay for four days, exploring arid steppes and semi-deserts. Proletarsk was a dusty town all but bypassed by the broad stride of Soviet history. Formerly a Cossack settlement (*stanitsa*), Proletarsk had buried its regal name, Velikoknyazheskaya (literally, "town of the Grand Prince"), in the battle-fields of the Revolution and Russian Civil War. Only downbeaten country roads led to Proletarsk. There was a gas station, but no hotel or hospital. Train tracks linked Proletarsk with large Russian cities: Volgograd to the northeast, Rostov-on-Don to the northwest, and Krasnodar to the southwest; and the trains' fretful hooting reminded the townies of faraway places they would never see. News of the arrival of Moscow students spread like wildfire through this "town of proletarians"; the local belles put on their best sundresses and strolled outside the town's post office, where our letters, addressed *poste restante*, awaited collection.

For the purposes of our expedition, Proletarsk had nothing but its location going for it. It stood near the northern shore of the long Proletarsk Reservoir, itself part of a series of waters stretching for several hundred miles and linking up the Don with the saltwater, miraculously shallow Manych-Gudilo Lake in Kalmykia. Staying at Proletarsk, one felt a nearness of boundaries, both natural and cultural. We were only a hundred fifty miles from the Kuma-Manych Depression, which naturally separates Europe and Asia, extending from Kalmykia down to the foothills of the Caucasus. Down below, on the other side of the Proletarsk Reservoir, lay the arid Salsk Steppe, once known for robust, durable horses. To the east and south of us was Kalmykia, an autonomous republic populated by Oirat people of West Mongolian origin, who had brought with them Tibetan Buddhism and echoes of the legacy of Genghis Khan. The landscape that revealed itself to us as we drove out of Proletarsk consisted of tracts of dry fescue-feather grass steppe and of semi-desert-like areas. Our column stopped right at the shore of the reservoir. Buff egrets stood guard in their reed sentry boxes, and there was a warm and tangible smell of salt in the air.

"Water, water! Let's go! Hurray!" Out of the uncorked bus we rushed to the end of the reservoir, men ripping off their shirts. We hadn't had a shower or swim since Kursk. "Return to the buses immediately. First we need to unload the trucks and set up. It's an order!" In vain the director tried to hold us back, delivering his operatic admonitions through a loudspeaker. There was no stopping fifty young men and women from jumping into the water and frolicking. It was one of those moments during the expedition when I felt a oneness with my mates, all of us behaving like grown-up children united in horseplay, screaming delightful obscenities. Finally, after the director promised us a day of rest, we returned to the trucks and went about our camp duties. After the tents were pitched and the kitchen and washing area set up, several of us found an old dingy lying on the shore, plugged up the holes as well as we could, dug up some greenish worms, and sent two men to procure fish. At dusk they returned with the catch—two pails full of crucian carp, lake perch, tench, and roach. After dinner, which mainly consisted of rice gruel, a fish fry was quickly organized. Two people gutted the fish, two others scaled them and washed them in a scratched enamel basin. I volunteered to do the frying. I had two cast-iron skillets each firing up on two bricks over embers from the campfire. Two girls were helping me by dipping the fish in salt mixed with flour. I would pour sunflower oil on the pan, throw in one or two whole fish, wait for one side to turn golden-brown and crusty and flip the fish over. All the while, somebody would hold a flashlight over my hand, aiming at the skillets. It took almost an hour to fry up the entire catch, and by the time a group of us gathered around the campfire for fish and song, all the instructors and some of the students had already retired.

I had a classmate by the name of Vova Sakharovsky. He rarely let his guitar out of his embrace. A talented performer and bard, he entertained us often, usually at the end of the day, by the campfire. Sakharovsky sometimes performed *romansy* ("romances")—Russian love songs infused with Gypsy cadences—in a duet with another classmate, Yulia I. That first night in Proletarsk, after we had gorged on fried fish and washed it down with weak swampy tea, the two of them sang from their usual repertoire of *romansy*—"The Campfire," "Dark Eyes," "The Gate." They took a break, and Sakharovsky laid his trusty guitar on his knees. I happened to be sitting next to him. I can't quite explain what force pushed me to pick up the guitar and to accompany myself, as I started singing: "Oseh shalom bimromav / Hu ya'aseh shalom aleinu / V'al kol Yisrael / V'imru, v'imru amen / Ya'aseh shalom, ya'aseh shalom / Shalom aleinu v'al kol Yisrael. . . ." I had picked up the lyrics and melody from my visits to the Moscow Synagogue. I knew, only vaguely, that the song was about praying and asking G-d—he who makes peace in heaven—to make peace for us here where we are and for all Jewish people. "Us" stood for Jews, and I sang a Jewish prayer to a group of my non-Jewish expedition mates under the glowing sky of the steppe by the rivers of Proletarsk.

"Could you translate, good pal?" asked none other than Sergei Khudoleyev, scion of a Cossack family.

"This is in Hebrew, the ancient Jewish tongue," I replied.

"I got that, but what is it about?" Khudoleyev pressed on.

"It's about a longing for one's homeland," I answered, a bit curtly.

The eyes of Inna Tolpeshta, a Ukrainian woman who hailed from Moldova, suddenly welled up with tears. No more questions followed. In fact, I was shocked how it had all come out and how the expedition director never reprimanded me for spreading "Zionist propaganda."

A journal entry from the first day at Proletarsk:

24 June 1986. Rest. A steppe viper snake, run over by a wheel, still alive, one meter long, fishnet body, lilac-gray-brown, oxblood spots, belly lighter and the color pattern paler; hanging on a steel wire. Everyone running to it; different opinions: let's kill it (a fat local boy with bright eyes); you can't kill snakes, they are useful; let's bury it in a hole, and make it deep; oh I feel bad for it, it's dying . . . ; a naturalist's dry silence (the mighty handsome Balandin[15] with dirty-blond hair and beard and blue eyes). . . . Digging the grave. The snake stares despondently, as if saying goodbye to everything. . . . At night, fried fish and fired up crawfish. Suddenly a turquoise-blue-milky area the size of two full moons, with a definite border, right in front of me bleeding over a quarter of the sky and then vanishing without a trace. At first very scary; in general, the elements overpower you, facing them one on one feels terrifying. . . . A sheep herd. A sheep farm. A dapple-gray stallion. The herdsman is bronze-faced, lean and muscular; pensive. The sheep herd like a single brain . . . moves across the steppe: head, eye, hand, phallus—a white horse with a rider's dark silhouette. I communicate with the herdsman almost entirely with hand gestures. An ornate lash. The stallion is like a rock. Trotting across a rivulet, past all the people, the campsite, the world, galloping. . . .

Riding horses in the wild fueled my imagination, and I was already carrying plans for a long narrative poem about the steppe. Two other strong impressions left a trace in my journal: visiting a local bookstore and seeing a salt marsh:

27 June 1986. Reyn[16] at the Proletarsk town bookstore, of the three copies I bought first one, then one more. Waxen white cherries. Dresses sold from a truck. Paper daises in the hair of a skinny high school senior. A *solonchak*[17]—first like water, a salt pond or a lake, a leaden surface, then

15. Sergei Balandin, who taught a field course in geobotany.

16. Evgeny Reyn, poet and screenwriter, see Chapter 6. Reyn's first collection, *Names of Bridges*, had been published in Moscow in 1984 and quickly sold out there.

17. *Solonchak*: a type of salinated soil with a crust of salt formed on top.

like snow, endless, pure white snow, crust, you feel like making snow-balls, rolling around in it, except your feet are getting bogged down.

It was a miracle of a bookstore, and I only wished I had more room in my backpack. My friend Max would have taken home the entire foreign literature section. So many titles that one couldn't get hold of in Moscow or Leningrad! And they clearly weren't in demand here. I bought a volume of Kafka and a stack of poetry collections, including one by my father's old friend Evgeny Reyn. And to counter this gift of culture, there was snow in the middle of a semi-desert, a crust of glimmering salt over this sensuous, un-Russian morass.

From Proletarsk we traveled to Northwest Caucasus, traversing the Stavropol Region, which sits atop the center of southern Russia like a molten church dome. West of Stavropol lay the Krasnodar Region with its double coast of the Sea of Azov and the Black Sea. On its northeast corner the Stavropol Region abuts the steppes of Kalmykia. East of where our expedition route traversed the Stavropol Region, lying in the foothills of the Caucasus was Russia's spa area with resorts historically developed around medicinal springs. Russian literary works about the conquest of the Caucasus, including Lermontov's *A Hero of Our Time*, abound in references to these spa towns. In them—especially in Pyatigorsk—civilians took the waters while wounded officers recuperated after having tasted the action on the Caucasus Line, throughout the 1820s to the 1860s. Just beyond the southern and southeastern border of the Stavropol Region there used to be the frontier between Russia and the yet-unconquered North Caucasus with its predominantly Moslem populations. Now the former frontier marked the northwestern boundaries separating the principal ethnic autonomous republics and enclaves of North Caucasus: Kara-chai-Cherkessia, Kabardin-Balkaria, North Ossetia, Chechen-Ingushetia, and Daghestan. It took the Russian Empire over half of the nineteenth century to colonize North Caucasus, and the Soviet Empire another half a century to contain the local unrest, but the legacy of resistance never died, especially in Chechnya.

One of my classmates, Akhmed, was a fierce, angry Chechen with a raven beard and unmastered Russian grammar. It had taken me two years to find a common language with him, both literally and figuratively. During the expedition, after a few clashes that nearly ended in fist fights, Akhmed had finally opened up to me, finally recognizing a Jew as a fellow alien. After that we spent quite of bit of time talking about his mountain village, family, and clan, and also about Israel, which he said he admired for its military might. Throughout this leg of the expedition, Akhmed served as my fist-clenched guide, telling me about the peoples and languages spoken in his Caucasus. In Akhmed, a native's protest against Russian domination clashed with North Caucasus traditions of hospitality, which had to be extended to individual visitors, however unwanted they might be.

But there was also the backdrop of Russian classical literature, in which privileged characters journeyed to North Caucasus, hoping to escape a life they had been destined to live. Over a decade after the 1986 expedition, I finally reread Tolstoy's *The Cossacks*, as I prepared to teach it, in English translation, to an audience of Boston College students. It was then that I fully appreciated Tolstoy's holographic depiction of leaving Russia and approaching the Caucasus. A wealthy Moscow playboy, Olenin, travels from Moscow to Stavropol more or less the way our expedition traveled there. Of his character's emotional state, Tolstoy wrote: "The further Olenin traveled from the center of Russia, the further removed from him seemed his memories, and the closer he got to the Caucasus, the lighter became his heart." Later Tolstoy reports Olenin's impressions: "Suddenly he saw, some twenty steps away, as it seemed to him at the first glance, pure-white enormities with their delicate contours and an ornate, distinct outline of their peaks and the distant sky." As I translate these lines, I recall my own expedition journey, and the sense of elation and wonderment I felt when seeing, from afar, the outlines of the ancient mountains.

My journal entries from the drive toward the foothills of the Caucasus are episodic, and I might have intended them as notes for future poems:

> 28-29 June 1986. The drive from Proletarsk to Teberda. Stopping for the night outside Stavropol. Eating mulberries in an orchard of an old man with teeth of steel. Rainbow roosters. . . .

On 29 June, lying under an alycha plum tree, I jotted down a whole poem, titled "Morning outside Stavropol." This unrhymed poem would later conclude my first poetry collection. Luxurious vegetation and southerly landscape evoked sensual thoughts, calling forth associations with the pleasures of serenity and rural beauty that are not attainable in Moscow. Here's a literal rendition of the third, shorter stanza: "And thyme is like a maelstrom / It smells of anything you want, / Of lemon and of cinnamon, / A smile dropped on the way,/ Steps of a moving train car, / A rainy Sunday, too, / A coffee shop in a passageway, / And a rose in the pale." In the conclusion of the poem I now hear something akin to a surrealist vision, which doesn't really surprise me, because the poem burst out from under my pen, hurrying to be set free: "And all of these analogies / Conflate into a melody/ Into cornflower threnodies / And stanzas of orache, / And the antler bug like a pendulum / Weighty he is and brassy, too, / And every hour he concludes / His daily chores and tasks, / While marking with a pungent smell / The foothills of a wild apple tree / Where transgressions ripen still / Living not by the clock." On rereading, the poem also makes me think of Henri Rousseau's paintings, which I had first discovered as a young boy, in my father's company, at the Pushkin Museum of Fine Arts in Moscow.

On the second day of the journey, North Caucasus opened before our eyes:

> The village of Tatarka on the road. Here the mountains begin. A donkey pulling a cart. Rider in a hat of soft felt. After Cherkessk: Ust-Dzheguta. . . . A dam on the Kuban river. [A banner]: "The waters of the Kuban river flow / Where the Bolsheviks command to go." After Ust-Dzheguta, three sources of Narzan mineral water—the most sulfurous, moderately sulfurous, the least sulfurous. . . . Aoul[18] Kumysh. Again the Kuban. A mustached sergeant and a woman wearing a gold headscarf (both dark) look with bemusement at our whole procession. . . . Fences made of natural limestone. A thread of a hanging bridge. A monastery

18. *Aoul*: a word in Turkic languages for "mountain village."

on the forehead of a mountain. . . . Karachaevsk. Women in orange skirts, dress coats, and snow-white nylons. A fat mustached Cherkess woman hangs over a balcony over the steep bank of the Kuban—probably waiting to be kidnapped.

By the afternoon of 29 June we arrived in Teberda, a town in the Karachai (southern) section of the Karachai-Cherkess Autonomous Province. Teberda was the place where Soviet lovers of downhill skiing would arrive before being transported further south, to the area of Dombai, a mountain peak and resort. In preparation for the week-long stay in the mountains outside Teberda, our teachers had been telling us how the Caucasus and the Alps were alike. They spoke about this with passion, even though not one of them, including our professor of geobotany, had been to the Alps. The week in the Caucasus was touted as the climax of our expedition, a chance to see for ourselves how changing climate conditions create altitudinal belts with their typical ecology. Natural wonders aside, for me the stop in Karachai-Cherkessia promised an opportunity to observe the workings of an amalgamated unit within the multiethnic and multireligious Caucasus.

The Karachais are a Turkic people and speak a Turkic language, Karachai-Balkar. With the neighboring Balkars they share both the language and the national symbol, Mount Elbruss. Most of the Karachais had been Sunni Muslims since after Tamerlan's (Timur's) invasion of the Caucasus. The Karachai lands were annexed by Russia in 1828, yet the Karachais continued to fight the Russians well into the 1860s. Some of the Karachai elders I saw in Teberda—and longevity into the nineties and hundreds was legendary in the mountains of the Caucasus region—remembered how in 1920 the Bolsheviks established the Karachai Autonomous enclave and soon merged it into an autonomous unit with the neighboring Cherkess lands to its north. The Karachais and the Cherkesses were unrelated ethnically or historically. Unlike the Karachai, the Cherkesses belong to the Northwest Caucasus ethnic group and speak a dialect of Kabardian, unrelated to the language spoken by the Karachai.

Throughout the Soviet years the province had changed its status and name several times. When I visited there in 1986, about 40 percent of the population were ethnic Russians, about 30 percent Karachai (or about 130,000) and only about 10 percent Cherkess, although the Karachai and Cherkess populations dominated in the rural areas, while other ethnicities also lived in Karachai-Cherkessia, including Abaza (Abazins), Nogais, and Ossetians. A visitor quickly learned that such conglomerations as Karachai-Cherkessia, effected against the will of the disparate ethnic groups, were Russia's way of quelling unrest and exerting control over the volatile North Caucasus. When I approached the locals in Teberda, some older people were willing to talk about their national tragedy. In 1942 the area was occupied by Nazi troops vying for control of the Caucasus and the Transcaucasian oil fields. In 1943, after the Soviet forces had cleared the area of the Nazis, the Karachais were accused of collaboration with the enemy. The Karachai civilian population—mostly the elderly, women, and children—were deported to Central Asia, while the Karachai men fought Hitler at the war fronts. About one third of some 70,000 Karachai deportees died within two years of exile, in what amounted to genocide. Stalin's plan was executed by organs of state security then headed by Lavrenty Beria, an ethnic Georgian like Stalin himself. In 1957, during Khrushchev's Thaw, the Karachais were "rehabilitated" and began to return to the native lands, which were once again co-opted into a Karachai-Cherkess Autonomous Province.

How does this place still function, I wondered, as I roamed the streets of Teberda. How had this bizarre product of Bolshevik rhetoric on nationalities survived after years of Stalinist repressions followed by decades of a status quo? We had pitched our tents on June 29, but I only got away to explore Teberda on the third day:

> 1 July 1986. Teberda. Men in the streets. Even mounted ones, with airs of self-importance. A fascinating fusion of civilization, urbanization, Russification, and tradition—things Cherkessian, wild, ancient. A velour sport coat on a mounted fellow; fishnet stockings on women. Cows with full udders weightily treading on construction sites, streets and lanes . . . Oriental-style coffee. Mustaches three-lips thick. "Mountain Air" Café.

Our camp sat on a large clearing in a mountain forest next to a stream. We did laundry by tying dirty clothes to a rope and releasing it into the swirling waters. To get to our campground from the outskirts of Teberda, one had to walk about two miles up a fairly steep and narrow road through a dense forest of beech, oak, spruce, and magisterial pines. Climate zones changed before one's eyes. I remember hearing from our geo-botany instructor that the firs here reached 200 feet—the tallest in Europe. In Europe? We were at the Caucasus, at the boundary of Europe and Asia.

The local forests were supposed to be rich in fauna, including bears and chamois goats. I lucked out by striking up a conversation with a game warden who came to fine our expedition for having damaged the road and the clearing:

> 2 July 1986. Game warden Vladimir Sh. of the Teberda Game Reserve. Game wardens have three stars on green boards. There are also senior wardens. Born in Yaroslavl, studied at Irkutsk Institute of Agriculture. . . . Six years at Teberda, then eleven years in the Altai Region. . . . In general [people who apply for warden's jobs] are attracted by romantic notions and don't realize the essence of the work. Difficult work, nerve-racking. Many violators, poachers. Locals kill *turs*,[19] just as they used to do. Here up to eighty different species sometimes roam together. Game wardens are armed with . . . hunting carbines; the commanding staff carry pistols. . . . He became a game warden, even though by training he's a chemical engineer, because "they've destroyed nature." A drinker's face, dark circles under his eyes. . . . In the reserve there are *turs*, bears, wild cats, ginseng, various rare trees and plants, birds—eagles, harriers.

Whether it was the pristine mountain air, or the altitude, or else being high on impressions, I distinctly remember requiring little sleep. At the Teberda stop, the nightly campfire sing-alongs lasted well past midnight. Amid waterfalls, mossy boulders, and ancient Nordmann's firs, summertime romance flared. We woke up at dawn, having only slept three or four hours.

---

19. *Tur*: a mountain goat-antelope found in the Caucasus.

The all-day ascent to the glacier started on July 6 at five in the morn-ing. As soon as we left the timberline, there were rhododendrons with blazing flowers everywhere. Only shrubs, and no longer any trees. Shrubs surrounded meadows, as if trying to contain them, and the meadows still looked more like flowering steppe than the Alpine meadows that I was about to see for the first time. As the ascent became steeper, we formed a single-person chain. Rocks fell from the baring slopes. We had no moun-tain-climbing equipment, no shoes with crampons. "Careful, you need to be 'on thou' with mountains," the expedition director announced through his throaty loudspeaker, but most of us ignored him. Only a couple of former paratroopers seemed to be taking heed. Snow-capped mountains beckoned from afar, and I experienced, for the first time ever, something akin to what petulant Alpinists probably feel as they brave the moun-tains—a soaring sensation of freedom enmeshed with a knowledge of liminality.

We approached a mountain stream propelling its way through the rockbed, banks grown with bright yellow flowers on tall malachite stems. We forded the stream, stepping from rock to rock while holding on to a makeshift rope handrail that the two biggest men in our group held from one bank, and two more from across the stream. Soon after that, we passed a glacial lake, one edge of it still frozen. The saturated aquamarine water made the lake look artificial, like a swimming pool. We made a pit stop in a flat area all grown in with the same, kinky yellow flowers. The geo-botanist identified them as *deviasil* (horse-heal), praising their medicinal properties. A portion was harvested and added to a growing regiment of folk remedies that we dried and maintained. Before the final section of the ascent our group took one more rest. I remember the words "closed zone" and "border patrol" burning the lips as they passed from one of us to the next. Who had started this? What sort of a "closed zone" and across what "border"? Not the foreign Turkey but "our" Georgia, a Soviet republic, lay across the main Caucasus ridge. What passes did the patrols guard? How could one "escape" across these unattainable peaks? And even if one did, wouldn't one just end up in Abkhazia, within Georgia? Yet the former servicemen, including my pals Khudoleyev and Chumachenko, nodded mysteriously, neither confirming nor denying the information. And the

Chechen Akhmed, a native of the Caucasus, only scratched his beard and grinned, grinned.

Finally we came up to the glacier, played a furious game of snowballs, and then ascended to a small plateau overlooking a gorge and a mountain pass. All around us, closer than ever, thick clouds were stacked upon toothy mountain peaks. We put down our backpacks and supplies and stood there, stretching and gaping. Before we started our descent, Lev Bogatyrev, our director, proposed a minute of silence for the climbers who had perished in the Caucasus. . . .

I write this on 22 August 2008, over twenty-two years after visiting North Caucasus. I haven't been able to write much for the past two weeks, since 8 August, the start of the Russian-Georgian hostilities over South Ossetia and Abkhazia. History itself seemed to be holding back my hands. A coincidence or a sign, but the Russian invasion gained speed as I tried to reconstruct the Caucasus leg of the 1986 summer expedition. Every morning for the past two weeks I have been poring over the coverage of South Ossetia and of Russian troops in Georgian Black Sea ports and on Georgian land. As I recalled standing in 1986 on the boundaries of a disjointed, often forcibly drawn political map of North Caucasus, I felt a wave of sadness and despair. I'm not interested in judging the rashness and opportunism of Mikhail Saakashvili, the Georgian president who is only a few months younger than I, and who grew up in Tbilisi just when I was growing up in Moscow. He and I come from the same Soviet generation; his father, like mine, is a physician. In our Soviet days, they used to refer to such families as Saakashvili's or mine as "the intelligentsia." Now, courtesy of Putin's oiled propaganda machine, Saakashvili was being vilified by the Russian media, by Russian journalists who would have been his peers—and mine—back in the Soviet 1970s and '80s. Instead of blaming on Saakashvili the faults and discontents of our ex-Soviet generation, I thought of a group of Moscow University classmates, among them sons of the Caucasus, resting after the ascent atop a mountain plateau. Young men and women from all over the former Soviet Union stood there silently taking in the mountains of Georgia. And I, too, stood and peered into the distant view as I recollected visiting Georgia as a young boy and loving her. . . .

In May and early June of 1977, I spent a month in Tbilisi. My father had been invited to Georgia to conduct collaborative research at Tbilisi's Institute of Vaccines and Serums, formerly the Institute of Bacteriophage. He arranged for me to skip the end of the school year and brought me along. We stayed in Adjaria Hotel, a modern high-rise named so after another autonomous region within the republic of Georgia. Father was spending mornings at the Institute, conducting experiments while also gathering material for a book about Félix d'Hérelle, the great French-Canadian microbiologist who worked in Tbilisi during two visits, in 1933-34 and 1934-1935. The liberal idealist d'Hérelle returned to Paris in 1935, contemplating a permanent move to the USSR. Then his Georgian disciple Georgy Eliava was arrested and purged by Beria, Stalin's associate and future head of the Soviet secret police. D'Hérelle never went back to the Soviet Union. Accounts of repressions against the Georgian intelligentsia during the 1930s fell under my father's double radar screen of medicine and literature as he interviewed eyewitnesses and survivors, gathering unpublicized evidence for *The French Cottage*, his book about d'Hérelle and Georgia. I was almost ten, an impressionable Jewish kid. I was spending a lot of time with my father's Georgian colleagues, going to the banquets and celebrations that my father's Georgian hosts threw in honor of the "dear Moscow professor." Georgians are renowned for their hospitality, princely feasts, and the art of toasting. Not infrequently, the subject of Stalin's legacy would come up in conversation. I remember quickly noticing that Stalin was still almost universally admired, despite his beastly crimes, while Beria, also an ethnic Georgian, was reviled and blamed for Georgia's misfortunes during the years of Stalinism.

When we visited Georgia in 1977, my father was at a doubly high point of his career, a senior research scientist and a member of the Union of Soviet Writers. And yet emigration was already on my parents' minds, as was the feeling that as Jews they could never break their professional glass ceilings. During the month we spent in Tbilisi, my father and I were taken around the country. Among other places, we visited the magnificent Alazan Valley, Georgia's wine country. A Jew visiting Georgia was immediately struck by the absence of tangible antisemitism, just as one would easily become aware of its endurance in Russia or Ukraine. To a

Russian-born Ashkenazi Jew, the experience of Georgian Jews was something quite incredible. Jews had been living in Georgian lands for over
two and a half millennia, perhaps since the captivity and exile to Babylonia. Georgian Jews were natives just as much as ethnic Georgians were.
We Ashkenazi Jews never had such a sense of roots in Eastern Europe,
and least of all in Russia. And of course, in terms of "street-borne" antisemitism, it was phenotypically hard to distinguish between the faces of
ethnic Georgians and Georgian Jews. In retrospect, I'm sure that not only
Georgian hospitality and abundant expression of feelings, but a sense of
Jewish rootedness in Georgia, had contributed to my falling in love with
the place. After visiting Georgia, I became the only kid in my Moscow
school who rooted for Dynamo Tbilisi rather than Moscow soccer teams
like the Central Army Club or Spartak. . . .

In Georgia, an unsteady armistice seems to be taking effect as I type
these unsure lines on 23 August 2008. It's Saturday morning, we're at my
parents' apartment in Brookline. We talk of Georgia constantly, my parents
and I, my wife and I. A column of Russian tanks is driving back into North
Ossetia. Yet ribbons of Russian troops remain in Georgia proper, both
inland and on the Black Sea coast. And Russia has recolonized Abkhazia
and South Ossetia, both of which had been parts of Georgia for many centuries. I understand the rage of the Georgians. I grew up thinking of the
Orthodox Christian Georgia as the friendliest nation to Russia in all of the
Caucasus. And now Russian planes bomb Georgian targets, setting the
protected Borzhomi forests on fire, destroying Georgian boats. How can I
possibly believe that Russia had been merely provoked in its aggression?
What a cruel and banal joke, blaming a victim for her own victimization.

As I excavated the memories of the 1986 summer visit to Karachai-
Cherkessia, the Georgian events of the past two weeks have made me
think about the two centuries of Russia's imperial game in the Caucasus. The czarist legacy of dividing and conquering, of pitting neighbors
against close neighbors of different ethnicity or religion, continued during the Soviet years. In order to wield more control over the Caucasus,
Stalin and his henchmen kept drawing and redrawing the map and exerting "punishment" on entire nations. The post-Stalinist Soviet leaders
never could set it right even as they repatriated and resettled the deported

Karachais, Balkars, Chechens, and Ingushes. Ethnic disputes, such as the one between the Ingushes and North-Ossetians or between Abkhazians and Georgians, lingered well into the 1980s when I visited the Caucasus. Numerous Caucasus tensions burst through the banners of friendship among Soviet nations, revealing the legacy of Russian imperial domination. Yet I couldn't imagine in 1986 that only a few years later the Caucasus region would once again erupt with conflict and war—in Chechnya, Abkhazia, South Ossetia. Nor could I see in my wildest dreams that Putin's Russia would be massacring Georgia in 2008, under the pretext of protecting South Ossetia. But I observed that ethnic Georgians were sometimes collectively blamed for the misfortunes that had befallen the people of North Caucasus in Stalin's time. Here's an entry from my expedition journal, penned the day before the departure from Teberda:

> 7 July 1986. An old Karachai man at a bus stop in Teberda: jackboots, black riding pants, black coat, black peaked cap, unshaven; white pockmarks on his chestnut face, a very stiff, walrus-like mustache, also gray, wrinkles run off like rays of an electric field from a charge; crafty, clever eyes, young, even with a glint of malice. A stick in his hand. Conversation with an old Nogai[20] man: Comrade Iosif Vissarionovich Stalin populated Karachai-Cherkessia with Georgians up to 40 percent and exiled the Karachais to Tashkent, Dushanbe, Frunze, and so forth. And there was also Lavrenty Pavlovich Beria—oh, this one was the most cunning Mengrel[21] in the world, and they were right to execute him. . . .

We were leaving Northwest Caucasus on June 8 and traveling to the Russian coast of the Black Sea. A direct route would have taken us across the Main Ridge down to the sea, and then up the maritime highway along the Abkhazian coast, past Sochi. But the route over a mountain pass wasn't available to our expedition column of buses and trucks, and

---

20. Nogai: ethnic group with a spoken Turkic language, living mainly in Russia (Daghestan Autonomous Republic) and Turkey.

21. Mengrels: one of the three principal subethnic groups of the people of Georgia. Beria was an ethnic Georgian, as was Stalin, born Dzhugashvili.

we took a long detour, first driving north past Stavropol and then going northeast and southwest through the Krasnodar Region. In some ways, departing from the mountains of the Caucasus and heading for the Black Sea accorded a sense of relief, of leaving behind someone else's strife. Such was the mood of my notes from the day of departure:

> 8 July 1986. Departure from Teberda. . . . A memorial museum of the defense of the Caucasus mountain passes. The first item on exhibit is a newspaper with the printed text of the radio address of 3 July [1941] and a large photograph [of Stalin], waist up, half-page. The guide, a Georgian woman, explains: "[This is] Comrade Stalin's speech." . . . Town of Armavir. Open-air market. Cherries strung on a stick. Motley folk costumes. Ice-cold apricot juice. An Armenian concession-stand-keeper with wilting eyes. In a smoky cafeteria, young chickens for take-out. Life goes on. Apricots are for sale. Rain falls on the fields . . . Stopping for the night some 70 kilometers from Kropotkin in a recently worked field. Apricot trees. Nectar. Sunset glow over the field. Fields of sunflowers and corn. You enter a field of sunflowers. . . .

The route from Karachai-Cherkessia took us through the western corner of the Stavropol Region over the Kuban River into Kropotkin, a town named after the great theorist of anarchic communism, Prince Pyotr Kropotkin. By the second day of the journey we had measured the whole girth of the Krasnodar Region:

> 9 July 1986. Passing the towns of Novo-Kubansk, Kropotkin (all covered in dust), *stanitsa* Tbilisskaya[22]—the Tbilissky administrative district—ha-ha-ha. Ust-Labinsk. A pit stop. Food store and bazaar. Pirozhki with sour cherries fifteen kopeks apiece. Melons by the roadside beyond Krasnodar—some lady gave us a few for free. The Sea of Kuban.[23] Town of Teuchezhsk. Goryachy Klyuch.[24]

---

22. *Stanitsa*: historically a Cossack town or big village; Tbilisi is the capital of Georgia, and this town in the Kuban region humorously points to the name of the Georgian city.

23. Krasnodar Reservoir: a large artificial reservoir.

24. In a literal translation, the name of this town means "hot spring."

After Goryachy Klyuch, it was straight down to the coast and then another hour along the maritime highway, before we came to Pshada, a small inland town about twenty-five miles down the coast from the resort of Gelendzhik. During the week we spent at the Black Sea I didn't make a single diary entry. This gap owes itself to several circumstances. Even though we still adhered to a schedule of lectures and digs, the Black Sea stop was a time of respite and relaxation, and I must have taken a break from chronicling or note-taking for future poems. The week at the Black Sea was also the culmination of a love adventure with an elusive classmate by the name of Anastasia. It was going absolutely nowhere, we both knew, and had no future in Moscow. Anastasia came from a Soviet diplomatic family and I surmised—she was reticent—that she had spent part of her childhood in East Germany. Once Anastasia alluded to having gone, with her parents, to a nudist beach on the Baltic Sea. I think she surmised—without asking questions—that I was from a refusenik family. Anastasia was smart, prankish, and open-minded. She was almost six feet tall—my height. Short-haired, slender, and blonde, she looked Scandinavian and sported lowcut summer outfits, braless and backless. Like some other members of Soviet golden youth I had met, Anastasia was sardonically contemptuous of the system. What was she doing in the School of Soil Science? She despised our expedition living, the dirt, the collectivism, acting in every way as though she were an inmate on route to penal servitude. She wore long dresses to supper and stared, with horror, at rusty-red stewed pork or khaki pea soup. Lying out in the sun and smoking was, perhaps, her greatest pleasure throughout the two months of the journey. Sometimes I shared Anastasia's solitude. We would sneak out of the camp—into the steppe or a mountain forest, later to a pebbly deserted beach. Once, both of us exhausted after an all-day ascent to the mountains, we tried to make love in Anastasia's tent but had to halt after one of her tentmates woke up and cried out, "Is someone here?" I crawled out before the roommate had time to reach for a flashlight. Anastasia and I knew that romance together, even under the most discreet of terms, was limited by the duration of the expedition. So the more delicious the adventure, and especially its last two weeks, right on the razor's blade of time.

We were staying near the village of Beregovoe in the valley of the Pshada River, which carries water from the foothills of the Caucasus to the Black Sea. Our camp was only a couple of miles from the coast, a lovely walk on a path of reddish clay. Around us were hills or low mountains covered with indigenous subtropical forest, sections of it under preservation. Where we were, the coast was not built up or developed; the beach was uncrowded as compared to the way I remembered from visiting Black Sea resorts as a child. There were a couple of shashlyk booths run by Armenian men in white shirts who acted like owners of big restaurants someplace in Miami or Los Angeles, and no changing cabins or benches. At the entrance to the beach, a handful of old local ladies in faded skirts and untucked blouses offered their wares—fruit, tomatoes, scallions and radishes, sunflower seeds by the glassful, and chunks of *salo* (salty pork) with red-peppery rinds. On our third day at the Black Sea, a group of guys got away to suntan on the rocks. We lay there naked, eating acromegalic peaches and tomatoes and slabs of salt pork that my pal Lyonya Chumachenko bought from an old Ukrainian lady. We stretched out side by side on the rocks, trading half-fictionalized accounts of romantic conquest. Upon arrival to Pshada I found an illuminated letter from my best friend Max. It was waiting for me, *poste restante*, and contained news of our circle of friends. Inserted in the letter was a drawing of Max as a bespectacled jack rabbit ravaging a naked woman.

Although presently in the Krasnodar Region, that part of the Black Sea coast hadn't become Russian territory until the 1830s. There had once been a small Greek outpost at Gelendzhik, and the area north of Colchis was known to ancient Greeks as Zygii. Ancient Pontus was across the Black Sea in modern-day Turkey; the coast of ancient Colchis was some two hundred miles down the coast in modern-day Georgia. Anastasia and I strolled under seaside groves. I treated her to shashlyk and then read my poems to her. We stood on the edge of the pebbly beach and imagined the Argonauts sailing across the "hospitable" Euxine in search of the Golden Fleece. We closed our eyes and tried to lose ourselves in history—far outside of Soviet time.

The day before leaving Pshada, and the Black Sea was filled with performances and celebrations. Our director Bogatyrev, obsessed as he was with singing in public, had arranged for a group of us to give a midday concert at a nearby workers' vacation home. In exchange for our entertainment, we were given a hot lunch at the refectory—slabs of tomatoes and cucumbers, rye bread, a rich spicy soup with rice and lamb, *kotlety* (Russian pan-fried burgers) with mashed potatoes, and a classic Soviet compote made of dried pears and prunes. Fortified after weeks of the leanest of diets, we went to perform at an open-air stage to a grateful audience of vacationing miners and millhands, local old ladies gnashing sunflower seeds, and two African students in plaid shirts. Bogatyrev sang *romansy* from the classical repertoire, then a timid blonde classmate of mine recited a selection of love poems by Sergei Esenin, who is universally admired all across Russia. After that, a chorus of five girls and I performed songs from postwar Soviet movies to the accompaniment of the baby accordion I had bought back in Krapivna, at the beginning of the expedition. The audience especially enjoyed hearing the song "The Daisies Have Hidden . . ." from the film *My Street*, and old ladies hummed all along. There was also a juggling number, a parodic Gypsy dance to a strumming, plaintive guitar, and then Bogatyrev returned to the stage, this time for a round of Soviet oldies from the 1950s. He usually concluded such performances, but this time he put me on the spot, announcing that "now Max Shrayer will sing in English for our African friends." I considered doing "Yesterday" but was a bit unsure of the chords. Instead, I performed "My Bonnie Lies Over the Ocean . . . ," which I had known since grade school and learned to play during the expedition. The two African students, who turned out to be Kenyans attending a university at Krasnodar, came up to shake my hand and thank me, in English.

In the evening, as had been the tradition of the Caucasus *zonalka*, we had a celebratory dinner and skits. One of my classmates, Alevtina Zayats, came from the Gelendzhik area and somehow arranged for a collective farm to sell us twenty or thirty plucked chickens at cost. They were spiced and roasted, and Bogatyrev also made an exception by buying carboys of cheap red wine with our contingency funds. Even though ahead of us lay another week of travel and one more major stop, we toasted the conclusion of the expedition. I sat by the fire, hand coasting the hem of Anastasia's skirt. I sipped sour red wine and thought of the nearing return to reality.

On July 17 we left the Black Sea and traveled, with an overnight stop somewhere north of Rostov-on-Don, to the eastern corner of the Voronezh Province. Throughout the expedition we would spend long hours on the bus, especially when we were making blitz-drives between major sites. For instance, between Pshada in Krasnodar Province and Khrenovoye in Voronezh Province we covered some 500 miles, and later, from Khrenovoye to Moscow, another 350 miles with just an overnight stop. By the standards of Soviet road travel at the time, these were supreme distances. There was only so much sightseeing one could do through dusty or mud-splattered windows. While in transit on the bus, I would catch up on sleep and reading. And I spent a lot of time chatting with my bus- and tent-mate Vanya Govorukhin. Son of an agriculture correspondent for a regional paper, Vanya came from Chkalovsk, a town outside the great city of Nizhny Novgorod (Gorky) on the Volga. Vanya and I had always been friendly, but we didn't bond until the expedition. We were very different, Vanya and I. He was a provincial to boot in everything—his store-bought clothes, his respect for the letter of the newspaper, his greasy dark-brown curls and pocket sewing kit, his abiding practicality, his insatiable desire to see everything for himself and to know the greater world. He was a fine chess player and did advanced math in his head. Poetry wasn't his thing, but he did harbor a special feeling for the workers of word.

Was it a mere force of circumstance that brought me and Vanya together? Or it could be that at one point or other, each inner Pierre Bezukhov encounters his own Platon Karataev. In volume three of *War and Peace*, Pierre leaves the house of his spiritual leader, the mason Bazdeev. Moscow has fallen to Napoleon's troops, and Pierre, disguised as a commoner, plans to assassinate Napoleon and save Russia. He gets arrested and taken prisoner by the French. In a prisoner camp outside Moscow, he meets a slightly effeminate, charismatic peasant by the name of Karataev. Platon Karataev has the same first name as the ancient philosopher, and he takes Bezukhov under his wing. Vanya Govorukhin was my Platon Karataev during the expedition. It's not a likeness of my condition to that of the aristocratic Pierre that intrigues me. During the expedition, I wasn't feeling lost or experiencing spiritual turmoil. And yet, like Karataev in Tolstoy's novel, Vanya compulsively offered me the wisdom of his Russian heart. He had a superior knowledge of provincial life, a knowledge which extended to all spheres of existence, from the most mundane issues, such as procuring a bar of soap in a small town where we made a rest stop, to the loftier ones, such as persuading an old cantankerous guard to let us see a museum during the lunch hour. He knew a great deal about things I knew nothing about. He taught me how to tie knots and to sharpen a penknife against the nether side of a belt and then to use the knife's blade as a shaving razor. His backpack was full of useful trinkets and contained a portable apothecary. He was a master of folk medicine and of fixing broken radios. His was, predictably, a storage box of trivia, from soccer scores to names of generals on both the Soviet and the Nazi side.

Vanya was bashful around girls, unprepared even to discuss women in men's company. When prodded or teased, Vanya would utter a sheepish laugh and try to change the subject—to chess, weather, or geography. A few times, later at night, when I crawled into the tent after having been out with Anastasia, Vanya would unclasp his moth-like eyelids and whisper, "Maxim, I worried about you." He might have been simply inexperienced, perhaps still a virgin. Or else. . . . He was sensitive and tactful, and I think he trusted me like a true friend. To this day I feel bad about not having told him I was a refusenik. I kept thinking of telling him during the last week of the expedition, but I couldn't, I just couldn't. And then the journey ended, I went to Pärnu with my parents, Vanya went home to Chkalovsk. The following October he was drafted into the army. He submitted with a Russian peasant's trust in Divine will, without even trying to get a deferral. We didn't have a chance to say goodbye. I was busy with my Moscow life and all its public and private orbits; Vanya had receded into the past along with the memories of the expedition, which I wouldn't revisit for over two decades, until I began to write this chapter.

What I experienced—and remembered—best in Vanya Govorukhin was that particular type of Russian ingenuity that cultivates an accepting way of looking at the world. Vanya's acumen, practicality, and street-smartness were coupled with a non-confrontational demeanor. Specifically, he never discussed the Soviet regime, never told political jokes, never commented on the poverty and backwardness of some of the areas we visited. Even if provoked by other classmates, he sidestepped

political debates—be it about Stalinism or Brezhnevism. I could tell that
Vanya was shocked when I sang in Hebrew at the campfire in front of
our classmates. Indeed, politics and Jewishness were outside the circle
of our daily conversations, our many hours of conversations on the bus
while in transit. I remember this well because of the two forbidden books
I was reading during the expedition. One was a wry literary critique of
the Soviet Bloc, the other a Jewish love story set on the eve of the Shoah. I
never got to tell Vanya about my reading; he sensed something forbidden
and asked not.

Both books were carefully wrapped in newsprint, for preservation
and to conceal their covers. Both were English translations, and the origins of the authors lay within the confines of what in 1986 was the Eastern
Bloc. A visiting American couple had given us these books not long before
I took them on the road. One was *Shosha* by Isaac Bashevis Singer, and the
novel transported me to the pre–World War II Jewish Warsaw. Hasidic
Jews were only vaguely known to me at the time, and I must have been
reading Singer less as fiction or poetry of imagination and more as history or truth. It was a novel about the destroyed world of East European
Jewry. I read *Shosha* as a nineteen-year-old refusenik on a bus traversing
the plains of Southern Russia, without being able to share my impressions;
the place and manner of reading made the sense of Jewish loss ever more
acute. The other paperback was *The Unbearable Lightness of Being* by Milan
Kundera. I have since re-read the novel a number of times while teaching it to American college students. I'm a forty-something expatriate as
I write these lines, the Eastern Bloc is no more, and the novel no longer
excites me the way it did when I read it for the first time as a Soviet university student. Back in 1986 I read Kundera's novel as the manifesto of an
Eastern Bloc artistic intellectual. I felt that Kundera had given his reader
a grammar of life in which sexually immoral conduct often stood in for
political protest against the totalitarian system. At the time, I could have
signed my name under each page describing the thoughts of the main
character, the Czech surgeon Tomáš. In many ways Tomáš's thoughts of
the totalitarian world—of love and sex, of art and music, conformism and
dissent—were also my thoughts. I could have sworn by Kundera's book,
and yet I couldn't even share my reaction with anyone around. . . .

On the afternoon of 19 July 1986, about fifty miles south of Voronezh, we turned off the highway connecting Rostov and Voronezh and drove east on a poor country road. We left behind Bobrov, a district center where trains made a quick stop before heading east toward Saratov and the Volga. Then we turned onto a dirt road. Beating out clouds of dust, our expedition column proceeded for another two miles until we almost drove into a fenced-off pasture. The pasture belonged to the Khrenovoye Horse Farm. On the edge of a pine grove, we raised our tents and assembled the field kitchen. A southerly wind carried a faint smell of resin to our nostrils. Red-capped boletus mushrooms grew abundantly near the campsite, promising to supplement our scanty diet. There was something inexplicably peaceful in the air, something enthralling in the fields heaving beyond the rickety fences. After breathing the dry aroma of this motherly Russian summer, one wanted to lie supine under the sheltering hands of old pines or disappear in nearby glens and pastures.

I had been looking forward to coming to Khrenovoye for two reasons, both having to do with horses and horseback riding. Some time in the fall of my sophomore year, in fact not long before my father's persecution had intensified, he told me about a new patient, a woman in her forties who suffered from bad hypothyroidism. A former jockey, she worked as a coach at the Moscow Race Track. My father, who had ridden horses when he was a young boy evacuated to a remote Uralian village during World War II, and later as a military doctor in Belarus, was intrigued by his new patient. In a couple of months, when she was feeling better and came to thank my father, armed with a token bottle of Armenian cognac, she also offered to get my father a pass to ride horses. He said he was too old for trotting, but suggested me instead. The Moscow Race Track had a school with serious students preparing for a career in riding, and also some open hours for amateurs. In theory, after taking a few paid lessons one could show up at a designated box office, purchase a ticket for a session of riding, and go around a smaller track with a trainer and seven or eight other riders. In practice, as I was soon to discover, the tickets were hardly ever available to the general public. Several horses always seemed to be reserved for foreign diplomats and their families; tickets were distributed through the back door. My father's patient first had one of her professional students show me how to saddle a horse and also how to clean and brush it. After lessons in the stable I was allowed to get on a horse for the first time. The riding coach arranged for me to come once a week and get my entrance slip in the back room of the ticket office. The race track was located near Begovaya (literally, "Racing") Metro station, just two Metro stops from where I lived. I usually went there on Saturdays, riding boots and whip in a rucksack over my shoulder. I would bring chopped carrots and sugar cubes wrapped in a napkin. In the winter the stables were dank and cold, milky bands of human breath mixing in with horse breath. Throughout the school year, at least two Saturdays every month, I would spend part of the afternoon at the riding school. Trotting would get boring, but it was exciting to go alone into the murky stable, greet a horse and saddle it, and then to lead it into daylight. Horses were perfect—wise, humble, patient, forgiving of our mistakes. Riding horses also boosted my chivalrous confidence. In my circle of friends, I was the only one to have been in the saddle.

At the racetrack I had heard of the Khrenovoye Stud Farm in connection with the famed Orlov *rysaks*—Russian trotters with extra-long shins. There were several of them in the riding school's stables. Retired from professional racing and the crowds, these veteran fast trotters now entertained mustached Latin American diplomats and their teenage daughters or else submitted themselves, never fully or completely, to odd city birds like myself. Khrenovoye, Orlovs, stud farm. . . . These words knocked about in my head like some equestrian incantation until one day I realized I had first read about them in Tolstoy's *Kholstomer: Story of a Horse*. I then reread the tale, this time with my eye on horse-related details. Kholstomer, Tolstoy's main character, is himself an Orlov trotter with a stride so broad and perfect and even that one imagines using its length to measure cloth. Hence the strider's name, literally "cloth measurer." Tolstoy's Kholstomer is born in Khrenovoye; near the stud farm, the decrepit trotter encounters his decrepit old master, an impoverished Russian aristocrat who has caused the horse's ruin. From the background Tolstoy provides, one can reconstruct the origins of his main character. Aged Kholstomer tells an audience of pedigree horses that he is a son of Lyubezny the First and Baba. Lyubezny, himself a great horse, was a son of the legendary

Arabian stallion Smetanka ("little sour cream"). In the late eighteenth century, Count Aleksey Orlov-Chesmensky, a favorite of Catherine the Great, had founded a stud farm in the Voronezh Province. Count Orlov's intention was to breed and rear horses with a spectacularly long stride. From Turkey he brought the priceless Smetanka, who, as the legend tells it, had extra vertebrae and ribs. Smetanka only lived for a year in Russia. The horses he sired were the founding parents of the breed that was developed at Khrenovoye in the late eighteenth and early nineteenth centuries. A direct descendant of Smetanka, Tolstoy's fictional Kholstomer is himself a fabulously fast Orlov. Yet he is not kept among siring stallions and is gelded because he is different, off color, piebald. History and fiction commingled in Tolstoy's *Story of a Horse*, and I was now to set foot in the real Khrenovoye, take in its atmosphere, and, if I was to be lucky, to ride the real trotters in the wild. . . .

At the sunset hour I walked down the sandy yellow road that girded the territory of the stud farm. Beyond a patchwork fence, propped up and repaired many times over, lay the long green stables and some dilapidated wooden structures, most of them predating the 1917 revolutions. The fields and pastures looked faded, lusterless, especially as compared to the blossoming steppe I had seen in Kursk in the middle of June. The sense of decay—not desolation but sweet decay and mystery—also stemmed from the absence of people. I only came across an old dreamy woman carrying loaded mesh bags from the bus stop on the edge of the village. She told me that most of the stud farm staff either lived on the territory in company housing, or commuted from nearby towns. Where were the main buildings? I asked her. Wasn't there a central pavilion, a museum, an office for visitors? Had nothing remained from the days when the place swarmed with visitors? The old lady put down her bags, stood with arms akimbo, looking me up and down, and explained that every year "the students" camped beside one of the back pastures where herds of unbroken horses were tended. For some reason she hadn't recognized a student in me. "The main facility is about a long walk from here," the old woman explained. (Two days later I would walk over and see the main offices, a stone Greek revival building which looked like an old train station or a watering pavilion at a German spa town.) "But we have a nice old building just a stone's throw from here. You go and look, my son, you go look."

The old woman directed me to a secluded path that led to an ornate, rust-eaten double gate. One side was slightly ajar, and a conifer-covered alley beyond the gates brought me to what looked like the former manor house. This was the site of a tuberculosis sanatorium, which, like the nearby stud farm, had fallen into oblivion. There was a time when many Russian consumptives were sent "for *kumys*." *Kumys*, a fermented product of the lactose-rich mare's milk, was once believed to possess medicinal properties. TB patients took it in a network of resorts and sanatoria that sprouted in the late nineteenth century along the lower Volga basin and in the steppes of southern and southeastern Russia. It wasn't just *kumys* but a combination of *kumys* and the dry steppe air that was believed to have healing powers. By the time I visited Khrenovoye in 1986, antibiotics and mandatory vaccination had ousted dietary and climatic treatments. For my generation, resorts for TB patients and *kumys* came alive in Chekhov's plays and stories. But here on the campus of a TB sanatorium where I strolled, shadowy patients still drank *kumys* and breathed the dry steppe air. A sanatorium from a romantic past, replete with consumptive waifs and coughing poets, still lingered here, on the sidelines of Soviet history. The whole thing felt nothing short of surreal, not just the slumbering sanatorium, but also the neighing farm. That the glorious legacy of the Russian trotters would have fallen into such disrepair seems hardly surprising. What I knew about the history of horse breeding in the USSR suggested a connection between its postwar deterioration and the disastrous early months of the 1941 Nazi invasion, when prided divisions of Red Cavalry proved useless against panzer tanks. More surprising was that the Soviet system would leave the famed Khrenovoye stud farm to decay in such peace and harmony.

My journal notes focus on the meetings with Uncle Vitya, a horseman. For the five days we stayed in Khrenovoye, Uncle Vitya took charge of my equine passion:

> 19-24 July 1986. Khrenovoye. Vit'ka, Viktor Fedorych, Uncle Vitya—
> bronzy-red face, age fifty, eagle nose, all skinny, native of Voronezh

Province, gold teeth. . . . A peaked cap. Speaks fine Russian. Extinguishes *mat*[25] or else swears along the lines of "It's a whorish business to milk horses and cut their tails for brushes." Speaks with horses: "Krokha, you girl, get up, you've been sleeping like a freaking log." In his eyes: a spirit of daring and desperate bravery, but the gaze is deep and substantial. He brings milk to a paralyzed friend. Divorced three years. Daughter lives not far from here, but hasn't been to see him (he hasn't been long in Khrenovoye after a hiatus, when for fifteen years he had been working in the Rostov Province in the Salsk Steppe with the Don and Budenny horses[26]); son lives near Kalinin.[27] Salary comes to about two hundred rubles a month.[28] A rundown hut—saddle and harness in the entryway; tins and cans, table, in the room I saw two beds. Smokes now filterless cigarettes, now rolls his own with great skill; his neighbor Lyoshka, also a sworn enemy of marriage, gives him homegrown tobacco. Vit'ka's friend Kol'ka recently visited him from Liski. He lives at the railway station, a refrigeration repairman, a boozer. Loves ladies. Now divorced and going with a thirty-six-year old woman (Kol'ka is fifty) who "paints her nails." Vit'ka doesn't like herbs and grass. Often refers to a horse breed as 'ordyn.'[29] They have a fat broad behind. Doesn't like "Arabs."[30] I shake his left hand (the right one is broken).

Sick of teaching and guiding, the instructors were cutting us slack. Even the morning lineups with Bogatyrev's big baritone streaming from

25. *Mat*: a special set of obscene swear words and their numerous derivatives in the Russian language.

26. The Don horse (*donchak*) is a known Russian breed, originally a Cossack horse; the Budenny horse (*budenovets*, from the last name of Semyon Budyonny, Red Army cavalry commander) was bred from among the Don horses as a specialized cavalry horse.

27. Kalinin (Tver'): a provincial capital north of Moscow.

28. In 1986, two hundred rubles was definitely an above-average monthly salary.

29. Not entirely clear what Uncle Vitya meant—*ordyn* is not a standard term for a horse breed. I suspect, given the etymology of the word (*ordyn* from *orda*=horde), that it suggests a horse's origin in the Asiatic steppes and association with the Golden Horde.

30. Arabian riding horses.

the loudspeaker were quickly becoming an anachronism. Did we study at all in Khrenovoye? A list of Latin taxonomic names in my notebook suggests that we must have, although I have little recollection of field trips or digs. The main reason the expedition stopped in Khrenovoye was to see the nearby Kamennaya ("Stone") Steppe. This is how the Russian peasant imagination had dubbed a drought-stricken steppe, where the lands were fertile if watered, but the climate was such that droughts abounded. In fact, something like every third year brought a serious drought to "stone steppes," hence the area's prominence in the history of Russian agriculture and forestry. We all knew the story from a freshman foundation course taught by the loquacious Professor Rozanov.

In 1891 a particularly severe drought hit almost thirty provinces of the Russian Empire. The government recruited Vasily Dokuchaev, a distinguished geographer and a founding father of Russian soil science, to examine the problem. Professor Dokuchaev's expedition led to his classic study, *Our Steppes Now and Today*. At a site in Kamennaya Steppe, at the turn of the nineteenth century, a research station was established. Dokuchaev introduced a method of protecting the steppe and minimizing the effects of drought. He started planting bands of forest and also building ponds to collect excess water from the fields. This method resulted in larger crops. The station grew in size and scope, and by the time we visited there, it had evolved into the Dokuchaev Research Institute of Agriculture. We drove there on the fourth day at Khrenovoye. The Institute was a short distance east of our camp, outside the town of Talovaya. There was a direct railroad between Bobrov and Talovaya, but only a roundabout driving route through the tousled town of Anna. The Research Institute of Agriculture at Kamennaya Steppe had a campus where the staff lived and worked. A nervous director gave us a tour, acting as though we were a troop of inspectors-general. He spoke of fifty Candidates of Science working at the Institute, of active research and publishing. There are even graduates of the School of Soil Science working there, the director pointed out. Graduates of *your own* institution. Poor souls, how did they end up here? I remember thinking. It must be deadly. Just imagine being graduated and then "distributed" to work here. Spending one's whole life in the Stone Steppe?

Somehow the day trip to the Research Institute of Agriculture, falling as it did on one of the final days of the expedition, added to my brewing sensation of having lost myself. There I was, tending herds with Uncle Vitya, not knowing what went on in the outside world. For almost two months I hadn't heard my parents' voice, had had no contacts with Moscow, save for a few delayed letters from my parents and Max. As a Jewish refusenik, what facts relevant to my future might I have snatched away from the occasional regional or local paper falling into my hands? Yet this chronic lack of information, this depersonalizing submission to a local Russian life, didn't seem to trouble me. I felt at peace with my surroundings. I would be lying if I said that, while at Khrenovoye, I was desperate to go back home to Moscow.

Out of this sensation of a young person's flight from reality, out of the exhilaration of riding horses in the wild, came some initial notes for a long narrative poem about horses and love. The poem's triangle of desire captured a Jewish student from a big city, a young woman (his love interest, who must have been modeled after Anastasia), and an older rider from a small town in the steppe. The horseman seduces the girl behind her boyfriend's back, even though the daredevil cannot offer her more than himself, his horses, and the wild expanse of the steppe. Born out of the expedition and inspired by my acquaintance with Uncle Vitya, this subject would preoccupy me for a long time, in poetry and subsequently in fiction, first in Russian, later in English. *Herd above the Meadow*, the long poem I started composing at Khrenovoye, would end with a scene of leaving behind an expedition campsite. I based the poem's finale on the real morning of our expedition's departure: "The tents as if exhaling life, / and having lost the quirks of their shapes, / now resembled / a pile of tanned skins, / we're leaving, / the camp has been dismantled in an hour, / now only a thread / a caravan of roaring / vehicles, I plunge myself into the thick forest, / so as to cut / directly to the stables. / The herdsman sits on a stump and nurses / a stogie, / only two vigilant cherries / his pupils / like a separate creature / stare from under his large curls / his crooked / peaked cap / slides down to the ground, / I say goodbye, shake his left hand, / the customary words, / —To visit? —Sure, visit, / we'll take out the herd at night, / Well, take care, / —Thanks. / My feet dance, / and I rush into the car, the conversation / with colleagues, / now pulling off / bus, cistern, kitchen, truck, / roll through the forest toward a meadow / after them / I also take off in flight, welcomed or dejected, / to grab onto a horse's mane, to feel / her heartbeat with my hand / over the river / to fly / embracing this blue sky, / the herd is flying over the meadow. . . . / Now I fly."

Having left Khrenovoye on 24 July 1986, we traveled to Chashnikovo, our school's summer campus north of Moscow, where I had spent two months in the summer of 1985. I was no longer keeping the journal, and of this drive with an overnight stop I remember mainly the feeling of hunger that had become particularly acute on the eve of returning to Moscow. We were finally depleting the remaining supplies without having to ration, which meant that for the last supper in the fields they allowed one can of stewed meat for three people. And they also decided to distribute our special stock of chocolate candy. I was delegated to take a plate of sweets to the drivers, as our last offering. "Maxim, you're a clever fellow," said the head driver, already drunk but not yet ugly, and I knew what he wanted to say to me but did not let escape from his chunky mouth.

Our caravan drove through the gates of the Chashnikovo campus in the late morning of 25 July. We were told that we wouldn't be released for another day, until all the gear had been cleaned and sorted. The thought of spending the night in the plywood barracks only thirty miles from home seemed blasphemous to the Muscovites among us. I managed to telephone my parents from the dispatcher's office. In the late evening our white Zhiguli collected me and took me home, and the next day my parents and I left for what would turn out to be our last summer vacation in Estonia.

On the way to Pärnu we stopped for the night in Leningrad and visited family graves. Throughout the drive from Moscow to Pärnu, as I recounted the expedition adventures for my parents, I stressed the exoticism and strangeness of what I had seen. It would take a long time, a new country, and a new language for me to realize that the summer expedition was my chance at seeing Russia before leaving her for good. This Russia I had been getting to know was rural, provincial, and, despite the paucity and desolation, it felt less Soviet, less touched by official lies and politics. This Russia—now both remembered and imagined—I could never unlove.

PART THREE

The Short Goodbye

8

LAST AUTUMN

STILL IN THE CAR riding back from Chashnikovo to Moscow, one of the first things I learned from my parents was that the Soviet chess magazine *64* had just printed an excerpt from *Drugie berega* (*Other Shores*), a Russian version of Vladimir Nabokov's autobiography, best known in the West as *Speak, Memory*. The excerpt, in which Nabokov discusses chess problems, was tiny. After two months on the expedition trail I was starved for information, and the news of Nabokov's first official publication in the USSR was scintillating. Nabokov had died almost ten years earlier in Switzerland. An aristocrat, bilingual genius, and unrelenting anti-Bolshevik, Nabokov had been persona non grata in official Soviet culture, and now two pages of his mellifluous prose had been finally sanctioned to be read by millions. "Is this a signal of change?" I asked my parents as we sped along the empty Leningrad Highway. The times may have been "a-changing," yet the dawn of Gorbachev's reforms still promised precious little to the refuseniks. Which is why my parents had used my absence from Moscow as a window of opportunity for renewed public protests. "Inaction is deadly," my father explained. "Desperate times call for desperate actions." And my mother added in her bashfully fearless voice, "Only open political protest can force them to let us go."

Still in the car I learned that while I had traveled and explored, my parents had gotten to know Wyatt Andrews, a rising star of American TV journalism who was then the Moscow bureau chief for CBS News. Andrews covered the Soviet Union in 1986–88, reporting on perestroika and glasnost, the Chernobyl catastrophe, and later on, the Reagan–Gorbachev summits. He didn't know Russian, but he was an astute journalist

217

who wasn't just walking the beat, in contrast to some of the reporters for the Western media we had met in Moscow over the years. After Moscow, Andrews would go on to cover the State Department and the White House, and seeing him on TV, silver-haired but with the same witty glint in his eyes, still brings back memories of our last year in Russia. While I was away on the expedition, Andrews arranged for my father to give a live interview. The occasion was the opening of the eighth Congress of the Union of Soviet Writers in Moscow on 24 June 1986. On 23 June 1986, as I rode on the dust-choked bus through the steppe toward the Sea of Proletarsk, my father sent an open letter to the Congress delegates. On the same day, my parents spoke to Andrews and his crew in the courtyard of the Union of Soviet Writers. My father read his open letter, my mother interpreting, and then answered Wyatt Andrews's questions on camera. The monument to Leo Tolstoy, a symbol of a Russian writer's consciousness, formed a visual backdrop as my father described his isolation as a writer and spoke of being punished for what the Soviet Constitution guaranteed. "With the CBS camera rolling, the bastards didn't dare touch us this time," mother said as we pulled into the front yard of our apartment building. "Perhaps there *is* hope, after all."

The other important event I had missed was a visit by Rabbi Harvey J. Fields and Sybil Fields in July 1986. Harvey Fields was then a senior rabbi of Wilshire Boulevard Temple in Los Angeles and an activist of the Soviet Jewry movement. While visiting under the official auspices of Intourist, the Fieldses came to the Soviet Union on a mission to see refuseniks. With my parents, whom the Fieldses saw twice during the visit, they shared a special connection: Harvey and Sybil were close friends of David and Gila Sharir, our Tel-Aviv–based cousins. Rabbi Fields was a prominent figure of the Reform Judaism movement in North America, whose name adorns each copy of *Gates of Prayer* and *Gates of Repentance*, the two New Union prayerbook volumes. Harvey Fields was not only a congregational rabbi, but also held a Ph.D. in US diplomatic history and was a Torah commentator and a creative writer. Already in America, when I met the Fieldses for the first time, I immediately understood why my parents had characterized their July 1986 meetings in Moscow as "electrifying."

Right away the Fieldses became involved in our case, joining other friends and colleagues already working to speed up our release. They engaged congressmen and senators, leaders of the literary and artistic community, and notable scientists to intervene personally on our family's behalf. In 1986–87, the US politicians who personally pleaded with the Soviet officials on our behalf included Senator Claiborne Pell of Rhode Island, Congressman Benjamin A. Gilman of New York, and others. But the support of Rabbi Fields and his family would become instrumental not just in pressing Soviet authorities at high levels, but in creating something of a political insurance policy that the Fieldses took out in our name.

I returned from the expedition very skinny and starved for decent food, with a "six-pack" of muscles on my gut, but also with a developing duodenal ulcer. I remember walking on a red-graveled park alley toward the Pärnu beach, and feeling much more "experienced" than my urbanite childhood friends. This new edge temporarily displayed itself through a swaggering body mechanics and a deliberate roughness of speech. Even my best friend Max, with whom I always enjoyed a harmonious friendship of equals, objected to the change. "This roughness thing is a bit much," Max said soon after we were reunited in Pärnu. "You've turned into one of those army guys we don't mix with." This external coarseness would rub off like crystallized sweat as I relaxed and soaked my body in the balmy shallows of the Gulf of Pärnu. But I also noticed an internal change: for the first time as a young adult I wanted to separate myself from our gang of old Pärnu friends and the group activities at the beach or in our outdoor cafes. I wanted to be alone with my notebooks. Hours, for the first time in my life, felt like a precious commodity. I had but three weeks in Pärnu—to rest, write, and ready myself for what I sensed would be a pivotal year.

I was composing *Herd above the Meadow*, the long poem for which I had started taking notes while still in horse country at the end of the expedition. For the first time, I was writing not in trance of inspiration— in subway cars or in bed upon waking up—but at my desk, steadily, for two hours daily. Writing itself was beginning to feel like a métier, and not just rapturous self-expression. Composing a long poem in parts, with a narrative structure, love triangle, descriptions, and other elements one associates more with prose than with short lyrical poetry, also signaled a growing interest in fiction-writing and in story-telling. Some time in the late fall of 1986 I would write the first short story that I wouldn't be ashamed of having reprinted today.

In those August Pärnu weeks I would work at home in the morning and then walk to the beach and meet up with my friends. I don't remember how my father and I negotiated the writing hours in the studio apartment my parents and I shared. Was father typing in the kitchen while I composed in longhand, in the bedroom? Did he leave the beach when I got there? Each of us had his own typewriter and brought it with him on vacation. The first draft of the long poem took about ten days to write, and I spent the rest of the Pärnu days revising and polishing the text. My first audience, at a reading held in our summer apartment just a few days before the end of the vacation, consisted of my parents and Max Mussel.

The next day after we returned to Moscow I called up Genrikh Sapgir and asked to show him my new work. Back in the spring of 1986, my father and Genrikh had rekindled their friendship, which dated to the 1950s. Genrikh and his wife Mila became my parents' trusted friends, and I visited the Sapgirs on many occasions. While I never wanted another mentor besides my father, it was important to get an unbiased professional opinion. Sapgir did not represent the Soviet literary establishment. I was quite sure that he would not be kind to me out of politeness or sentimental attachment to my father and their literary youth. On 1 September 1986, the day school traditionally started in the Soviet Union, I spent the morning at the university and then visited Sapgir in his professorial apartment located near Butyrka, Moscow's old transit jail where a number of writers had been held in czarist and Soviet times. Sapgir received me in his study, walls lined with canvases by Soviet avant-garde artists, among them Oskar Rabin. Sitting on the ottoman and laying pages of the manuscript on a low coffee table, I read the entire of *Herd above the Meadow*. Sapgir sat across from me at his desk, by the window overlooking a courtyard with maples shedding blackened gold. He liked the long poem, especially what he deemed "Nabokovian moments." At the time I had only read a little bit of Nabokov, but it felt good to hear this. "You know," Sapgir said, "you have those spaces within spaces within other spaces. That's very good." He asked to see the typescript, passed his eyes and thumb over a few pages, and cited the episode where the protagonist brings a bunch of cornflowers to his girlfriend: "you can put them next to your pillow, / they are like an orchard where swifts dash to and fro, / they are like a dream. . . ." Sapgir advised me to avoid verbal clichés, even if the pathos of the poem—be it a declaration of love or a description of sunset over the steppe—seems to justify recycling them. "Easier said than done," I retorted.

As he saw me out of the apartment, Sapgir told me to seek publication, "here or elsewhere." Sapgir's imprimatur gave me confidence. I went home determined to submit my long poem to a literary magazine and also to put together a manuscript for a poetry collection. Over the next two days I only got as far as typing up about forty shorter poems plus *Herd above the Meadow* and arranging them in a manuscript, which I titled *End of August*. *End of August* meant the end of summer, but also suggested something Roman, something about an emperor's death. An emperor's death and an empire's fall must have been on my mind. I put together the manuscript but had to postpone the quest for publication until October. On 3 September 1986 I left for Chashnikovo, to harvest potatoes in the meager fields north of Moscow.

Being sent to assist the rural population with the collection of agricultural crops was a common experience of Soviet studenthood—and also of life in Soviet cities. Throughout my childhood, my father and his fellow researchers at the Academy of Medical Sciences would spend two or three autumn weeks outside Moscow, helping collective farmers. The agricultural dispatches stopped for my father after we became refuseniks, and as a physician in his local health center he was so needed that the potato-picking ceased to be mandatory. For Moscow University juniors, the fall semester started almost a month later. We contributed virtually free labor to the Soviet agricultural economy. The colloquial expression in Soviet Russian was to be sent *na kartoshku* (literally, "for potatoes"), although the nature of the crops changed, depending on climate and location. In the spring of 1993, when I was doing research in Prague, I was surprised to learn from a young Czech woman that in the Eastern Bloc days she, too, had been sent on agricultural works. Except the students in Prague were mainly used to pick hops, an agent in brewing beer. "Therein lies all the difference," I remember saying to the Czech woman.

Chashnikovo was a sorry sight. Protracted rains, common in Central Russia in September, quickly turned dirt roads into sleeves of mud. The barracks where we had so merrily lived in June and July after freshman year had no heat and were made of plywood; roofs leaked and windows were missing glass panes. To most of us this really felt like a penal colony without strict work enforcement. Not the tired Soviet motivational mottos like "To fulfill and overfulfill the norm!" but pot-boiling and time-passing were our slogans of the day. We were paid some fantastically low wage per unit of "workday." Only a few of my fellow students, all of them the army veterans from rural areas of the country, preferred the manual chores to studying, worked with verve, and opted for overtime.

Our work week, like the school week, consisted of six days, with Sunday off. The day started with some bronchial song of labor enthusiasm blaring from the loudspeaker, with gruel and tasteless tea at the refectory, and the daily lineup and headcount. Then we would trudge through muck to one of the naked, flooded fields surrounding the Chashnikovo campus. Most of the days we were harvesting potatoes or carrots. A tractor would plough a row across the field, and a group of us would follow with buckets, picking up some and stomping what remained under the surface of the thin clayish soil. Sometimes we were too lazy even to cover up, leaving the smaller tubers and roots for the local population to prey on after dusk. This was a student operation, and there was practically no local supervision. Only once or twice I remembered being called "lazy city sons of bitches" by a bristly manager yelling from the cab of his pickup truck.

By the end of the day our Chashnikovo-issued quilted jackets and pants would become heavy with water and mud. At night, we would leave our boots and wet, dirty clothes in a small communal room with heaters, and when they were dry, the clay-splattered pants and coats would stand on their own like petrified life-size puppets. The puppets would spend the night in the communal "drying-room," and in the morning we would have to break them apart from their hardened embraces. There was heat only in the central cottage with its community room, TV set, and telephone line, on which we could receive but not make calls. I would steal away to Moscow at every opportunity, and not just on Sundays but sometimes, if the rain was too heavy to work in the afternoon, for half a day and the night.

Six months had passed since Lyuba and I had parted, and I was still free of strong romantic attachments. In fact, after Lyuba, I would not have a serious girlfriend until after leaving Russia. Was I protecting myself? In Pärnu I had met Lenochka, a friend of an old childhood friend. By coincidence, Lenochka was a student at Max Mussel's Institute of Communications (nicknamed the "Institute of Liaisons"). She was two years my junior, with wavy blonde hair, shapely eyes of cinnamon, and full lips. Her maternal grandmother still looked like the Russian peasant girl she had been when she came to Moscow in the 1930s, part of a giant influx of rural dwellers seeking big-city opportunities. Lenochka was intelligent and stylish, and ambitious in an understated fashion. She designed and made her own smart clothes after what she observed in magazines at the apartments of wealthier, modish girlfriends. Because Lenochka had entered our circle of Pärnu friends, the fact that I was a refusenik was known to her from the get-go. One might say, in retrospect, that she may have had a penchant for Jewish boys; her first serious boyfriend had been Jewish, as was the man she ended up meeting through me and later marrying. I suspect that Lenochka's mother, an engineer and aspirant member of the Moscow intelligentsia, might have preached to her that Jews made good husbands. But her peasant grandmother had her own wisdom and tried to talk her out of seeing Jewish boys. The grandmother was right: Jews did not bring Lenochka luck. I didn't fall in love with her, despite the good times we shared in the summer. Throughout the autumn and winter of 1986–87, Lenochka and I would sometimes get together while leading our own, disparate lives. The man Lenochka later married, my former Moscow friend Valera Valdman, took her away from her family and country but couldn't make her happy. But I'm running ahead of my story. . . . During those weeks of the agricultural work—summertime romance still fresh on our hearts—I saw Lenochka in Moscow when I escaped there. In Chashnikovo I slacked off as inventively as I knew how.

One time I arranged for a doctor's note documenting an acute attack of hay fever and recommending bed rest. One had to be creative to avoid Soviet fields of muck.

I felt a chronic lack of privacy while stuck in Chashnikovo. A romantic aura of itinerant brotherhood and sisterhood had lost its appeal for me, even though the same classmates surrounded me. The weeks of potato-picking are a blur of sunless days, drenching rains, and repulsive food. The episode that has stuck in my head most vividly occurred one evening in the heated community room, where many of us would gather to watch TV. It was cold in the barracks, even in double layers of sweaters, and there was no way to read except with a flashlight. When I entered the community room on that particular evening, I saw a group of my classmates, mostly girls, glued to the TV screen. "What's on?" I asked but only got "hush, be quiet" in response. It was a regular TV show, *The Camera Faces the World*, something of a Soviet cross between ABC's *20/20* and CBS's *Sixty Minutes*. As my luck would have it, the show host announced that the Soviet viewers would have the opportunity to see a re-broadcast of an American documentary titled *The Russians Are Here*. The title must have been a play on Norman Jewison's film of 1966, *The Russians Are Coming*. The host explained that the documentary had been released in the United States and focused on the lives of those who had left the Soviet Union and settled in America. The host added that four years after the documentary's release a Soviet TV crew located some of the émigrés featured in the film and interviewed them for the show. These interviews, said the host, were supposed to serve as a tacit commentary on the "hollow" (I think this was the epithet he employed) lives of the former Soviet citizens "in emigration."

I must have been the only one in that community room full of university students who had heard of the PBS documentary prior to its showing on Soviet television. I had learned about it from the letters of my parents' friends living in America. The film, after it was first shown on PBS in 1983, generated protest among Soviet émigrés, who accused the makers of a strong bias. The émigré papers were abuzz with discussions of the film, and one friend living in Washington, D.C. even enclosed a clipping from a New York Russian daily. They found particularly objectionable the film's portrayal of Soviet immigrants as unable to integrate and assimilate, as unappreciative of the "freedoms" and "values" of American society. This much I did know, and now before me, unfolding on the screen, were scenes of immigrants suspended between Soviet past and American present. Old depressed-looking Jewish-Russian women someplace in Brighton Beach were watching a video of a Soviet film, watching and weeping. The documentary featured an interview with Lev Khalif, a poet who had been a friend of my father's in 1960s Moscow before emigrating in the 1970s. Khalif stated that in the Soviet Union at least the KGB was reading his work, whereas in the United States, nobody did. This portrait of a Russian poet in America, unwanted, dejected, deprived of his readers, was particularly jarring to me, considering that Khalif was my father's peer and a real person, not an unknown, abstract Soviet "émigré." I haven't seen the documentary since 1986, but I do remember clearly that in its thrust and tenor the American film was disdainful of "the Russians."

So there I was, a refusenik hiding beneath the tattered façade of a regular Soviet student relaxing after a day of work in the fields of his motherland. I was watching an American documentary wrapped inside a Soviet show about Soviet immigrants abroad. There were about twenty-five of us in the community room, and several of my female classmates openly wept when the camera showed old women crying over a Soviet movie they watched in a darkened living room in Brooklyn. My classmates' tears were unforced and spontaneous. The propaganda was working, I could see it for myself. See how miserable our former citizens are abroad, the show was saying to the mass Soviet audience. As the show rolled on, gazes kept turning at me, the only Jew in the room, and those were not gazes of hostility but only of pity. I didn't return the innocent, tearful looks. I just sat there in the community room, sipping sweet tea and pretending I had no idea what they were talking about. Jewish emigration? No idea. Refuseniks? Who would those be? Brighton Beach? Whatever. Doubly the double life . . .

Back in Moscow in October, I resumed my research with Professor Samoylova. She was unsentimental about work expectations and respectful of my private life and literary pursuits. Did Samoylova know that I had a suspect background? Never once had Samoylova brought up the subject of Jewish emigration or refuseniks, which were by then slowly becoming matters of public conversation in Soviet society. I would meet with her every other week, present results of my literature review, and discuss the progress on what would become my third-year research project, a long paper on the evolution of soils in the Kulunda Steppe, especially in relation to the area's salt lakes.

The research at the library took up a fair amount of time throughout the autumn semester, but I didn't mind it. I also had a part-time job as a research assistant in Samoylova's lab, mostly preparing and labeling soil samples. It was not onerous and I received something like thirty-five rubles for it, which, combined with my monthly cash stipend of forty rubles, brought my monthly contribution to our family budget to a lofty seventy-five rubles, almost as much as a full-time hospital orderly made a month. At home, we stored an oversized wallet in one of the drawers of my father's desk. There we kept all the cash. My parents deposited their earnings, and I proudly placed the cash stipend and recompense I received at the university. Money wasn't divided into my parents' or mine, and I just took what I needed for everyday expenses. This was so different from the prevailing model I would later observe in American families, where children had separate bank accounts and spent the earnings from their part-time jobs on themselves, without contributing to the family budget.

Following all the misfortunes of the autumn of 1985, things were looking a bit better in the autumn of 1986. My position at the university seemed more stable, and I had struck a workable balance between studying and literary pursuits. After a summer of political protests and the absence of reprieve or punishment by the authorities, my parents felt ready for further political action. And we were doing fairly well financially. My father had a real following of patients. In keeping with the signs of the time, the enrollments had doubled in the English classes my mother taught at the House of Culture. And my father even received substantial honoraria from reprints of his literary translations in anthologies and collections. He had discovered them by pure chance, while browsing at a central bookstore, and the publishers were legally obligated to pay him. In one of the publishing houses they apologized to my father: "We thought you had emigrated." In another, the cashier paying out the honorarium whispered to him: "We were told you'd died."

Over the refusenik years there may well have been occasional other reprints of my father's literary translations. He hadn't been able to emigrate, yet as a literary professional he was "dead" to the Soviet reading public. This is, perhaps, the reason why my father pinned his hopes on my breaking into Soviet magazines. After the tradition of non-Russian, especially Jewish, authors' adopting Slavic pennames, and also in keeping with our family's own history, my father advised me to take up a penname. His literary name in the Soviet years had been David Petrov, after the Russianized first name of his late father. My *nom de plume*, Maxim Davydov, short-lived as it would turn out to be, was derived from my father's first name. While masking my Jewish last name, it also air-brushed my father's starkly non-Russian first name by replacing the vowel *i* with y. Davidov was a most unlikely Russian last name; Davydov was a fairly common one. There had even been a Russian poet of the Romantic age with this last name, Denis Davydov, recognized for his military valor and exuberant consumption of "the Widow."

With my own Russian penname in hand, I typed up selections of poems and started peddling them around Moscow's editorial offices. There were two main types of magazines, the so-called "thick journals" and the glossier monthlies or weeklies. Among the "thick journals" was the legendary *Novy mir* (*New World*), where Solzhenitsyn's works had appeared in the wake of Khrushchev's Thaw. Depending on their printing size and place in the Soviet literary hierarchy, each of the thick monthlies had a coterie of staff poetry editors and freelance contributing editors. It's difficult to imagine such a magnitude, but the official printing runs of the leading thick journals of the Soviet 1980s well exceeded 100,000 copies. A poem published in one of them would instantly accord the poet a mass audience. Besides the traditional "thick journals" clothed in plain covers, Soviet versions of glossy magazines also published poetry. Some of them were supposed to target a specific audience: students, young people in the rural areas, female collective farmers, aspiring authors in a country of mass graphomania, and so forth. One always had the option of submitting work by mail, and one would even get a reply from an assistant editor or editorial "consultant"; in the land of people's culture the editors were obligated to respond to citizens' submissions. But the more familiar fashion was to visit editorial offices and call on editors in person. This experience of editorial office-crawling differed starkly from the impersonal, self-addressed-stamped-envelope mode of the Anglo-American literary world. Editorial offices had open visiting hours, when authors were supposed to commune with editors. More commonly, if you were an unknown, aspiring author, you would be received by a freelance "literary consultant," for whom the job was frequently a sinecure. The "consultants" were mainly paid to serve as concierges while pretending that Soviet literature was a house with many open doors. During my visits to editorial offices in the autumn of 1986, I came upon established poets as well as the ones still struggling to gain the privileges of official Soviet writers.

I remember talking with Anatoly Parpara, a reactionary who guarded the poetry portal at the monthly *Moskva* (*Moscow*). Once or twice I brought poems to Arvo Mets, a soft-spoken Estonian writing slightly gawky *vers libres* in Russian and working at *Novy mir* as a poetry consultant under Evgeny Vinokurov. Vinokurov, a prominent Soviet poet of the war generation, had the nickname "doughnut with shit" and, in his later years, discouraged young talent, unless it came in a skirt with pretty legs. I recall bringing poems to the magazine *Yunost'* (*Youth*) and being intercepted by Viktor Korkiya, a poet and playwright of Georgian descent, who acted the role of a sympathetic cop to his senior colleague Yury Ryashentsev. A poetry "consultant" at *Youth* magazine, the Jewish-born Ryashentsev was an established songwriter and translator. After Korkiya mumbled something about being unsure the poems would "pass the editorial board," he brought me over to Ryashentsev's nook. Ryashentsev sized me up and down, as though looking for some clues in my face. Then he glanced at my poems diagonally across the page and returned them with a verdict: "The syntax is wobbly. Come back once you've mastered the Russian literary language."

The offices of several monthly magazines targeting students and young readers were located in two low-rise modern buildings in the same area of Moscow, near the Savelovsky Railroad Station. About every other week, throughout the autumn of 1986, I made trips to the two low-rises.

Five or six of the editorial offices I visited were affiliated with the publishing branch of the Komsomol, of which, strangely enough, I was still
a member. On the way there from the Novoslobodskaya Metro stop I
would pass Genrikh Sapgir's apartment building. I so much wanted to
get published, to break in. Looking up at Sapgir windows from a trolleybus car, I was reminded of Sapgir's refusal to compromise, even if it
meant remaining unpublished in the Soviet Union. I also thought of my
own father's career.

Leaving aside issues of form and professional quality, of which the
author himself is not always the best judge, I think the poems I composed
in 1986–87 weren't anti-Soviet, just un-Soviet or a-Soviet. It's easier to say
what they were not than what they were: not conformist, not patriotic, not
ideologically opportunistic. There was one exception, though. Some time
in the autumn of 1986 I tried my hand at concocting what in literary slang
was called a "steam engine": an ideologically-marked text that would help
steer a selection of other poems into print. In my case the steam engine
I attempted was a poem of solidarity with Leonard Peltier, the Native
American leader, who was something of a hero of Soviet anti-American
propaganda. Peltier was a pretext, the poem itself was an exercise at rhym-
ing creatively and violently, and the whole thing didn't come off.

My Russian penname, "Maxim Davydov," concealed my Jewishness on a typewritten page or in a byline. When I personally interacted
with editors, they quickly discerned a phenotypical Jew while also being
alerted by my non-Russian patronymic. Not all editors and literary consultants harbored racial prejudice, yet almost all served as gatekeepers
and entry-level censors. In my efforts, I also encountered several official
Jews who were especially apprehensive as they faithfully served at the
tables of Soviet culture. What was I trying to get myself into, a young Jew
writing in Russian, a refusenik attempting to place poems in Soviet magazines? Why was I so keen to get published in the country which I wanted
to leave for good?

In all fairness, it was not all about a Jew knocking at the doors of Russian poetry. I relished the aura of being an almost-published young poet,
the sort of Russian (Soviet) aura that hardly exists in the United States,
where writing is regarded by and large as a professional activity, not a

special calling or a guild of the chosen few. Being a published writer-in-waiting already gave one some social advantages. You could speak to your peers of promises by magazines, of manuscripts under review or consideration, and it sounded special and "cool." I recall, for instance, picking up the phone and asking to speak to the manager of Blue Bird, a trendy club in the center of Moscow. At the time this was one of the hottest spots, with drinks and dancing, and there was always a queue and a long wait. I introduced myself to the manager as a "young poet Maxim Davydov" and asked if he could get me in. On my part this was part-truth, part casual mythmaking, and all bravado. Without so much as a moment's hesitation the manager of the bar replied "but of course, just tell the doorman you spoke to me." My date and I circumnavigated the long queue and approached the doorman. Here I encountered an unexpected snag. The doorman and I recognized each other. We had recently met at the apartment of Bill F., an American diplomat. The handsome, well-dressed man with Mediterranean looks struck me as something of a mysterious figure: at the diplomatic party he had introduced himself as a journalist working—I wasn't sure in what capacity—for a Western newspaper. And now I encountered him in the employ of a doorman in a fashionable Soviet night spot. In the years leading to the collapse of the Soviet Union, M.D., as was the name of the "doorman," would become a well-known political commentator and columnist. "You must be trying to figure out where we met," the doorman asked. "No . . . yes," I mumbled, bewildered. He led me into the manager's office, and the manager cleared seats for me and my date at one of the tables. He didn't even ask for proof or under the table payment. My date was duly impressed, and for the rest of my time in Russia I would continue to bring dates to this bar, still a "young poet," still unpublished.

I was getting mostly oral no's or written rejections, which was all to be expected, but I got some positive feedback and a few maybes. At the three magazines and the daily newspaper where I had bites, each editor or literary consultant played her or his own game and fashioned himself after a certain Russian cultural stereotype or an esteemed Russian poet of yore. At *Student Meridian*, the sarcastic Igor Tarasevich, who looked like an

1850s Russian nihilist, selected a poem of mine about running into an old friend, and suggested that I change one line, "without finishing our wine," to "without finishing our cigarettes." "We have an anti-alcoholism campaign in the country," he said. "But I like your poem." Before I even had a chance to agree, Tarasevich opened a fountain pen and scribbled the correction across the page. "I'll recommend it at the next editorial board," he promised. Another magazine where I felt I was getting somewhere was the monthly *Rural Youth*. I had made a connection with this magazine a year earlier, when, in the midst of a crisis at Moscow University, I was thinking of becoming a science writer and writing about agriculture. At *Rural Youth* I dealt directly with the poetry editor, Mikhail Pozdnyaev. Pozdnyaev, who had published a collection of verse and had a second one on the way, looked like a Russian Orthodox seminarian with his longish hair and cropped beard and mustache. We would have long conversations in his office overlooking veiny railroad tracks, and he was particularly intrigued by my recent expedition experience and my pantheistic poems set in the south of Russia. Pozdnyaev kept asking for more poems to build up a "portfolio" he was going to advocate at an "opportune" moment. He never elaborated, but I had the feeling he either knew I was my father's son or suspected something. I finally ran out of patience and confronted Pozdnyaev, and he blew up on the phone and rejected my poems altogether. In the years of Soviet transition and collapse, Pozdnyaev became a writer about the Russian Orthodox Church, and I would come across his articles in leading newspapers and magazines. The third magazine where I was getting encouraging signals was *Rabotnitsa*, literally *The Female Worker*. Its poetry editor, Oleg Khlebnikov, was a tall robust man with straw-colored hair. He shared his last name with the incomparable Velimir Khlebnikov, the great poet-philosopher of Russian Futurism. The Khlebnikov of *The Female Worker* fame had published clever and technically accomplished poems which I liked for their marriage of peasant folklore and urban Soviet mentality. He complimented me on the "colorful" rhymes and promised to "do something." For some reason the heat wasn't working when I saw him last in December 1986, and Khlebnikov received me in a sheepskin coat. The most heartening news came from the culture editor at *Moscow Komsomol Member*. Despite the name and affiliation, since the late 1950s and early '60s, when the country was going through de-Stalinization, this daily with a huge circulation had had the reputation for liberalism. Among its columnists was the poet Aleksandr Aronov, known for his lyrics for movie songs and for polemical poems circulating in the literary underground, among them a poem about the Warsaw Ghetto Uprising. The culture editor at *Moscow Komsomol Member*, Natalia Dardykina, was a cantankerous, chain-smoking woman in her late forties, with an eviscerated face and a slicing speech manner. She read a selection of my poems as I sat, waiting, in her smoky office, and asked if I had shorter poems. "We're a daily, our readers don't have the time for more than four stanzas," she said to me. When I was leaving, she gave me a stack of typewriter paper that was thicker and whiter than the wafer-thin paper then available at the stores. Through her brown teeth Dardykina pressed out: "Bring me shorter poems, and no symbolism, I beg of you." Some time in December I gave her a cycle of short poems. Dardykina gobbled them up, told me to check back in a few weeks, and then things got very busy and I didn't follow up. In September 1987, soon after my parents and I had settled in Providence, Rhode Island, after a summer in Austria and Italy, my friend Max mailed me a clipping from *Moscow Komsomol Member*, dated 1 September 1987. It was my poem "Spring in a Provincial Town," abridged from the original five to three stanzas. On the newspaper page my short poem neighbored a poem by Arvo Mets, the poetry consultant at *Novy mir* who had tried but failed to get me published. This was, to the best of my knowledge, my only poem published in the Soviet Union, and also the only one I'm aware of that came out under the penname "Maxim Davydov."

My father encouraged me to seek publication in the Soviet Union while he, a refusenik writer, had been living in a state of isolation. The circulation of his texts in the underground or abroad did not bring much satisfaction. The first part of the refusenik saga he had written in 1979–1982 was about to come out in Israel, but even this news didn't gladden enough. What could I do to support my father? My mother was already at work translating into English sections of my father's memoir about Leningrad writers. I was nowhere near ready to translate my father's prose, but I decided to try my hand at rendering his poems in English. Some of the poems we selected went back to my father's youth and the Thaw and included "King Solomon" and "The Six-Pointed Star." They couldn't have been published in the USSR because of their openly Jewish themes and perspectives. We also chose refusenik poems such as "Lot's Monologue to His Wife." Dedicated to my mother, the poem was a parable of my parents' condition.

What were they like, those first translations? You can imagine how little I knew or understood about idiomatic English or the living texture of Anglo-American poetry. I tried to match the meters of the Russian originals, beat by beat, and the translations sounded like Russian poetry in some sort of textbook English. I tried very hard, and I think one or two lines in each of the translated poems might have come alive in English. We had no English typewriter at home, and I copied them in longhand, in my schoolboy's handwriting, which was better in English than in Russian. In the late autumn and winter of 1986-87 I began to show my translations to foreign acquaintances and visitors, some of whom I would never see again. My first audience included diplomats stationed in Moscow and American academics spending a year or a semester in Russia. One of them was a political scientist from a Jesuit college on the Eastern Seaboard, a tall patrician. I remember how he read my translations in our kitchen, snow falling outside, a Moscow winter night. The American professor perused my translations while leaning on our refrigerator, an unfinished drink in his other hand, and then launched a tirade, in his impressive Russian, about the prospects of making a living as a writer in America, and also about the way the American academy had its own "games and politics," and why wouldn't I think of law or medicine instead of literature. "Its own games and politics," I remember thinking. "How very enticing."

I found a more helpful audience in the Cooper family from Madison, Wisconsin. John Milton Cooper Jr., an American historian, came to Moscow on a Fulbright to teach at Moscow University. We met him, his wife Judith, a lawyer, and his children John (Jamie) and Elizabeth (Betsy), through our friend Bill F. at the embassy. Betsy was going to a Soviet high school for the semester they were in Moscow, and Jamie explored Moscow, studied Russian, and later worked for the Moscow CNN bureau as an errand-boy. In my eyes the Coopers epitomized American decency, generosity of spirit, intellectual curiosity, and firmness of convictions. Jamie, a year my junior, became my first American friend. Jamie and Betsy were roughly my age and we made a connection instantly. They read my translations with discernment, although I could tell they were hesitant to comment unless—and until—I directly asked them for specific suggestions. The translations evolved, going through a number of drafts, and it was exciting to hope, naïvely, that I was creating something in the English language while also carrying out a mission. Some time in late December my translations, among them "Lot's Monologue to His Wife," were laid flat on the floor right in the middle of my room and photographed by a visiting activist of the Soviet Jewry movement. The film was delivered to Rabbi Fields in Los Angeles. December bending its snowy back under the calendary whip, our family wondered if, through translation, the English language would magically deliver us to freedom.

Some time in December of 1986 Max Mussel and I ditched classes on Friday and Saturday and went to Leningrad for a long weekend. It was a familiar routine: two or three times a year during 1984–87, Max and I would go to Russia's westernmost city just to get away from our inland capital. We would either take the cheapest overnight train and ride in a car with doorless sleeper compartments, or, when money was particularly tight, we went by day train with its seats made of uncushioned wood. Our monthly university stipends were about forty to forty-five rubles, and the cheapest round-trip student ticket to Leningrad cost about ten rubles, so with some help from our parents we could almost afford these occasional trips. Waxing poetic about the architectural splendor of St. Petersburg, this last of the great European cities, would be like saying that Paris is romantic in the spring—equally true and trite. And while Max and I loved what was left of St. Petersburg in the Leningrad of our student years, it wasn't the Western architecture that so attracted us. Rather, going to Leningrad accorded the uplifting sensation of being at the boundary, the Gulf of Finland literally and figuratively separating Russia from the West.

On that particular December visit we took a train Thursday night, expecting to arrive in a northern city choked with snow and icy chill. Express overnight trains arrived early in the morning, and in winter,

immediately upon getting off the train, Muscovites would take comfort
in knowing that our climate was less severe. This time, as we walked up
the long platform of the Moskovsky Station, songs about the city of Lenin,
the cradle of Revolution, booming from up on high, Max and I were surprised how unseasonably warm it felt. Buttons were undone and winter
hats stuffed in our weekend duffle bags. Katya Tsarapkina, who met us
on the platform by the entrance to the station, remarked with only a bit
of irony that we both looked like "young Western authors or filmmakers"
visiting her windy city. Years later we would refer to that December visit
to Leningrad, my last one before leaving Russia, as our "surrealist" trip.
The word *siur* (short for the Russian *siurrealizm*) was considered chic, and
we used it not always correctly or judiciously. But my recollections of that
visit are enveloped with a film of strangeness, and not just tinged with
spellbinding illusions of loss. Such was the light, crisp and bright, with
strips of azure and magenta around the edges of buildings and monuments. Such was the air our lungs gulped that morning; not the arresting
air blowing from the Gulf of Finland, but a warm, southerly breeze, as
though wafting in, impossibly, from the Mediterranean. And such was
the mood that overtook us at the train station platform and held us, happy
and serene, for the rest of the warm December day. We dropped the bags
at Katya's; she, too, was blowing off classes at her Chemical-Pharmaceu-
tical Institute. The three of us rode the Metro back to the Nevsky and
walked along the embankment of the undulating Griboedov Canal, heading for Leningrad's Theater Square, site of the Kirov Theater (now, again,
Mariinsky) and the Leningrad Conservatory of Music. There, at the college attached to the conservatory, our Pärnu friend Marina Evreison was
studying piano. Marina's last name means "Jewison"; when she said her
name in public, people turned around. This petite woman with percep-
tive eyes of Nevan grey was something of a legend in the circles of young
Leningrad musicians, owing both to her talent and to the quiet dignity
with which she carried her most Jewish of names. We had all known each
other for years. Katya, Max, and I swang by the wing of the conservatory
where Marina's class was about to end. We ran down the conservatory's
granite steps cracked by wartime bombardments and polished by the
feet of many great musicians. We were all feeling free and rebellious. All

day, while it was still light out, we wandered around Leningrad, soaking in its beauty. At some point we chanced upon a movie set. It must have been an episode about the 1900s revolutionary unrest. We saw barricades, upturned carts and broken-off wheels, all sorts of odd pieces of antique junk, student greatcoats with a row of silver buttons, old-fashioned worker's caps, and even a whip lying on the cobblestones. The film crew must have been taking a lunch break, there was not a soul on the site, not even a security guard. We walked around without obstruction, trying to put the scene together. Had a unit of Cossacks just rushed by, charging at a group of street protesters? Had the czarist police just carried away the bodies?

The movie set was just a few blocks from the editorial offices of *Aurora*, one of Leningrad's monthly reviews. I left a batch of poems in the hands of an editor with bushy eyebrows, who had looked them over and promised to recommend them. I was still hoping to get my poems published in Soviet magazines, but my efforts would soon come to a halt. In January, political currents would pick me up and carry me, and I wouldn't resume my publishing efforts until the summer of 1987, already in Italy, already an émigré.

I didn't know this was to be my last visit to Leningrad before leaving Russia. In January 1987, while on student vacation with Max at a ski lodge outside Moscow, I cast the impressions of that December visit to Leningrad into a cycle of three poems. I would ski in the morning and then lounge in bed in the afternoon, composing, while Max read a Russian translation of *Look Homeward, Angel*. In writing these poems I pictured myself as an American journalist embedded with Soviet students so as to understand their lives and gain their perspective. In the poems there was a "girl in a short coat" and a "friend in misted-over spectacles." Based on Marina Evreison and Max Mussel, the characters in the poems were painted from an estranged, otherworldly point of view. They were, I now understand, poems of parting in advance of the parting itself.

When I re-read these Leningrad poems today—and also try to work them out in English—I'm struck by the near-absence of a gruesome Soviet existence: "that—games of a tame autumn deity / that—we who fell for these games / shaking the train station frenzy away / that—our girl never asking she blindfolded us / with a scrap of mist saved under her flap / the misty orb is open."

References to historical time are faint, and if it weren't for a mention of the streets of Leningrad and an evocation of the movie set that we had come upon, one couldn't even tell that the poems described the Soviet 1980s. In its last lines, the cycle spoke of "notes of farewell notes of forgiveness." As an émigré, I have long been a student of saying goodbye. But I'm surprised when I find notes of forgiveness in the poem. Whose forgiveness—and for what—could I have possibly had in mind?

INTERLUDE

READERS' REPORTS

WHILE PURSUING PUBLICATION of my poems in periodicals, I also attempted a more wholesale approach. I had assembled a typescript of a poetry collection. It was originally called *End of August*, but I later retitled it *Herd above the Meadow*, after the title poem about horses and the steppe. The logical first choice was the publishing conglomerate Molodaya gvardiya (Young Guard). Young Guard had a separate editorial office set up for working with "young authors." "Young and younger authors" might have said it better, since in the Soviet Union one's literary youth could be defined loosely, and writers in their late thirties were in some cases still branded as "young." The editorial office for young authors not only handled individual collections but also sponsored the so-called "cassettes," volumes in which first collections by four or five authors would be put out under the same cover.

Back in October of 1986 I had made an appointment with a senior editor, Galina Roy, a puff-pastry of a lady who kept looking to her right and left before she would say something in a soft, perfumed voice. She asked where I went to school and seemed encouraged by the fact that I wasn't another "humanist" or a student at the Moscow Literary Institute, where future professionals were being trained and mostly messed up. Roy took my manuscript upstairs to have it stamped and "registered," as was the standard in those days. I would be hearing from them in about a month, after the reader's report came back. A part of me—the part that to this day refuses to believe in so-called collective wisdom—was buoyant with hope as I left the editorial office.

238

In early January, the mailwoman wearing my mother's old paisley jacket brought a large grey envelope to our door. The manuscript was returned to me with a perfunctory note from G. Roy and her boss S. Rybas. Wishing me to persist in mastering "the Russian poetic tradition and rich-most culture," the editors echoed the enclosed, three-page reader's report. Although it wasn't vicious in tone, the report contained certain coded expressions. It hinged on three points. One was the author's "youth and inexperience," and needing to study with the "masters." Since I was nineteen years of age, this part was neither here nor there, platitudinal. Lines and phrases from my poems were quoted piecemeal, and the reviewer might have been correct in some of his criticisms. The more disturbing part of the report spoke of the absence of values, life experience, world vision, and spiritual "accumulations" in my manuscript. Maxim Davydov, the reader claimed, has a "vague idea of ethics." To support this point, he quoted lines describing the woman's body and openly speaking about desire and sexuality. From the report, I remembered the phrase "a complete abandonment of the ethical foundation." Something in the diction of the reader's report made me think of the anti-cosmopolitan campaign of Stalin's last decade, when Jewish artists and writers were targeted as "bourgeois nationalists" and "rootless cosmopolitans," both un-Russian and unpatriotic. The poison was spilled in the closing paragraph. "In Russian poetry," the reader stated, "there are many to learn from."

Incensed by the rejection, I charged Young Guard like a young bull. This time I ran past the office of Galina Roy and stormed into the office Svyatoslav Rybas, who was Roy's boss. A novelist, Rybas belonged to the right wing of the Russian nationalist movement within official Soviet literature. He was one of those burly, mustached, physical Slavic men who tend to intimidate intellectuals and Jews with macho body language and raucous voice.

"I've come to file a formal complaint," I said, tossing the manuscript and reader's report on Rybas's desk.

"What about?" Rybas asked, eyes unswerving.

"This is a classic case of Grand-Russian chauvinism," I blurted out.

"Are you referring to what's in your manuscript?" Rybas asked again, baring his teeth.

"You know very well that I am referring to the treatment of me by your editorial office and your reader's report. You just don't want to let any Jews in, do you?" I felt my voice teetering on some low verge of tears.

"Stop accusing us," Rybas barked at me. "I see nothing of the sort in the report. But I'm willing to make an exception and instruct Galina Roy, our most experienced literary editor, to work with you on revising and resubmitting the manuscript."

Rybas asked me to wait outside as he made a call. He then directed me to Roy's office. She acted embarrassed and mumbled something about being young and daring, about playing fife (as did the hero of one of my poems), and about the importance of compromise. She promised to select something for the annual poetry anthology *Sources* and also to go over the manuscript and then sit down with me.

But the promises didn't ring genuine, as though Rybas had furtively instructed her to placate me. I didn't have a good feeling as I left the editorial offices of Young Guard. Over the next few days I added some new poems to the manuscript, retyped the title page, and took the Metro to the editorial office of Sovremennik (Contemporary). Why did I bother with Contemporary, a publisher known for its nationalistic orientation and its patronage of younger provincial poets working in the "peasant" vein? On the surface, I did it because Contemporary published many first collections of poetry and was a second logical choice for a young author. However, a part of me just wanted to ram my head against the closed doors, to challenge the establishment. A young Jewish-Russian poet brings a manuscript to a publisher with a xenophobic reputation, and the publisher is obligated to respond with a statement, a report, a letter of rejection. In the changing Soviet times, I saw this as a culture war. At Contemporary I was dealing with an assistant editor for poetry, who had already published a few poems and told me she had a manuscript of her own under consideration. "Your collection could be considered for our series *First Book in Moscow*," said the poet-editor, and put my manuscript in a cardboard file with rope ties.

Here I need to suspend linear time and explain that by the time I had received the reader's report from Young Guard and submitted an expanded manuscript to Contemporary, I had been selected to participate in a series of readings under the auspices of the Commission for Young Authors of the Moscow branch of the Union of Soviet Writers. The readings, I believe three or four of them, were held in late November and December in the Maly (Small) Auditorium of the Central House of Writers. As the winds of change were beginning to fill the sails of Soviet culture, the organizers of the readings decided to resurrect the traditions of the Thaw. In the late 1950s and early 1960s, annual open tournaments of poets took place in Leningrad, and the winner was chosen directly by the audience. (My father had won the Leningrad poets' open in 1958.) The organizers also emulated the celebrated readings at the Polytechnic Museum in Moscow, at which the young stars of the 1960s, among them the poets Yevgeny Yevtushenko, Bella Akhmadulina, and Andrey Voznesensky, had captivated the audiences. The selection process involved bringing a manuscript to an office on the ground floor of a mansion in one of the side streets off the Arbat in the center of Moscow, and leaving it in the hands of two functionaries in their mid-thirties. The screeners asked some personal questions and said they would get back to me, and I really didn't think I would get in. And yet I did get a call back about a week after the interview, and my name (the *nom de plume*) was added to a list of poets scheduled to read in December. By mail I received several copies of an invitation that looked like it had been produced by an ancient letter press or else a dying photocopy machine. A copy has survived among family pictures in an album that traveled from Russia in a foreigner's suitcase. Printed on the invitation were the words: "January 14th. Poetic Wednesday (second session). Young poets are invited to take part in the winter tournament. Moderated by Valentin Ustinov. 19.00 Small Auditorium." The names of the readers weren't listed, making it look like an open-mike competition, even though they had already been selected.

Valentin Ustinov, as I was soon to find out, oversaw the discovery evenings from his perch at the Union of Soviet Writers. He had moved to Moscow from the northern city of Petrozavodsk. In Petrozavodsk Ustinov had been poetry editor at the moderately nationalistic magazine *Sever* (*North*) and rose through the ranks. Although he didn't seem like a visceral chauvinist, he allied himself with the Russian cultural right, representing its grassroots. He wrote ballads and laments about the damaged yet glorious heritage of the "Holy Mother Russia"—without articulating, like some of his literary brethren, just who exactly was to be blamed for the seventy years of Soviet rule. Ustinov shared his last name with that of the Soviet Minister of Defense, Marshal Dmitri Ustinov. In Moscow, Ustinov was installed as Secretary of the Union of Soviet Writers, a culture apparatchik. He was my father's age, a mellow guy with the looks and garb of a director of a regional House of Culture, a party man almost by default. He spoke with a dash of northern Russian *okan'e*, a peasant's cunning smile swinging in his squinted pale eyes.

To restore the time frame, I went to the reading at the House of Writers with the knowledge that my poetry manuscript had already been once rejected by Young Guard and would probably soon be rejected by Contemporary Publishers. Twelve poets read that evening at the Central House of Writers. At nineteen I was the youngest, and also one of the two visible Jews on the program. In the group that read on 14 January, not all of the poets were Muscovites and some looked like they were a generation older than I was. That group of readers included those who had already published their first collections and were making a living as professional authors, and those who, despite being in their thirties, hadn't yet broken in. In fact, in 1986–87, as I actively pursued publication, I intersected with a number of "young" and "younger" poets at various sanctioned and unsanctioned events and literary seminars. Several of the poets I met at the time have become coordinates of today's Russian literary scene; others, even though quite talented, have drowned in the post-Soviet inky waters, leaving no trace of published verse.

I was anxious throughout the evening, both because it was my first public reading at such a venue, and because I could feel my father's unease. From that January reading I remember only one face, that of Tatiana Bogatova, a stately woman with long loose hair who took either the second or the third prize. I remember her because my friend Max immediately nicknamed her "Bogatova-Neradova" (something like Ms. Wealthy-Stealthy, after the Russian saying *chem bogaty tem i rady*, literally "we're glad for whatever we have"). In my recollections I'm aided by the surviving invitation. On the back of the leaflet, in her very legible handwriting, my mother listed the names of the twelve readers in the order of appearance. In reproducing the list, I will furnish the names with parenthetical comments, drawn from what I know about the post-Soviet careers of these "young" literary men and women: 1. Vyacheslav Ananyev (I still encounter his name in print, but very occasionally); 2. Vyacheslav Sablukov (disciple of Vadim Kozhinov; *éminence grise* of the Russian cultural right, Sablukov is virtually unseen in print); 3. Vladimir Aristov (mathematician and poet, very visible and successful in both capacities); 4. Aleksandr Levin (an engineer-turned-poet and well-known chansonnier); 5. Vyacheslav Kazakevich (an actively-publishing Russian author living and teaching in Japan); 6. Natalia Bogatova (her name occasionally appears in print); 7. Ivan Bessonov (???); 8. Olga Grechko (in the 1990s I ran into several folklore-infused publications of Grechko's poetry, only later to find out that she died in 1998, age forty-one); 9. Leonid Volodarsky (best known today as an active Russian theosophist and author of esoteric treatises, both in verse and not); 10. Maxim Davydov (???); 11. Yusuf Sozarukov (???); 12. Igor Boyko (???).

To return to the tournament, the rules stipulated that each poet read for under five minutes. At the end of the evening each audience member got to vote. The three poets who received the greatest numbers of votes would make it into the next round; if I remember correctly, their poems would be chosen for an anthology. The audience of about a hundred and fifty was diverse in age and status. Sitting across the aisle from me was Semyon Babaevsky, a smiley, hairless octogenarian, author of the postwar Stalinist bestseller *Cavalier of the Golden Star*. When it came to voting he kept raising his plump hand, a bit coquettishly, not for three but for each of the readers.

Standing and rocking before the mike that evening, I felt like a fishing rod bent near the point of breaking. I was wearing blue jeans and a crew-neck wool sweater. I introduced myself with these words: "It so happens that I study at Moscow University's School of Soil Science." I recited from memory and I kept looking toward the back where my parents were sitting. My reading included a poem based on my expedition experiences in Teberda in the Caucasus. It was a lovers' tryst on a bridge over a mountain stream, with the muttering of an old Karachai man as a historical backdrop. Ironically, one of the poets reading that evening was Yusuf Sozarukov, an ethnic Karachai writing in Russian. He read about the deportation of the Karachai in 1943. When the votes were cast and tallied, I came in fourth. If I'm not mistaken, the third prize went to the Karachai poet. In Russian poetry, as in other spheres of Soviet life, the nationalities game was continuously playing itself out.

Less than a month after the 14 January reading at the Writers' Union, I received the reader's report from Contemporary. It came from a poet about ten years my senior, and compared to the Young Guard report, which wasn't exactly sympathetic, this one read like an openly vicious diatribe. The opening sentence got stuck in my memory: "We must not publish this book." In the original Russian, it was the same phrase one would use for such expressions as "smoking prohibited" or "no soliciting." The report referred to the prospect of my book's publication as "harmful" to Russian poetry. This was not just a polite attempt to steer away those who were aesthetically or ideologically suspect. This was prejudice unbridled.

I read the report and immediately called the office of Valentin Ustinov at the Secretariat of the Union of Soviet Writers and made an appointment to see him. A few days later he received me in his office behind two doors, one of them yellow and lacquered, the other padded and soundproofed from the outside. Ustinov sat me down and asked me what brought me to him, speaking at first like a senior colleague and avoiding the kind of coded chancellery language one might have expected from an apparatchik. I felt more relaxed and I told him that I as encountering antisemitism in trying to place my poems. Ustinov sighed, like an old swineherd at the sight of a storm cloud, and said to me:

"What's happening with your manuscript isn't good." He spread his arms and continued, still in a trusting voice: "And I feel bad about this, and about the reader's report. You're gifted and you write good Russian poetry. Not my cup of tea, but gifted, interesting. The report was unkind."

He paused, as though trying to choose his words carefully. I silently listened.

"But I can't do anything for you," Ustinov finally said, lowering his gaze.

I was still looking at him in silent bemusement.

"And I can tell you from my own experience," Ustinov said. "It's sometimes hard to be a Russian writer."

Hard to be a Russian writer? Was Ustinov talking about Tolstoyan existential imperatives? Of a Russian writer's moral responsibility to speak out against injustice? I didn't think so. He was, I believe, speaking in code to a Jew writing in Russian. By "Russian writer," Ustinov meant "ethnic Russian writer" as opposed to Russian-language writer, who could come from many backgrounds in the vastly multiethnic Soviet Union.

I didn't get the sense that Ustinov was, like some of his cohorts, a Jew-hater by his gut. But I think he subscribed to Russian nationalistic versions of the common anti-Jewish myths that had gained currency in the Soviet 1970s. These myths alleged that Russian Jews dominated the Soviet media, the literary translation establishment, and the ranks of playwrights and screenwriters, and also that Russian Jews among the literary critics stifled the expression of religious and national sentiments by ethnic Russian authors. Such Soviet myths went back to the 1930s and found their first open expression during the late 1940s and early 1950s, the years of Stalinist anti-Jewish paranoia. They were old-fedora by the 1980s, and yet I was shocked to hear this unthreatening Russian functionary venting out his frustrations at me, a young Jew without status or connections who had come to seek his help.

When I think back to that conversation with Valentin Ustinov in his office at the Union of Soviet Writers, I truly cannot believe this man my father's age wasn't embarrassed about his rhetoric. In the early Soviet decades there were still quite a few Russian writers of Jewish origin serving in official capacities in literary journals, newspapers, publishing houses—and in the apparatus of the Writers' Union. By and large, the ranks had been cleansed of decision-making Jews by the early 1950s. In the 1980s, only a token number of Jews born in the 1910s through the 1930s, notably such "official" Jews as the novelist Anatoly Rybakov and the poet Margarita Aliger, still influenced Soviet literary politics. But their relative weight in the official Soviet apparatus was extremely low, and was especially low in Russian poetry.

"Can't you see what's happening!?" I said to Ustinov. "You're pushing us to emigrate. Is this what you want, to have no Jews left in Russian literature? Then why don't you just let us leave?"

This was more than what Ustinov was willing to discuss. In fact, in adhering to the code, he hadn't once pronounced the word "Jew." He was after all an official, a functionary. Discussing the Jewish question openly would have been much too much for him.

As I was getting up to leave, Ustinov said: "Wait, there's one thing. I'm hearing of a new initiative called April, a journal or publishing house. They would be sympathetic to people like you. I wish you good luck."

I had already heard of the nascent April movement. Behind the project was a group of official liberals, several of them Jewish. There was talk of a publishing venture without censorship, perhaps a cooperative of writers. The initiative later evolved into the Committee of Writers in Support of Perestroika. It didn't publish its first annual collection, *April*, until 1989.

At home, I told my father about the conversation and Ustinov's advice. My father had personally known some of the writers behind the emerging April movement; not one of whom had voiced support for the persecution of Jewish refuseniks. The April initiative worked handily for the Russian nationalist wing: Jews were being channeled out of the literary mainstream into some sort of an officially sanctioned liberal ghetto. April also smacked of Khrushchev's failed Thaw, of broken post-Stalinist promises, of a compromise of the weak. Of course my father wanted the best for me, wanted me to publish my poems. But for himself he wanted no palliatives, no aprils or thaws. He only wanted to leave Russia, finally to emigrate—or so he thought at the time. Back in the spring of 1986 my father had started to write works of shorter prose he called *fantellas*— "*fant*astical nov*ellas*." In his imagination, the refuseniks' exclusion from the Soviet society had been coupled with the absurdity of being a Jewish writer who is both silenced by and shackled to the Russia that has rejected him. In the fantellas, love, talent, and miracle opposed (and sometimes defeated) forces of totalitarian vulgarity. Central to these new works was the autobiographical figure of a Jewish artist clashing with the regime. Throughout the fall of 1986 my father read the fantellas at refusenik seminars and literary gatherings, including one at Genrikh Sapgir's apartment. Although he didn't put much hope in the changing literary climate, on the suggestion of Evgeny Reyn and one other writer, he clenched his teeth, put together selections of his *fantellas*, and visited editorial offices of two magazines which had placed themselves under Gorbachev's unfurling banners of glasnost. The first, *Znamya* (*Banner*), was a leading Moscow literary monthly; the other, *Ogonyok* (*Little Flame*), was an illustrated weekly with a colossal circulation. The editor of *Banner*, Grigory Baklanov, was a Jew who had made a career of writing about his experiences as a young serviceman in World War II. The likes of my father, refusenik Jews writing about Jewish questions, were the last thing Baklanov needed in his Soviet abode. "If you had been Bunin and had emigrated and died," unflinchingly he said to my father, "we might have published you today." The other editor, Vitaly Korotich, was less concerned with life and death or with barriers of Jewish identity. An opportunist, Korotich said to my father: "Perestroika is out in the streets. Change your plans for emigration. Retract. And we'll run your stories in the next issue." Both the prospect of having died and the one of betraying his dignity and the whole community of fellow refuseniks didn't exactly appeal to my father.

As for myself, the attempts to place my manuscript at two Soviet publishing houses and the subsequent candid conversation with Valentin Ustinov had cured me of remaining illusions. I would resume my efforts at seeking publication in the summer of 1987, already abroad. From Italy, in July of 1987, I would mail a selection of my poems to New York, to *Novyi zhurnal* (*The New Review*), the oldest Russian émigré quarterly and an heir to the Parisian *Contemporary Annals*. I addressed my submission to Roman Gul, a former White Army officer, turned Berlin-based émigré writer, turned editor of *The New Review*. I accompanied the submission with a note along the lines of "who but you would appreciate the feelings of a young poet who has recently left behind his entire world. . . ." I didn't know that Gul had already passed away in 1986, age 90. I still don't know how it happened that two of the poems I had sent to Gul appeared in the Fall 1987 issue of *The New Review*, commencing my career as an émigré Russian author.

9

PURIM-SHPIL

DISPASSIONATE STATISTICS now tell us that throughout the entire calendar year 1986, only about 900 Jews were allowed to emigrate from the entire Soviet Union. We didn't know the exact number at the time, but we knew that Jewish emigration had stood at a near standstill. Unlike some of the dissident activists who wanted to ameliorate or to improve the Soviet society from within and were trying on the pink-colored glasses of reformism, for the coming new year, 1987, veteran refuseniks wanted nothing but deliverance. The prospects of Jewish emigration had not improved, even as perestroika slowly gained momentum. If anything, our legal status had become worse when the Soviet Council of Ministers passed the August 1986 resolution "Concerning the additions to the principles for entering the USSR and leaving the USSR." According to the amended emigration rules, leaving the USSR permanently was only allowed if one had "direct family members" abroad. Of the tens of thousands of refuseniks, how many could claim parents, children, or siblings living abroad? Was my father's elderly Uncle Munia in Israel a "direct family member"? The August 1986 resolution also contained various clauses and conditions, in light of which citizens might not be allowed to emigrate. For the most part, they were formulated with deliberate vagueness and nonspecificity that would make it easy for the authorities to bend and manipulate them. Refuseniks felt vulnerable as ever, yet there were signs that the position of our community might be changing for the better. There were fewer crackdowns by the authorities on refusenik seminars, such as the one my parents ran at our apartment.

To me, a nineteen-year-old living a double life, the next major signal of change had been sounded just a week before the coming of the new year of 1987. Andrey Sakharov and his wife and fellow activist Elena Bonner were allowed to return to Moscow from internal exile in Gorky (Nizhny-Novgorod). There was talk about Sakharov's triumphant arrival, about a small crowd of foreign journalists, about his having refused to bow to the Soviet authorities. University students talked about Sakharov almost unabashedly, in cafeterias and during breaks. Slava Len, a colorful Moscow bohemian whom my parents and I had met through Genrikh Sapgir, wrote an ode on the return of the "great Russian man Andrey Sakharov" to Moscow. In the early months of 1987, Len performed his ode at various underground literary gatherings as the word "underground" itself was beginning to lose its Dostoyevskian significance.

In January 1987 a plenum of the Central Committee was finally convened. It had been twice postponed. At the plenum, perestroika and glasnost were finally announced as official policy. Gorbachev, who in his public remarks no longer minced words about the course of reforms, appeared to be fully in charge. Or, at least, he appeared to be under the impression of being in control of the Soviet freight train that was beginning to speed out of control. Immediately after the January 1987 plenum we began to hear of an "amnesty" for refuseniks. Gorbachev had to show the West he was serious about doing business, refuseniks pundits ventriloquized. On 5 February 1987 Gorbachev received a delegation of high-caliber US officials in the Kremlin. Among the US dignitaries were two former secretaries of state, Henry A. Kissinger and Cyrus R. Vance, as well as Harold Brown, former secretary of defense. Some aspects of the visit were reported in the Soviet press, and we were hearing more from broadcasts on Voice of America, BBC, Kol Israel and other "voices." We knew that members of the delegation requested and were allowed a meeting with Sakharov. In the few days following the visit, both the official Soviet media and the foreign media, which we heard intermittently on the unscrambled broadcasts, began to report the favorable reviews from the US delegation. The reports seemed grossly upbeat, as though some of the main American players in the Cold War arena had mellowed with age and decided to give Gorbachev's perestroika praise still unearned. To my

parents and me, and to many other refuseniks, the visit by the US delegation and the thumbs-up for Gorbachev looked out of touch with our own
reality. Or was it we who were out of touch?

In 2002, at an academic symposium in upstate New York, I referred to
the peculiar historical choices refuseniks faced in the winter of 1986-87.
A historian of Russian Jewry, a man just slightly older than I, challenged
me during a public discussion. He claimed that the official repressions
against Jewish refuseniks and activists had stopped by 1987 as Gorbachev's reforms gained momentum. He was in Moscow at the time, the
historian said, glibly, and he didn't see any more signs of persecution. I,
too, was there at the time, I replied. Except that I observed the repressions
not as an American scholar in Moscow, but from within the refusenik
community. I tried to speak unheatedly, like an academic. Yet I could feel
the anger rising from my solar plexus. The evidence, you want the evidence? In my head, I kept seeing my mother as I left home for school on
that particular Friday morning in the middle of February 1987. The way
she saw me out the door, a stamp of mournful solemnity on her face. . . .

. . . Week-long refusenik demonstrations had been scheduled to take
place in the center of Moscow. Their goal was to protest the condition
of Yosef Begun, but also to let the world know that refuseniks were still
oppressed in spite of perestroika. Begun was a legendary Jewish activist,
a Hebrew teacher, and one of the emblems of our movement. He was a
Prisoner of Zion serving a third sentence. His third trial took place in 1982,
when refuseniks and dissidents alike were being terrorized into silence.
In February 1987, Begun was fifty-four, a few years older than my own
father. He was being held at the infamous Chistopol Prison in Tatarstan,
where the dissident Anatoly Marchenko had died only two months earlier. Begun was a refusenik hero, and at home we had frequently talked
about his arrests, trials, and sentences. I remember hearing fragments of
my parents' conversation about a refusenik demonstration in support of
Begun. The initial intention had been just for women refuseniks—wives,
mothers, sisters, and daughters—to stand with Begun's wife and son in a
busy Moscow street.

To this day I feel guilty about the way I said goodbye to my mother
on the morning of the day she was going to stand at the demonstration for

Begun's release. I sensed that my mother was planning to participate in a political action, but I didn't know for sure and I didn't ask. I'm not sure my parents had even told me. I'm not sure I knew. My memories of that February day are blurry, recollections of details blunted. Had I truly not known most of it or have I suppressed the details?

On that February day, my mother was beaten up by plainclothes agents at the demonstration. She was knocked off her feet and thrown on the pavement. I was not by her side. I didn't even stand in the sidelines supporting her. I was in class or eating lunch at the university refectory or wherever else I was at the time. Having a good time, flirting with a classmate, playing the normal Soviet student?

When I came home that evening, my mother was lying in bed. Usually she is quick-witted and razor-sharp in her reactions to the world. But that particular evening there was unusual slowness to the way mother spoke and even to the way her smile spread out over her face. The way her hand floated up to touch my face as I bowed to kiss her.

My father was bustling around like a private nurse, giving mother now soup, now a cup of tea, now a little cognac. In the hallway my father whispered to me that mother had taken a bad fall. When my parents talked of the demonstration in front of me, they sounded less like parents and husband and wife and more like two tired conspirators. They were discussing the timing of the demonstration: a large international forum for disarmament was to open in Moscow the following weekend, and foreign scientists and cultural and public figures were already converging on the capital. I remember my father mentioning the name of the American writer and activist Norman Mailer. The phone kept ringing, and father kept saying to me that he "got it" and then disappearing in his den. Mother asked me about my day, held my hand. I described the minutiae, the classes, the breaks, the food at the cafeteria, the banter. She listened and nodded with her eyes only. Soon she dozed off and I left my parents' bedroom. Later my father and I had tea in the kitchen, and he told me that "mamochka was a hero" and that she "had it pretty bad today." It was an eerily quiet evening. My father didn't want to leave mother alone in the apartment, and we didn't go on our usual evening walk around the neighborhood.

I have pieced together the story of that February day. It was on the Arbat, a sometimes hectic pedestrian area in the heart of old Moscow a bit like Newbury Street in Boston. I knew practically every building and store on the Arbat. When I close my eyes I can visualize the setting, the stores, the window signs. But I don't see my mother; I wasn't there with her on the day of the demonstration. The main sources of how I picture my mother at the demonstration are a lone photograph and a short clip from a US news broadcast.

By the time the photograph appeared in *Newsweek* on 23 February 1987, just over a week after the Yosef Begun demonstrations, a brief news clip had already aired on *ABC World News* with Peter Jennings, reported from Moscow by Walter Rodgers. Taken by Andrew Rosenthal, the photograph in *Newsweek* accompanied Mark Whitaker's article titled "Countering Gorbachev: How Should the West Respond to Moscow's 'glasnost' campaign?" The caption under the photo reads: "The limits of 'openness'; Begun's son (left) and other protesters just before attack." Cinematographers call this type of a medium-long shot *"plan américain."* It's a knee shot of a group of three people standing in the street in winter clothes. On the left is Boris Begun, to whom the *Newsweek* caption refers only as "Begun's son," without a first name. He is only two or three years my senior, but he looks much older. A thick, bristly beard covers his sunken cheeks. He wears a knit woolen sweater and an almost-matching woolen cap with a pompom on top. His hooded coat is unbuttoned. In front of his chest he holds a piece of brown cardboard with the words "Freedom to my father Yosef Begun." To the right of Begun's son stands my mother. She looks so beautiful in her men's muskrat fur hat and short fur jacket. Beautiful and condemned. I can see her opaque lip gloss and shadows of rouge on her chalk-white cheeks. Her eyes are looking inwardly, as though she's facing imminent danger. Shades of determination, fear, calm, and irony are ensconced within her features. I look at the picture, I know this is my mother, and yet I cannot physically believe she's there, in a small defenseless formation of refuseniks. My mother is not identified in the *Newsweek* photo or in the news broadcast. The magazine caption describes her and the older refusenik gentleman standing next to her as "other protesters." They are anonymous to history. The white hair of the older gentleman has come undone at his left temple. He's old enough to have fought the Nazis, but it's not the Nazi enemies he is eying from under his heavy brow. My mother's gaze is turned upward and inward, as though she refuses even to make eye contact with the thugs lined up in front of the demonstrators. But the old gentleman clearly sees something coming their way. To the right of the older refusenik gentleman I can make out a woman's fur hat of another demonstrator. But there are two more bodies in the photograph. One is just an outline of what looks like a torso and hat, standing very close to the protesters. But the other one is much more tangible. In the right corner of the shot, facing the older gentleman and my mother, there is a man wearing a blue-gray striped hat with the Russian words "Sports Sports Sports." One can only see his left cheek, jaw, and temple, and there's something disciplined, militaristic in his posture. The man's light brown barn jacket with a small faux-fur collar and his "Sports Sports Sports" hat were a Soviet everyman's clothes. They had no style or fashion. In them one merged with the crowd, looked Sovietly nondescript. Some of the brutes who beat up my mother and the other refuseniks might have been not KGB operatives but "volunteers." It's possible these young jocks were *lyubery*, members of an organization that had been gaining notoriety in Moscow. Around the autumn of 1986, when I first heard the term *lyubery*, it referred to gangs of young ultrapatriotic men who would descend upon the streets of Moscow from Lyubertsy. Lyubertsy was a southeastern suburb of Moscow that grew in the 1930s during the construction boom, when peasants-turned-construction workers were settled there. By the time I was growing up, a final stop of Moscow's busiest Metro line was built close to the Lyubertsy town line. A commuter train also stopped directly in Lyubertsy. Moscow was easy to access, and in the winter of 1987 Muscovites heard, more and more, about *lyubery*. Bodybuilding was their leisure of choice. They worshipped the Soviet military and Soviet sports. They came across as ultrapatriotic, anti-Western, and anti-intellectual. One heard, not just anecdotally but from the Soviet press, about their attacks on punk rockers and "heavy metalists," whom *lyubery* associated with the West's "corrupting" influence on the mind and body. Underprivileged young men from a working-class suburb, *lyubery* took anger out on various targets they both envied and reviled. Would a group of Jews protesting on the Arbat in the center of Moscow have made an attractive target for the *lyubery*? Would it have taken much for the KGB to manipulate and direct their anger?

The *Newsweek* photo captured the moment just before the attack, and the ABC news broadcast actually showed the demonstrators being attacked, encircled by plainclothes agents, pushed around and harmed. The violence against refusenik protesters was widely reported in the Western media, both in print and on television, as was the fact that even the journalists themselves were attacked. That people outside the Soviet Union knew about the demonstration and crackdown became evident to us over the weekend. We were getting call after call from the United States, from Canada, from England, from France. Millions of people saw the demonstration on television. Among them were our old friends who had emigrated back in the 1970s and early 1980s, as well as some of the foreign emissaries who had visited us. To them my mother, whether or not identified by caption or commentary, was absolutely real. They saw her right on the brink of the attack. A camera was knocked out of the reporter's hands. They could hear a woman's screaming. Then the recording was ruptured. I later heard that to the people who knew my mother, this was a scary moment, as they didn't know what happened and imagined the worst. With trepidation, they telephoned us from overseas, to ask about her condition.

Different—a sign of changing times—was that the Yosef Begun demonstration received press coverage inside the Soviet Union, and that the coverage showed variation of tone. I'm looking at copies of two articles. The first appeared in *Vecherniaia Moskva* (*Evening Moscow*) on 20 February 1987 under the title "What They Raised Their Arms Against," signed "V. Slavin." The second one was printed in *Izvestia*, one of the two largest Soviet dailies, on 22 February 1987. Titled "When Arguments Aren't Enough," the article was signed "L. Vladimirov." The article in *Evening Moscow* described, with unreformed Soviet hysteria, how the protests were orchestrated by the American embassy as spectacle with the Western press, diplomats, and local "jesters" contorting themselves before the camera. The article referred to the refusenik protesters, not the dispersers, as "hooligans": "At the end of the repulsive performance, [Muscovites] appealed to the city authorities with a demand that next time they not treat the hooligans liberally, regardless of their citizenship." The *Izvestia* article attempted a more objective tone, yet presented the demonstration as an anti-Soviet "action" by the West, designed to tarnish the image of the USSR in its new reformist course.

Yosef Begun was released from prison on 20 February and arrived in Moscow on 24 February 1987, just a week after the refusenik protests. At the train station in Moscow he was greeted by cheering refuseniks and Jewish activists. Begun's release was an official gesture comparable to the release of Sakharov at the end of 1986. The refusenik protest was, by that measure, a great success. Luckily, my mother was not physically maimed. As for me, the whole episode yielded one immediate result, actually a visceral response to the way the Soviet state and its agents had violated my mother. Instead of the feeling of hope one might have expected in a young person, a student at a time of a national upheaval, I felt violent wrath against the state. I felt I could no longer stay, if pro forma, in the skein of official ideology. Political grand gestures were running through my head, including a solo protest on the Moscow University campus. In the end, I decided that I could not remain a member of the Komsomol. I had joined fairly late in high school, and did so calculatedly, for opportunistic purposes, to be able to get into a good university. On the surface of it, I had been what they might call an average Komsomol member "in good standing." An idealistic part of me felt that I should have resigned earlier, back in the autumn of 1985, in protest over my father's persecution and defamation. But there was another part, the pragmatist, which felt that such an act would have simply given the system an open invitation to take revenge on me—ostracize me, dismiss me from the university, send me away somewhere. All along, my parents had been trying to support the pragmatist in me by encouraging me to pursue some semblance of a Soviet career at the university and by delaying my open involvement in refusenik politics. Something about the political moment registered in me personally after the February demonstration. I could no longer endorse the Soviet system by remaining, along with the vast majority of its young people, a card-carrying member of the Komsomol. This sounds quixotic, but I felt that I was doing morally the right thing. I wanted to share with my parents the status of having openly challenged the system.

On a standard sheet of paper, the same as my father and I used for our typewriters, I wrote a short resignation note: "Please remove me from the membership of the Komsomol for personal reasons." During a break between two lectures I went up to the office of the School of Soil Science's Komsomol Committee. The chairman of the Komsomol Committee was a graduate student by the name of German Kust. He was tall, unprepossessing, with a head of thick chestnut hair. In his simple two-piece suit and plain white shirt, he looked like a turn-of-the-century Russian naturalist from lower–middle-class origins. As I slowly walked up the double flight of stairs, I reflected (and in moments like this, one often latches on to details completely extraneous to the matter itself) on the slightly parodic combination of German Kust's first and last name. His shared his first name both with the name of the protagonist in Pushkin's *Queen of Spades*, and also with German Titov, one of the first Soviet cosmonauts. Kust's last name, which in Russian means "shrub" or "bush," underscored his innate link to the soil. They say a last name can affect one's choice of occupation, and this seemed true in the case of German Kust. He actually went on to become a professor of soil science and an expert on evolution of arid soils and desertification, and as of the writing of these pages, Kust was teaching at Moscow University.

Kust was about six years my senior, and I had always felt that he was pulling the cart of Komsomol activism with the sanguine professionalism of a work horse on a hot summer afternoon—drunken peasants, gadflies, and all. In the autumn of my freshman year, Kust had recruited me, on the basis of my high school record of school service in the "Club of International Friendship," where the activists had traditionally been the Jewish "rootless cosmopolitans." I helped him with a few events for international students. At the end of the year, Kust had asked to meet in person and invited me to join the School Komsomol Committee and serve as his assistant for "international work." I politely refused, claiming health problems and a "difficult situation" at home. Kust didn't press me on details and suggested that I remain involved in some other capacity.

I handed my resignation note to Kust and stood in the office, waiting, as he looked it over. He shook his head, glanced at me in disbelief, and mumbled something like "I see." Later that day, while I was out somewhere with my friend Max, Kust telephoned me at home. My mother took the call. Kust introduced himself, with excessive care and politeness, and went on to describe my resignation to her. He must have thought my parents didn't know. "Is something wrong with Maxim?" he asked my mother. "Sick, perhaps, or having some mental difficulties?" My mother told him that I was fine, not having mental difficulties, not sick. In the eyes of German Kust, I was doing something crazy, doubly crazy for a Jewish student at Moscow University. In my eyes, the resignation from the Komsomol was not an action, but simply a belated acknowledgment of being one with my parents, finally, in our Jewish refusenik plight.

In the old Soviet Union the day of 8 March, the International Women's Day, enjoyed an official status. By the time I was growing up, rituals of this "women's day" had conjoined scraps of the rhetoric on women's equality surviving from the heyday of Soviet revolutionary feminism with abundant, macho-sentimental signs of attention paid to the "weaker sex" by Soviet boys and men.

Preparations were under way to hold a refusenik women's hunger strike on 8 March 1987. The refusenik community itself was riddled by politics, cliques, and power struggles, and various internal tensions had been exacerbated by the climate of Gorbachev's equivocal reforms. Something could soon change, and the main question was how to make it happen sooner for all refuseniks and for one's individual family. Following the Yosef Begun protest on the Arbat, my mother had become an influential presence among the Moscow refuseniks. This irony of anti-government movements wasn't lost on our family: you had to have been beaten by the KGB in the street in order to be recognized by fellow activists.

A blunt motto had been chosen for the three-day hunger strike: "Let us go." My mother was one of the organizers. Her professional English skills made her a spokeswoman for the nearly seventy strikers. In the morning they would gather in groups, in several designated apartments.

At our place, a group of ten refusenik women held vigil. Word about the upcoming hunger strike had been sent to the West and to Israel, and Russian-language broadcast services covered it while it was still happening, which was exhilarating. Part of the plan was that in solidarity with the refusenik women, women abroad would also protest, including a group of them right near the Wailing Wall in Jerusalem. Women's organizations abroad were involved in supporting and publicizing the protest.

The striking refusenik women had received instructions, in fact more than one version of instructions, on how to ready oneself for not taking food for several days. There were recipes for cleansing one's body, for what to eat in the coming days. 8 March 1987 was a Sunday, and I stayed home for part of the day. While women in my mother's group shared a sense of danger, there was also a feeling of celebration and even some humor. "They won't come and arrest all ten of us, will they?" one of the women said, laughing. The spirits soured a bit by the end of the day. The strikers at our apartment were expecting a telephone call from Los Angeles, from Rabbi Fields, but the call didn't go through. Instead, it was postponed for a whole day, and the telephone company notified my mother that she would be taking the call at the district post and telegraph office, not at the apartment. At the time, one couldn't direct-dial to or from the Soviet Union, and there were also all sorts of regulations regarding international calls. The prospect of having to leave the apartment on the second day of the hunger strike, and of talking in a public place, was unnerving. My mother had a poor night of sleep from all the excitement of the first day and from thinking of the upcoming phone call with Harvey Fields. The second day of the hunger strike was a Monday, and I was at the university most of the day. In the evening I found my mother exhausted, but very hopeful of the outcome of the protest. She had been to the district telegraph office with several other women from her "group." This time, luckily, the call had come through. It was morning in Los Angeles when they called from Wilshire Boulevard Temple. The telephone conversation was being broadcast on speakers directly to the sanctuary, where women members of Rabbi Fields's congregation were holding a hunger strike in solidarity. My mother spoke with Rabbi Fields on behalf of the other women refuseniks, and she later told me it felt like she was speaking to the world. When I read a transcript of the broadcast, which was published in a Jewish newspaper in California, I'm amazed by my mother's composure and by the toughness of her voice. She was certain she was addressing not only an audience of supporters in America but also a KGB audience listening in at home.

As part of the conference call with Rabbi Fields, mother read a prepared statement, calling on the people in the West to send telegrams *directly* to Gorbachev. And send telegrams they did, both to Gorbachev and to the hunger strikers. Over the next two days the mailwoman kept coming to our door with batches of telegrams from across the United States and from Europe. They included expressions of solidarity by individuals in small towns across America, from politicians, from women's organizations. Words fail to describe how much being supported this way meant to the striking refusenik women.

The intimidation continued, although it was now taking new, perestroika-adaptive forms. As in the case of the Yosef Begun demonstration, there was official press coverage. What's more, certain Soviet journalists were becoming designated "specialists" in refusenik affairs. I'm looking at a copy of an article titled "Hunger Strike on Special Commission." Signed "R. Anatolyev, Sh. Ilyin," it appeared in *Evening Moscow* on 9 March 1987, the second day of the women's hunger strike. The journalists portrayed the strike as an action orchestrated by the West and a "farce." The apartments where the women gathered are referred to, mockingly, as "headquarters." The article contrasted the hunger strike by women refuseniks with the hunger strike by Dr. Charles Hyder, an American astrophysicist who had been camping out in Lafayette Park near the White House in order to call the world's attention to nuclear disarmament. Hyder seemed convinced that the ball was in the American, not the Soviet court. His hunger strike was being widely and sympathetically covered in the Soviet media. Gorbachev had apparently urged Dr. Hyder to halt the strike and invited him to the Soviet Union for medical treatment, but Dr. Hyder refused. The real gem of glasnost hypocrisy was when the article called on those "citizens" who identify themselves as "refuseniks" to "open [their] eyes, look out the window" and see that "spring is outside." This was becoming the new government rhetoric on refuseniks: we have perestroika and glasnost, and you still want to leave?

My mother's name had appeared in the paper among seven or eight other names of refusenik women treated like saboteurs of perestroika. The intimidation by newspaper coverage also felt to us like a form of official courtship, aimed at cajoling veteran refuseniks into laying down their arms and reconsidering their wishes to emigrate. On balance, the coverage of the women's hunger strike in the Soviet press might have done us more good than harm. At least it showed us that the regime had placed the refusenik problem on the agenda of the day. As the holiday of Purim approached in the middle of March, my mother was busier than ever with refusenik activism while my father was in the throes of rehearsals. He had written a Purim-shpil play to be performed by an underground Jewish troupe.

If these pages lack in laughter and merriment, it's not because my intention has been to make this book gravely serious. I've been trying to recapture the daily mixture of anxiety, uncertainty, and even fear that defined our lives as refuseniks. In this regard, the Purim season of 1987/5947 stands out as one of the brightest memories of, and also one of the few carnivalesque episodes in, those bitter years. The Jewish holiday of Purim celebrates survival. Told in the Book of Esther, the story of Purim is an exilic tale, set in Babylonia, then governed by the Persian King Axasuerus. Haman, a vizier to the king, is working on a plot to exterminate the Jews living under Axasuerus's rule. Haman's genocidal plan is undercut by Esther, a Jewish woman and the new Persian queen (Axasuerus doesn't know she is Jewish). Working jointly with her foster father and cousin Mordecai, who is a courtier in Axasuerus's palace, Esther saves her people. Haman is killed and the plot against Jews prevented. One of the ways the Jews have celebrated the joy of Purim is by mounting Purim-shpiln—Purim plays based on the kernel story about the beautiful Esther, the villainous Haman, and the wise and enterprising Mordecai. Myth and memory have mingled and lived on.

For Soviet Jews of the postwar years, associations with ancient Babylonia rang close to home. From early childhood I had been hearing from my father how his paternal grandmother would joke that "she and Yossele" had the same birthday in December (by Yossele she meant Joseph Stalin).

Great-grandmother Fanya, who outlived Stalin by ten years, spoke of the day Stalin died as a day of Jewish liberation from what looked like a certain death at Stalin's hands. She was referring to the antisemitic campaign of Stalin's last years that culminated with the so-called Doctors' Plot. At the time of Stalin's death on 5 March 1953, many Soviet Jews expected deportation to remote areas and feared the worst. In my refusenik youth, the idea of a miraculous escape through some divine or fatidic intervention, which lies at the heart of the Purim story, resonated with special significance. As we watched the Purim-shpiln in crowded Soviet apartments, we would relish the Jewish victory over ancient enemies and dream of our own escape from Soviet Babylonia.

Some time in late January of 1987 an unofficial troupe consisting mainly of refuseniks approached my father with the idea of writing a Purim-shpil. Roman Spektor, the troupe's charismatic leader, appeared in minor parts and referred to himself as the "acting director." He was a tall, sinewy man in his thirties, a mane of unkempt black hair, a curly beard, and charcoal eyes. Spektor and his troupe had sought out my father because he was a professional author with playwriting experience, a veteran refusenik who had chronicled the lives of refuseniks in a novel, and a poet who had written many song lyrics. I remember Spektor and two core members of his troupe coming to our apartment to meet with my father for the first time. They said they wanted something more than a Russian-language rendering of the Book of Esther puffed up with Yiddish and Hebrew songs. That sort of thing had been done to death, they said. Something different was on their mind, a Purim-shpil infused with contemporary politics, to set them apart from the other troupes active in Moscow. They wanted my father to create a Purim-shpil that would be poignant, topical, biting. Spektor brought up traveling troupes of the Commedia dell'arte coming to a new town, learning the local news and politics, and quickly writing these facts and rumors into a new show. They wanted my father to come up with a play that would incorporate both perestroika politics and prevalent moods of the refusenik community. Father treated the commission as though not an amateur troupe but Moscow's leading theater had asked him to write a play. In two weeks he had the Purim-shpil play written, and the troupe began its rehearsals.

I was fortunate to observe the composition of the Purim play from within. Father and I discussed it almost daily as he worked on it. From the outset he resolved to shift and alter the historical timeframe by setting the play not in ancient Babylonia ruled by a Persian king, but in a composite totalitarian empire experiencing pangs of reforms. The reforms were rather reminiscent of perestroika, and yet my father was very careful to coalesce contemporary Moscow and ancient Babylonia in such a way that politics, however captivating in the spring of 1987, yielded to the spectacle of art. My favorite thing in the Purim-shpil were the *chastushki*, folk-inspired couplets, that my father composed for Queen Vashti (Axasuerus's previous wife) and for the evil Haman himself. In those couplets, performed either to the accompaniment of a small klezmer-style band or a lone guitar, one heard about the beating of refusenik women by athletic thugs. One of the most hilarious couplets told of the American talk show host Phil Donohue, who came to Moscow in January 1987 to tape a week's worth of episodes of his syndicated TV show. Donohue laughably sought to find a silver lining in every aspect of the Soviet authorities' behavior.

Over the Purim-shpil season of 1987 I got to know the members of the troupe very well. Most of them were in their twenties and early thirties. Most were refuseniks, although the male lead, Aleksandr Ostrovsky, who brilliantly played King Axasuerus, was not. In March and early April of 1987, I must have attended at least ten performances of "our" play. When my father couldn't go, I acted as his representative. My friend Max Mussel accompanied me to some of the performances. It was a lovely group of people, remarkably free of jealousies and intrigues that often underlie the lives of thespians. Besides the explosive "acting director" Spektor and the hedonistic and witty Ostrovsky (Axasuerus), the core members of the troupe included the brother and sister Shchyogolevs, Lev (Hamman) and Irina (Esther). Lev was a Jewish fighter with the heart of an unrealized Russian civic poet. Irina was a true Ashkenazi beauty, the prima donna of our Purim-shpil. There was also the gentle Gennady Milin, who played one of Haman's two henchmen. The youngest performer was my peer Nadya Ilyina, daughter of our refusenik friends Pavel Ilyin and Mikaella Kagan. Nadya, a pianist with loose red hair and a pale freckled face,

played Queen Vashti and sang punchy, political couplets. Nadya wasn't
the only professional musician in the troupe. There was also the violin-
ist Alla Dubrovskaya, without whom there would have been no plaintive
or joyful Jewish tunes filling the backstage; the guitarist and songwriter
Aleksandr Lantsman; the guitarist Aleksandr Mezhiborsky; and Feliks
Abramovich on tambourine and melodica. And there were also various
"groupies" and family members serving as support staff. Traveling to an
underground Purim-shpil performance at someone's apartment, often by
a combination of subway, bus, trolleybus and streetcar, with bags full of
costumes and props and musical instruments in their beat-up cases, we
behaved like members of an itinerant troupe. We would arrive early to set
up, feed on whatever we had brought with us or were offered by the hosts,
and sometimes stay after the performance, singing and partying. And yet,
even through the most bohemian moments of sharing a drink or a kiss or
a raunchy joke or a line from a beloved poet, not for a minute did I forget that this was a brotherhood and sisterhood of refuseniks, a transient
commune that would fall apart and be dispersed when its members were
permitted to leave Russia for good.

Those motley gatherings, those Jewish spectacles in overheated apartments with windows wide open onto Soviet streets. One never knew for
sure who would be in the audience besides refuseniks. Friends of friends
would invite friends of their friends. Foreigners, including American students doing a semester in Moscow, often turned up. There would be various odd characters, bohemian artists, silent frowning old men in derby
hats, bejeweled and heavily scented ladies. Once my father simultaneously invited our friend Genrikh Sapgir, a poet and a playwright, and
two visiting American college girls to join us at a performance, and we
all shared a ride in a crowded, smelly trolleybus while communicating
in metaphorical Rusglish. Another time a shy-looking young man took
me for a foreigner and whispered, at the end of the performance, "Do
you not speak any Russian?" "I'm Russian, I mean Jewish, I'm one of us,"
I replied, choking with laughter. On another occasion I invited Jamie and
Betsy Cooper, whom I had already befriended, to attend a performance
at some posh apartment building not far from the Pushkin Art Museum.
We had met outside Kropotkinskaya, the Metro stop named after the

anarchist Prince Kropotkin. We rang the doorbell. The stern Jewish lady who opened the door wouldn't let us in until I pleaded with her I was the author's son. "And who are these two?" she asked, pointing to the Wisconsinite brother and sister who looked utterly un-Soviet. "They are my friends, from America, they are with me . . ." I answered. "Too many young foreigners, that's my crummy opinion," she grumbled and finally undid the security chain, letting us in. Another time I remember arriving and being told by the apartment's owner, a man who forced his children to speak Hebrew at home, that the performance was only for those committed to going to Erez Israel.

The whole Purim-shpil experience, the goings around town and the chance encounters, allowed me to interact with Soviet Jews from many walks of life. I met refuseniks so uncompromising in their insistence on going to Israel or in their religious observance that it was difficult to have an open conversation with them. I also ran into refuseniks who, even after years and years of being stuck, still had no time of day for Israel and considered it a repressive regime. Especially meaningful to me, considering that my closest friends identified as Jewish but didn't come from refusenik families, were random conversations with Jews teetering on the verge. How many had been wanting to emigrate or considering emigration? Thousands of undecided Jews? Hundreds of thousands of vigilant and waitful ones? I also came across Jews, including my peers, who said they could not imagine leaving Russia yet wanted to express themselves, freely and openly, as Jews.

The refusenik rumor mill kept burbling on about clandestine funding somehow coming from Israel to support a grassroots refusenik troupe or even a full-fledged theater. Such talk was not entirely new. For over two decades, two forces had been shaping the intellectual life of the Jewish movement in the Soviet Union. The *politiki* ("politicians") firmly stood on the rock bed of Zionism and aliya. The *tarbutniki* or *kul'turniki* ("culturists," from the Hebrew *tarbut* or the Russian *kul'tura*) fantasized about legal cultural autonomy while seeking to revive Jewish life in Russia. With Gorbachev's reforms moving beyond rhetoric in the spring of 1987, the prospect of reopening Jewish emigration seemed real. At the same time, there was also the sense that the reformist Soviet leadership may want to ease or remove the various state-sponsored anti-Jewish restrictions, and give a green light to a restoration of the virtually suppressed Jewish religious and cultural life. But the emigration door may not reopen for a while, refuseniks were musing. And shouldn't we, at least for the time being, take advantage of the moment and press for greater Jewish autonomy in Russia?

Toward the end of the Purim-shpil season, two members of "our" troupe paid my father an unexpected visit. I was home, it was late, a wet April evening with earthen smells of spring wafting in through the kitchen *fortochka*, a quarter-size ventilation window. "We heard, actually well, we've been told, there was going to be a theater. Yes, we've been told it would be under your tutelage," they said to my father. "Not our troupe but 'David's Theater.' And we weren't even consulted?" My father was puzzled by their words and assured them he hadn't heard of any plans for "David's Theater."

In just a couple of days, though not unexpectedly this time, Yuli Kosharovsky came to see my father. An aura of mystery surrounded this man with a slender frame and eyes of wolfram. An electrical engineer by training and an underground Hebrew teacher, Kosharovsky had been a refusenik since the early 1970s. Kosharovsky was a man of few words. When he spoke, he did so with elegance, wit, and resoluteness. My father's junior by about five years, Kosharovsky was known to be one of the generals of the refusenik community. In contrast to the former Prisoner of Zion Vladimir Slepak, whom I got to know well in 1985–87, Kosharovsky came across not as a man on the barricades but as a quiet leader behind the scenes of refusenik protests and demonstrations. Kosharovsky and my father spoke behind closed doors in my father's den, then went outside to continue their conversation. When they returned, father looked a bit distressed. I joined them in the hallway and we made small talk for a few minutes. For some reason I remember that Kosharovsky inquired after my university studies and then mentioned his son, who was younger than I, perhaps still in high school.

"He has but one fiery passion," he said, slightly paraphrasing a poem by Lermontov.

"Erez Israel?" my father asked.

"No-no," Kosharovsky replied with a thin half smile. "Computers."

After he left, my father and I went on our evening stroll, which took us around the wrought-iron fence of a KGB hospital and also past the maternity hospital where I had been born almost twenty years earlier. I could see why Kosharovsky's visit had upset my father. I learned that at first Kosharovsky spoke with admiration of my father's literary work and the Purim-shpil play. He had a copy of the collection *Being a Refusenik*, in which part one of my father's novel *Herbert and Nelly* had recently appeared in Israel. A refusenik writer like my father needed support, Kosharovsky said. Would my father be interested in directing a Jewish theater? Regular productions and performances? New plays? All of this sounded very attractive, yet my father reminded Kosharovsky that local Jewish autonomy wasn't what refuseniks ultimately wanted. How about for the time being, while we're still waiting? Kosharovsky asked. Well, perhaps, father conceded. And even if you received the permission to leave, might you consider staying behind and taking charge of the newly founded Jewish theater? Kosharovsky inquired. My father replied that he didn't want to stay in Russia, that all he wanted was to get his family out. Will you go to Israel? Kosharovsky asked then point blank. My father felt cornered. Both he and my mother had very close relatives in Israel, he answered, a living uncle and a number of first cousins. But whether or not we would go to Israel was our family decision, a decision by all three of us. He couldn't and wouldn't give Kosharovsky or anyone a guarantee that we would definitely go to Israel. Kosharovsky silently nodded, signaling that the conversation was over.

The last performance of my father's Purim-shpil play took place at our apartment. It was a sunny afternoon, with glass beads stringing themselves on the rivulets of water formed by molten snow. All the moveable furniture had been cleared from my parents' bedroom. Windows were opened to let in fresh air. Chocolate-brown drapes with printed clusters of blue gardenias fluttered in the April wind, forming a backdrop for the actors and musicians and blocking the view. Behind the drapes there were crooked pine trees and wrought-iron spikes on the fence of the Institute of Atomic Energy.

Over fifty people crowded the room, feet extending onto the narrow proscenium. The performance was videotaped by an American diplomat. He was young and physically fit, with red hair and long, pale eyelashes. He had a wife who excitedly described the abundance of goods in US supermarkets, and two little kids who would later inherit my favorite stuffed dog and my East-German-made toy train set. It's hard for me to watch the surviving recording. I choke with tears when I see my father being called by the director to join the cast on stage at the end of the performance. I see my father dancing *freilechs* with the members of the troupe, levitating in his heavy tortoise shell frames, a sky blue suit, and an embroidered *kipa* of blue velvet. He looks exhausted from years of being fenced in, yet somehow unimaginably happy among the younger Jewish performers. He twirls around first with Esther, then with Queen Vashti. He kisses the actors and actresses on stage like a father would his own children. He seems at home in their element, a refusenik author for refuseniks, a dancing outcast among the dancing children of refusal.

In late March, just as the 1987 Purim-shpil season had been winding down, the refuseniks had mulled over the news of a visit by Edgar Bronfman, then President of the World Jewish Congress, and Morris Abram, at the time President simultaneously of the Conference of Presidents of Major Jewish Organizations and of the National Conference on Soviet Jewry. They were received in Moscow by high-level Soviet officials. We heard from various sources that on the table was the condition of Soviet Jews, specifically refuseniks, and emigration. The Jackson-Vanik and the Stevenson Amendments, the former only repealed in 2012, restricted US trade relations with the Soviet Union. The linkage of Jewish emigration and the trade relations between the two countries was hardly new. New were concrete and real promises that Soviet officials had reportedly made. The refusenik community was on the verge of change.

Something had also changed in my parents' attitude to my direct involvement in refusenik politics. They weren't encouraging me, but they weren't trying to stop me, either. A Komsomol membership no longer weighed me down or hindered me. Nor was I any longer particularly concerned about being thrown out of the university. I finally felt free to protest the authorities alongside my parents and other refuseniks. The demonstration I remember most vividly took place in early April in the center of Moscow. My father and I took the direct Metro line to Pushkin-skaya, then walked briskly for ten minutes from the Pushkin monument along the Tverskoy Boulevard toward the Nikitsky Gate. There was still a chill in the air, despite the late morning hour and the sun, and the buds on the limes and poplars were only beginning to unfold and show green. The *grande dame* of Moscow's boulevards, with its dark-green benches, smaller monuments, and play areas with seesaws, was empty, save for an occasional retiree reading a newspaper posted on a billboard or an old lady pushing a pram. We passed the Literary Institute on the right, the new building of the Moscow Art Theater on the left. Practically every inch of the street here was a museum, of either public or private memories. In that mansion Maria Ermolova, one of the greatest Russian actresses, once had her home. On that peeling bench I had sat kissing a Jewish girl I had met in front on the Moscow synagogue, both of us recent high school graduates waiting to take university examinations. Tverskoy Boulevard was a legendary rendezvous terrain, and I was now treading it with my father on the way to a refusenik protest. We approached the end of the boulevard with its public garden and circle of benches surrounding the monument to Kliment Timiryazev, eminent Russian botanist and plant physiologist. Past this point was a busy intersection where the Boulevard Ring veered to the right and continued for a few blocks under a different name, only to hit the Arbat. From here one could see the yellow confines and gilded cupolas of the Grand Ascension Church where Pushkin was married to Natalia Goncharova in 1831. More or less straight ahead lay Herzen Street, which took one past the Moscow Conservatory of Music and toward Red Square. Across the street on the left, the modern gray building of the Telegraph Agency of the Soviet Union (TASS) stood out among its teal and tea-green old neighbors with ornate stucco façades. I was tempted to come out of the boulevard and turn right onto a quiet lovely street called Malaya Bronnaya, with a struggling Russian theater occupying the building that had once belonged to the Moscow Yiddish Theater. A short stroll brought one to an enchanting area of Moscow, the Patriarch Ponds, and to what had once been an area of Moscow seething with Jewish life, around the former synagogue at Bolshaya Bronnaya Street.

Timiryazev, Russia's student of photosynthesis, stood tall on a granite pedestal, his hands crossed in the front over his lap. From a certain secret angle his knuckles formed a protruding something, probably unintended by the sculptor. At eighteen or nineteen it was considered a special sign of cultural subversiveness to point this protrusion out to a girl on a date and elicit a sexy giggle. I couldn't shake this association even as my father and I joined a group of eight or ten refuseniks already lined up in front of the Timiryazev monument. I had met two or three of them before; my father knew almost all of these men and women, grown middle-aged or even old during the refusenik years. Clipped or sewn to the breasts of several protesters were small posters with slogans. Having survived among my parents' papers is a sheet of white paper with a number of such slogans written out, crossed out, or edited: "Freedom of Emigration to All Refuseniks!"; "People of All Faiths, Fight for the Freedom of Jews–Refuseniks"; "Auschwitz, Babi Yar, and Refuseniks—a Jewish Tragedy," and others. Which one was my father to wear on his black leather coat with a row of buttons? I don't remember. The memories begin to falter and spin out of control. We arrive beneath the botanist's feet and greet the other refuseniks. Young men, some of them dressed in sporty attire, jump out of one of the buses parked right nearby. From another bus, slowly, descends a group of old men in derby hats; military decorations and badges are pinned to their chests. Several uniformed cops stand on either side of the low wrought-iron fence separating the inner, pedestrian space of the boulevard from the street and late morning traffic. The young men have short hair and broad shoulders; their mouths are twisted with ferocity. They are moving closer to our small chain of refuseniks. The war veterans shuffle their feet behind the broad backs of the jocks. Maybe a reporter or two are flashing cameras from a distance, but otherwise we're alone. Uniformed police are not interfering, just standing there and barking into their walkie-talkies. The jocks come up to the refusenik protesters and methodically rip off the small posters. The refuseniks continue to stand in place, some of them turning their heads to the side as if offering the other cheek to their detractors. Why are these Jewish men and women passive?

I wonder. Are they prepared to face annihilation with silent determination? Father and I are standing on the leftmost flank of the demonstration. Everything is unraveling so quickly that father hasn't even attached his poster when two thugs have stepped forward to rip one off the rain coat of a refusenik woman right next to us.

"What are you doing?" I yell at the two "athletes." I cannot control myself.

"What do you want, sissy? You stay out it," one of them replies, stepping toward me. Face to face, I get a good look at my enemy. He is not a *lyuber*, not a bored youth from a working-class suburb seduced with ultra-patriotic hogwash. This one is a professional, a well-groomed man in his late twenties, with a clean shave. His athletic cap and jacket must be a costume he was issued at his office that morning, to look like a Soviet nobody. But a thug he is all the same, doubly the thug because he takes a salary and state benefits for persecuting defenseless refuseniks.

"What right do you have to do this?" I scream right in his face, and in place of this one thug I suddenly see brigades of other thugs as they call Jewish kids "kike" in the school courtyard, assault Jewish girls in secluded park alleys, knock Jewish mothers off their feet on the Arbat Street. "What right?" the thug now brings his barrel chest inches away from mine. I can smell his cologned sweat, see a faint scar beneath his right eye. "Yes, what right," I scream back. I don't know what I'm doing anymore. "These people have a constitutional right to free speech," I scream.

"Get him out of here," a war veteran's bleaty voice emerges from behind the thug's back. "Why isn't he paying his debt to the motherland?"

In my state of extreme agitation I can still process the fact that the old goat is referring to me and to military service. I know I should stop and retreat, but I cannot. I want to fight the thug, I want to rip his throat out. I feel as though years of bottled-up rage are about to burst out of me. I want revenge for what he had done to my mother just a few weeks ago. I can feel that our bodies are about to collide, that he's just waiting for me to shove him first. Fortunately my father brings his right arm around my chest and restrains me.

"Stop, he's provoking you," father whispers loudly as he drags me away from the thug, who still hasn't moved. Only after a few minutes of being pulled away from the scene and in the direction of the Pushkin monument do I begin to come out of the trance.

I was lucky, very lucky. I had escaped unscathed. My father didn't say anything to me afterwards. I think he wanted to, but held back. Only now, as a father of two children, a man in my mid-forties, have I begun to understand what my father was feeling.

INTERLUDE

FAMILY TREE

HOW MUCH LONGER, my parents and I would ask ourselves. How much longer could our family remain uprooted on our native soil, before our roots would wither away and die? In the spring of 1987, as leaving the USSR consumed my daily existence, I developed something of an obsession with our family tree. I perused family albums (some of which wouldn't survive emigration), and I pestered my parents with questions that seemed quite idle, given the daily pressure of their lives. It was an oral, truncated family history I was parsing, and in collecting our ancestors' Jewish, Russian, and Soviet past I was finding some of the keys to my family's refusenik present. I discovered, for the first time, that family history comforted but also filled one's life with pain.

All four of my grandparents came from the Pale of Settlement, from what are now independent Ukraine and Lithuania. Up until 1917, the vast majority of Russia's Jews had been constricted to the boundaries of the Pale, originally the empire's western and southwestern frontiers. All four of my grandparents had made sweeping—and in many ways successful—transitions as young people. As did tens of thousands of children of the Pale, in the late 1920s and early 1930s they actively sought a place and a career in a new world, which during the first two Soviet decades still intoxicated the Jews with a promise of equality, if not acceptance. All four of my grandparents were culturally Russianized, and yet for each one of them, Jewishness was inescapable. Over the decades of living outside the former Pale, even their first names and patronymics had become palimpsests of acculturation, a Jewish past still echoing in my parents' own birth certificates issued before World War II. My paternal grandfather Peysakh

Borukhovich became Pyotr Borisovich, a name free of Judaic tell-tale signs. My paternal grandmother Bella Vul'fovna, a Lithuanian rabbi's daughter, metamorphosed into Bella Vladimirovna. My maternal grandfather Aron Ikhilovich put on the tidy clothes of Arkady Ilyich. And only old university friends from Kharkov remembered my outwardly Slavic grandmother Anna Mikhailovna as the once Jewish Nyusya Moshkovna.

Both of my mother's parents grew up in the Ukraine (which has since lost its definite article). My mother's mother, Anna (Nyusya) Studnits, was born in 1914 in the town of Bar, presently of the Vinnitsa Province of Ukraine. Around the time of my grandmother's birth, almost half of Bar's population, or 10,000, were Jewish. She lost her mother as a young girl. After living with the family of her father's sister, she left home as a teenager to go to junior college. My maternal grandmother came of age at the time when the Soviet Union was moving at a fast clip toward Stalinism. She was, in many ways, a typical member of that first all-Soviet generation, collectively orphaned during the 1917 Revolution and the Civil War, later schooled and brainwashed in the late 1920s through the early 1930s into accepting Stalin's collective fatherhood. Although never a member of the Party, my grandmother lived much of her adult life in the Soviet Union by pretending to believe in the official ideology. Like so many women of her generation living through Stalinism and World War II, she had learned to be a survivalist. My grandmother told me about being a student at Kharkov Economics Institute in the 1930s. After Grigory Petrovsky, an "old Bolshevik" and then President of the Ukrainian Soviet Republic, was purged in 1937 (he would be released from the Gulag in 1953), my grandmother and two girlfriends stayed up all night sifting through their photo albums in search of their pictures taken alongside Petrovsky at a gala for top university students. The pictures with the deposed Ukrainian leader were either eviscerated or burned altogether.

As a young boy, I spent a great deal of time either alone with grandmother Anna Mikhailovna or together with her and my cousin Yusha, daughter of my mother's sister Zhanna. For a number of years I would spend a whole summer month with my grandmother at the Estonian resort of Pärnu, and curiously I don't recall my grandmother's Sovietness spilling into our conversations. Perhaps I just don't remember or don't wish to remember? What I do remember about my mother's mother, from early childhood, was the striking degree of her Russianization and assimilation. While she remained "Jewish" in her official papers (in the Soviet Union "Jewishness" was defined as nationality or ethnicity, not religion), in the street, blonde and gray-eyed, she looked and deliberately acted Slavic and un-Jewish. Whenever possible, she tried to conceal Jewishness in her public life. In their communal apartment, where privacy was hardly attainable, grandmother Anna Mikhailovna forbade her elderly father to speak Yiddish in public and tried hard to hide matzos from the non-Jewish neighbors. Instead, she made traditional Russian blinis during Maslenitsa (Shrovetide), the Orthodox Christian festival marking the last week before Lent. Around Orthodox Easter (a week after Passover), my grandmother used to bake the traditional Paschal sweet bread (*kulich*) to blend in with the rest of the neighbors. She had been raised in a Yiddish-speaking household, with a father who until his death in 1953 started his days with putting on the *tfillin* (phylacteries) and mouthing his prayers. And yet, by the time I was growing up, my grandmother had lost (or suppressed?) the ability to speak Yiddish almost entirely. Only occasionally would I hear words like *makhteneste* (daughter's or son's mother-in-law) or *abisale* (a bit) coming out of her mouth as though they lived a life of their own in the depths of her memory. While technically semi-native, her Russian was perfect, virtually free of any Jewish or Ukrainian accent, save for an occasionally misstressed past tense feminine verb. After over two decades in America and until her death in 2009, her unhurried Russian speech with its languorous intonations still betrayed a long-term resident of old Moscow.

My mother's parents were as different as two people could be. My grandfather, Arkady (Aron) Polyak, was passionate, life-loving, obsessive; my grandmother was rational, exacting, ascetic. Fate shouldn't even have accidents, and yet an "accident of fate" brought them together. After graduating with a degree in economics, my grandmother had been sent to my grandfather's home town of Kamenets-Podolsk to work in the regional planning department. In 1939 my grandfather stopped in Kamenets-Podolsk on the way back from a vacation in North Caucasus. He called on my grandmother at her office to deliver a message from a fellow engineer from Moscow, one of my grandmother's old suitors. The suitor had proposed to my grandmother in a letter a year earlier, and she replied that "her plans for the future were still wide open." After calling on my grandmother, my grandfather (a young engineer whom her co-workers described as a "tall, very handsome man"), invited her to his sister's house. To maintain decorum, my grandmother brought along a girlfriend. There was a little party at the house of my grandfather's sister Sonya, with food and dancing in the yard under the ripening April stars. A few weeks later my grandmother visited my grandfather in Moscow for the May First holiday, the International Worker's Day. He was living in a tiny closet of a room, in a communal apartment. "If we get married," he told my grandmother, "then they can't force you to go back to Ukraine." It wasn't what they call a "harmonious marriage," and in the middle of the 1950s my maternal grandparents divorced, only to get back together over a decade later. Unlike her younger sister, who was conceived during the jubilant months following the victory over Germany and Japan, my mother owed her conception to the signing of the Molotov-Ribbentrop pact of 1939 and the brief prewar interlude of calm. My mother was born in Moscow in May of 1940, one year, one month, and three days before Nazi Germany invaded the Soviet Union.

My maternal grandfather Arkady died when I was eight, but I remember him very well. Even in his latter years, after going blind (a complication of poorly treated diabetes), he still charged those around him with an intensity of mind and a generosity of heart that I have hardly encountered since his departure. In the projection room of memory, grandfather Arkady acquires Olympian proportions. One of my strongest memories of him is coming to visit him as a child and finding him in his den playing cards with two old friends, drinking vodka, smoking, and treating his company and himself to the abundant *zakuski* crowding the side table next to his divan. For me as a Soviet first-grader, there was something incredibly mystifying and liberating to see my gourmand grandfather playing *Preference* with his pals.

Grandfather Arkady came from a solid middle-class Jewish family and attended *cheder*, the Jewish religious school. Three of his siblings, a brother and two sisters, were Zionists and escaped to what was then the

British Mandate of Palestine, while another brother and two sisters stayed in the Soviet Union. As a young man, in the late 1920s, my grandfather moved to Moscow from Ukraine. After two or three years of working as a stone-mason he had managed to obliterate his "bourgeois" past, join the ranks of the proletariat, and get himself accepted to an engineering school. By the time he had met grandmother Anna, both of his parents had already passed on: my great-grandmother Khana-Feyga in 1935 in their native Kamenets-Podolsk, and my great-grandfather Ilya (Ikhil) Polyak in 1933 in the faraway Birobidzhan, an enclave on the Soviet-China border where he was building the Jewish Autonomous Province. Grandfather Arkady went on to have a career as a communications engineer. Unlike his wife, even after decades of living in Moscow, he never quite shed the skin of a Jew. Jewishness defined him, broadcasting itself through his overachievements, his questionings of received wisdom, his bitter-sweet humor, and, above all, through his distinctly Jewish view of history. Something in the way my mother's father carried himself left even me, a Moscow Jewish boy, with no illusions about assimilation. He passionately hated the Soviet regime, while also managing not to lose to the system at its ideological games and machinations. He was—not even through what he said but through what he didn't say, or better yet, *how* he said it at the dinner table—the source of my mother's early ideological dissent. His inner opposition counterbalanced my grandmother's Soviet conformism. His whole life, grandfather Arkady ached for Israel.

Following the early 1950s, as the Soviet policies towards Israel became increasingly hostile, grandfather Arkady was having to avoid a direct correspondence with his siblings and family there so as not to damage his career and his children's happiness. He employed the services of a Jewish woman who had few concerns about her own career. Through this woman, my grandfather corresponded with Israel. To this woman's address, his siblings, and especially his sister Tsilya, to whom he was the closest, sent occasional gifts from Tel Aviv, Haifa, and Be'er Tuvia. In 1965, taking advantage of a brief interlude that preceded the complete severing of diplomatic relations with Israel during the Six-Day War, Tsilya, a chief nurse at the Hadassah Hospital, traveled to the Soviet Union and stayed in Moscow for over a week. She and her brother hadn't seen each other in forty years. Being with sister Tsilya ignited anew grandfather Arkady's desire to get his children out of Russia. At the time my young parents were storming the career heights and wouldn't hear of emigration. But the first seeds of a Jewish yearning to emigrate had been planted in my parents' hearts in 1965, still two years before I was born.

Was it destiny or the legacy of my grandfathers' origins that brought my parents together in 1962? It was a family wedding in Leningrad, where my father's people had been living since the early 1930s. The wife of my father's eldest uncle Yanya happened to be a cousin of my mother's father, and the wedding gave the Polyaks and the Shrayers a chance to remember their place of origin. Natives of Kamenets-Podolsk lovingly referred to it simply as "Kamenets." A place quite mythological to me when I heard about it during my Moscow childhood, Kamenets had been absolutely real to both my grandfathers, who grew up there and even played soccer together.

Located on the banks of the Smotrich River close to the border of the Austro-Hungarian Empire, Kamenets-Podolsk had been the capital of the Podolia Province and an important regional center of commerce. On the eve of World War I there were 23,000 Jews, or nearly half of the population, in Kamenets-Podolsk. The family of my father's father, Peysakh Shrayer, had been living in the environs of Kamenets-Podolsk at least since the first half of the nineteenth century. For several generations, a milling business was the Shrayer family enterprise. My father's grandfather, Borukh-Itsik, who was born in 1875 in the village of Dumanov outside Kamenets-Podolsk and died in Leningrad in 1946, was the last one in our loud dynasty of millers. He raised five children into adulthood. His first wife died in childbirth after giving birth to a little girl who only lived for a year. Their other children, Yanya (Yakov) and Berta, were two and three when their birth mother died. In 1906 my great-grandfather married Fanya (Freyda) Kizer, who came from a poor family and was interested in socialism. She raised her husband's two children like her own. Great-grandmother Fanya Shrayer and great-grandfather Borukh-Itsik had three boys, Munia (Moisey), Pusya (Peysakh, later Russianized to Pyotr), and Abrasha (Abram). Pusya, my grandfather, was born in 1910. In the 1910s the family moved from the countryside, where stood the Shrayer mills, to Kamenets-Podolsk, a city by today's standards. My father's father grew up in an established, financially secure family where Judaic religious rituals were loved, but not fanatically obeyed. As children, the Shrayer siblings had received instruction in Judaic law and custom and a solid European education. Yiddish was spoken at home, and the Shrayer children were also exposed to colloquial Ukrainian and Polish, and later, in Gymnasium, to literary Russian. As far as I can tell, my great-grandfather Borukh-Itsik didn't shun modernity but respected Jewish traditions. In 1917, on the eve of the two revolutions that brought the Russian Empire to its collapse, my grandfather's father bought a white stucco house on Sobornaya (Cathedral) Street from a Polish count and installed his family in an upper–middle-class neighborhood. In 1917–21 regimes and occupation forces came and went in Kamenets-Podolsk: Provisional Government, Bolsheviks, Ukrainian Directoriat, General Denikin's White Army, Simon Petlyura's Ukrainian units, Polish troops, and Bolsheviks—this time, to stay. Still aspiring to the lifestyle of the urban haute bourgeoisie during the years of the New Economic Policy, even my shrewd great-grandfather hadn't anticipated the voracity and destructive pace of the Soviet experiment. In 1924 my father's Uncle Munia, who had been active in the local left-wing Zionist movement and interested in agriculture, left Kamenets-Podolsk and sailed off from Odessa to Jaffa. The family had been broken up and never recovered after his departure. The presence of a son and brother in Israel would later become a verdict in the hands of the Soviet system.

In 1927 my Shrayer grandfather moved to Leningrad and started working there, first as a plasterer and later as a hospital orderly. In 1928, when the country was about to close the door on the New Economic Policy and private entrepreneurship as it entered the Five Year Plan, what remained of the Shrayer milling business was levied with excruciating state taxes and shut down. The family in Ukraine had fallen into hard times. By 1933 my great-grandfather, the former Merchant of the First Guild Borukh-Itsik Shrayer, having already spent two months in jail for allegedly concealing assets from the Soviet authorities, was living in Leningrad in tiny rooms he shared with his wife and eldest children. Yet even in Leningrad his business talents didn't lie dormant. He became a "requisitioner" for the film studios, spending his days in a mad chase after clothes, props, equipment, and whatever else was needed to shoot a picture. In the Venice of the North, life went on for the Shrayer family, a life without Kamenets and against all Jewish and Soviet odds.

The Shrayers had uprooted themselves and emigrated—yes, emigrated from Ukraine in the former Pale—to Leningrad. It was a different world, the Soviet world that all four of my grandparents encountered in the late 1920s. To the young Jewish men and women born in the late 1890s and early 1900s, the large Soviet cities seemed aglitter with career opportunities and escape routes. In the late 1920s, when the Shrayers made the move from the former Pale to Leningrad, my grandfather and his siblings had all managed to whitewash their origins by working menial jobs and earning workers' status. It was a struggle—"friends" from Kamenets sent anonymous letters to their places of work and study, denouncing them as "bourgeois elements." Yet by the middle of the 1930s, my grandfather Pyotr and his three siblings, Yanya, Berta, and Abrasha, had graduated from colleges and universities to become Soviet professionals ("specialists"). In the late 1930s and 1940s grandfather Pyotr had the most glamorous career of the four of them. He joined the Party while studying mechanical engineering at the university and was favored for his practical talent and leadership skills. In the late 1930s my grandfather, still a young man, rose to the position of chief engineer of Leningrad's "department of trams and trolleybuses." He volunteered for the Soviet–Finnish War of 1939–40, serving in a mechanized unit, and during World War II he was transferred to the Navy and decorated for valor. A lieutenant-commander at thirty-four, he had commanded a unit of torpedo boats and saw his last war action during the capture of Königsberg in April of 1945. In 1949, my grandfather was dismissed from a prominent position at the transportation branch of the Ministry of Internal Affairs, because the Soviet policy towards the young Jewish state had taken a sinister turn, and my grandfather, a Party member, had a brother in Israel. The postwar years brought not only professional but also personal devastation. In 1934, grandfather Pyotr had married my grandmother, Bella Breydo, and my father was born two years later. In August of 1944, some six months after the siege was lifted, my father and grandmother returned to Leningrad from a remote village in the Ural Mountains, where they had been evacuated to as the siege had closed on the city in 1941. Soon after their return, grandmother Bella discovered that her husband had been having a wartime affair with another Jewish woman. He had a baby daughter with her, born in March 1944. Grandmother Bella refused to take her husband back in spite of his supplications. He was not happy in his second marriage, which his parents and siblings never quite accepted.

Because I was born and grew up in Moscow, and my grandfather Pyotr was living in Leningrad, I saw him only a few times in my early childhood. Above all, I remember an aura of charm and nobility that he exuded. Only three episodes have survived in my memory, the first in Technicolor, the other two in black and white. The summer of 1968, one of my first distinct memories. Soft, gentle, faded colors. I'm fourteen months old. We're spending the summer at my grandfather's *dacha* in Beloostrov on the Karelian Isthmus. It has rained earlier that August afternoon, my grandfather is standing on a sandy path laid with dry pine needles near a crooked wooden fence, in a striped blue and gray pajama coat, eating small raspberries off the wet bushes and zestfully telling something unbelievably funny to my mother, who is laughing the way a teenager laughs at hints of the forbidden, and here everything vanishes into fog, and we're now in our old Moscow studio apartment. I'm already three, and I see an extreme close-up of my father's trusty typewriter, Olympia. A photo of "Papa Hem" in a fisherman's sweater hangs above my father's desk in the corner of the living room, which doubled as our bedroom; when I was asleep, my father often typed in the kitchen or bathroom, typewriter enthroned on the toilet. My parents are both sitting on a couch upholstered in charcoal wool. My mother looks like a young girl and sports a Brigitte Bardot haircut. On the coffee table there's a platter of Crimean pale elongated grapes called *damskie pal'chiki* ("ladies' little fingers"). It's October, grape season in the south of Russia. Across from my parents, my grandfather and his third wife Adelina, whom I had dubbed Auntie Yo, are sitting on crab-legged kitchen stools. Milky light is pouring into the room from the balcony behind their back. In my hands I hold a bow and arrows, my grandfather's present. And the third episode, the briefest, shot a year later, in the fall of 1971. Grandfather Pyotr is dying of cancer at the age of sixty-one. My father brings me to the hospital ward to say goodbye. The light in the hospital room is a scary, lumpy gray, and my grandfather smiles so tranquilly that I cannot understand how someone so charming could be dying.

Of my four grandparents, only my mother's mother Anna Studnits, *Babulia* as we called her in Russian, had been a constant presence in my life. I loved my maternal grandfather Arkady Polyak but lost him when I was eight, in 1975. I only got a few glimpses of my paternal grandfather Pyotr Shrayer, far too few to be able to judge his character, but perhaps enough to appreciate how little of his outer composure and wit I have inherited. But I never knew my father's late mother, my grandmother Bella Breydo. Nor did my mother, as my parents wouldn't meet for almost two years after her death. In the autumn of 1960, my father was serving as a military physician in Belarus. My father's first cousin Boris Breydo, a dastardly Soviet engineer, son of my grandmother's older brother, found my grandmother dead in her bedroom. Heart attack was deemed the official cause of death. She had never recovered from the unfaithfulness of her beloved husband. Before the Nazi invasion, my father's parents had been together for seven years. To Grandmother Bella, her husband's wartime infidelity meant *betrayal*, and not just weakness resulting from temptation in the face of death. I suspect that my grandmother's heart was forever broken in 1945, not only by my grandfather's unfaithfulness, but also by her own inability to forgive him and take him back—a war veteran in the country which had lost millions of its men. Bella's heart must have been breaking and breaking yet again when she saw how much her Jewish son, growing up in a rough neighborhood of the postwar Leningrad, needed a functional family and a present father. By today's American standards, at thirty-four she still was a young woman when the war ended in 1945, and could have probably remarried. She was only forty-nine when she left this world.

The noun "grandmother" tastes bitter on my lips when I speak of my father's mother, stranger and even bitterer in English than it is in Russian. I always missed her growing up, more acutely than I missed my late grandfathers. I miss her every time I recognize in myself a trait that my father had inherited *not* from his father's side and that I don't know to be of my mother and her parents. It must be from my grandmother's ancestors, the stern *mitnaggedic* Lithuanian rabbis, that my father and I have taken an idealistic belief in universal fairness, a low tolerance for cowardice, a resistance to compromise. Growing up, I felt my Lithuanian grandmother's blood flowing in my veins and reminding me of Lithuania, where we come from. My grandmother's blood pulsates in me as I write of Jewish revolutionary fervor, its atheist illusions, and hopes of acceptance and equality.

Bella Breydo (Broyde is an alternative spelling) was born in 1911 in Šiauliai (Shavel) and grew up in Panevėžys (Ponevezh). At the turn of the century the Lithuanian town of Šiauliai had about 10,000 Jews out of the total population of about 17,000 residents. Her father, Rabbi Chaim-Wolf Broyde, had descended from a long line of Litvak rabbis, which may have included the Gaon Rabbi Yitzchok Aizik Broida. Grandmother Bella rebelled against her father and left home as a young woman. In her youth she admired the Blue Blouse, an agitprop performance group founded in 1923 and touring the country all through the 1920s and early 1930s. The blue-blousers preached an aesthetic of new proletarian simplicity of style, disdaining the bourgeoisie and mocking its cultural accoutrements. Grandmother Bella moved to Leningrad to study organic chemistry. Daughter of a rabbi who scorned secular art, she sang Russian songs and wrote poems. Pushkin and Esenin were her favorite poets. During my father's childhood and youth, his mother's Jewish pride manifested itself in her contempt for ethnic prejudice, and also in the culinary traditions that she faithfully followed. On Fridays, while living in a communal apartment with Russian neighbors, she made gefilte (stuffed) carp and noodle *kugel*. After the Nazi invasion, her elderly father, who since the 1920s had been living in the Belarusian town of Polotsk in the Vitebsk Province and worked there as a Jewish teacher, refused to leave his home despite his children's entreaties. After the war, a Belarusian neighbor told my grandmother that her father was shot by a Nazi hand while praying over his sacred books. My grandmother's elder brother Eyno Broyde, who had been a banker in Panevėžys, was believed to have been killed with his entire family in August 1941. A photos of Eyno's two sons, Ruvim and Meyr, dated "Panevėžys 1931," has been preserved in the family archive, alongside a later photo of my father's cousin Ruvim Broyde, dated "16 August 1940 Panevėžys" and inscribed, in Russian: "For good remembrance to all of you dear ones. Yours, Ruvim." Growing up, I learned from my father that after the war his mother and her siblings heard an unconfirmed rumor that their brother's family had escaped to South Africa, where Lithuanian Jews had been immigrating through the Baltic seaports. Grandmother Bella had even tried to locate them through the International Red Cross, but to no avail.

When I look into the almond-shaped, slightly downsloping eyes of my older daughter Mira and my father, I imagine Grandmother Bella's eyes. I like to think that the spirit of my Litvak grandmother looks gladly upon my family, safeguarding us from the brutalities and betrayals of time.

10

TAKING LEAVE

IT WAS ALREADY THE BEGINNING OF APRIL, past the point of no return for the Russian winter. OVIR, the Office of Visas and Permissions, was still silent. We had no choice but to remain a thorn in the side of the authorities. My father decided to hold a solo six-day demonstration in the same place where he had given an interview to CBS's Wyatt Andrews in the summer of 1986. He planned to read from his poetry and fiction right in front of Tolstoy's monument in the courtyard of the Union of Soviet Writers, something almost unprecedented since Solzhenitsyn's "calf" head-butting the Soviet "oak tree." This time father sent letters of notification to the Union of Writers, the Moscow Soviet (City Government), and a number of newspapers and magazines. He also notified foreign journalists and diplomats. My father drafted a statement, typed it up several times with three rounds of carbon copy paper, and mailed off the statements along with copies of the notification. My mother translated the statement into English and read it by telephone to an American contact.

In preparation for his readings, father shared his plans with refusenik friends and acquaintances. Not all of them were supportive of his new action. Some felt that further refusenik political protests, however peaceful, would irritate Gorbachev. "David, don't do it. Your action would be flying in the face of their glasnost and perestroika," I remember a distinguished aeronautics designer, a virile Mediterranean-looking man whose head had grown completely white after a decade of refusenik living, telling my father in our kitchen. The logic that, after everything we had been through, we should give Gorbachev's policies a chance seemed completely backward to us.

On 8 April 1987, just two days prior to the first date of my father's planned demonstration, we got a call from the Office of Visas. It was in the afternoon, I was walking leisurely across the campus toward the University Metro station. I loved this time of the year in Moscow, the sooty wind, the opening buds, the undone coats. It felt so good to be outside after three lectures and a lab. I was contemplating a longer walk, perhaps with a stop at the university book shop and another stop to drink a glass of watery coffee with a rum baba. There were payphones outside the wrought-iron fence of the Moscow University campus. From those payphones I often called home after classes to check in before taking the Metro downtown, where I would meet Max and other friends.

"We just got a call from the Office of Visas," said my mother's voice from the heavy black receiver. And then my mother's voice halted, choking on the unpronounceable words. "They said they would be 'granting our request,'" mother's voice laughed and cried into the heavy black receiver. "Yes, 'granting,' that's what they said. I called papa at the clinic, but couldn't get ahold of him."

"Mamochka, I'll get a cab, be there soon. . . ." I ran across the street and flagged down a mud-covered yellow Volga. "Hurry, please, I'll take care of it," I said to the cabbie in some other person's voice. The driver cocked back his hat, looked at me through the rear-view mirror, and nodded, a smoldering *papirosa* dangling in the corner of his grubby mouth. He ended up speeding the whole way and got me home in just over half an hour.

My father had been visiting a sick patient when I had called home, and he had just gotten home when I walked in the door. Mother immediately filled me in on the details. The caller said he was from the OVIR and identified himself as "Andreyev." He said that we would be getting our exit visas in ten days. There was one hook, however. The person who called my mother requested that my father cancel his demonstration. For many years my mother had been preparing herself for this conversation. "I just ignored his words," she told me as the kettle whistled on in the kitchen. "Instead I told them I wouldn't leave without my sister, mother, and niece." The voice of the man from the OVIR changed from frosty-polite to fuming. "Don't you tell us what to do," barked "Andreyev," but my mother said she heard defeat in his voice.

There it was, now, it seemed, almost a done deal. We were finally getting our permission, nine years too late. There was something anticlimactic in the way we came to face the news of our leaving. We were uprooting ourselves, something we had been preparing for and yet never could have prepared ourselves for. We couldn't have known this at the time, but the exit visas granted to veteran refuseniks in the spring of 1987 commenced a new wave of Jewish emigration. In April alone over 700 people, mostly veteran refuseniks, would receive permissions, and after that the numbers would rise to thousands for each of the remaining months of the year. Almost 8,000 Jews would emigrate in 1987, a wave that would rise exponentially over the next three years, to reach well over 200,000 in 1990, the penultimate Soviet year.

Despite the call from the OVIR, my father was adamantly proceeding as planned with his readings. "I'll believe it when I see the postcard," he kept saying. By "postcard" he meant the open-face notice the OVIR would mail to an applicant's home. On 10 April my father held the first of the announced readings in the inner courtyard of the Union of Soviet Writers. We drove to the center of Moscow in our white Zhiguli all splattered over in Moscow springtime mud. We turned off Gorky Street, leaving behind the Pushkin monument and the early afternoon *flâneurs* on the boulevards. One of the smaller arteries connecting Moscow's Boulevard Ring with the Garden Ring, Vorovsky (now, again, Povarskaya) Street was among old Moscow's fanciest addresses. Known as Moscow's embassy row, it housed gems of Art Nouveau architecture—mansions and larger buildings with gingerbread façades. We passed the Institute of World Literature and also the Film Actor's Studio Theater and the Gnessin College of Music.

The older section of the Union of Soviet Writers occupied a yellow palace with white columns. This was the legendary city estate of the Dolgorukov family, a late–eighteenth-century building that served as the prototype for the Moscow house of the Rostovs in *War and Peace*. The Central House of Writers, where as a kid I had gone many times with my father, was located in the modern, adjoining section of the Union. We entered through a wrought-iron gate, passing on our right the editorial offices of *People's Friendship*, one of Moscow's leading monthly reviews. My father had earlier published there and had received a literary prize co-sponsored by this magazine. This, too, was all in the past, our pre-refusenik past. From the main street entrance to the spacious courtyard of the "Rostov House," a path led to the monument to Tolstoy through a landscaped area with last year's wilted grass and naked trees. It was a postwar Soviet monument, and a muscular Tolstoy sat on an armchair pedestal, clad in a roomy peasant shirt with steely folds, his back turned to the classical front of the old palace. My father stood a distance from the monument, facing Tolstoy and the offices of the Union of Soviet Writers. A group of about fifteen to twenty supporters, my mother among them, formed a semicircle before my father. In the audience were refuseniks, several foreign journalists, and two or three unknown observers. My seventy-three-year-old maternal grandmother Anna Mikhailovna, who had never before gone to any refusenik political actions, stood in the semi-circle, nervously clutching her handbag. A police car and an unmarked black Volga were parked in the inner courtyard. A short distance away from the path and monument, athletic men in plain clothes stood, arms folded, faces stupefied. I positioned myself behind my father's back, guarding him from being hit from behind. Father read "In the Reeds," a *fantella* about a group of dissidents and outcasts. It was studded with darkly aphoristic humor, and I distinctly remember Bengt Eriksson, a Swedish diplomat and a translator of Russian authors, earnestly laughing at the punch lines. The reading ended without confrontation with the official observers.

There was still no news from the Office of Visas, no postcards delivered to our door or left in our mailbox. On the eve of Passover, word had reached our family that Rabbi Fields had arranged for my father's poem "Lot's Monologue to His Wife" in my translation to be printed as a Supplemental Haggadah Reading (a "plea for freedom") for the Passover of 1987 and recited in synagogues in the United States and Canada. Some time before Passover my parents had been invited to attend the first Seder at Spaso House, the residence of the US Ambassador, then the recently appointed Jack F. Matlock Jr. Ambasasor Matlock's predecessor, Arthur A. Hartman, who had been US Ambassador to the USSR in 1981–87, had personally done a lot to ease the plight of refuseniks. "Please join us for a Seder Dinner. Monday, April 13, 1987 6:45 p.m. Spaso House . . . ," read the invitation to the new ambassador's Seder, which also included an incantation, "R.S.V.P."

Standing in the center of old Moscow, close to the Arbat Street and the Garden Ring, Spaso House received the name from its address, Spasopeskovskaya Square, 10. My parents had been at the ambassador's residence for prior activities, including film screenings and concerts, but never on such an occasion and in such company. They came home from Spaso House transfigured with new hope. Secretary of State George P. Schultz was there at the Seder, wearing a *kipa* and sharing the Passover table with veteran refuseniks. Among the refusenik guests were our friends Vladimir and Maria Slepak and Yosef Begun, Aleksandr Lerner, author of *Fundamentals of Cybernetics* and a world-famous scientist, Viktor Brailovsky, former Prisoner of Zion and the last editor of the underground magazine *Jews in the USSR*, Ida Nudel, also a refusenik hero and former inmate, and the pianist Vladimir Feltsman. This was a high point for my parents, and I felt immensely proud of them.

We tried to wait patiently, but struggled with waitfulness. I barely remember the next two weeks. I do remember one curious detail: the famed pianist Vladimir Horowitz came to Russia to give recitals. He was eighty-two and hadn't been to Russia since leaving it, sixty one years before that. I remember the buzz around his concert in the Grand Hall of the Moscow Conservatory of Music. Scalpers were selling tickets for upwards of 50 rubles, about ten times the official price. America was coming to us in the shape of a former Russian Jew, and we were still trying to leave.

It was already the end of April, Moscow spring in full swing, and we still hadn't received the notification from the OVIR that we should pay for the processing of our exit visas, a notification that usually amounted to a formally issued "permission." My parents began to think the phone call from the OVIR had been but a ploy to stop my father's protests and readings. Then, suddenly, a second phone call came from the OVIR, and my parents were asked to come in for a meeting. The official who received them "invited" them to submit our applications anew, formally to reapply. This meant gathering all new paperwork and another deferral, possibly by several months. Now my parents clearly felt they were being manipulated. "Why are you yanking us around?" father said to the visa official.

"You know nothing has changed, you have our dossiers, you know everything you need to know to release us."

My parents came home furious. On the same day, 28 April 1987, my father made a second appeal, a short one, to the Soviet and foreign media. In the statement he summarized the promise made on 8 April, the pressure to stop demonstrating, the lies and machinations. He also notified the Soviet authorities and the media that on 5 May 1987 he would demonstrate in front of the Union of Soviet Writers and read from his literary works, to protest the fact that the authorities still had not given our family the official permission to leave the country.

At his 5 May demonstration, father focused exclusively on his writings about the Jews of Russia. Some of the core supporters attended the second reading, although new ones turned up, including a reporter for *Evening Moscow*. My father first recited poems, including "My Slavic Soul," "Lot's Monologue to His Wife" and a long, hallucinatory poem about Yosef Begun, in whose release my mother had played a part back in February. In this allegorical composition, which I would later translate into English, my father related a haunting dream. The dream itself had been informed by refusenik affairs and also by the emergence of ultrapatriotic paramilitary groups such as *lyubery* from the underbelly of glasnost and perestroika. In the dream, Begun (whose name, pronounced "be-goon," literally means "runner" in Russian), was running around a stadium ring while thousands of ululating, Jew-hating plebeians ominously cheered and brandished fists from the grandstands. He had previously read this poem at refusenik gatherings, including one at the Beguns' apartment soon after the hero's release from prison.

Then my father read an excerpt from *Herbert and Nelly*. In this novel, the story of the Levitins, a refusenik family with a Jewish husband and a non-Jewish wife, is interlaced with the author's autobiographical digressions. Facing the monument to Tolstoy, a supporter of legal equality for all religious and ethnic minorities, who had at one point studied Hebrew with a Moscow rabbi, my father read an episode about searching for the remains of the Karaites in Soviet Lithuania. In the fourteenth century the greatest Lithuanian warrior and conqueror, Grand Duke Vytautas, brought from Crimea about 300 Karaite men with families, settling them in Trakai

(Troki), then the Lithuanian capital, and making the men his personal guard. The Karaites, a Jewish sect rejecting the Talmud, originated in the eighth century in the Near East. During the Shoah, the Karaites survived because they had successfully pleaded with the Nazi authorities that they were neither ethnically Jewish, nor Judaic, but rather a Turkic tribe with a spoken Turkic language and a faith of its own which recognizes the Old Testament and incorporates traditions of Islam. After the war, Lithuania's Karaites (Karaims) found themselves self-isolated, mainly living in Trakai and Vilnius and continuing to insist that they were not of the Jews. By the late 1970s their numbers had dwindled to under 500, only slightly higher than the number of Crimean Karaites that Vytautas had originally brought to Lithuania in the fourteenth century.

In the episode of the novel that my father read that day, he walks around Trakai, querying the dark-haired, swarthy, eagle-nosed Karaims: Aren't you like us? Aren't you Jews? Only one old lady acknowledges the group's Jewish roots while all the others rigorously deny them. What becomes of Jews' descendents when they sever themselves—or are severed—from their Judaic roots? That was the crux of my father's reading that amounted to a Soviet Jew's lamentation. Then an unexpected thing occurred. While the observers, both with and without uniform, stood at a distance and took notice, they did not attempt to interrupt my father. Just as my father was finishing the episode, a woman in her fifties, with graying curly hair and a tenebrous face, emerged from the offices of the Union of Soviet Writers and joined the audience. She stood and listened for a little, then interrupted my father and screamed in his face:

"Why are you doing this? They already gave you a visa!!!"

"I beg your pardon," father replied, very softly. "And if you don't mind my asking, how do you know this?"

"How? How?" replied the frenzied messenger. "I just know. It's . . . it's known."

"Forgive me," father asked, remaining calm. "And who might you be?"

"Me, I'm a *karaimka*," the lady blurted out and dashed back to the side door whence she had come. My father finished his reading without further interruptions.

Another week went by. I had practically stopped going to classes. On 12 May we opened the mailbox to find the long-awaited postcard: "Pay . . . for the visas." We finally had our official permission, in writing. Our relatives, my mother's mother, sister, and niece, also received the notifications. Immediately we went to the Aeroflot ticket office and booked tickets to Vienna, for 7 June 1987, giving ourselves under a month to make all the arrangements. There was more availability in first class, and we didn't regret having to spend more of our soon-to-be worthless rubles on the tickets.

The happy panic of taking leave quickly got ahold of us. Even of individuals who have already been granted permission, the OVIR required a whole range of additional documents. A Russian colloquial term for such units of bureaucratic paperwork was *spravochka*, a diminutive of *spravka*, a reference or a supporting note. As we entered the OVIR building we ran into a family of refuseniks we had known for years. They had a son with a disability that required the kind of special care that would have been routinely provided in the civilized world but was absent in Soviet elementary schools. Holding hands, the parents of the sick boy were skipping and hopping across the vestibule toward the exit doors. "Spravochka, spravochka, spravochka," they screamed in the voices of rapturous children. We understood this to mean that they were just one last piece of paperwork away from the issuing of the exit visas.

The main *spravochka* I was expected to provide was a Kafkaesque note confirming that I had been "withdrawn from Moscow University." To request it I went to the Office of Student Affairs at the School of Soil Science. There I fell right into the hands of my old nemesis, Ms. Hairbun. "Aha, OVIR, going to Israel, I see. Betraying your Motherland, Shrayer," my nemesis spoke so loud that all the other students waiting in the office turned and stared. By an impure coincidence, Professor Rozanov happened to be there, taking care of a grade-related matter. "Stop by my office," he said through his teeth. After I was done at Student Services I knocked on his door. Rozanov was sitting at his desk, the photo of Marilyn Monroe winking at him from under a heavy piece of glass. "You'll regret it," Rozanov said, lighting a *papirosa*. "Too bad, a smart guy. I've seen people like yourself at international conferences. Some from Israel, some from the States and Canada. We had one or two here at the School. They all regretted their decision to emigrate."

I did not engage with Rozanov. Perhaps I should have reminded him that Jewish academics were leaving in part because of the complacency and cowardice of people like him, members of the Soviet intellectual leadership, elite professors who silently witnessed or assisted the system, or worse yet, peddled half-truths to academic colleagues abroad. I thanked Rozanov for his advice and left his office, never to see him again. I had better things to do with my time. I needed to go around the university and collect various signatures. Before the withdrawal note could be issued, I had to prove that I had returned balls to the gym, books to the library, and paid all the dues to the Komsomol (even though I had resigned two months earlier).

My parents and I had divided the dizzying number of tasks we had to complete in three weeks. Among the tasks falling in my lap was the handling of our home library. Back when we had first set our feet on the emigration path, my father had shipped many books to a friend's address in New England. The friend PS'ed in his occasional letters that our parcels were "still waiting" for us in his dry basement, but it was hard to imagine their survival after so many years of exile. We used to have a terrific collection of books, the foundation of which my father had laid as a medical student in Leningrad, when the city's bustling used-book market still offered first editions of Silver Age and early Soviet poetry at affordable prices. After we had already become refuseniks, during the year when my parents scrambled to find employment and my severely myopic father worked at night as an unlicensed cab driver, we had to sell valuables, including our rare editions. Over the refusenik years, as things eased financially, we started to buy books again. It was a compulsion. For my father's fiftieth, I had gotten him a slim brick-red volume of Pasternak, paying a book dealer half of my monthly university stipend for the book.

In dealing with our newly accumulated library of about five hundred volumes, I first went through all the books and divided them into three categories. First, there were books we were prepared to leave behind; these were mostly Russian translations of Western literature and books in English. Then there were books we knew we wouldn't ever be allowed to take with us or ship, including rare editions and books inscribed to my father by their authors. These would travel out of the country in diplomatic luggage, and we wouldn't be able to reclaim all of them. Finally, there were books that are Russian classics, and books by authors of the Soviet period, that we thought we couldn't live without.

A set of byzantine rules and regulations governed which books could be taken out of or shipped from the USSR. Books supposedly constituted Russian cultural patrimony and belonged in Russia, and yet a foreigner could buy many of the same books in a Beryozka store for hard currency and take it abroad. For the books that Soviet citizens were not automatically allowed to take or ship out of the country, one had to obtain special permission slips from an inspection office at the Lenin Library (now the Russian State Library).

Over the weeks of leave-taking I must have made a dozen trips to the inspection office. There was a small waiting area crowded with book lovers, many of them Jews emigrating from the USSR. One was only allowed to bring a limited number of books for inspection. I would haul from home a duffle bag filled with books. Outside the waiting area I would divide them among my friends who came along. Each of us would go in separately, with his or her own passport, pretending these were their books. After five or six such raids the chief inspector, a gallantly dressed woman with red hair arranged in a double bun (were buns the hairdo of choice with the Soviet inspectresses?) confronted me in her office.

"I know what you're doing here, bringing your friends and passing your own books for inspection."

"What difference does it make?" I asked, no longer caring to appease.

"What difference?" the inspectress repeated my question, voice straining.

"Yes, what's the big deal?" I continued. "Plus you have perestroika, so why don't you reform these bogus rules."

"Don't teach me perestroika!" yelped the inspectress, so loudly that my friends waiting outside could hear it. But she couldn't legally stop my friends from submitting my books as their own, and we continued with the exercise for two more weeks.

During our final weeks my parents and I drank more than our fill of the absurdities of Soviet life. For some reason, several of the absurdities were related to books. A stranger telephoned, introducing himself as a friend of so-and-so (who, in turn, was a friend of a refusenik friend), and asked to see the books we had for sale. He came over the same evening, lugging a black cello case down the corridor into my father's den. The visitor turned out to be a cellist from a distinguished Moscow orchestra. He wasn't Jewish and had no plans to emigrate. But he was particularly interested in émigré authors, in Russian-language books and magazines published in the West. "I'll pay you whatever you ask," he said, removing a wad of cash out of his chest pocket. "Just let me have them. You don't need them any longer, you're going. And I'm staying here," the cellist licked his lips like a hungry bookeater and pointed to one of the half-empty shelves, where he had spotted issues of the Paris-based *Continent* magazine and an anthology of émigré poetry. After paying and receiving an Israeli-printed Russian translation of Joseph Roth as a bonus, the cellist packed the books into his hard cello case and carefully fastened the clasps. "I'll have to take a taxi," he said in the doorway. And he added: "Have a good life."

Selling or giving away our Russian-language books turned out easier than getting rid of the numerous English-language books we had accumulated over the refusenik years. Visitors from abroad often left us with volumes of the classics and books by contemporary Anglo-American authors. Not surprisingly, we had a whole mini-library of works by Jewish-American writers, including books by the greats—Bellow, Malamud, and Philip Roth—but also novels by the lesser lights such as Chaim Potok or Herman Wouk. And there was also a nice stack of books by James Baldwin, including *Giovanni's Room* and *Another Country*, which must have been given us by a visiting admirer of the writer. I filled our plaid East-German-manufactured shopping bag on rollers with English-language books and took them to a foreign-language bookstore with an extensive second-hand section. The manager, an ashen-blonde with ropy lips, looked through the books, selected all the Steinbecks, Updikes, James Joneses and even Jacqueline Susanns, but didn't want to take Potok, Malamud, and the other Jews. She also tossed all the James Baldwin books back into my East German bag. Had Moscow been so deluged with books by Jewish-American and African-American authors that the bookstore didn't want them? I was so puzzled that I could think of nothing better than to ask the manager: "But why?" "What now?" she replied, tartly but also lazily. "Are you going to accuse me of antisemitism? Or perhaps of racism or some other prejudice?" I did not accuse the bookstore manager of anything. Instead I quietly planted a pack of Salem cigarettes behind her counter; she nodded in acknowledgment of this small bribe and bought all of my books, Jews and Baldwin included.

As I was walking out of the bookstore, I bumped into an old acquaintance, Kristina Chernova, whose grandfather had been a Soviet publishing executive. Kristina was my age, we had met in the winter of 1978 in Maleevka, a writers' resort outside Moscow. In senior high school and during my freshman year at the university, Kristina and I would occasionally get together, alone or with some mutual friends. Her mother had remarried, Kristina now told me. The mother's new husband was a German citizen, and they were in the midst of relocating to West Germany. If I'm not mistaken, Kristina had brought a bagful of German language books to sell to the bookstore. We compared notes about leavetaking; she too, had to furnish the OVIR with various ridiculous documents from her university. Kristina promised to write to me *poste restante* or to locate me in Italy through the Jewish organizations sponsoring Soviet refugees. Both prospects seemed utterly fantastical at the time.

The closer I get to the memories of my last days before leaving, the harder it is to reconstruct the texture of the physical time. I remember not whole days but only certain events ornately woven from the remaining threads of my Soviet existence. I cannot recall the exact evening when a neighbor from three floors below rang our door. His name was Rogozhkin; I had known him since we moved into our co-op building in 1971. Rogozhkin was a member of the co-op board and had been charged with the task of assessing the condition of our place. I was home alone, it was past 10 p.m., my parents were out of town, in Leningrad, visiting the family graves. A tipsy smile on his face, Rogozhkin followed me to my father's den, now half-dismantled of its furnishings and belongings. I offered him a drink of Armenian cognac. Rogozhkin showed no signs of hostility or curiosity on account of our emigration. All he wanted to do was drink our cognac, pick out tunes on our piano and sing, in chorus with me, to his own boozy accompaniment. Thus we sang for about an hour, mainly wartime songs, and I couldn't just show him out. We needed his assessment in order to withdraw from the co-op and get our money back. Finally Rogozhkin, now formidably drunk, took a spin round the apartment, concluded it was in splendid condition, and assessed it at full value. The apartment had been paid off, and my parents ended up receiving all of the 4,500 rubles it was officially worth. At the time, the official exchange rate was around 1.4 rubles per US dollar, while the black market value of an American dollar was more along the lines of 4 rubles. (A two-bedroom apartment like ours now sells for around $250,000 in that area of Moscow.) At that time, we truly wanted nothing to do with that building, land, or country. We didn't even consider holding onto the apartment by fictitiously transferring the ownership to a trusted friend.

Saying goodbye to friends, most of whom believed they would never see me again, or I them. I wasn't just going abroad, I was relocating to a different universe. I wanted to spend at least some time alone with each of my friends, doing something memorable. We visited art museums, went to concerts, or just strolled through the boulevards in blossom. One evening in May I took my friend Vlasta to see a play. I had met her during the spring of my sophomore year, through my musician friends Dima Kovalyov (stage name Dimitri Perets) and Masha Barankina. Vlasta was studying violin at the college affiliated with the Moscow Conservatory of Music. We went on a few dates together, but then I left for the summer expedition, and in the Fall of 1986 we resumed seeing each other as friends. Vlasta was half-Czech, half-Russian, with long strands of wheat-colored hair and bright blue eyes, and she always seemed to have her violin case with her. She never asked questions she suspected I wouldn't be comfortable answering. Sovremennik (Contemporary), where Vlasta and I went to see a play, was one of the best theaters in town, having broken off, in the 1960s, from the Moscow Art Theater. And it wasn't just any play, but a production of *Incident at Vichy*. Years later, already an American college professor interested in Jewish authors, I would come to value this play above all of Arthur Miller's, including *Death of a Salesman*. In May

1987 I had only seen a production of Miller's *The Price*. But this much I did know about Miller: he was one of American theater's greats, he was Jewish, he had been married to Marilyn Monroe, he had spoken out against the repression of artistic freedom in the USSR. And his plays had been virtually banned in the Soviet Union since 1970. In fact, *Incident at Vichy* had been originally produced in Moscow in 1967, my birth year, by Marlen Khutsiev, a legendary film director of the Soviet New Wave. Soviet authorities shelved Khutsiev's production for twenty years. It finally had its premiere in the spring of 1987, when the director Igor Kvasha had it restored and finally released. In a city where getting tickets to any half-decent theater was an ordeal, *Incident at Vichy* was one of the hottest productions of the season.

The cast was phenomenal, and I had the feeling that the actors played as though this could be the last production. Kvasha, the director, also starred as Leduc, the Jewish doctor and war veteran, and the play's voice of conscience. Gennady Frolov played the German Wehrmacht major who executes death orders, although not without some stirring of guilt. And Valentin Nikulin was brilliant as the Austrian prince von Berg, a lover of music and of young Jewish musicians, now living in the south of France. To this day I remember Von Berg—no, imagine Von Berg—as having Nikulin's long, slight frame, refined features, and melodic speech. I don't know what my friend Vlasta, a musician and a Slav, was thinking as she watched the event unraveling on stage, but I remember turning her way to see single tears in her eyes at the end of the play, after Prince von Berg had offered his pass to the Jewish doctor, himself choosing to remain in the antechamber of the Nazi interrogation room. In this play about rounding up Jews and Roma in Vichy France, so much spoke to me about our condition as refuseniks and as Soviet Jews. Miller's play was about the Shoah, about denial and self-denial, about resistance, collaboration, and complicity. How perfectly intoned and enacted were the words and body language of von Berg directed at the "professor" of racial anthropology: "Hände weg!" ("Hands off!" or "Ruki proch!" in Russian). Don't touch me, I'm not one of you. I was sitting in the audience and thinking: How many Russian aristocrats of origin or spirit would say "Hands off!" to Soviet professors of antisemitism? After the performance, Vlasta and I went to see Nikulin backstage. My parents knew him through our friend Mark Portnoy, a friend of many Moscow actors, and Nikulin himself had gotten us the coveted tickets. In the dressing room, his white shirt undone and revealing a silvery chest, Nikulin hugged me and warmly wished me luck in the "new life." He knew we were leaving the country; at the time he couldn't imagine emigration. Son of a Jewish mother, Nikulin would repatriate to Israel in 1991, but return to Moscow seven years later. In Moscow he would die, unable to find thespian happiness in the post-Soviet world.

Within a day or two of seeing the production of *Incident at Vichy*, I attended a farewell party thrown by my Moscow University classmates. Max, who had known some of my classmates since the Chashnikovo summer after my freshman year, accompanied me to the House of Graduate and Professional Students, or DAS, as it was known in its abbreviation. Out-of-town students at the School of Soil Science were given rooms in this high-rise. We entered a dormitory room, normally shared by four or five students, and saw a long table stretching across the room and about twenty-five classmates, all clapping and cheering. I unloaded the two bottles of vodka we had brought along and immediately descended into a scene almost straight out of Dostoevsky's *The Idiot*. Was I the *idiot*?

The fare was simple—herring, sardines, and *vobla* (salt-dried fish), boiled potatoes, a gloppy "Russian" salad overflowing with mayonnaise, brown bread, pickled vegetables, slabs of Ukrainian peppered pork fat. The number of bottles far exceeded the number of dishes weighing down the centipede table. Girls drank port, boys—shots of vodka or vodka–beer cocktails known in Russian as *yorsh*, after a spiny and spiky freshwater fish. Very soon I was being asked left and right why I was leaving "home." Max and I dashed glances at each other across the table. Drunk as I was, I understood that scenes like that could quickly metamorphose into a scandal or even a brawl. Yet I couldn't, in part because inebriation accords a greater clarity of consciousness, placate the people with whom I had shared a university life for nearly three years.

"I'm leaving because of antisemitism," I replied, rather loudly.

"But look around, good friend," said Lyonya Chumachenko, the one who used to paint houses in Odessa with a Jewish partner. "Look, we are no antisemites, you know that. We all see you as one of us."

"The ones who came here, yes," I replied, feeling like I was about to slip. "But the others . . ."

"They were probably just afraid, or busy with the exams, that's all," Lyonya said in a guilty voice. "Let's have a drink to stainless friendship."

We all toasted and drank bottoms up. A silence had set in, and I thought of a Russian wake and remembering the soul of the deceased. Then a strained voice interrupted the silence.

"They'll kill you, pal, they'll kill you over there." This was the former marine "Stepasha," the one with whom I had clashed over interpretations of Russian history. "There's a war going on in the Near East," Stepasha continued. "They like to send cannon meat like yourself to battle Muslim fanatics." All the while Stepasha had avoided referring to Israel by name.

At this point a blonde, blue-eyed student with a handsome face and a mouth full of rotten teeth sat next to me. Like Lyonya Chumachenko, he hailed from the port of Kherson on the Black Sea. He was a year behind us but shared the dorm room with a few of my classmates. I didn't know him well and was surprised by his outspokenness.

"Listen, Maxim, you can still call the whole thing off," he said. "I tell you what, my dad's in the KGB, not the lowest man in the establishment, either—I can call him right now and ask him to stop the whole thing if you like. It's not too late . . ."

I said nothing in reply, smiling drunkenly at these fantasies of Dostoevskian boys.

The farewell party was occurring the night before my parents and I were supposed to surrender our Soviet passports. We were being stripped of our citizenship as a price for the exit visas. I remember this well because a disaster had nearly occurred when I left. With me was Max, also quite tipsy, and a classmate of mine by the name of Katya Pyndyk, an honest, politically savvy woman whom I got to know while we both harvested potatoes in September 1986. Max and I were planning to flag down a cab, give Katya a lift, and then decide how to finish off the revelries. As I entered the elevator, I tripped and fell. Making a perfect parabola, my Soviet passport fell out of the chest pocket of my sport coat and landed over the crack between the edge of the floor and the edge of the elevator.

I sobered up in a split second as I saw my passport lying over the elevator shaft, barely an inch from falling in. Max blocked the door with his foot and I retrieved the passport, having nearly dragged my family into a bureaucratic hell.

From that farewell party I brought home a small notebook. Now it lies on my desk as I type these lines on the eve of the 2010 Halloween. Downstairs, my daughters are decorating with sparkles the home-made tiaras to go with their costumes. Mira, the older, is going as Tinkerbell, and Tatiana, the younger, as a ballerina. My present American life lies only two flights of stairs below as I leaf through the notebook and read the Russian inscriptions. My classmates had made them during the party, taking turns. A combat veteran wrote this for me: "Maxim. . . . I will always be anxious about your destiny. You've left in my heart a nice, remarkably warm trace; you're loved by all of us. How sad that you're leaving [the expression used in the Russian is *ty ukhodish'*, the way one might speak of passing, leaving this world]. Be happy." And this is from a melancholy woman from the ancient city of Vladimir: "Remember all of us. You're very kind, fun . . . in a word, it's really sad. . . ." Another woman wrote the lyrics of "Yesterday" in the notebook. A dreamy Bulgarian student, Petya Peneva, copied a short poem by Marina Tsvetaeva.

Over the next week, two or three classmates who hadn't been at the party stopped in to say goodbye. One of them came with his wife asking to locate his relatives, former Displaced Persons (DPs), in West Germany.

"Are you thinking of emigrating?" I remember asking him.

"Well, no . . . maybe," my visitor hesitated.

"For the children," his wife added, handing me the information on a sheet of paper.

On 26 May 1987 we surrendered our Soviet passports, and our exit visas were formally issued by the OVIR. Just in case, I had jotted down the serial number before handing over my Soviet passport: Series XXIX-MYu No. 679429.

Israel hadn't had diplomatic or consular relations with the Soviet Union since 1967, when the Soviets had broken them off in response to the Six-Day War. The Netherlands represented Israeli interests in the Soviet

Union, and those leaving for Israel had to visit the Dutch embassy and consulate to complete the required paperwork. My parents and I had previously met the Dutch consul, a young, flamboyant man in tight-fitting suits. On the late morning when we visited the consular office, our Dutch acquaintance came out of a back office to shake our hands. "You're going to love it," he said cryptically.

From the Dutch embassy my parents drove home, and I took the subway to Moscow University. My goal was to pick up my transcript; I knew I would be needing it abroad as proof of my almost three years of university studies. This was to be my last visit to the campus, and while riding in the subway car, this time of day empty like a disemboweled fish, I readied myself for all sorts of last-minute surprises. The surprises came flying at me almost immediately as I entered the building. A young woman with braided hair intercepted me in front of the Office of Student Services. She was ideology secretary of the School's Komsomol Committee. I can't remember her name, but I associate both the name and her demeanor with that of Ulyana Gromova, a member of a mythologized anti-Nazi youth underground organization in occupied Ukraine; every Soviet kid of my generation would have studied Ulyana Gromova as a fictionalized character in Aleksandr Fadeev's novel *Young Guard*.

"Wait, Shrayer," the reincarnated Ulyana Gromova yelled as she stood in my tracks. "You're a coward. You didn't show up at the school-wide Komsomol assembly to answer the charges. We have expelled you from the Komsomol."

"You can't expel a non-member," I replied, trying to contain my welling anger.

"What are you talking about, a non-member?"

"You know that I had resigned from the Komsomol on my own accord," I said, relaxing as I thought of the absurdity of the scene.

"Shrayer, they won't let you out of the country," said the ideology secretary. "They told us about such cases."

"I'll take my chances," I said, sidestepping her and placing my hand on the doorknob in front of me.

At Student Services, the inspectress looked at me with silent contempt and handed me a handwritten transcript with official blue stamps and signatures. Just down the corridor, I bumped into Irina Sergeevna Reshetova, the assigned faculty mentor for our class. Already in her late forties but still only a lecturer, Reshetova had just recently defended her Candidate's dissertation. A mothering figure to many out-of-town students, Reshetova always seemed overloaded with university service, with helping students secure part-time jobs, arranging trips, pleading with professors for an extension.

"Maxim, is it true?" Reshetova whispered as she pulled me aside by the sleeve.

"Yes, Irina Sergeevna, it's true. In a week," I answered.

"Oh my Lord," she clasped her head with both hands. "What am I going to do? They'll now expel me from the Party."

"Irina Sergeevna, you didn't do anything."

"I'm in charge of your entire class, they'll blame this on me," Reshetova mumbled.

"Dear Irina Sergeevna," I tried to comfort her. "I'm emigrating legally, this couldn't possibly be blamed on you, plus you've got perestroika."

"What perestroika?" Reshetova said despondently. "Who, me? Where did you see this perestroika?" And she scurried down the corridor.

In part as a consequence of the encounter with Reshetova, I didn't say goodbye to Professor Samoylova, my academic advisor. Perhaps I should have, out of respect for her scholarship. She was a dedicated scientist, focused on research and expedition work and oblivious to almost everything else. I had been working with her for about a year, and she had not once asked me a personal question. We would meet periodically, I would show her my results, get feedback, and not think of her until the next consultation. Reshetova's fright, her fear of being complicit, had instantly convinced me that I had better not say anything to Samoylova. This way, I decided, if I said nothing to her, abstaining even from saying goodbye to her, I wouldn't compromise her in any way. If asked about me, Samoylova would be able to say, hand on heart: I didn't know, he never told me, and he didn't even say goodbye. I brusquely walked past Samoylova's office and was about to duck into the staircase landing when a member of her research group, a woman I knew only slightly, accosted me:

"Shrayer, it's time to fill out the paperwork for the summer expedition. We're leaving for West Siberia at the end of June."

"But I won't be going," I answered, "I'm leaving the country."

"Oh my goodness, so it's true what I heard. Oh dear, so young and uprooting yourself like that." She hugged me and whispered: "May the Lord keep you."

This kindly woman would have been my supervisor in the upcoming expedition to the Kulunda Steppe.

The last "official" I ran into at the School of Soil Science was German Kust, the first secretary of the School's Komsomol committee. He had a thick trimmed beard à la the middle-aged Karl Marx.

"Maxim, I wanted to ask you about your plans," Kust asked in a tentative sort of voice.

"I don't know. . . . Live life, study," I replied.

"Who do you have over there?" By "over there" Kust meant Israel.

I didn't really want to get into the whole Israel versus America conversation with him, but I explained that my father had a living uncle in Tel Aviv, a land surveyor by trade. Kust seemed genuinely intrigued by all this, and he said goodbye to me without spite or malice.

In the afternoon of 28 May 1987, about a week before we left Russia for good, my father and I came home to discover a poster crookedly pasted to our apartment door. On the poster, in black Biro pen, were the words: "Traitors Get Out" (*Predateli ubiraites'*). Within thirty minutes the poster had been ripped off our vinyl-covered black door, just as hastily as it had been attached to it, leaving glue marks and pieces of stuck paper.

That same day, a young citizen of the Federal Republic of Germany by the name of Matthias Rust had flown from Finland over the Soviet border across Estonia without being shot down. Around seven in the evening he landed his light plane in Moscow just steps from Red Square. The incident was on everybody's lips. It seemed that everyone in the city of eight million knew someone else who was in Red Square at the time of Rust's landing. Not exactly lightly policed on a normal day, the streets of Moscow suddenly seemed peppered with officers and police vehicles. Later in the evening, my parents were stopped by a cop in front of our building and asked to show their passports. My father told the young warrant officer that his police superiors should know that our family was leaving the country and we had already given up our passports. The officer blushed and muttered something about Moscow being overrun with visitors. At home I leafed through the address book and started dialing foreign news bureaus. Lines were either busy or not answering.

Our family did get its share of journalistic attention as we prepared to leave Russia. In late May, Dan Rather visited the Soviet Union with a large crew of news people in order to film a two-hour CBS special, *Seven Days in May: The Soviet Union*, which would air nationally in the summer of 1987. This was an ambitious proposition: by showing various slices of Soviet life, the film would document the country at the threshold of what her leaders couldn't fully control or her people fully comprehend. Rather brought with him nine reporters with crews, among them Diane Sawyer. Besides Moscow and Leningrad, they taped segments in Tbilisi, Georgia and Tallinn, Estonia. Some of the chosen subjects were obvious: Yeltsin, then boss of Moscow and reformist already on a collision course with the Party establishment; the Soviet Navy; Soviet socialized medicine. Other stories focused on notorious topics then besetting the Soviet press, such as *lyubery*. Some segments sought to highlight societal problems, to which the Soviet Union was reluctantly and finally admitting: crime, drug addiction, widespread abuse in psychiatric wards. Quite a bit of attention was paid to cultural issues, from interviews with official authors and editors to stories about unsanctioned artists. One segment featured Boris Grebenshchikov, leader of the cult Leningrad rock band Aquarium. The producers also wanted to document refuseniks at a time when the floodgates of Jewish emigration were about to reopen.

It was Wyatt Andrews who had suggested my father's name for a segment on Jewish emigration. Andrews had interviewed my father back in June 1986, when he had first demonstrated in the courtyard of the Writers' Union. They stayed in touch throughout our last year in Moscow. The selection process had been under way for several weeks before the arrival of Rather and his crews. I remember the evening when Wyatt Andrews paid us a visit and brought along a jittery American colleague by the name of Jonathan Sanders. Sanders, a historian of Russia with a Columbia Ph.D., was serving as a consultant on the project. (Later, already in America, we would watch Sanders's live reports from Red Square during his stint as a Moscow CBS correspondent.) He acted like a know-it-all, and spoke passable Russian with a proclivity for the bon mot, used both correctly and incorrectly. We sat around the coffee table in my father's den, drinking tea with sweets. During Sanders's visit we learned that the segment on Jewish emigration would also include Vladimir Feltsman, a fellow refusenik who would subsequently enjoy a successful American career as a performer and mentor to younger pianists. We also found out that CBS planned to interview Anatoly Rybakov, an official Jew whom the authorities had permitted to speak of being Jewish and of the Shoah in his novel *Heavy Sand*. Rybakov's rhetoric presented the Soviet Union as a welcoming international home to the Jews, a home from which they should not seek to emigrate.

After discussing in English the topics that might come up in Dan Rather's interview with my parents, Sanders turned to me and asked, in Russian, "What's your relationship with *komsomolka*?" He probably intended for the question to be: "What's your relationship with the Komsomol organization?" (meaning: "Are you a member of the Komsomol?") The Russian word he used, *komsomolka*, meant a female member of the Komsomol or, colloquially, the organization's central daily newspaper, *Komsomol'skaya Pravda*. This was hilarious and I cackled, probably a bit inappropriately, then answered in English that I had resigned from the Komsomol back in late February. Wyatt Andrews beamed, but Sanders appeared unimpressed, ogling me like an irritated professor would regard a pest of a student.

A CBS crew came to tape our segment during the week after we had traded our Soviet passports for the exit visas. Dan Rather, smiling crisply and wearing a blue blazer, looked less like an American reporter and more like an ambassador from a different world. He was not just extremely polite, but was deferential with my father and mother. While the crew set up, he made small talk with us, and my father mentioned his poems that I had translated into English. Rather asked to see them, and I brought two pages from my room. He took the time to look them over and said he liked them, particularly the way they rhymed. I was surprised by the comment and wasn't sure what to make of it.

During the taped interview Rather asked my father—my mother interpreted consecutively—about the life of a refusenik, and whether he could imagine staying in the Soviet Union today, with perestroika knocking at our windows. Actually, outside the windows, alongside the CBS vehicles, there were several police cars parked at our curbside. Father hesitated for a few seconds, then said: "*Net, ne mogu*" (No, I cannot imagine [staying]"). Rather finished the interview and departed with his entourage, leaving behind just the cameraman and the soundman. They asked my father to do something he would do every day at home. Father sat at his desk, freed his typewriter from its well-worn hard-sided black case, and started to type an impromptu opening for a new short story. Chekhov used to say to young writers: Why do you keep asking for special topics to write about? I can pick up this ashtray on the table and write a story about it. In the CBS special one can hear the knock-knock-knock of my father's typing and see a close-up of the page he typed under the camera's gaze. If you extract a frame and blow it up, you can see the title of the story, "Dismemberers," and read the opening paragraph. In the story, subsequently included in my father's collection *Jonah and Sarah*, Olympia, the beloved typewriter of a dissident author, continues to crank out subversive stories even after her owner has left Russia for good. Of course CBS ended up using only a fraction of the recorded interview, just a few questions. When I watch the tape of the documentary today, I shiver when my father repeats the word "limbo" after Dan Rather, and then my mother says, in English: "We've done away with everything in this country. We no longer love it." Eleven years later, in a Washington, DC restaurant just around the corner from the CBS offices on M Street, Wyatt Andrews and I reminisced about the Dan Rather interview. "Your mom was a tired but young-looking forty-seven-year-old," Andrews said to me. "When I first met your dad in 1986," he added, "I thought he was a very old fifty-year-old." Even though it's hard for me to think of my father as old, I admit that he looks stronger as a seventy-six-year-old American than he did as a fifty-one-year-old refusenik preparing to take leave of Russia.

Dan Rather and his crew returned several days later to tape the arrival of guests to our farewell party. They came by the apartment early, to avoid the crowd that was about to descend on us. In the documentary you can see Rather entering with the air of solemnity and shaking hands with a couple of Americans, our supporters from the embassy. We must have had two hundred people stop by throughout the evening, among them old friends and relatives we hadn't seen throughout the refuseniks years, including my father's half-sister. To each other, veteran refuseniks were saying not only "see you in Jerusalem" but also "see you in Rome," and one couldn't quite tell if they were being facetious.

In my memory the whole gathering rocks and sways like filmy water in a busy harbor. My father had asked me to look after Jüri Arrak, who was in bad shape. He and Urve had come from Tallinn to say goodbye and were staying with us. Their marriage had disintegrated. When drunk, Jüri would let his demons out, the demons of protest against the Soviet regime in Estonia and against marital domesticity. At the party, Jüri managed to clash with an American diplomat. "Estonia is not Russia," Jüri yelled at the top of his lungs. Urve didn't know what to do. Jüri had quieted down by the end of the evening, and at some point I walked into the living room to find him and Genrikh Sapgir sitting on the floor, by the piano, on either side of Nadya Ilyina, their heads resting against Nadya's hips. Nadya, who had been Queen Vashti in our Purim-shpil, was playing Russian *romansy*, and Jüri and Genrikh hummed along, tears running down their cheeks. I also remember talking with our downstairs neighbor, Galina Kornilova, a fiction writer and a follower of the masterful Konstantin Paustovsky. "Soon enough Russian won't be enough for you, Maxim," Kornilova told me. "You will start writing prose in English."

It was time to start saying goodbye to my dearest friends. Katya and her mother, Inga, had come down from Leningrad. Katya was in the middle of exams and could only stay for two days. We kept postponing the inevitable. We ended up saying the last goodbye in Pushkin Square, near the poet's monument. Katya was meeting her mother, and they were going directly to the train station. Max waited on the bench nearby.

"So does this mean we won't see each other ever again?" Katya asked and started to weep in my arms.

"Of course not, silly girl, of course we'll see each other," I comforted her, not very convincingly.

I really wasn't sure. I knew I was leaving Russia for good, but my friends? That evening I gave Max a suitcase full of books and cassettes I wasn't taking with me. I also gave him a little notebook, the one in which my university classmates had made inscriptions. In it, as neatly as I could, I had copied contact information for some of the foreign diplomats and journalists we knew in Moscow. "If anything happens," I said to Max, "if anything happens here, use these contacts." In the notebook, which Max has preserved for me, the names of journalists and diplomats were entered according to a code I must have devised: Serezha for Serge, Villi for William, Filya for Philip, Felya for Felicity, etc. Then I probably ran out of time and just transliterated the foreign names: Dzheremy, Dzhek, Styuart, and even Toshiko.

5 June 1987, my twentieth birthday, fell on a Friday. Our apartment was missing about half of the furniture and looked bare without the photos and paintings on the walls. A long table was set in my parents' bedroom. Through the open windows and balcony door one could hear the clanking of children's bicycles and the sounds of feet hitting a soccer ball. The air was saturated with the smell of sap from the pine grove growing in the back of our building. Wind carried in pieces of poplar cotton, and they floated round the apartment and fell onto our heads like summer snow. My parents had helped set up and bring out the hors d'oeuvres and champagne, greeted my friends, and left for the evening. Of about fifteen guests who came that evening, there were some old Pärnu friends and some friends I had met already as a university student. So many times I had partied together with these boys and girls, dancing and drinking and feeling free inside the apartment walls, but this time the mood wasn't one of revelry. My musician friends saved the party. First Dima Kovalyov sang from the album of songs he and I had composed together, accompanying himself on the piano. After him Dima Malikov, who would become a Russian pop star in the 1990s, performed some of his own songs. Our black

piano, not a Red October but a less fancy brand, was still in the apartment. We were leaving the apartment keys to our friend Mark Portnoy, who was to liquidate the remaining furniture and then turn the keys over to the co-op management office. The piano would end up in "44," one of the first private cafés in reform-era Moscow, which Mark Portnoy would open and run for the next several years.

The guests left early, some of them planning to see me off to the airport in two days. Father and I spent most of the next day at Sheremetyevo-2 dealing with the customs police. In those days we had to submit the luggage through customs in advance of the travel date. It was a grueling and humiliating affair. The customs officers opened each suitcase and rummaged through all the belongings, making crude jokes and innuendos. We were in their power, but not for much longer. In fact, my father and I both felt a certain indifference, if not contempt, toward the material baggage gathered in our four suitcases. The clothes, bed linens, Russian souvenirs, tins of caviar . . . What did it matter! I got into an argument with a customs officer over a bound notebook he had unearthed from one of the suitcases. It contained my notes from art history lectures. "There's nothing here that's important for the state. See for yourself," I told the officer. He ran the edge of one notebook against his thumb, paused, then tossed it back in the suitcase. When we got home around midnight, mother told us she had received two harassing phone calls. "I had no way of reaching you," she said. "I was worried. This spooky male voice kept repeating into the receiver: 'We still haven't settled the score with your husband.'"

I collapsed and slept until about 7 a.m. Mother was making our last breakfast in the apartment, which had been our home since 1971. It turned out father couldn't sleep and had taken a long stroll around the neighborhood at dawn, saying goodbye to our old haunts. It was 7 June 1987, a Sunday, our last morning in the Soviet Union. Genrikh Sapgir rang the doorbell before 8 a.m. From an attaché case he removed a bottle of cognac.

"I can't go to the airport," said Genrikh. "Too much." In the 1970s Sapgir had sent off to emigration his ex-wife and daughter and a slew of friends from among writers and nonconformist visual artists. He couldn't bear the physical act of parting at the border. We had a drink and said goodbye.

Outside the windows the Sunday streets lay quiet. I stood on our back balcony and stared at the grounds of the Institute of Atomic Energy, at the crooked pines amid which I had played cowboys and Indians, at the one- and two-star generals doing their morning calisthenics in the courtyard of the nearby apartment building. This was a world I knew so intimately, and was now leaving behind.

By nine, the apartment had been filled with neighbors and friends. We ended up riding to the airport in a roomy black BMW that belonged to our friend Bill F., an American diplomat, and his wife Catherine. He had offered to drive us so as to avoid any last-minute KGB surprises. As we drove to the airport, the sidewalks lay under a dainty shroud of poplar fuzz. I wore a glen plaid suit that my father's Israeli uncle had sent me, and black Italian wingtips I picked up at a local department store. The moment we got out of the diplomatic BMW and stepped into the terminal I felt dazed and numb. I remember a CBS crew waiting at the terminal to film the end of our segment. I remember saying goodbye, hugging and kissing Max, who was choking, while all the while I kept registering that we may never see each other again. Then it was time to rip ourselves from the small crowd of friends. We had to go through customs with our carry-ons. My parents and I went first, then my grandmother, my aunt and her daughter, my little cousin. Shorn like a lamb, my cousin Yusha, as if realizing for the first time that her father was staying behind in Russia, burst into tears and couldn't stop crying in her mother's arms.

Our Aeroflot flight was bound for Vienna, the first airport of call for the emigrating Jews. In Vienna some would stay a week or two, anticipating a transit to Italy and a refugee's summer of waiting for America, while others would get on a flight bound for Israel.

A leery customs junior officer, only a few years my senior by his looks, asked me as he fingered my blue backpack, "Where are you going, pal? Down south or to the States?"

I didn't answer. Instead, I turned around to steal one more glance at my dear friends. I remember wanting to cry but being unable.

My parents and I marched in place, lingering and waving our hands—just one more last goodbye. Then my father produced our exit visas for examination and stamping.

We went through the turnstile of the Soviet passport control.

Upon crossing over to the other side, my parents' first words were: "We got you out. Finally, we got you out."

EPILOGUE

IN AMERICA?

PRIOR TO COMPLETING THIS BOOK, I had written and published a literary memoir of the summer of 1987, which my parents and I spent as US-bound refugees in Austria and Italy. After *Waiting for America: A Story of Emigration* was released in 2007, critics and readers queried if I was working on another memoir. I would reply that in fact I was working on *Leaving Russia: A Jewish Story*—not strictly speaking a prequel, but a story that leaves off there, where *Waiting for America* begins its course, on the day we left Russia for good. "Does this mean there will be a third book, a kind of sequel to both *Leaving Russia* and *Waiting for America*?" I was then asked. And also: "Are you thinking of these books as part of a would-be trilogy?" I would quickly call up possible titles and subtitles for a third memoir—*City of Providence* or *A Russian Jew in America*—and my heart would grow heavy. Yet another story of immigrants' struggles and victories after coming to America, I would ask myself? But life—and literary life—makes its own arrangements, and I'm not ruling out the possibility of writing one day about the way I had failed to store my old Soviet self in the attic of American history.

It has taken me quite a number of years to complete *Leaving Russia*. Several other books had knocked it out of the queue, clamoring to arrive first. But more importantly, when I resumed writing this book in 2007, after a hiatus of several years, I had become a father of two children. Now that I'm sending *Leaving Russia* off to press, I'm tempted to make one final comment about the things I learned through writing this story. I say this, specifically, with my young daughters in mind.

Who am I today, twenty-five years after leaving Russia and coming to America?

A believer in causal scenarios would say that I'm a product of the historical and political circumstances that surrounded me during the formative years of my childhood and youth in the former Soviet Union. And this causalist wouldn't be wrong. A believer in psychoanalytical explanations is likely to suggest that my present self exhibits signs of trauma I experienced during my Soviet years—and especially the scars that remain from antisemitism and the persecution of refuseniks. How could I disagree? A metaphysician, whether in an organized or a self-stylized fashion, might say or at least think that some benevolent and omnipotent force has guided and guarded me through the Soviet years and brought me to America. For me to disappoint such a metaphysician would be an act of ingratitude to various individuals and powers who have helped me along, above all to my own parents.

I had a happy childhood but difficult teen years, I like to say, half in jest. My wife sometimes tells me I need to unburden myself of those painful memories, and I don't like to hear it, even though she is probably right both as a person who knows me and as a practicing physician.

A few years ago, on the urging of an American poet, I set out to translate into English a section from a cycle of poems I had composed in the countryside outside Moscow in the winter of 1987, not knowing yet that we would soon be leaving for good. The original Russian version had appeared in my first collection, *Herd above the Meadow*, published in New York in 1990. While I was attempting to render in English an exact translation, I found myself rewriting all but the first two lines of the Russian original. This impulse surprised me, as both a literalist and a formalist when it comes to translation. A cry of my Jewish-Russian past, I felt, had materialized from inside me, seeking to find expression in English. The result, still imperfect, amounted to this: "Remember, papa, the oaken leaf that spiraled / Downward, desperately, into mama's open hand? / The blazing yellow, the red, the autumn sprawled / Across the woods and took the gasping land. / Those pine trees split and bent like ancient lyres / On which the captive Jews refused to play. . . . / We were those captives, and for those stolen years, / O daughter of Babylon, o, Russia, you shall pay."

Earlier I had rendered, quite faithfully, another section from the same Russian cycle, and it appeared in a West Coast literary magazine. The part I quoted above had been sitting in my laptop's proverbial desk drawer until one day another American colleague asked, in an email, whether I was translating any more of my Russian poems. Without rereading it, I dashed off the grunted section to him. The colleague, a third-generation Jewish American, was very surprised. "I had no idea you're still so bitter," he commented.

Am I indeed so bitter after all these years of outward peace, family happiness, and what probably qualifies as the "American dream"?

In final reckoning, I must say that writing *Leaving Russia* has not been a therapeutic experience. I may have purged my memory of some vestiges of Jewish and Russian past in the Soviet Union, but I have not unburdened myself. Unburdening myself of the things from the past that to this day make me furious would probably mean unmaking him who I am today, and I don't think I'm capable of this. I'm not suggesting that art is not or cannot be healing, both for the author and for the readers. Indeed, committing some of one's memories to writing can be a form of healing. But in itself, remembrance is not. At least it hasn't been for me.

Once a year for the past many years, when my dear friends Katya Tsarapkina and Maxim Mussel and I get together for our reunions, sometimes here and sometimes in Europe, we talk for hours about what if. Both of them still live in Russia and call it their home, that despite their Jewish heritage. Both of them have children growing up in Russia. What if I hadn't left back in 1987, we often wonder. It's impossible to tell how things would have turned out had I stayed in Russia. And yet, for better or for worse, Russia had made me who I was at the time of the leaving, in 1987. And America enabled me, a twenty-year-old Jewish-Russian immigrant, to start unlocking the hyphens of my self. She let me in and took me as her own—Soviet lock, Russian stock, and Jewish barrel.

INDEX OF NAMES AND PLACES

Abkhazia, 101, 107, 194–95, 198

Abolits, Israel, 63

Abolits, Olympida, 63

Abolits, Zoya, 63

Abram, Morris, 267

Afghanistan, xix, 30, 40, 46–47, 81–82, 104

Akhmadulina, Bella, 34, 241

Akhmatova, Anna, 130

Aksyonov, Vassily, 34

Aliger, Margarita, 245

Altai Region, 193

Ananyev, Vyacheslav, 243

Anatolyev, R., 259

Anchorage, 80

Andrews, Wyatt, 217–18, 284, 304–6

Andropov, Yuri, 46, 80, 126

Anna (Voronezh Province), 211

Antonioni, Michelangelo, 115

Aristov, Vladimir, 243

Arkhangelskoye (Moscow Province), 7–8

Arkhipov, Abram, 111–12

Armavir, 199

Armenia, 90, 142

Aronov, Aleksandr, 232

Arrak, Arno, 67–68, 71

Arrak, Ivi, xiii, 71, 74

Arrak, Jaan, 67–68, 71

Arrak, Jüri, xiii, 65–74, 127, 307–8

Arrak, Urve Roodes, 67–73, 127, 307

Astrakhan, 103, 182

Austria, 297, 312

Averbakh, Ilya, 51

Axasuerus, King, 260

Azerbaijan, 101, 103

Babaevsky, Semyon, 243

Babel, Isaac, 19, 59, 155

Babi Yar, 269

Babylonia, 260–61

Bagritsky, Eduard, 130, 155

Baklanov, Grigory, 247

Baku, 103

Balandin, Sergei, 187

Baldwin, James, 294

Balzac, Honoré de, 133

Bar (Vinnitsa Province, Ukraine), 273

Barabinsk (Novosibirsk Province), 160

Barankina, Masha (Maria), 296

Bardot, Brigitte, 280

Barnaul, 160

Bashkortostan, 101

Begun, Boris, 252

Begun, Inessa, 250

Begun, Yosef, 250–52, 255, 257, 259, 288–89

Belarus (Belorussia), 14, 35, 165, 206, 281–82

Belaya Kalitva (Rostov Province), 182

Belinsky, Vissarion, 172

Bellagio, Italy, xiii

Bellow, Saul, 294

Beloostrov (Leningrad Province), 9

Beregovoye (Krasnodar Region), 201

Beria, Lavrenty, 192, 196

Berlin, 154, 247

Bernshtein, Boris, 65–66

Ber Tuvia, Israel, 276

Bessarabia, 124

Bessonov, Ivan, 243

Binz, 56

Birobidzhan, 276

Bizet, Georges, 37

Blok, Aleksandr, 154

Bobrov (Voronezh Province), 180, 211

Bochkarev, Igor (Gosha), 58–61

Bochkareva, Olga (Lyalya), 58

Bogarde, Dirk, 117

Bogatova, Tatiana, 242–43

Bogatyrev, Lev, 167, 177, 201–3, 210

Bogliasco, Italy, xiii

Bonnard, Pierre, 10

Bonner, Elena, 249

Boston, vxii–xviii, xx, 166, 189

Boyko, Igor, 243

Brabant, 56

Bradbury, Ray, 131

Brailovsky, Viktor, 288

Brest (Brest-Litovsk), 6

Breydo, Bella, 34, 273, 279–90

Breydo, Boris, 281

Breydo, Maria (Manya), 14

Brezhnev, Leonid, 21, 46, 78, 89, 126, 205

Brighton Beach (section of Brooklyn, New
York), 225

Brodsky, Joseph (Iosif), 57

Broida, Yitzchok Aizik, Gaon Rabbi, 282

Bronfman, Edgar, 267

Brookline, Massachusetts, xxii, 197

Brown, Harold, 249

Broyde (Breydo), Chaim-Wolf, Rabbi, 282

Broyde (Breydo), Eyno, 282

Broyde (Breydo), Meyr, 282

Broyde (Breydo), Ruvim, 272–83

Budyonny, Semyon, Marshal, 210

Bulgaria, 102

Bunin, Ivan, 172

California, 23, 153–54, 259

Canada, 71, 73, 113, 142, 147, 254, 287

Carter, James Earl "Jimmy", Jr., 40

Caucasus, 101, 103, 118, 163–64, 177, 183,
188–90, 193, 195, 198, 201, 243, 274

Central Asia, 102–3

Ceylon, xviii

Cezanne, Paul, 10

Chashnikovo (Moscow Province), 118–19,
122–25, 213, 217, 221–22, 224, 298

Chechen-Ingushetia, 188

Chechnya, xix, 101, 164, 198

Chekhov (Lopasnya, Moscow Province),
167

Chekhov, Anton, 5, 37, 47, 122, 128, 209,
306

Cherkessk (Karachai-Cherkessia), 190

Chernenko, Konstantin, 126

Chernobyl (Ukraine), 165, 180, 218

Chernova, Kristina, 295

Chertkovo (Voronezh Province), 180

Chestnut Hill, Massachusetts, xxii, 3, 23

Chile, 109

Chkalovsk (Nizhny-Novgorod Province),
203–4

Chumachenko, Lyonya (Leonid), 104, 179,
194, 201, 298–99

Cooper, Elizabeth, 233

Cooper, John Milton, Jr., 233

Cooper, John Milton, III, 233
Cooper, Judith, 233
Cortázar, Julio, 63, 115
Cranston, Rhode Island, xx
Crimea, 53, 163, 165, 289
Cuba, 46
Cui, César, 17
Cuxhaven, 56

Daghestan, 101, 188, 198
Dante Alighieri, 133
Dardykina, Natalia, 232
Dargomyzhsky, Aleksandr, 17
Davydov, Denis, 227
Denikin, Anton, General, 278
Devitsa (Voronezh Province), 179
D'Hérelle, Félix, 196
Dobrovolsky, Gleb, 83
Dokuchaev, Vasily, 211
Dombai (Karachai-Cherkessia), 191
Donohue, Phil, 262
Dostoevsky, Fyodor, 131, 249, 298
Dubrovsky, Alla, 263
Dumanov (Khmelnitskiy Province,
    Ukraine), 277
Dushanbe, 198

East Prussia, 102
Edelstein, Yuli, 158
Egypt, xx, 4
Eisenstein, Sergei, 117
Eriksson, Bengt, 287
Ermolova, Maria, 268
Esenin, Sergei, 130, 202, 282
Esther, Queen, 260, 262, 267
Estonia, xiii, 3, 6, 14, 53–54, 60, 65–66,
    71–73, 75, 95, 102, 127–28, 165, 213,
    303–4

Evreison, Marina (Masha Arshinova),
    235–37

Fadeev, Aleksandr, 301
Feltsman, Vladimir, 288, 305
Fet, Afanasy, 57
Feuchtwanger, Lion, 59
Fields, Harvey, Rabbi, 218–19, 234, 258, 287
Fields, Sybil, 219
Finland, 153, 234, 303
Fitzgerald, Ella, 9
France, 27, 69, 147, 254, 298
Freud, Sigmund, 62
Frost, Robert, 38
Frunze, 198

Galkina, Yulya, 106
García-Viardot, Pauline, 173
Gelendzhik (Krasnodar Region), 164,
    200–203
Genoa, 178
Georgia (Democratic Republic of Geor-
    gia), 165, 194, 196–97, 200–201, 304
Germany, xvi, 55, 200, 208, 267, 295, 300,
    303
Gilman, Benjamin A., 219
Glinka, Mikhail, 17
Gorbachev, Mikhail, 126, 148, 152, 154, 217,
    247, 249–50, 252, 257, 259, 264, 284
Gordon, Raisa, 78, 80
Goriachy Klyuch (Krasnodar Region),
    199–200
Gorky, Maxim, 78, 149–50
Grashchenkov, Viktor, 138–40
Great Britain, 30, 254
Grebenshchikov, Boris, 304
Grechko, Olga, 243
Grigorenko, Petro, 33

Grishin, Viktor, 126
Gromova, Ulyana, 301
Gul (Goul), Roman, 247

Hague, The, 56
Haifa, 276
Harlingen, 56
Hartman, Arthur A., 287
Heine, Heinrich, 132
Helsinki, 71
Hemingway, Ernest, 38
Hesse, Hermann, 63, 115
Horowitz, Vladimir, 288
Hyder, Charles, 259

Ilyin, Pavel, 262
Ilyin, Sh., 259
Ilyina, Nadezhda, 262
Irlin, Iosif, 42
Iskander, Fazil, 34
Israel, 4, 13, 30, 38, 69, 82, 124, 135, 142,
    248–49, 258, 264, 266, 291, 294, 301, 310
Italy, xvi, 312
Ivan IV (the Terrible), Czar, 141

Jackson, Henry, Senator, 40, 257
Japan, 31, 37
Jennings, Peter, 252
Jerusalem, 34, 258
Jewison, Norman, 224
Jordan, 4
Joseph, xx
Jūrmala, 56

Kabardin-Balkaria, 188
Kafka, Franz, 188, 291

Kagan, Mikaella, 262
Kaliningrad (Königsberg), 102, 279
Kalmykia, 176, 182, 184–85
Kamchatka, 102
Kamenets-Podolsk, Ukraine, 14, 121, 274,
    277–79
Kamensk-Shakhtinsky (Rostov Province),
    182
Karachaevsk, Karachai-Cherkessia, 191
Karachai-Cherkessia, 164, 188, 198
Karelia, 58, 71
Kazakevich, Vyacheslav, 243
Kazakhstan, 159, 176
Kazakov, Matvey, 145
Kenya, 109, 202
Khalif, Lev, 225
Kharkov, 273
Kherson, 104, 299
Khlebnikov, Oleg, 231
Khlebnikov, Viktor, 231
Khrenovoye (Voronezh Province), 203,
    209, 212–13, 297
Khrushchev, Nikita, 5, 152, 227, 246
Khudoleyev, Sergei, 174, 183–84, 186, 194
Khutsiev, Marlen, 297
Kiev (Kyiv), 16
Kirgizstan, 102
Kissinger, Henry A., 249
Klyuev, Nikolai, 130
Kogan, Inga, 61
Kolomenskoye (area of Moscow), 141
Kon, Yuzef, 58
Korkiya, Viktor, 228
Kornilova, Galina, 307
Korotich, Vitaly, 247
Kosharovsky, Yuli, 265–66
Kovalyov, Dmitry (pseudonym: Dimitri
    Perets), 296, 308
Kovda, Viktor, 83
Koyfman, Evgeny, 157–58

Kozhinov, Vadim, 243

Kozintsev, Grigory, 127

Krapivna (Tula Province), 171, 202

Krasnodar, 184, 188, 199, 201–3

Kropotkin (Krasnodar Region), 199

Kropotkin, Pyotr, 199, 264

Kuban (Krasnodar and Stavropol
    Regions), 104, 174

Kulunda (Altai Region), 160

Kundera, Milan, 205

Kunyaev, Stanislav, 44

Kurchatov, Igor, 88

Kursk, 164, 173, 175–79, 208

Kust, German, 256–57, 303

Kvasha, Igor, 297

Lagerkvist, Pär, 63

Ladonin, Dmitry, 179

Lasser, Karen Elizabeth, xiii, 3, 23, 71–72,
    75

Latvia, 14, 102

Lefortovo (district of Moscow), 115

Len, Slava, 249

Lenin, Vladimir, 6, 101, 235

Leningrad. See St. Petersburg

Lermontov, Mikhail, 188, 265

Lerner, Aleksandr, 288

Leskov, Nikolai, 172, 175

Lesnykh, R., 157

Levin, Aleksandr, 243

Lipetsk, 173

Lippi, Filippino, 139

Liski (Voronezh Province), 210

Lithuania, xvi, 14–15, 34–36, 272

London, 9

Los Angeles, 201, 234, 259

Lübeck, 56

Lucca, 178

Lugansk (Voroshilovgrad), 179

Lugovskoy, Vladimir, 130

Lyubertsy (Moscow Province), 253–54

MacDonald, Lawrence, 80

Madison, Wisconsin, 107

Maeterlinck, Maurice, xiv

Magazanik, Norbert, 47

Malamud, Bernard, 294

Malikov, Dmitri, 308

Mandelstam, Osip, 130, 179

Mann, Heinrich, 59

Manucharov, Aleksandr, 94, 140

Marchenko, Anatoly, 250

Marcus Aurelius, Emperor, 139

Markin, Vladimir, 19–20, 89–90

Marx, Karl, 303

Massachusetts, xxii

Matisse, Henri, 10

Matlock, Jack F., Jr., 287

Maugham, William Somerset, 5, 110

Mayakovsky, Vladimir, 116, 149, 151

Melovoye (Lugansk Province, Ukraine),
    180–82

Mérimée, Prosper, 37, 58

Mertvovodsk (Rostov Province), 182

Mets, Arvo, 228, 232

Mezhiborsky, Aleksandr, 263

Mezhirov, Aleksandr, 14

Miami, 201

Michurin, Ivan, 182

Mikhalkovo (Moscow Province), 7

Mikkus, Evald, 54

Miller, Arthur, 296

Minsk, 14, 91–92

Mitić, Gojko, 55

Moldova, 121, 186

Molotov, Vyacheslav, 275

Mondale, Walter, xviii

Monet, Claude, 10

Monroe, Marilyn, 138, 291, 297

Morozovsk (Rostov Province), 182

Moscow, xv, xvii–xviii, xxii, 4–5, 7, 9, 13–15, 17, 23, 28, 33, 36–37, 39, 44–46, 48, 50, 56, 66, 69, 75, 80, 83, 101–2, 104–6, 110–11, 114–15, 118, 123–25, 134, 137, 145, 147, 149, 152, 156–57, 161, 164–65, 169, 172, 175, 177, 184, 186, 188–89, 200, 203, 212, 217, 219–21, 223, 226, 228, 230, 262, 268, 274, 284, 288, 304, 314

Moses, xx

Mtsensk (Orel Province), 171, 175

Muravyova, Irina (Ira), 174, 176

Murmansk, 103

Muscovy, 170

Musil, Robert, 63

Mussel, Maxim (Max), xii, 5, 17, 48, 61–63, 71, 112, 114–15, 124–25, 201, 212, 219–21, 234–37, 262, 298–300, 307–8, 310, 314

Mussorgsky, Modest, 17–18, 32

Myshkino (Moscow Province), 167–68

Nabokov, Vladimir, xviii, 121, 217, 220

Nairobi, 109

Napoleon I (Buonaparte), Emperor, 203

Narragansett, Rhode Island, 117

Neizvestny, Ernest, 57

Nekrasov, Nikolai, 57

New England, 292

New York (city), 9, 37, 59, 80, 129, 224, 247, 313

Newport (Rhode Island), 117

Nikitin, Ivan, 57

Nikulin, Valentin, 297

Nizhny-Novgorod (Gorky), 103, 203, 249

Nogin, Viktor, 111

North Ossetia, 188, 197

Novo-Kubansk (Krasnodar Region), 199

Novosibirsk, 160

Nudel, Ida, 143, 288

Odessa, 59, 65, 103, 155, 278, 298

Okudzhava, Bulat, 34

Olesha, Yury, 155

Omsk, 160

Orel, 164, 171, 173, 175

Orlov-Chesmensky, Aleksey, Count, 208

Orwell, George, 71

Ostende, 56

Ostrovsky, Aleksandr, 262

Palanga, 56

Panevėžys (Ponevezh), Lithuania, 282–83

Panga-Rehe (Jüri Arrak's homestead, Estonia), 66–68, 70–71, 73, 75

Paris, xviii, 59, 294

Pärnu, Estonia, 4, 53–56, 60, 62, 66, 68–69, 72, 80, 95, 127, 152, 204, 214, 219–20, 223

Pasternak, Boris, 130

Pell, Claiborne, 219

Peltier, Leonard, 229

Peneva, Petya, 300

Peter the Great, Emperor, 56, 115, 170

Petrovsky, Grigory, 273

Petrozavodsk, 58, 241

Picasso, Pablo, 10–11

Pinochet, Augusto, General, 109

Platonov, Andrey, 179

Podolia, 14

Poland, 58

Pollock, Jackson, 38

Polotsk (Vitebsk Province, Belarus), 282

Polyak (Katsenelson), Tsilya, 277

Polyak, Arkady (Aron), xx, 273–76

Polyak, Ilya (Ikhil), 276

Polyak, Khana-Feyga, 276

Portnoy, Mark, 309

Posner, Michael, 142

Potok, Chaim, 294

Pozdnyaev, Mikhail, 231

Prague, 221

Proletarsk (Rostov Province), 182, 184, 186–87, 189

Proust, Marcel, 63

Providence, Rhode Island, 232

Pryanishnikov, Dimitri, 108

Pshada (Krasnodar Region), 200, 201, 203

Pushkin, Aleksandr, 15, 56, 115, 256, 268, 271, 286

Pushkina (née Goncharova), Natalia, 268

Putin, Vladimir, 195, 198

Pyatigorsk (Stavropol Region), 188

Pyndyk, Ekaterina (Katya), 299

Radonezh (Moscow Province), 105

Rastrelli, Francesco Bartolomeo, 178

Rather, Dan, 304–7

Reagan, Ronald, xviii, 217

Renoir, Pierre-Auguste, 10

Reshetova, Irina, 302

Reyn, Evgeny, 131, 187, 246

Rhode Island, 117, 219, 232

Ribbentrop, Joachim von, 275

Riga, 53, 56

Rimsky-Korsakov, Nikolai, 17

Rio de Janeiro, xviii

Rodé, Aleksey, 108

Rodgers, Walter, 252

Rosenthal, Andrew, 252

Rostov-on-Don, 182, 203, 206, 210

Roth, Joseph, 234

Roth, Philip, 294

Rousseau, Henri, 10, 190

Roy, Galina, 238–40

Rozanov, Boris, 138, 155–58, 211, 291

Rozenbaum, Aleksandr, 59

Rudzish, Zinaida, 84

Russia, xvi, xvii, xix–xx, 23, 28, 31, 35, 47, 75, 108, 118, 164–65, 177, 179, 183, 188, 197, 199, 202–3, 217, 222–23, 233, 237, 242, 277, 307, 313

Rust, Matthias, 303

Ryashentsev, Yury, 228

Rybakov, Anatoly, 245, 305

Rybas, Svyatoslav, 239–40

Rybkin, Rostislav, 131

Saakashvili, Mikhail, 195

Sablukov, Vyacheslav, 243

Sakhalin, 80

Sakharov, Andrey, 249, 255

Sakharovsky, Vladimir (Vova), 186

Salita, Ilia, 102

Salsk (Rostov Province), 185, 210

Samary, Jeanne, 10

Samoylov, David, 34

Samoylova, Elena, 159–60, 226, 302

Sanders, Jonathan, 305

San Francisco, 9

Sapgir (Rodovskaya), Lyudmila, 220

Sapgir, Genrikh, 132, 220–21, 229, 246, 249, 263, 307, 309

Saratov, 206

Sawyer, Diane, 304

Schultz, George P., 288

Scott, Sir Walter, 58

Selikhovy Dvory (Kursk Province), 175

Selvinsky, Ilya, 130

Semipalatinsk, 160

Shaferman, Polina (Polya), 14

Sharansky, Natan (Anatoly), 154

Sharir, David, 218

Sharir, Gila, 218

Sharir, Moisei (Munia), 37, 142, 248, 277–78

Shchekino (Tula Province), 169

Shchepkin, Mikhail, 173

Shchyogolev, Irina, 262

Shchyogolev, Lev, 262

Shklovsky, Viktor, 32

Shklyarevsky, Igor, 34

Sholem Aleichem, xx

Shostakovich, Dmitry, 176

Shrayer (née Polyak), Emilia (Mila), xiii,
   xx, 5, 7–9, 13, 30–31, 36–37, 39, 41–43,
   46, 49–50, 54, 69, 73, 89–90, 95, 126–29,
   141, 146–54, 218, 250–54, 258–60, 280,
   285, 305–8

Shrayer (Sharir), Moisei (Munia). See
   Sharir, Moisei

Shrayer, Abram, 277, 279

Shrayer, Berta, 277, 279

Shrayer, Borukh-Itsik, 277, 278

Shrayer, David (penname: David Shrayer-
   Petrov), xiii, xx, 5–10, 13, 15, 20, 30,
   31–36, 39, 42–49, 51, 54, 61, 66, 69, 70,
   76, 86, 89–90, 95, 112, 126–28, 130–32,
   142, 145–54, 158, 218, 220, 227, 232–33,
   251–52, 261–67, 279–80, 284–91, 305–6,
   309

Shrayer, Freyda (Fanya), (née Kizer), 13,
   260–61, 277

Shrayer, Maxim D., 12, 15, 85–87, 94–95,
   156, 202, 212–13, 219–20, 227, 238–47,
   257, 314

Shrayer, Mira Isabella, xiv, xx, 3, 309

Shrayer, Pyotr (Peysakh), 9, 32, 97, 154,
   273, 277, 279–81

Shrayer, Tatiana Rebecca, xiv, xx, 300

Shrayer, Yakov, 277, 279

Šiauliai (Shavel), Lithuania, 282

Siberia, 35, 159, 183, 303

Simferopol, 166

Sinatra, Franck, 9

Singer, Isaac Bashevis, 205

Slavin, V., 254

Slepak, Maria, 142–45, 288

Slepak, Vladimir, 142–45, 265, 288

Slutsky, Boris, 32, 44

Sochi, 198

Solzhenitsyn, Aleksandr, 227, 284

Sopot, 56

South Ossetia, 195, 197–98

Soviet Union. See USSR

Soyfer, Valery, 142

Sozarukov, Yusuf, 243

Spasskoe-Lutovinovo (Orel Province),
   172, 174–75

Spektor, Roman, 261

Stalin, Joseph (Iosif), xvi, 101, 135, 174,
   198–99, 205, 261, 273

Stavropol, 188–90, 199

Stevenson, Adlai E., III, 267

Stockholm, 71

St. Petersburg (Leningrad), xx, 5, 9, 14,
   16, 23, 28, 58, 62, 70, 95, 106, 118, 145,
   152–53, 178, 188, 217, 234–37, 241, 277,
   279, 281, 292

Studnits, Anna (Nyusya), xx, 24, 273–76,
   281, 287

Suslov, Mikhail, 126

Syria, 4

Tallinn, 53, 56, 65, 95, 97, 304, 307

Talovaya (Voronezh Province), 211

Tambov, 164

Tarasevich, Igor, 231–32

Tashkent, 58, 103, 198

Tatarka, Karachai-Cherkessia, 190

Tatarstan, 101, 105, 250

Tbilisi, 196, 304

Tbilisskaya (Krasnodar Region), 199

Teberda, Karachai-Cherkessia, 177, 189, 192, 198, 243

Tehran, 37

Tel Aviv, 218, 276

Teuchezhsk (Krasnodar Region), 199

Timiryazev, Kliment, 268

Tintoretto, 139

Titov, German, 256

Tolpeshta, Inna, 186

Tolstoy, Leo, 184, 189, 203, 208, 218, 245, 286

Töstemaa (Estonia), 66

Trakai (Troki), Lithuania, 290

Tsanava, Pyotr, 106–7

Tsarapkin, Vladimir, 61

Tsarapkina, Ekaterina (Katya), xiii, 59–61, 63, 71, 114–15, 235, 307–8, 314

Tsimlyansk (Rostov Province), 183

Tsirkunenko, N. B., 142

Tsvetaeva, Marina, 130, 300

Tula, 169–70

Turgenev, Ivan, 172–73, 175

Tuscany, 178

Turkey, 194, 198, 201

Tver (Kalinin), 210

Tyutchev, Fyodor, 172

Ukraine, xvi, 14–15, 35, 102, 121, 157, 165, 181, 197, 272–73, 279

USA (United States of America), 40, 111, 113, 117, 135, 147, 161, 224, 249, 259, 287, 311

USSR (Union of Soviet Socialist Republics), xvii, xx, xxii, 4, 16–17, 21, 23, 30–31, 36–37, 47, 49, 51–52, 54, 69, 71, 83, 89, 96, 110, 114, 117–18, 134, 217, 220, 230, 248, 259, 264, 272

Ust-Dzheguta, Karachai-Cherkessia, 190

Ustinov, Dmitri, Marshal, 242

Ustinov, Valentin, 241, 244–47

Ust-Labinsk (Krasnodar Region), 199

Uzbekistan, 102–3

Väike Lubi, 72–74

Vance, Cyrus R., 249

Van Gogh, Vincent, 10

Vanik, Charles A., 40, 267

Vashti, Queen, 262, 263, 267, 307

Vassily III, Czar, 141

Vedder, Stephen, xiii

Venice, 117, 279

Vertov, Dziga, 116

Vichy, 296–98

Vienna, 22, 291, 310

Villon, François, 106

Vilnius (Vilna), 290, 349

Vinnitsa, 279

Vinokurov, Evgeny, 228

Visconti, Luchino, 117

Vitebsk, 282

Vladimirov, L., 254

Volgin, Igor, 131

Volgodonsk (Rostov Province), 184

Volgograd (Stalingrad), 174, 182, 184

Volodarsky, Leonid, 243

Vologda, 55

Volynskaya, Julia (Yusha), 273, 310

Volynskaya-Levy, Zhanna, 273

Voronezh, 164, 179, 203, 206

Voznesensky, Andrey, 34, 241

Vytautas, Grand Duke, 289

Warsaw, 205

Washington, DC, 225, 259, 306

Whitaker, Mark, 252

Wilder, Thornton, 117

Wisconsin, 107
Wolfe, Thomas, 236
Wouk, Herman, 294

Yan, Vassily, 58
Yaroslavl, 193
Yasnaya Polyana (Tula Province), 170
Yeltsin, Boris, 152, 304
Yevtushenko, Yevgeny, 34

Yuri I Vladimirovich (Dolgoruky), Grand
    Prince, 144

Zabolotsky, Nikolai, 130
Zamoskvorechye (area of Moscow), 146
Zayats, Alevtina, 202
Zelenograd (administrative okrug of
    Moscow), 118
Zivert (Siewert), Svetlana, 121